Walking Out

WALKING OUT

America's New Trade Policy
in the Asia-Pacific and Beyond

Michael L. Beeman

Stanford | Walter H. Shorenstein
Asia-Pacific Research Center
Freeman Spogli Institute

Shorenstein APARC addresses critical issues affecting the countries of Asia, their regional and global affairs, and U.S.-Asia relations. As Stanford University's hub for the interdisciplinary study of contemporary Asia, we produce policy-relevant research, provide education and training to students, scholars, and practitioners, and strengthen dialogue and cooperation between counterparts in the Asia-Pacific and the United States.

Walter H. Shorenstein Asia-Pacific Research Center
Stanford University
616 Jane Stanford Way, Encina Hall
Stanford, CA 94305-6055
650-723-9741 | aparc.fsi.stanford.edu

Published by the Walter H. Shorenstein Asia-Pacific Research Center

Distributed by Stanford University Press

Library of Congress Cataloging-in-Publication Data Is Available

ISBN 978-1-931368-74-2(paper)
ISBN 978-1-931368-75-9 (eBook)

For Anna and Maya

Contents

Preface and Acknowledgments

This book is about policy choices. Specifically, it is an account of the origins and characteristics of America's policy choices since the mid-2010s that are fundamentally transforming its foreign trade policy. Molded by America's hyper-polarized domestic politics, these choices are also reshaping and resetting many of its foreign relationships and engagements. Nowhere has America's new trade policy impacted its relations more than with the countries of the Asia-Pacific, which is a particular focus here.

While these impacts have been profound, this book intentionally and unapologetically adopts an America-centered view of its trade policy choices. Bringing to light the worldviews and new goals of America's decision-makers, as they see and express them in its trade policy toward Asia and beyond, is essential to shed greater light on the origins of this dramatic shift in the trajectory of American trade policy and on its probable future course.

America's detachment over most of the past decade from numerous trade policy goals it has pursued for over 75 years has confounded and disappointed many at home and abroad, but this sea change also is strongly supported by important constituencies in America. Initially viewed widely as a series of principally reactive actions, its disparate threads are gradually revealing a greater coherence and trajectory. America's new trade policy now appears sufficiently entrenched and, for the foreseeable future, appears likely to remain America's new normal.

Nothing in this book is intended to minimize the trade challenges that America's decision-makers face. Its trading partners, broadly speaking, continue to advance their individual interests, often directly or indirectly similarly undermining their commitments to the international trade rules. Their approaches to trade are likewise impacting America's new normal. China, by far, is the most significant challenge to global trade interests and easily requires the most aggressive response. Rather than critique these choices, this book instead aims to contrast those made by America's past generations of trade policy decision-makers with those of the present, to highlight both the enormous differences in approach and reasoning used to respond to these challenges in new ways.

To better illustrate this new normal, some of the issues and questions this book seeks to answer are: What are the definable characteristics that make policy choices identifiable as "new trade policies," as opposed to policies that are merely reactionary and ad hoc in their approach? Moreover, who or what is driving these policy choices? As often portrayed, is it America's response to the emergence of a new great power competition with China? Or, is it a response to challenges of the 2010s and 2020s that some U.S. officials claim are significantly different than those of past decades? Alternatively, is it driven by other influences and causes?

There is a surprising degree of consistency in some of the trade policy choices made by America's two most recent presidential administrations, particularly when set against their striking, sharp differences on many other issues. In other ways, however, their trade policy approaches and choices are more at odds in ways that reflect those larger differences. I argue there is regularity and predictability to both these consistencies and differences in their trade policies, shaped as they are by America's new political geometry forged from extreme new levels of domestic political division. On trade, it is a geometry of acute angles and no longer one of curves and tangents.

Politics is always at the forefront of these decisions because trade policy lies at the intersection of every nation's domestic economic and foreign relations interests. It is not surprising that a dramatic transformation of a political system would also give rise to choices to overturn policies viewed as relics of the old system and assumptions. Along the way, revisionism is employed to redefine prior goals, assumptions, and strategies by those who seek to justify and prove their new theorems. These changes and the revisionism underpinning them are all products of America's new politics of trade.

Correspondingly, as political as trade has almost always been in America, it is now more challenged, politicized, and transformed than at any point since at least the early 1930s. At that time, Congress was still unable to chart a consistent approach to U.S. tariff policy, which remained punctuated by dramatic swings in America's external tariffs as its political parties alternated control of the institutions of power in Washington. Those swings began to be tamped down starting with the 1934 enactment of the Reciprocal Trade Agreements Act, when Congress began to routinely share with the executive branch its constitutionally derived responsibility for foreign commerce. This first step was to grant the executive branch the authority to negotiate and implement reciprocal tariff reduction with its trading partners. Strongly influenced by the progressive vision of Franklin Roosevelt, America's thirty-second president, and his administration, reciprocal tariff reduction with America's trading partners was initially pursued principally as a tool of domestic recovery from the Great Depression.

Soon after, America emerged victorious from war and became the new leader of the free world. Congress continued to share new grants of trade authority with different U.S. administrations, enabling Washington to pursue a more consistent, effective, and strategic trade policy. The defining feature of that policy reflected America's emerging bipartisan consensus in favor of freer, more open global trade. Stability in policy and (relatively speaking) politics at home enabled America to carry this vision into the world to help create and expand a new rules-based international trading system to promote joint prosperity and help prevent a return to global war. Out of America's leadership and this new bipartisan consensus came its responsibility and commitment to follow these rules, which were largely shaped by Washington, and to further promote the system. This helped over many decades to, for the most part, contain and turn back the political challenges on trade that inevitably arose at times to undermine it, as well as to energize new efforts to shape this order in the direction of greater fairness for America's interests.

Throughout the book, I briefly revisit this and other stories in America's trade policy history for two reasons. First is to recall the arguments, objectives, successes, and failures that defined that history, in light of recent efforts to revise these motives and events in the attempt to justify contemporary efforts to remake and reform trade policy. Second is to chart and compare other transformations made to U.S. trade policy over many decades to confront numerous challenges, both domestic and foreign. These were pursued in ways that enabled

America's postwar bipartisan consensus on trade to evolve but remain intact for over 75 years, which stands in stark contrast to the new areas of alignment and disagreement that have emerged in the attempt to redefine and replace it.

A few style notes about the book: first, I have attempted to simplify and clarify as much as possible the main political issues and trends by avoiding overly technical explanations of trade rules, norms, and exceptions. Acronyms and jargon are also kept to a minimum for this reason. This has made this book more challenging to write, because it requires searching for an accurate-as-possible degree of generality in descriptions and accounts to do so. It, therefore, may prove unsatisfactory in places to trade lawyers, economists, and other specialists who know the full extent of these technical complexities. I, nonetheless of course, take full responsibility for any substantial lapses in explanation and interpretation. I hope, however, that keeping the descriptions and language as uncomplicated as possible will help make the book easier to read and thus better enable an understanding of the new politics of trade in America and its impacts. I encourage anyone with a deeper interest in the specifics to refer to the wealth of technical publications on these topics for more.

Second, I intentionally use "America" instead of "United States" throughout this book. While some may question this choice, I am attempting to convey that all the choices made in Washington, when viewed from abroad, are perceived as *America's* choices. Much effort is made in this book to delineate and differentiate among the various factions in the United States that are shaping it. Once shaped and decided, however, the rest of the world often sees it singularly–as "America's trade policy."

The final point is one of perspective. My personal privilege is to have worked as a U.S. trade official for over 16 years. During that time, I became deeply familiar with the perspectives of four different U.S. administrations on trade, both as explained and debated within America and as negotiated and pursued with its trading partners. My perspective is necessarily that of a former trade official, whose responsibility it was to always look in both these directions to advance each administration's goals and a wide range of American interests. As trade officials often say, it is always different than others might imagine when sitting in *the* chair. I am only and always honored to have done so.

With that perspective, I have attempted to write this book in an even-handed manner, giving greater clarity to the views, influences, and obstacles at home and abroad that have shaped America's trade policy decisions. Some may find these descriptions and portrayals inelegant, while others may insist that I am flat wrong. The central point of this book is that America has lost much of its ability, in this new highly politicized environment, to recognize, allow for, and find compromises among these views. My attempt with this book is to restore balance and perspective to many of these issues. I hope others, whether having served on Capitol Hill or in the headquarters of America's labor unions or in business, will step forward to tell their own stories and that when doing so, they at least attempt to treat fairly the full range of *other* perspectives, interests, and challenges. In my view, recognizing the multiplicity of interests and telling the real story is the essential first step to helping America ease its divisions.

To conclude, here are some words of sincere appreciation. My first shout-out goes to my former colleagues at the Office of the U.S. Trade Representative (USTR). I have worked with and been educated by the best of the best of America's civil servants at the most special place to work in Washington. I also have truly enjoyed my professional relationships with the political appointees of every one of these administrations. We fight for America together, and it is a special place because everyone at USTR makes it so. Almost no other job in Washington derives the same privilege in such a direct way—one of working for both America's economic and foreign interests. I am deeply grateful.

I also wish to express my deep gratitude to the entire team at Stanford University's Walter H. Shorenstein Asia-Pacific Research Center. You have allowed me the space, support, and opportunity to pursue this and other projects after leaving government. Particular appreciation goes to Kiyo Tsutsui and Gi-Wook Shin, along with Cheryll Alipio, Denise Masumoto, and Kristen Lee, for making my stay at this prestigious and important institution possible. A further profound thanks to Tom Fingar, Don Emmerson, and Kristian Kender for so many wonderful conversations and points of advice. An additional thank you to Andy Grotto of the Freeman Spogli Institute who, having also moved through the policy-to-academia tunnel, has provided invaluable advice and support.

While writing this book, I have reached out to several former government officials to help make sure I am striking the balance and accuracy I am attempting to achieve in the following pages. So that you will not be deemed, in this current political environment, guilty by association with my manuscript, I will not mention specific names other than to say you know who you are and that I want to express my deep thanks to each of you.

Mike Breger and Noa Ronkin more than deserve special recognition for their advice and support, among others at Stanford who have provided constructive comments and feedback. I also owe special thanks to George Krompacky, Jr., for his patient and expert skills in laboriously helping me turn my former government official prose into, well, something that is more generally understandable. I also wish to thank Michael, Richard, and James for your beautiful California gardens, from which I have drawn so much inspiration while writing this book.

Finally, I cannot express sufficiently my endearing gratitude to my family, beginning with my wife and children, for whom I have boundless adoration and appreciation. Thank you. To my mother, who has always been there in support, and to my siblings and other family members, I am also greatly indebted.

Abbreviations

AFL-CIO	American Federation of Labor and Congress of Industrial Organizations
AGOA	Africa Growth and Opportunity Act
APEC	Asia-Pacific Economic Cooperation
BIT	bilateral investment treaty
CED	U.S-China Comprehensive Economic Dialogue
CHIPS	Creating Helpful Incentives to Produce Semiconductors
CPTPP	Comprehensive and Progressive Trans-Pacific Partnership
EGA	Environmental Goods Agreement
EU	European Union
EV	electric vehicle
FFR	Free, Fair, and Reciprocal (trade talks)
GATT	General Agreement on Tariffs and Trade
GPA	Government Procurement Agreement
GDP	gross domestic product
GSP	Generalized System of Preferences
ILO	International Labour Organization
IMF	International Monetary Fund
IP	intellectual property
IPEF	Indo-Pacific Economic Framework
IRA	Inflation Reduction Act
ISDS	investor-state dispute settlement
ITO	International Trade Organization

KORUS	U.S.-Korea Free Trade Agreement
MFN	most-favored-nation
NAFTA	North American Free Trade Agreement
P4	Four Pacific nations of Singapore, Chile, Brunei, and New Zealand
RCEP	Regional Comprehensive Economic Partnership
TiSA	Trade in Services Agreement
TPP	Trans-Pacific Partnership
TRIPS	Agreement on the Trade-Related Aspects of Intellectual Property Rights
UK	United Kingdom
USMCA	United States-Mexico-Canada Agreement
USTR	(Office of the) U.S. Trade Representative
VER	voluntary export restraint
WTO	World Trade Organization

Walking Out

ONE

Walking Out

I n this age of economic hyper-competition among trading nations, America is walking out on the very trading system it helped establish, shape, and promote.

After decades of American leadership, the way it is turning its back on the system is sometimes reminiscent of a tired and disappointed parent who has suddenly thrown up their hands at a grown child who did not turn out as hoped.

There have been threats to tear up prior U.S. trade agreements; the United States has also intentionally hobbled certain functions of the World Trade Organization (WTO) system, on which the core international trade rules are based. It repeatedly failed to renew a decades-long trade program to help many of the world's poorest countries improve through trade with America. And who can forget the previous leader of the free world declaring, "I am a tariff man," or the finger-wag of a recent prominent Democratic presidential candidate railing against America's "disastrous trade agreements."

Over the past decade, America's sharp trade policy swerves to the New Right and the progressive Left have bent both ends of the U.S. political spectrum back toward each other and into rough alignment in a new policy dimension. This new space is where many of its political leaders, the new mainstream of its two political parties, and its two most recent presidential administrations have now converged on America's trade policy.

It is a gathering place for those who have soured on the type of international trading system that America long led and championed, guided as it was by the fundamental belief that freer and more open international trade, based on rules to help ensure it is also fair, is a positive generator of global peace, economic prosperity, and opportunity for America.

America's walkout, therefore, is far more extensive than the headline-grabbing acts of a single U.S. president. Rather, it is an attempt at a fundamental shift in policy aimed at forcing a reset of many of America's past trade priorities and choices, as well as many of the global trade norms that America itself had a dominant hand in shaping over the past 75 years.

Backing away from America's past approaches toward trade and flipping over the table of some of the system's rules and norms on the way out means that America is increasingly surrendering its place in the ongoing competition among nations for new external markets and the new jobs and wealth that trade can help create.

It also has created some sharp, new inconsistencies in America's foreign policy and foreign relations. It comes as America and many of its self-defined "allies and partners" seek to shore up and strengthen the so-called rules-based international order against profound external challenges. America's leadership and ability to take the high ground in global affairs—especially economic affairs—lose substantial credibility when America cannot confidently define which rules and values it is still prepared to support or defend.

If America's new approach to trade policy continues as it has, its critics fret that America will only completely surrender and willfully deny itself its historic leadership role in shaping the more open international trading system that it meticulously tried to champion, and thereby eliminate its ability to reap the benefits from that leadership and that system. By doing so, this internationalist view goes, America is just walking out on its own interests since it is effectively handing the keys to others to define and lead the system in a direction that fulfills their priorities.

Conversely, America's free trade skeptics embrace this new approach as progress toward a long-sought domestic policy prize. It is an opportunity, in defense of local jobs and communities from import surges, to reset and rewrite what the trade rules dictate. It also is an opportunity to wean America off the idea that market-opening agreements and freer trade should aim to serve foreign policy goals. Should more fundamental reforms fall short, America's new approach at least brings a respite from the mantra of market opening, which these critics view as a decades-long failed economic philosophy and approach to trade.

Both why this is happening and where America's trade policy might be heading next have left many scratching their heads—and wondering how deep the domestic economic and foreign policy consequences of that trade policy may prove to be. This book aims to explore and explain the principal factors driving America's great new walkout on trade, outline some of the significant ways in which its trade policy has changed, examine some of the key impacts on both domestic and foreign policy, and offer some conclusions to predict what might be in store ahead.

It is important to point out that "walking out" most often is not, in the immediate term at least, the same as "walking away."

In international trade diplomacy, walking out can be a straightforward, spontaneous act of protest in response to some action or position taken by a counterpart. Most often, it is a more calculated tactic used to signal a desire to fundamentally reset the terms of a discussion or negotiation or respond to a circumstance viewed as heading off course in an unfavorable direction.

The classic scenario is a trade official in an unfinished meeting with a foreign counterpart dramatically standing up to head for the exit. The much more common version of the walkout is subtle, or even passive, and accompanied by no fanfare. In this form, a negotiator can simply refuse to meet again or engage seriously with a trade counterpart on pending business until some condition is met, or they can just decline to continue to engage meaningfully at all any longer.

As defined here, a "walkout" is thus a familiar and widely used tactic in negotiations of all kinds—and so it also goes in the conduct of international trade relations. Since it aims to force a desired change in terms to enable an acceptable outcome, a walkout *does not itself imply a desire to completely walk away for good.*

Political decision-makers who have served in the Donald Trump and Joseph Biden administrations and many who hold similar views on trade on the key committees in the U.S. House of Representatives or Senate would reject the generic assertion that they ever "walked out" on America's trade interests. These American trade policy "realists," "reformers," or perhaps even "restorationists," as some might prefer to be called, will point to a handful of significant trade agreements or actions or legislative initiatives, either launched or completed during these administrations and legislative sessions, to make their case.

In each instance, they will also stress that their efforts aimed to reform or reset America's role, rights, or place in the prior trading order with the world or with individual trading partners. They will further point to the past, often citing generations-long mistakes, failures, or incorrect assumptions in trade policy as the motivation for these efforts.

All of these meet the definition of walking out as outlined above and agree with this book's central point for examination.

Yet, as any trade official also well knows, even if one hopes or intends to come back to the table on new terms, a walkout often instead triggers a complete stalemate or an interim period of drift in engagement that quickly dims the chances of re-engaging in further talks or negotiations. This is the tipping point where walking out leads to a dead end and thus effectively becomes the same as walking away.

This is where America's decades-long global leadership on trade has most often run aground as its decision-makers insist on going their own new way.

<hr />

On what and whom, exactly, is America walking out?

America's trade agreements, initiatives, and other commitments cover hundreds of rules, norms, and other objectives. These range from the very general, such as new tariff liberalization and general prohibitions on discriminatory import licenses and fees, to the very specific, such as individual product tariff elimination commitments and rules to ensure international express delivery companies are provided an expedited means for customs clearance at the border.

America's objectives for these agreements have routinely evolved and changed, be it opening new markets, creating trade rules for leading new growth sectors such as the digital economy, or updating and filling in gaps in previous rules to respond to new conditions in its trade relations and trade flows. As it negotiated to achieve its latest goals, it did so by working within and often building further on these rules. Those core rules and principles, in turn, underpinned thousands of other detailed commitments that America expected from other agreements and deals with individual countries. The primary difficulty in these deals was convincing trading partners to agree to America's terms, or at least a satisfactory version of them. Accepting these agreements was rarely problematic for America because the terms overwhelmingly reflected its pre-existing policies and practices, underscoring its unique leverage over the global system.

Since 2017, however, the hallmark of America's approach has been to directly challenge or ignore—and thus walk out on—many of these same core rules and norms. It has done so in different ways. These include pulling back its own attempts or obstructing other attempts to build on them further to advance them and, thus, reinforce the status quo. More aggressive has been its insistence on changing or securing new terms for these rules by threatening to withdraw from entire agreements— in other words, accept America's new conditions or else. It has also pursued both external trade objectives and domestic policy objectives by simply ignoring its standing obligations to these rules rather than working within them.

The cumulative significance of these policy shifts has been to profoundly shake the trading system, one that America, after 75 years, no longer prioritizes remaining tethered to. Instead, America has consciously disassociated itself from and openly questioned the wisdom and efficacy of many of the rules and norms it helped create for itself and the world.

One potent response is that since other countries sometimes have acted less constrained by the need to prioritize or follow these rules and norms, America is similarly justified in detaching itself from them, with little inhibition or restraint, to pursue and protect its interests. While the former point is certainly true, legions of American officials and members of Congress have aggressively mounted challenges, formed alliances, and used other leverage to push back on these trading partners while maintaining the belief that fundamentally undermining the rules and norms to do so would itself be a disservice to America's interests.

Thus, the central question is not whether America is justified in asserting its trade interests—it has always done so. Instead, it is why and how America's decision-makers today have redefined those interests and come to make sharply different choices about how to advance them. They have done so by turning away from the postwar rules-based trading system, profoundly impacting its future viability and stability.

This book aims to explore these and other fundamental changes in greater detail. It begins by framing the choices America made to separate itself from the core rules and norms underpinning the international trading system before looking at the impact of America's new policy in its trading relations across the Asia-Pacific region. To provide context, I outline four fundamental elements of the international trading system that the United States played a leading role in creating in 1947 and continued to shape decades after, set against decisions made starting in 2017 that have undermined that very system.

The Biden administration and the U.S. Congress walked out on the first core element of the international system, the "open trade" norm of advancing ever-more liberalized trade. While America has at times wavered in its commitment to this norm, it has routinely still engaged with other countries, collectively or individually, to advance successive negotiations to cut tariffs and remove other barriers to trade.

Since coming to office, the Biden administration has turned down all opportunities and proposals to join new reciprocal tariff-cutting negotiations, along with placing a much lower priority on efforts to remove non-tariff barriers to American exports in pursuit of other objectives. Similarly, since 2015, the U.S. Congress has failed to approve any agreement or pass legislation to further open America's market to anything other than only token new access. In fact, by failing to act for over three years to renew limited, conditional programs providing tariff breaks on certain imports, including one program supporting mutually beneficial trade with the world's developing countries, it has effectively only moved in the opposite direction by curtailing access.

The Trump administration walked out on the second core element, the principle of most-favored-nation treatment. Sometimes referred to as the reciprocity principle, this obligation in the rules requires each system member to provide the same terms of access to its market as it provides to all other system members. For goods and services, each country designs its own liberalization "package" to negotiate with other members that do the same, allowing each to maintain greater control over which sectors it liberalizes over others. Once trade-offs are made and these packages are agreed upon through negotiation, each must, in turn, provide its access package to all members of the system. While a limited number of important (and sometimes quite significant) exceptions can be used, the goal is to prevent countries from later offering better terms to some than they do to others.

The Trump administration flouted this core principle of non-discrimination by first threatening and following through with large, unilateral tariff increases against multiple countries. These included large tariff hikes directed at specific partners, such as China, as well as against global exporters of steel and aluminum. These tariffs, widely viewed as violating the international trade rules, have been kept in place by two U.S. administrations.

The Biden administration and the U.S. Congress walked out on the third core principle, called national treatment, which requires members to provide equitable treatment for imported and domestic products and services. The goal of this principle, sometimes called the level playing field rule, is to prevent countries from erecting discriminatory barriers through laws, regulations, or other practices aimed at putting imports at a disadvantage vis-à-vis their domestic producers. Because of the complexity of the barriers countries can use to discriminate or disadvantage, scores of additional rules were subsequently developed to cover more specific situations. Some of these cut across the economy, such as minimum standards for government regulatory transparency or rules on anti-corruption. Others were targeted to establish a level playing field for foreign exporters and firms in narrow industry sectors, whether for financial services or agricultural goods.

When the U.S. Congress approved and President Biden signed a new law in 2022 establishing billions of dollars of U.S. government-funded consumer subsidies for the purchase of electric cars, they willfully ignored this fundamental core principle of non-discrimination. The program was opened for American-made goods to qualify, but then tight limits were set on the other countries from which cars and some of their components could be sourced and still qualify.

The Trump administration walked out on the fourth element, which is to provide a dispute resolution mechanism to enable system members to hold each other accountable to their obligations. The mechanism has evolved over the years, but the fundamental approach remains unchanged—a member that alleges another is violating a trade rule can file a claim that is then reviewed by a panel of experts. If the plaintiff succeeds in its claim, it is authorized to take action, most often to raise its tariffs proportionally against the other member until it ends that practice.

The Trump administration exploited a loophole to break this trade dispute resolution mechanism and then made it clear that it was perfectly comfortable to leave it unfixed. In practical terms, breaking it for the world also allowed the Trump administration to ignore, more easily and at will, America's own trade commitments. The Biden administration, only after much delay, finally committed to work with other members to explore a compromise to make this mechanism functional again, but it continued to insist that it would only do so if fundamentally reformed. As of the publication of this book, whether such a compromise can be reached to make it functional once again remains unclear and the focus of much concern.

These and other examples explored in the following pages underscore the radical shift in America's trade policy since the mid-2010s, changes that have led it to turn away from much of what it aimed to achieve since the 1940s. These developments also raise the question of where America is headed next. The last time America's trade policy appeared so unpredictable was during the late nineteenth and early twentieth centuries when the U.S. Congress exercised its constitutional prerogative over foreign commerce more independently. That period was punctuated by episodic waves of dramatic hikes and then cuts to U.S. import tariffs depending on the party in power; the international rules that would later be created were intended to prevent the United States and other countries from returning to embrace such gyrations in trade policy.

Having poked large holes in the commitments it forged to help wean itself and the world away from volatility in global trade, today the postwar rules-based international trading system remains afloat but has taken on water and is listing heavily. Some have gone as far as to pronounce it dead, already "sclerotic," then pushed onto the tracks to be run over by America's unilateral pursuit of its own goals.[1] Trade continues, but with a new sense today that just about anything goes in a system that is left helpless to stop it.

If the rules and the system are no longer sufficiently in its interests, America has failed to develop a convincing vision of the kind of system it seeks instead. Even if it could formulate this vision, it is unlikely to be a system that the rest of the world would agree to live with. More likely, America will instead continue down its current path of poking holes in the system when needed to respond to the country's new political alignments, testing its limits as it goes until it has stirred up enough waves to finally sink it. Meanwhile, the world is closely watching and hedging its bets on the future of the international trading system in the wake of America's disruptions, in the expectation of more to come, and absent America's leadership to provide a compelling and workable alternative.

---

1   See Jeffrey Schott, "The WTO Is Dead . . . Long Live the WTO," *Milken Institute Review*, May 4, 2020.

Before America started walking out as it has in recent years, its political decision-makers managed for seven decades to instead walk and chew gum on trade policy. When new challenges or political concerns from America's openness to global competition arose, policymakers responded by layering on additional, new policy tools to respond—all while maintaining their overall commitment to advancing freer and more open trade as in America's best overall interest. These responses included insisting on new rules to keep foreign governments from replacing their tariff barriers with other forms of discriminatory barriers. They also included developing programs in America to aid workers who lost their jobs from global competition and new domestic laws that expanded definitions of unfair trade and the means for American business owners to obtain remedies against it. As important as these tools became, they were imperfect and often proved insufficient, especially since many did not even kick in until after substantial harm had already been done.[2]

As more globalized trade advanced and new countries such as China, with different economic systems and motives, negotiated their way into the international trading system, America responded yet again by seeking another round of new trade rules. These aimed at setting standards abroad to help stem imports of cheaper goods before they arrived at U.S. ports by requiring them to take on the greater costs of meeting environmental, labor, or other regulations that helped make for cheaper production abroad. These also included tightening existing and developing new rules and obligations to prevent unfair government aid and other non-market benefits coming from state ownership of its exporters. With these additional goals incorporated into its negotiating agenda, America tied acceptance of these new standards to its leverage of offering better market access in exchange for reciprocal, tariff-free access abroad for its exports.

Initially skittish about upsetting domestic critics over trade, the Obama administration was the last U.S. administration to embrace America's traditional trade priorities as it attempted to layer on these new trade rules to improve its terms for trade. It called its approach a "transformational trade policy," and once it got started, it threw every-

---

2   For a sober overview of some of these programs and their shortcomings and failures, see Edward Alden, *Failure to Adjust* (Lanham: Rowman & Littlefield, 2017).

thing into an ambitious market-opening agenda. It launched significant new free trade negotiations with 11 other trading partners in the Asia-Pacific region and with the European Union, comprised of 27 member countries. It also took more selective approaches to global free trade talks, supporting further negotiations to achieve what was possible in smaller groups than what had proven perhaps no longer possible among the WTO's 160-plus members. One such effort was a negotiation by a few dozen countries to eliminate tariffs on a list of "green goods," such as components for wind-powered electricity generation, where tariff-free trade could further facilitate their deployment to help meet climate goals.

The Obama administration's vision and these efforts proved insufficiently transformational, however. Just as the administration was hitting its stride, Washington's shifting consensus on trade was building steam, and America's commitment to open, rules-based trade hit a wall just as the administration sought more of it. Nearly every one of its new trade liberalization efforts, from goods to services, collided with awaiting domestic opposition, and then, in 2017, the new American administration walked out.

———◆———

What took America so sharply off course from its 75-year commitment to these rules and norms?

One explanation is the historic impact of China's post-2001 export deluge on the U.S. economy—with sharper and more exaggerated political adjustments and reactions made in response to it than to past challenges presented by other trading partners. In numeric terms, America's annual $83 billion goods trade deficit with China in 2001 ballooned to an annual $375 billion deficit by 2017. While estimates of job losses from plant closings and other economic dislocations from offshoring range widely, even conservative estimates are that a few million jobs were affected. Economists have sharply different views about the impact on the overall American economy, with some pointing to record low unemployment into the early 2020s as a sign of a resilient economy that weathered and successfully adjusted to the China shock. Others argue that the hidden impact of maintaining an open market to China is suppressed wages for other jobs over the longer term, in addition to the often-incalculable short-term costs to individuals and communities from these "adjustments." The elimination of American jobs and industrial capacity, coupled with Washington's insufficient responses to these losses, led to an untenable situation sufficient to enable and trigger a political response that moved sharply away from prior trade policies and approaches.

Another explanation centers on a seismic political reaction to broader economic challenges. The basic argument goes as follows: heightened economic discontent fueled by the 2007–08 financial crisis, further compounded by dramatic technological shifts and their associated impacts on automation and competitiveness, focused political attention on vulnerabilities that cut across the economy. These changes have been further exacerbated by America's open market posture toward the world.[3] External shocks that include China's impacts on the U.S. economy have added further to these pressures, giving more momentum to political opposition to America's openness to global trade.

All of these factors are relevant and have contributed significantly. However, they still fall short of sufficiently explaining the dramatic break in America's political consensus on trade—one that proved sufficient enough to cause its leaders to walk out in such a fundamental way. America has faced these challenges before and has responded with high-stakes threats and actions to confront foreign trade practices that it viewed as unfair. It similarly weathered, adjusted to, and emerged from deep recessions and major economic transformations during periods of criticism that faulted its open trade approach as a leading contributor to those recessions and adjustments. Although pausing at times from pursuing more open markets, its political leaders recommitted themselves to maintaining the system with further efforts to evolve instead of walking out on its postwar vision and goals.

Not long ago, Japan was deemed the greatest external challenge to America's economic competitiveness and leadership. For thirty years, especially throughout the 1970s and 1980s, Japan's export machine led to major acute dislocations and U.S. job losses across several industrial sectors. This occurred amidst major economic transitions that included some of America's deepest recessions and, notably, periods of strong growth. Similar to today's concerns about China, Japan leveraged its (initially) lower wages, pursued state-supported targets that led to export deluges into the U.S. market, manipulated its currency, poached U.S. industrial designs, and used innovative approaches to work around the

---

3   See Monica de Bolle and Jeromin Zettelmeyer, "Measuring the Rise of Economic Nationalism" (Working Paper 19-15, Peterson Institute for International Economics, Washington, DC, August 2019).

core rules of international trade—at least as the United States had anticipated them to be followed—to gain a competitive trade and industrial advantage. This, too, shook America's confidence in the international trading system and brought strong resentment and calls for action at home that blossomed into major political issues and pressures. In response, America developed and used defensive and offensive trade tools against Japan, just as it has with China today.

Few in America remained complacent in the face of these and other challenges from abroad, fighting back and leveraging the size and influence of the U.S. market to carve out new advantages in global markets. Even as the most taxing of these times routinely stretched America's commitment to the rules and norms of the international system, U.S. presidents and the two major political parties largely resisted taking steps that fundamentally turned away from open international trade and the core attributes of the trading system.[4] Instead, sufficient political space was maintained to keep the lane clear for pressing ahead with more open, rules-based trade.

Have today's trade and economic pressures and challenges become simply too overwhelming compared to the past, forcing America's decision-makers to finally close off the political safe space to advance free trade? Or has something qualitatively new and transformational emerged to finally tip the balance?

This book argues that among the many external and domestic influences shaping U.S. trade policy decisions, the cause of the collapse in America's decades-long, bipartisan consensus supporting freer trade and the rules-based trading system has been principally homegrown. This consensus ultimately succumbed to the emergence of America's zero-sum-centered politics as the new, defining feature of its political system. As this stark political divide deepened throughout the 2010s, reaching a level that polling found to be "exceptional" by international standards,[5] America's new zero-sum-driven politics fundamentally transformed its trade policy choices along two dimensions—domestic and foreign.

4   See, e.g., Richard Gephardt, "Commanding Heights," interview, PBS, April 26, 2001, https://www.pbs.org/wgbh/commandingheights/shared/minitext/int_richardgephardt.html. The Democratic congressman was the U.S. House of Representatives majority leader during the height of U.S.-Japan trade friction.

5   Michael Dimock and Richard Wike, "America is Exceptional in the Nature of Its Political Divide," Pew Research Center, November 13, 2020, https://pewrsr.ch/2JZY9fb.

Along the domestic axis, opposing Right and Left camps in Washington could no longer forge consensus on new ground rules for the economy within America's borders. As a result, America could no longer support its own rules for global trade, much less lead the way to help forge new ones. Along the foreign axis, a strikingly aligned view emerged from these polarized camps on the new mainstream of the Right and Left: America's experiment with free trade had become a greater source of harm than opportunity. With these seismic shifts in play, the middle disappeared. America's political leaders found it easier to walk out on their predecessors' commitments rather than maintain them by forging other compromises to solve America's challenges. Much more on these key points is discussed in the final chapter.

One manifestation of this homegrown shift has been America's turn toward results-based, instead of rules- and principles-based, trade and related industrial policies. Turning America's external trade deficit into a scorecard of trade policy success and failure is a straightforward example. Soaring trade deficits have often created acute political demands on Washington. Yet even its most hawkish political leaders on trade long recognized that foreign barriers to America's exports were only one part of that story, with the sustained impacts of massive macroeconomic imbalances triggered by America's recurring large national budget deficits and the overall gap in national savings and spending also playing an outsized role in it.[6] A belief that America's external trade deficit instead is the zero-sum result of failed trade policies that can be eliminated by getting tough with its trading partners leads, in stark contrast, to fundamentally different assumptions about the necessity and means of trying to eliminate that deficit.

Another result has been a fundamental transformation in views around the role of America's large, multinational corporations in the trading system. Public opinion toward large corporations has markedly deteriorated in America in recent years, whereby supporters of both American political parties today equally share in their broad distrust and disapproval of big business.[7] Whether rooted in public anger toward tax unfairness ("corporate tax dodgers"), high prescription drug prices ("Big Pharma"), gasoline price-gouging ("Big Oil"), or profiting from

6   See, e.g., Peter T. Kilborn, "Working Profile: John C. Danforth; Twisting Tokyo's Tail on Balance of Trade," *New York Times*, July 10, 1985.
7   Amina Dunn and Andy Cerda, "Anti- Corporate Sentiment in U.S. Is Now Widespread in Both Parties," Pew Research Center, November 17, 2022, https://pewrsr.ch/3ApCrsw.

the trade of personal information ("Big Tech"), familiar public out-rage directed at large U.S. companies for years was typically limited to narrower, issue-specific politics. In the case of America's international trade agreements and other commitments, these issue-specific criti-cisms have combined in an omnibus way into the political smear that such agreements are nothing more than "corporate deals" principally subservient to these narrow corporate interests. Longstanding political support for other efforts to open new markets for American companies, whether large or small, has particularly retreated amid the Democratic Party's embrace of its progressive mainstream's zero-sum claims about winners and losers.

The shift toward zero-sum-centered politics and policy choices also has ushered in sweeping new efforts on the New Right and the progres-sive Left to wall off America's markets against imports, including in ways that flout the international trade rules. These include Washington's new practice of slapping steep new tariffs on hundreds of billions of dollars of imports and then continuing to develop novel justifications for keeping them in place. Other efforts include attaching discriminatory domes-tic production and purchase preferences to massive new government subsidy programs and additional steps to curtail foreign access to U.S. government procurement contracts. Finally, it has resulted in America walking out on nearly all negotiations that would further open its market, as well as its failure for over three years and counting to renew its 50-year commitment to providing limited tariff-free access for the world's developing countries.

⸺⸺◇⸺⸺

America's trade policy today stands in opposition to the positive sum idea that guided its politicians and officials to create and lead the expansion of the international trading system in the first place—freer, rules-based trade was a tide to help lift all boats, making it good policy for both America and for the world. Initially a progressive priority of the Franklin Roosevelt administration to aid America's economy in recovering from economic despair and depression in the 1930s, the approach soon after was accorded a central place in America's postwar foreign economic vision to help ignite a new era of global economic prosperity to prevent the world from sliding back into conflict. The idea solidified into a new mainstream, bipartisan consensus after the Republican Party turned in the 1950s toward its new internationalist orientation on trade, after its nearly century-long support for high tariff policies to benefit the U.S. industrial sector. By leading and promoting the expansion of this system, America often took on the extra burdens and responsibilities that came with its role while also affording it a position of even greater influence over the system.

By the mid-2010s, America's two political parties came together again on trade, but with a different cause and new goal. Even as the Republican mainstream New Right and the progressive Democratic mainstream Left engaged in fierce, gridlock-inducing disagreements over domestic policies, often taking the form of fights around preserving or reforming the status quo at home, each found themselves in alignment against America's openness to international trade and many of the policies and approaches that had enabled it. Justified as everything from the need to reassert America's sovereignty by reneging on its previous international commitments to the need to stem globalization and foreign supply chain overdependency, they converged on a similar set of choices for America's external policies that rusted through the anchor chain mooring America to existing trade rules and norms. With these new choices, America emerged as one of the world's leading trade rule disrupters, ceding its role as the most influential rule-maker.

The international implications of this shift have been more than profound. Beyond the international trading system sliding from its state of paralysis into increasing irrelevancy, America's shift is acutely seen in the Asia-Pacific region as a self-inflicted flag of surrender to China's aggressive efforts to expand its trade relations and influence. America has lost the confidence of many in the region as it expects them to welcome its presence but also accept and tolerate its new discriminatory practices and consistently flip-flopping priorities. It has alienated its allies and then, while professing to wish to re-engage with them, only further discriminated among them. It has sparked a new global subsidies race that leaves the poorest countries behind while failing to renew tariff preferences that it had routinely granted for a half-century to help the economic development of these disadvantaged countries through exports. It has also lost the confidence of its own businesses and exporters, which long depended on the American government to support their interests abroad.

The problems facing America's trade policymakers in the late 2010s and into the 2020s are as politically significant as in the 1970s and 1980s when America's commitment to freer trade was arguably more deeply tested. It is hard to argue that the external trade challenges America faces today are any starker than they have been over much of the past 75 years. Most modern-day problems, such as several dozen ships waiting to unload at the Port of Long Beach amid a short-lived, post-COVID supply chain crisis, have not matched the severity of chaos and disruption that faced global trade in the aftermath of World War II. At that time, unfair manipulation of commodity markets, excessive concentration from wartime production, high tariffs, and trade barriers were the norm, not the exception, leading America to create and commit to, and then continually readjust its approaches to remain committed to its vision of fair, rules-based global trade. It was never shy in asserting its interests along the way, which at times also pressed and undermined America's strict adherence to this commitment. Incredible progress was made over the past 75 years to achieve America's self-defined objectives for the kind of global trading system it set out to create.

The weakness that America's negotiators of the 1947 General Agreement on Tariffs and Trade and, later, the WTO did not anticipate was the country's inability to solve its problems and challenges at home. Other books have focused on these domestic policy failures in the face of America's growing openness and exposure to expanding international trade and globalism.[8] This book focuses on the choices made in America's trade policy to adjust and respond—choices that have always been deeply political.

If current trends persist, the Asia-Pacific region, other trading partners, and American export-oriented businesses that rely on government advocacy will be left to wonder about the impact of America's inward-facing policies. Will America irreversibly hobble and destabilize the regional and global trading order by continuing to walk out, or will it decide to make a cleaner break by deciding to simply walk away?

---

8   Especially powerful among these is Alden, *Failure to Adjust*.

TWO

Walking Out on the WTO

Twenty-one trade ministers from around the Pacific region gathered in May 2017 in Hanoi, Vietnam, for their annual Asia-Pacific Economic Cooperation (APEC) forum meeting. President Trump was starting his fifth month in office and had already taken several actions to follow through on his presidential campaign bluster on trade, putting many of the gathered trade officials on edge. With confirmation that U.S. Trade Representative Robert Lighthizer would attend the meeting days after being sworn into office, attention turned to what message President Trump's new trade ambassador would deliver to the 20 other trade ministers gathered at the venue.

On the surface, Ambassador Lighthizer's opening message to the APEC trade ministers was not as sharply antagonistic as some expected, particularly in relief against Trump's actions and rhetoric. It was nonetheless stern and clear: America remained committed to freer trade, and the new administration supported competing on that basis—but only if, and only where, fair conditions of competition first existed. This, at least, was not unfamiliar language from past U.S. administrations.

When the ministers' agenda turned to the topic of the WTO, its director general, Roberto Azevedo, came to present his overview of the challenges and opportunities ahead for the organization and its ongoing negotiations. Each APEC minister then joined a speaking queue to offer their views on how best to support further progress in the WTO. All, that is, except for Trump's new personal representative on trade, who declined to offer one.

At that moment, America's posture and position toward the WTO and the international trading system were far from fully formed in the public domain. Candidate Trump said very little about the WTO beyond his familiar trope of calling it and other U.S. trade agreements "a disaster."[1] The new administration signaled more specific concerns soon after Trump's inauguration. These included accusing the WTO of having usurped America's sovereignty and highlighting its inadequacies as a tool for America to defend itself from Chinese and other unfair foreign practices.[2]

At that early moment in his tenure, Lighthizer did not join the APEC forum queue to share his vision with his new counterparts. In a different room, however, American officials had begun to reveal the administration's new positions on the WTO to other APEC delegates. Their demands for the meeting's ministerial statement made clear that America was ready to walk out on the WTO and its system of global trade rules and norms. Statement negotiators met around the clock to successfully resolve countless issues, but they refused to accept America's objections to two phrases that had been among the most routine, uncontroversial passages from past statements.

American officials first objected to acknowledging that the WTO was the world's central rules-based trading system. As the United States was a principal leader in creating the General Agreement on Tariffs and Trade (GATT), the postwar trading system's core agreements and foundational grouping, and then in helping build new institutions such as the WTO, the GATT's successor, along with others such as APEC to foster economic cooperation and support free and open trade, refusal to agree to this basic acknowledgment was profoundly bewildering and alienating for just about all gathered.

The second objection was against renewing a pledge that had appeared routinely in the statement since the 2007–08 financial crisis. It was a voluntary commitment among APEC members to avoid taking new protectionist trade measures and to roll back any that they had

---

1   Ian Mount, "Donald Trump Says It Might Be Time for the U.S. to Quit the WTO," *Fortune*, July 25, 2016.

2   USTR (Office of the U.S. Trade Representative), "The President's 2017 Trade Policy Agenda," in *2017 Trade Policy Agenda and 2016 Annual Report of the President of the United States on the Trade Agreements Program* (Washington, DC: USTR, March 1, 2017), 1–7.

implemented. Since the pledge was an empty and thus meaningless commitment by some other members, America's new position went, America was no longer willing to endorse it. Delegates correctly suspected that the actual reason was America's new unwillingness to have its hands tied by the pledge. Trump's own rhetoric already pointed to America's intention to break the pledge, giving the opening to others who had already done the same to pin the blame on America for refusing to renew it.

Negotiations for the APEC trade ministers' statement ultimately ended in a stalemate, the same fate for most similar trade statements over the four years of the Trump administration.[3] With America the only APEC member blocking agreement, Vietnam's meeting chair was left to issue his own version, conveying the "ununified but prevailing views" of the APEC members in support of upholding the WTO's rules-based system. Because America refused to agree to renew the pledge to avoid protectionism, the chair left out that commitment altogether.[4]

Most gathered in Hanoi viewed America's positions as sharply antagonistic. America had long insisted others sign onto these and similar principles, both in specific policy terms and in the form of these broader political commitments. While just a statement of political commitments, the message America's positions were sending was unmistakable and reverberated across these meetings as though the very floor was preparing to fall out from beneath global trade. Delegates could only wonder what to expect from Washington going forward. Meanwhile, America's complete isolation was welcomed by its adversaries, which joined America's allies in poking it for turning its back on its longstanding positions and values, and in pressing it to reconsider.

America's long list of concerns and grievances with the WTO and the international trading system came into full relief as the Trump administration's trade policy unfolded. Many of these concerns also found a new home in the Biden administration's approach to the WTO, albeit with some differences.

---

3   On similar U.S. objections over trade language in other statement negotiations, see, e.g., Jenny Leonard, "Sources: Language on WTO, 'Reciprocal' Trade Causes Roadblocks in Negotiations for G20 Communiqué," World Trade Online, July 7, 2017.

4   For part of the story, see, e.g., Nguyen Dieu Tu Uyen and Luu Van Dat, "APEC Trade Ministers Omit Protectionism Pledge in Statement," Bloomberg, May 21, 2017. For the APEC chair's statement, see Tran Tuan Anh, "Statement of the Chair (Ha Noi, Viet Nam, 21 May 2017)," APEC, May 21, 2017, https://www.apec.org/meeting-papers/sectoral-ministerial-meetings /trade/2017_trade/chair.

This chapter first provides a broad overview of why and how America's careful support and nurturing of the postwar international trading system began to unwind over time, setting the stage for a dramatic series of reversals in America's long-held positions. It will then turn to cover three major ways that America, starting with the Trump administration, walked out of the WTO in pursuit of its new trade policy: by breaking the WTO's system that held America and others accountable to the rules, by paving a wide boulevard to have an argument to skirt around the WTO's rules when imposing new tariffs on the world, and by its use of tariff unilateralism against individual trading partners, which drove an American truck directly over the WTO system. The final section will evaluate the implications of these actions for America's foreign relations. The next chapter will take up America's efforts to undermine the WTO's other key function—its role in advancing new global negotiations to achieve freer trade and new trade-liberalizing rules.

AMERICA'S PROBLEM WITH THE WTO

Lighthizer, who served as a deputy U.S. trade ambassador in the Ronald Reagan administration, returned to government in May 2017 as President Trump's lead U.S. trade ambassador. In the 30-plus-year interim, he had developed a successful practice at a leading Washington law firm, specializing in cases helping U.S. companies—often American steel and other manufacturing companies—seek temporary tariff protection from cheap or other unfair imports. His practice focused on the flip side of the free trade coin, which was the business of protecting the rights of America's industries that, under U.S. law, sought the shelter of these higher tariffs.

Highly skilled at parlor talk, Lighthizer liked to recount the story of a social encounter he had witnessed that ended in a humorous chain reaction of glasses crashing to the floor. Decades after the incident, he would describe it with great fondness, ending by confessing his love of "a good train wreck." Given the glasses about to be broken over America's new trade policies, there was no better person to relish in it than Trump's new trade representative.

Fluent in the ways he believed the WTO had itself become a harmful train wreck, Lighthizer nonetheless often insisted that he was not anti-WTO per se. He sometimes remarked that "if the WTO didn't exist, you'd have to create it" and even called it an "important institution." Later in his tenure, he wrote more clearly about his support for the WTO and the international trading system, albeit with extensive qualifications.[5] As an attorney who had spent much of his career defending U.S. companies and industries against harmful and unfair imports, he also was always happy to find a balcony to make clear the many bones he had to pick with the WTO and the harm that it had done. Cumulatively, in his view, the WTO's shortcomings and overreaches allowed its fundamentally flawed system to prevent America and its industries from rightfully challenging and defending themselves against these unfair trade practices. He was more than ready to knock the WTO off its pedestal.

Lighthizer's objection in Hanoi to draft statement language affirming the "rules-based multilateral (international) trading system with the WTO at its core" was premised on doing just that. Keeping the WTO system at the core of America's trade policy decisions and commitments, in Lighthizer's view, unhelpfully subordinated U.S. trade laws and trade rights to the nation's obligations under the WTO's flawed system and agreements. Prior American administrations similarly held that U.S. law was ultimately superior to WTO rules and rulings but spent their energy working within the WTO system to improve it and America's position in global trade competition. Lighthizer's sharp shift in emphasis signaled that America instead would no longer be constrained by the WTO rules when deciding and implementing its trade policies and priorities. The approach also mirrored the Trump administration's highly negative view of other global organizations and America's international obligations to other countries participating in them.

Lighthizer took this further by also objecting strenuously to describing the WTO as a "rules-based" system. With hundreds of agreed rules in the WTO and a process to help enforce them, delegates in Hanoi could not understand what this new objection even meant, much less what kind of system Lighthizer believed that the WTO represented. He posed that same question in response. In his view, the WTO's expanding body of jurisprudence—new "rules" in the form of interpretations of the WTO rules by expert judges helping settle disputes among its members—had acquired precedential significance and metastasized into harmful overreach. Much like the conservative lawyer's distaste for "activist" judges, he insisted that these rulings trampled America's rights by erasing some of the key red lines that America had already built into the WTO agreements. This was especially true for rules relating to the

---

5   Robert E. Lighthizer, "How to Set World Trade Straight," *Wall Street Journal*, August 20, 2020.

right to raise tariffs to defend domestic industries from unfairly priced or otherwise advantaged imports. On that basis alone, Lighthizer refused to agree that the WTO was still a "rules-based" system, even though that was exactly what it was.

With his concerns, Lighthizer was in very good company on both sides of the political aisle in Washington, especially around the perceived overreach of the WTO's appointed dispute settlement judges in their decisions. By the mid-2010s, America's labor unions and other activists, many Capitol Hill lawmakers, and Lighthizer's predecessors serving in the George W. Bush and Barack Obama administrations had come to hold similar concerns. To deal with these, America continued to work within the system as it nearly always had by, for example, stepping up its public criticism of some WTO judicial decisions and conducting more comprehensive vetting before agreeing to the appointment of any new WTO judges.

Amid these growing criticisms, the WTO's dispute process had evolved into its busiest and most consequential area of work. Its other most important function—as a forum for concluding new tariff-liberalizing and trade rule negotiations—was spectacularly failing to deliver virtually any new agreements. Scores of negotiations were launched in the WTO that were both broad (e.g., the Doha Round of global tariff reductions) and narrow (e.g., industry-specific tariff reductions, such as for environmental goods) in scope, as well as focused both on specific sectors (e.g., WTO-related negotiations to liberalize services markets) and across thematic areas (e.g., issues such as competition policy). Despite these efforts, only one significant WTO agreement was reached among all its members during its first 25 years of existence.[6] As explored in the next chapter, the Trump and Biden administrations only further encumbered the WTO's negotiating agenda, stalling any prospect of reaching new trade liberalization agreements.

Since unanimity was required to conclude most WTO agreements, each new member added to the organization made that goal more challenging to achieve. Following the original 1947 GATT agreement among just 24 countries, its membership had expanded to nearly 130 nations when the GATT was succeeded by the WTO in 1995. By the mid-2010s, membership had reached over 160 countries, accounting for roughly 95 percent of world trade. Even as consensus and agreement became

---

6   The notable exception is the WTO's Trade Facilitation Agreement, concluded in 2014. Other, significantly more limited agreements were reached in 2022.

harder over time, members still managed to eke out, every decade or so, large and important new agreements to liberalize tariffs further and create new rules. The 1994 agreement to form the WTO was among these major new agreements. It also was the membership's last major negotiation to conclude successfully and the last to further liberalize trade among all members.

After 1995, the WTO's membership expansion added not only to its numbers but also to the diversity of economic systems, levels of development, and views of its members, including their views toward the international trading system's rules and norms. Major developing economies came to have stronger voices, further shifting the WTO's negotiation dynamics. Instead of the mostly Western democracy–led group setting the main commitments, with developing countries allowed special status to make less ambitious commitments to the same, multiple new power centers emerged, each able to exert independent influence and demands, further adding complexity.

By the 2010s, the cumulative effect was a WTO that was failing to keep up in the most basic ways. For example, countries that originally had joined the GATT as developing countries, such as Singapore and South Korea, had been able to keep the advantages of that status, often for decades after becoming developed economies. As important as its role and function were in maintaining the global trading order, the WTO was becoming more unwieldy and quickly losing organizational credibility in key ways, whether from accusations of its overreach or inadequacy.

Dropped like a ton of bricks into these shifting dynamics was the 2001 agreement to admit China into the WTO. To be admitted and access the preferential (lower) tariffs that all its members offered to each other, China, like other candidate countries, first had to demonstrate satisfactorily that it met the WTO's rules. It also had to secure the membership's agreement that its market opening offers on tariff rates, services, and in other areas provided a sufficient package of new access in return for the levels each member had offered other WTO members. After lengthy negotiations, which lasted well over a decade, America joined others in finally admitting China in 2001 as the WTO's 143rd member. What was not anticipated at the time was that the WTO would fail to reach new tariff-liberalizing agreements, leaving China locked in at a higher average tariff rate than the developed world, although still lower than most of the least developed countries.

America's decision to admit China was based on the belief and presumption that by undertaking reforms to its own system to join the

WTO and committing to the organization's nondiscriminatory principles and rules, China would proceed on a transformational path of market-oriented reforms and opening. The decision also anticipated large new opportunities for American exporters to access and sell into its rapidly growing market.[7] The view was similar to other decisions made following the collapse of the Soviet Union in 1991, grounded in a belief that the attractiveness of a liberal democracy and supporting international institutions like the WTO would foster the spread of a liberal, market-based economic order.[8] In terms of trade and investment, the Golden Arches Theory of Conflict Prevention was in its full ascendency—the theory that war and other serious conflict would not break out between countries having embraced economic integration between them, as measured symbolically by whether a country had agreed to allow McDonald's to operate within its borders.[9] China, which already had roughly three hundred McDonald's stores by the time it joined, was viewed by many as a welcome, if not long overdue, member of the WTO (today, there are nearly five thousand McDonald's in China).[10]

America's early vision for global trade liberalism, which took hold with the establishment of the GATT system in 1947, quickly found the potential of its global reach limited by the sudden emergence of the Cold War. With the end of the Cold War, the founding of the WTO in 1995 was a new opportunity to bring countries such as China, the former Soviet states, and eventually Russia itself into the international system as the squaring of the global circle that America had envisioned for the international trading system in 1945. Inevitable clashes in values and systems were important issues in these WTO accession discussions, as they had been decades earlier when some of America's postwar allies sought gaping carve-outs to the core trade rules to take any measures they deemed necessary to meet full employment objectives.[11] China, Russia, and others had to accept the rules as they were. Their candida-

7   For a summary of the views at the time on China's WTO candidacy, see Phelim Kine, "China Joined Rules-Based Trading System—Then Broke the Rules," Politico, December 9, 2021.

8   Francis Fukuyama, *The End of History and the Last Man* (New York, NY: Penguin Books, 1992).

9   Thomas L. Friedman, "Foreign Affairs Big Mac I," *New York Times*, December 8, 1996. As a counterpoint, see Paul Musgrave, "The Beautiful, Dumb Dream of McDonald's Peace Theory," *Foreign Policy*, November 26, 2020.

10   Sara Murphy, "How McDonald's Became a Fast Food Giant in China," Mashed, April 4, 2023; and Shawn Baldwin, "How McDonald's Won Over China," CNBC, February 28, 2023.

11   William Diebold, Jr., *The End of the I.T.O.*, Essays in International Finance, no.16 (Princeton: Princeton University, October 1952).

cies were instead judged by each wto member by the adequacy of the reciprocal access they offered and by their commitments to reform and abide by the rules.

By the mid-2010s, many in America came to believe that these prior assumptions about China's trajectory were either a critical error by America's decision-makers or, somewhat more charitably, the result of them having been skillfully duped. Either way, after reaping large financial gains from the export revenues from its new wto-enabled access to global markets, China soon turned sharply toward a heavy-handed, state-directed, and state-subsidized model of economic development and trade across many large and important industries. As successful as it was in many ways, China's serial theft of industrial secrets and intellectual property, use of forced labor in the production process, massive state subsidization of key industries leading to below-cost export deluges, currency manipulation to maintain trade advantages, and opaque application of rules and regulations to pressure and disadvantage foreign firms created major new strains on global markets and within the wto. The wto rules could deal with many of these issues only in limited, sometimes unhelpfully narrow ways.

Even though straight number crunching, measured as overall economic welfare effects, showed that America benefited in some ways from China's membership in the wto, the numbers masked the direct harm inflicted on many industries, communities, and individuals.[12] The consolation that jobs lost to China were picked up elsewhere in the economy was of little consequence to the growing number of communities left without the resources to overcome business closings and job losses. China increasingly presented a new and more alarming type of trade challenge in terms of America's new dependence on these imports and the traceable loss of jobs to them.

The Bush and Obama administrations both responded by stepping up more aggressive enforcement of the wto rules against China. When brought to the wto, these cases were nearly all successful. At the same time, the challenges brought by Chinese trade grew exponentially and far outpaced what could be achieved by bringing new cases to the wto. Worse, China's new policies and practices increasingly lacked the trans-

---

12   See Xavier Jaravel and Erick Sager, "What Are the Price Effects of Trade? Evidence from the U.S. and Implications for Quantitative Trade Models," Finance and Economics Discussion Series 2019-068 (Washington, DC: Board of Governors of the Federal Reserve System, August 2019), https://doi.org/10.17016/FEDS.2019.068.

parency necessary to gather proof and successfully litigate them through the WTO, or they took greater advantage of gaps in the WTO trade rules and operated in plain sight. When it faced similar problems with Japan's system in prior decades, America had to, at times, work outside of the GATT to pressure Japan over these concerns. The problems with China, however, were even bigger and broader.

Both administrations also engaged with China to seek unilateral commitments to reform and change. This approach, often with meager leverage behind it, yielded little in results. America worked with others to develop new rules for the WTO to address the issues, but with China now a member able to wield a veto, no meaningful progress was likely to be made there either. By the early 2010s, political finger-pointing picked up in Washington on the need to do more to stem the harm. Maintaining faith that the WTO was an adequate answer to confronting China became politically unsustainable and unconvincing.

In this environment, the Obama administration continued to express support for the WTO as it also began to step up calls for needed change. By late 2016, America's ambassador to the WTO reflected that dual message well in one of his parting messages to the WTO membership. He called for actions to "strengthen" and "revitalize" the WTO, considering "distressing trends in the dispute settlement functions" and the need to "move beyond negotiating structures that had . . . long ceased any promise of success." He then went on to underscore America's pledge to continue to work within the WTO rules and norms to accomplish this goal, stressing America's longstanding "commitment to open markets and to the rules-based multilateral trading system as embodied in the WTO" and noting that it remained "a vital part of the United States' trade and investment policy" and that it was "firmly in our national interest to promote a rules-based system"—all phrases and concepts that Lighthizer would flatly reject just a few months later.[13]

During his campaign, Trump made unmistakably clear that, if elected, he would directly deal with the unfair trade practices of China and other countries. By implication, it was unlikely they would be handled through an intermediary process like WTO dispute resolution panels or by worrying over the need to follow WTO obligations and procedures. Whether they were intended to blunt China's low-wage export machine

---

13 Michael Punke, "Statement of the United States by Ambassador Michael Punke at the 13th WTO Trade Policy Review of the United States of America," USTR, statement transcript, December 19, 2016.

or to threaten China's or just about any other foreign leader to achieve other outcomes, these threats were precisely the kind of unilateralist approach that the international trading system, and especially the creation of the WTO, had aimed to curb.

Another core theme of Trump's campaign was an insistence on restoring trade balance and tariff reciprocity, including for America's trade with China. The GATT and the WTO were built on the most-favored-nation (MFN) approach to reciprocity, whereby each member offered the same market-access package to all other members. This approach allowed each country to set different tariff rates for different imported products depending on their needs and import sensitivities, such as charging no tariff on imported raw cotton but setting a higher tariff for imported cotton clothes to encourage domestic textile production. Each product tariff rate, in principle, was then uniformly assessed on imports from all GATT and, later, WTO members. Members used global tariff-cutting rounds to negotiate better overall access packages across a wide range of products in other members' markets in exchange for offering a better package of lower tariffs for imports into their own market. As countries agreed to lower their average tariff rates through these negotiations, product-specific tariff rates continued to vary significantly among countries. As average tariff rates were cut over several decades, America's rate remained among the very lowest but still comparable to the average rate charged by other advanced countries such as Canada and Australia. Even as average tariffs came down globally, lesser-developed countries were still given room to keep the highest average tariff rates. Rapidly industrializing countries, meanwhile, often resisted expectations that they should lower their average tariff rates further and faster as their economic development progressed.

Trump's goal of achieving absolute tariff reciprocity turned the principle on its head, insisting instead on matching each U.S. tariff to each WTO member on a country-by-country, product-by-product basis. This approach harkened back to thinking from the nineteenth century and aimed to upend the MFN principle. Its simplicity has undeniable intuitive appeal, but if applied consistently, the approach would also entail potentially undesirable and politically unacceptable outcomes. For example, America would raise its 2.5 percent tariff on passenger car imports from the European Union (EU) (to match the EU's rate of 10 percent on imports) while raising it still higher on imports from China (to meet China's 15 percent rate). Going the other way, each could be expected to reciprocate by raising their own (lower) tariffs on imports of American pickup and other similar light trucks to match America's tariff rate of 25 percent for those vehicles. In the case of trade with Japan (which has a zero percent tariff on all vehicle imports), absolute reciprocity would be achieved either by eliminating America's tariffs on vehicle imports from Japan—an improbable scenario—or by Japan also seeking reciprocity for itself by charging new tariffs on vehicle imports from America. Regardless of its upside-down consequences at times, Trump insisted that his zombie brand of absolute, complete reciprocity, which had been dead and buried since the middle of the twentieth century, was the only commonsense means of restoring fairness while slashing the U.S. trade deficit.

Given Trump's campaign positions, once he took office, there was no need to consciously choose to walk out on the international trading system. The administration's new trade objectives made clear that it just would. The only question left was how it would go around, or directly over, the WTO. To do so, administration advisors and officials clarified early on that they were considering different ways to bypass America's accountability to the same WTO rules that it helped write decades earlier.[14]

The cleanest but most extreme path would have been to withdraw and walk away entirely from the WTO. While the administration never decided to pull America out of the WTO or from any of its individual stand-alone agreements, hints and direct threats that the option was on the table nonetheless were made throughout Trump's presidency.[15] Inside the administration, serious discussions about pulling America out of the WTO were also held occasionally, with draft paperwork to put the withdrawal into effect even drawn up early in the administration.[16] The level of consideration and initial preparation given to withdrawing from the WTO was significantly greater than ever generally understood or appreciated by those outside the administration.

For all of America's frustrations, even a flirtation with pulling out of the WTO was by itself a dramatic turn of events. If it had been carried through, it likely would have proven catastrophic for the U.S. and global economies by triggering monumental economic uncertainty across

---

14   Shawn Donnan and Demetri Sevastopulo, "Trump Team Looks to Bypass WTO Dispute System," *Financial Times*, February 27, 2017.

15   See, e.g., John Micklethwait, Margaret Talev, and Jennifer Jacobs, "Trump Threatens to Pull U.S. Out of WTO If It Doesn't 'Shape Up'," Bloomberg, August 30, 2018.

16   See, e.g., Bob Woodward, *Fear: Trump in the White House* (New York: Simon & Schuster, 2018), 264.

nearly every major sector, with firms and markets left calculating the implications of fundamentally resetting and changing the terms for much of America's annual $5.5 trillion in two-way trade in goods and services with the world.[17] Withdrawal would allow America to set its tariffs and other trade policies as Trump wanted, constrained only by Congress, which holds the ultimate constitutional authority over tariff policy, and and by its liability to its free trade agreement partners, which have their own written tariff obligations with America. Withdrawal would also free America's trading partners to practice their version of reciprocity in return, hiking their tariffs against U.S. exports and adjusting other policies to exclude U.S. exports as they wish.

Withdrawal thus risked returning America and, because of the country's size and importance, much of global trade to the routine practice of tit-for-tat adjustments in tariff and other trade barriers that existed before the 1940s. Because that approach had often pulled countries apart and sometimes even helped to propel them into wars, America pushed to create the new GATT-based international trading system to break this repeating cycle of retaliation and retribution. Having created the system, America now seemed newly ready to consider tossing it all aside in pursuit of its new aims, premised on the faith that America's size and leverage would allow it to do as it wished with fewer consequences.

Had WTO withdrawal been attempted, Congress, if able to muster veto-proof majorities, could have reasserted its authority over trade policy by pulling back on some of the tariff and trade authority discretion it had given to the executive branch to exercise its own approach. These existing authorities ultimately gave Trump enough latitude, along with some creative interpretations of U.S. law, to hike tariffs in some instances without the need to withdraw from the WTO agreement or obtain Congress's approval. By exercising these flexibilities, instead of taking more drastic steps, a major executive-congressional standoff to curtail Trump's tariff policy goals was avoided.

Many in Congress were similarly concerned by the WTO yet never appeared as ready as Trump to weigh withdrawal. Among those more sympathetic to withdrawal was a small group of mostly Republicans who held the extreme view that America's WTO membership was unconstitutional, along with a larger group of mostly Democrats who, in a more blanket way, were opposed to America's trade liberalization pathway in the WTO. Congressional resolutions calling for America to withdraw

---

17   As of calendar year 2017, the first year of the Trump administration.

from the WTO were introduced in the House and the Senate as early as 2000, resulting in symbolic votes taken at times to register disapproval. One of these efforts, in 2005, ended in defeat when the House voted 338 to 86 against the resolution to withdraw. In May 2020, congressional leadership prevented another withdrawal resolution effort from ever making it to a vote—one that might have been a lot closer.[18]

Even so, Washington's frustration and unhappiness with the WTO were in full stride by Trump's inauguration on January 20, 2017. Afterward, America gave up on addressing these concerns with the WTO and working within its rules and framework to effect change. The remainder of this chapter explores these new approaches taken by the Trump and then Biden administrations, which instead aimed to work outside of the WTO's rules in three main areas and would fundamentally undermine and erode the WTO's core functions and principles.

BREAKING THE WTO—AND AMERICA'S ACCOUNTABILITY TO IT

Of all the Trump administration's trade war artillery, its most important attack against the WTO's rules-based system was never launched in any ordinary sense. It was not even announced or tweeted. Instead, it was accomplished with a slow, methodical squeeze that took advantage of the goodwill on which the WTO system was based. By late 2019, and after two years of patience, the administration achieved its goal of completely kneecapping the WTO's dispute resolution system. It did this by breaking the system that held all its members accountable, successfully leaving America itself and others essentially untethered from the rules.

The WTO dispute settlement mechanism was its rules-based system's only bulwark against the type of actions and outcomes that America's new trade policies sought to achieve. As highlighted in the previous chapter, America's original design for the GATT trading system included a procedure to peacefully resolve disputes among members as one core feature. The inclusion was vital to provide the means to encourage and then help enforce accountability among all its members to live by their commitments. Its procedure, rudimentary at first, was later beefed up with the WTO's more judicial-style structure. However, its success ultimately depended upon member countries' goodwill to agree to change their practices to comply with the rules.

---

18   Keigh E. Hammond, *Major Votes on Free Trade Agreements and Trade Promotion Authority*, Congressional Research Service, R45846, July 22, 2020, 7–8.

Maintaining this goodwill depended on two general presumptions. The first was the expectation that other GATT and, later, WTO members would comply to maintain stable foreign relations among themselves. However, this often was an insufficient check on trade policies and behavior as countries consistently created new ways to skirt around or take advantage of gaps in the rules to pursue policies and practices to gain trade advantages. The second presumption became most important: that each member would need to preserve a functioning GATT and WTO dispute system in the expectation that they would later come to rely on that system to preserve their access to foreign markets.

Any system that ultimately relies on broad parameters of goodwill to resolve disputes is also vulnerable to opportunism and exploitation. While far from perfect, it still mainly proved successful at meeting one of America's founding goals—preventing the vast majority of disputes from escalating to a point that caused serious rifts among its members. A basic understanding of how the WTO dispute system worked is necessary to understand why and how America proceeded to break it and sever the country's overall accountability to the global trade rules.

Before the WTO, the original GATT dispute resolution system, which operated from 1947 to 1994, strongly encouraged negotiated settlements between countries. If a settlement could not be reached, it also provided a procedure for seeking independent rulings by a neutral panel of experts. As long as no other GATT members objected, any member could request the formation of this panel to hear both sides of a case and make a judgment on a claim. If the panel agreed that a rule was broken and no GATT member objected to the panel's judgment, the complaining party could retaliate until the defendant country changed its practice or policy. By allowing member countries to potentially block both the initiation of a panel hearing and its final decision, the GATT system also left to all members, including the defendant, a great deal of final discretion over how accountability was ultimately enforced among its members.

Authorized retaliation gave the plaintiff the right to take away an equivalent level of access to its market that the defendant had taken from it by breaking the rules. The plaintiff did this by raising its tariffs on a carefully selected list of exports from the defending country until it ended the violation. By limiting authorized retaliation to a proportional level of affected trade, as opposed to allowing a plaintiff to impose tariff hikes of a more punitive nature, the approach aimed to give members tools to incentivize compliance by others while preventing disproportionate actions in response that could lead to broader tit-for-tat tariff escalations.

While allowing for proportional retaliation to encourage compliance, the GATT and WTO dispute processes lacked the means to force a trading partner to comply with a panel decision. This meant that members could maintain rule-breaking policies for as long as they were willing to tolerate authorized retaliation by others. Ultimately, therefore, reliance on goodwill became critical to achieving eventual compliance with the rules for countries that were otherwise willing to live with perpetual, approved retaliation.

The rudimentary GATT dispute resolution system was amended over several decades to tighten some procedures. By the late 1980s, dissatisfaction with the system also had grown. This came as new GATT trade rules in areas from subsidies to technical regulatory barriers brought new types of conflicts into the dispute system. America and other members also expressed a growing list of concerns with it, including informalities in the system that failed to provide a requisite level of responsiveness, fairness, and predictability.

Moving to a more judicial approach for the dispute system won out. The new system was launched with the establishment of the WTO in 1995. Countries were still encouraged to resolve their differences, but complainants could now automatically—and without the risk of any one member blocking it—request a panel to review and decide on the facts presented. A new appeals-level review was added above it to provide either party the right to seek another independent review of the panel's initial decision before a final judgment was reached. These appeals were handled by a new seven-member Appellate Body established within the WTO. Decisions by this body were final, with no ability to appeal its decisions or block their adoption. This completed the WTO's new-look court-style approach, with appointed judges empowered to make final, binding decisions on countries involved in trade disputes.

America's evolving concerns with the efficacy of the GATT dispute system led it to join others from the early 1980s to promote its reform, advocating for a new structure that leaned much more toward a judicial-style approach for resolving disputes. The approach was predicated on the belief that America would be better off with a more robust, courtroom-style system to press these claims. Others disagreed, believing a shift to a more judicial-style approach would only expose America to more claims from other members without the ability, as had been available under the GATT mechanism, to block those claims and panel rulings that it found disagreeable.[19]

To provide the Appellate Body a degree of further independence, each of its seven judges, subject to the final approval of all WTO members, were appointed for seven-year terms. By the WTO's rules, the Appellate Body was charged with reviewing appeals for "issues of law covered in the panel report and legal interpretations developed by the panel."[20] Originally expected by some to be limited to providing straightforward legal reviews of panel decisions, appellate judges also began issuing rulings on fact and on the interpretations of the WTO rules made by lower panel decisions to determine the consistency of trade measures with WTO obligations. With this, the Appellate Body's role and function began straying far off course from the more limited review role that American negotiators and some others saw for it when agreeing to its mandate.[21] Others welcomed the Appellate Body fulfilling a role they preferred, which was more akin to that of an international court with the ability to interpret WTO rules and make judgments based on those interpretations.

The Trump administration made its strenuous objection to the WTO's "judicial activism" the centerpiece of its first official trade policy agenda statement, reminding everyone that WTO's dispute settlement process, according to the agreement creating it, could not "add to or diminish the rights or obligations" of its members.[22] Two groups of decisions, among Lighthizer's other complaints, stood out among the WTO Appellate Body's rulings and jurisprudence he most often pointed to as its greatest transgressions. They also had been obstacles to Lighthizer's ability to secure more favorable and lasting client outcomes in his law practice, which focused on helping U.S. companies secure temporary protection from subsidized or unfairly priced imports.

---

19   Lighthizer recounts his fundamental disagreement with then U.S. Trade Representative Bill Brock over this point as the United States made decisions on negotiating positions that eventually led to the new WTO dispute system. See Robert Lighthizer, *No Trade Is Free: Changing Course, Taking on China, and Helping America's Workers* (New York: Broadside Books, 2023), 67.
20   United Nations, Marrakesh Agreement Establishing the World Trade Organization, Annex 2, Article 17.6: "Understanding on Rules and Procedures Governing the Settlement of Disputes," April 15, 1994.
21   See, e.g., Hannah Monicken, "Four Years in, the U.S. Appellate Body Block Has Changed the Game," World Trade Online, August 23, 2001.
22   USTR, "The President's 2017 Trade Policy Agenda," 2.

The first relates to a long series of WTO cases surrounding the topic of zeroing. Zeroing is a calculation method long used by the U.S. government to decide the appropriate level for temporary tariff hikes permitted under U.S. law on below-cost imports from abroad. The zeroing methodology tended to result in higher levels of protective tariffs compared to other approaches, giving its supporters a stronger motive to fight for its use against unfairly priced imports.[23] By the mid-2010s, zeroing also had emerged as the most litigated single issue in the WTO's dispute system and a top focus of America's broader concerns with it.

In the 1980s and 1990s, producers, particularly from Japan but also from South Korea and several other countries, faced frequent unfair dumping claims against their exports to America, often resulting in substantial tariffs against these exports that lasted as long as a decade. Japan was among a few governments that pressed hard for renegotiating the GATT rules on these trade defense measures to narrow their scope and impact. Agreement was reached on updated rules within the broad 1994 agreement that founded the WTO. This agreement included language that arguably left less clarity on whether zeroing was still allowed within the updated rules. American negotiators, at least, believed that it was still permitted.

With these new rules in effect, Japan, India, and others subsequently brought dispute cases in the WTO against the zeroing practice. These were successful at the new WTO appeals level after its judges looked at the rules and made final determinations that zeroing was not allowed. With these judgments, other countries still using the zeroing calculation gave up using it and moved on to other methods. Calling the rulings unjust and to avoid a domestic political blowback from surrendering to these rulings by giving up the practice altogether, America attempted a series of tactical tweaks to how it implemented the zeroing methodology to claim it had complied with the latest WTO appellate decision. This only triggered new complaints from its trading partners, which argued that America was still not complying, leading to another time-consuming round of litigation through the dispute system. America's resistance to just ending the practice principally rested on its argument that since the WTO rules did not disallow the use of zeroing, the Appellate Body had unfairly made up a new WTO rule by finding against it.

---

23   See, e.g., Chad P. Bown and Thomas J. Prusa, "U.S. Antidumping: Much Ado about Zeroing" (Policy Research Working Paper no. 5352, The World Bank, Development Research Group, June 2010).

Outrage in Washington spread and grew as WTO rulings against zeroing continued to stack up, stoking and escalating anger from U.S. steel, lumber, seafood, and other producers (and their unions) that relied on these temporary protections. American officials attempted to use the next round of WTO negotiations, the Doha Round, to amend the trade rules to clarify the legality of its use, efforts that ultimately ended in vain after the round collapsed nearly a decade later. Although America eventually clawed back some recognition of the validity of the zeroing practice through additional WTO dispute cases, the political damage was done.

While never on the radar of the American public, the relevant political circles widely perceived this issue as a challenge to America's sovereignty—one where appointed WTO judges, through their decisions, were denying an integral and longstanding U.S. right to appropriately defend its industries from unfair foreign competition. The accusation landed with more potency when more colloquially expressed and deployed as a case of unelected foreign bureaucrats preventing America from protecting itself from unfair imports.

The second Appellate Body interpretation of deepest consternation to Lighthizer went to the heart of America's ability to shape its means of defense against government-advantaged exports from China. The Chinese government challenged claims by the United States, the EU, and others to their right to assess tariffs against exports they alleged as benefiting from government support or other control. Initial WTO dispute panels found against China, but the Appellate Body ruled the other way, citing insufficient evidence of informal government support and control. Considering China's nontransparent, state-capitalist system, the practical effect of the ruling meant that the Appellate Body's findings dramatically narrowed America's ability to enact trade defenses in the form of tariffs to protect U.S. industries against China's state-supported juggernaut.[24] Washington's inevitable reaction was that this ruling showed the WTO dispute resolution system spun out of control, once again violating America's sovereignty to act in its defense.

Once president, and with Lighthizer in his ear, Trump began to routinely publicly target the WTO, lobbing a range of accusations that included the claim that America loses "almost all of the lawsuits in the

---

24   See Dukgeun Ahn, "Why Reform Is Needed: WTO 'Public Body' Jurisprudence," *Global Policy* 12, supp. 3 (April 2021).

WTO" as proof that it "was set up for the benefit for everybody but us."[25] Given the president's large public platform and social media reach, this was the framing by which many Americans first came to be familiar with the WTO, both in name and in its dubious reputation.

The claim was also untrue. In terms of the simple win/loss record, America's success in the WTO dispute process closely mirrored the same general pattern experienced by other WTO members. Namely, countries that brought cases against others tended to win them most often, while those defending against claims from others most often lost. Similarly, America won approximately 90 percent of the cases it filed and lost roughly 90 percent of the cases it defended against.[26] By the mid-2010s, it was true that America had become the country most targeted by trade claims from others. It also was the country that most frequently brought claims against others.[27]

However, simple win/loss numbers say little about the qualitative importance of these decisions. When creating trade rules in the GATT and later the WTO, American officials aimed to make them broadly consistent with U.S. laws and practices to avoid having to change them to comply. However, the practical experience of two decades of WTO rulings suggested that those efforts were either insufficient or that some of the WTO rules were being interpreted in unanticipated ways. This was especially true for U.S. laws, methodologies, and procedures used to grant temporary tariff relief as defenses against dumped, subsidized, and other advantaged imports. These are, in principle, allowed according to WTO rules, but WTO panels and the WTO Appellate Body took a narrower view of their consistency with the agreed international trade rules than American negotiators believed they had achieved in the WTO agreements.

25 Ian Schwarz, "Full Lou Dobbs Interview: Trump Asks What Could Be More Fake than CBS, NBC, ABC and CNN," Real Clear Politics, October 25, 2017.

26 One estimate puts the U.S. case loss percentage at around 90 percent when the United States is the defendant. Precise percentages depend on whether split decisions, or positive settlements, are included in the "win" column. Most estimates place America's success rate at around 90 percent when bringing WTO cases against others, including against China. See, e.g., Jeffrey J. Schott and Euijin Jung, "The United States Wins More WTO Cases than China in US-China Trade Disputes," Peterson Institute for International Economics, November 22, 2019; and Andrew Mayeda, "America Wins Often with Trade Referee that Trump Wants to Avoid," Bloomberg, March 27, 2017; and Dan Ikenson, "US Trade Laws and the Sovereignty Canard," Forbes, March 9, 2017.

27 As of the end of 2023, the United States had initiated 124 cases as a complainant and been the recipient of 158 claims as a respondent. WTO, "Disputes by Member," https://www.wto.org/english//tratop_e/dispu_e/dispu_by_country_e.htm.

When America was on offense and overwhelmingly successful in pressing its claims, the record of WTO rulings showed the greatest success when specific and definable foreign government measures could be identified and clear discrimination against U.S. exports and firms over domestic goods could be proven. Cases brought against broader systemic or informal barriers used by foreign countries proved much harder to win. Therefore, the WTO rules and dispute process proved to be a much less dependable tool than American negotiators originally anticipated to effectively fight against some of the informal and non-transparent practices used in countries like Japan for decades and later in China and other markets.

Lighthizer's answer to these problems with the dispute system and the Appellate Body was not to try to reform or to change it, which would have taken years and almost certainly failed to gain agreement among all WTO members. His answer was instead sublimely simple: to withhold approval of new nominees to the Appellate Body and eventually starve it of the judges it needed to operate. New cases could still be filed, and initial panel rulings could still be issued. If any party appealed the decision further, the Appellate Body would be unable to meet and make final decisions. America, and any other WTO member, could simply then "appeal (cases) into the void," a zone of perpetual legal limbo with no sitting judges to hear and finalize a ruling in a case. The fact that no rule existed to prevent a country from doing this is emblematic of the trust that America and other members originally had in the good faith of the undertaking. As Appellate Body judges reached the end of their terms or left for other reasons, America blocked nominations to replace them. Lighthizer stepped further on the Appellate Body by pressing to slash its budget by 87 percent.

Trump's mid-2017 unilateral announcement that a renegotiation of the U.S.-Korea Free Trade Agreement was underway, which did not officially begin until six months later, provided the critical opening for Lighthizer to begin his squeeze on the Appellate Body. This announcement caused South Korea to recall its former trade minister to Seoul to handle the negotiation after serving only one year of his seven-year Appellate Body term. Combined with the expiring term of another Appellate Body member on June 30, Lighthizer's plan was set in motion by blocking all the proposed nominees to replace them, cutting the Appellate Body's body count from seven to five by August 2017. Only three more departures were needed before it would lose its quorum.

Without bluster or press releases, Lighthizer's quiet plan to bleed to death the Appellate Body finally succeeded in late 2019. In February 2020, Lighthizer left behind a 174-page, softbound obituary detailing for the court of international public opinion the multiplicity of Appellate Body transgressions, mistakes, and overreaches over its 25-year history.[28]

Beyond settling Lighthizer's score with the Appellate Body over its rulings over zeroing and China's state-centered model, breaking it also facilitated almost any trade action the Trump trade agenda could imagine. America still had separate obligations and enforcement mechanisms with its 20 free trade agreement partner countries, and thus, some potential liability for its trade actions with those partners. Otherwise, as long as the WTO dispute system was left paralyzed with no means for providing accountability, the administration could proceed confidently by steering around, over, or straight through the WTO rules to implement Trump's tariff and other trade restrictions.

With accountability through the WTO severed, countries were left to use their own sources of leverage to respond to the administration's new trade restrictions. America's traditional allies, from South Korea to Europe to Japan, which were also targeted at times by Trump's tariffs and other threats, expressed dismay with America over its betrayal with a single-handed takedown of the WTO dispute system. Some, like the EU, quickly hit back with their own retaliation outside of the WTO rules. Others like Japan and South Korea sought other ways to soften the impact of Trump's new tariffs on their exporters. As Lighthizer continued to block appointments of new WTO judges, trade representatives from all these countries routinely visited Washington to urge the administration's commitment to work with them to keep the WTO functioning. Instead, they were greeted with clear signals of disinterest in doing much about it. By mid-2018, it became apparent to most that America was neither serious about discussing reform nor willing to back down on its approach of blocking the nominations.

Countries like China, with significant market power, had the leverage to engage in direct, tariff-war-style retaliation if needed. Smaller countries, by contrast, had little leverage and market power and thus mainly relied on the WTO dispute system to protect their interests.[29] These countries generally knew they were not likely to be among Trump's trade

28   USTR, "Report on the Appellate Body of the World Trade Organization," February 2020.
29   See Jacqueline Spolador Lopes, "Dispute Settlement System of the WTO: A Powerful Weapon for Developing Countries," in *The WTO Dispute Settlement Mechanism: A Developing*

targets. Still, many were deeply upset with America for, in their view, cavalierly choosing to break the WTO for everyone just to meet its own purposes. Some of them were still hit with tariffs when the administration hiked tariffs on global imports of steel and aluminum, discussed below.

As each Appellate Body judicial term ended and America refused to agree to any replacement, the looming crisis for the WTO and the international trading system was set in motion. Earlier in the 2000s, when America's concerns with the dispute system began to grow, the Obama administration expressed its displeasure by blocking the approval of certain Appellate Body candidates. Eventually, however, it agreed to other nominees to keep the Appellate Body in business. By refusing to agree to any new appointments to keep the Appellate Body alive, the Trump administration positioned America as the largest and most existential threat to the WTO system's legitimacy.

In an interview weeks before stepping down at the end of the Trump administration, Lighthizer was asked about his handiwork in crippling the Appellate Body. As dry as a gin martini among the glasses crashing to the floor in his "train wreck" anecdote, Lighthizer quipped: "No one's really missed it."[30] Most WTO members did, in fact, miss it. Some also created their own stop-gap, voluntary appellate system to fill the void, as discussed below.

AMERICA'S NEW TARIFF WAR WITH THE WORLD

With Lighthizer's slow Appellate Body squeeze quietly underway from late summer 2017, the administration was already moving to set Trump's tariff agenda in motion. By the time any complaints against these tariff actions were filed, heard, decided, and ready for an appeal in the WTO, the Appellate Body would be out of business to hear them.

Severing America's accountability in the WTO was helpful, but, as shown below, it proved insufficient to avoid triggering tariff wars with its trading partners. Not often appreciated was another critical factor in the form and justifications the Trump administration used to raise U.S. tariffs, which was the legal necessity of working within the limited authorities that Congress, with the ultimate power under the U.S.

Country Perspective, eds. Alberto do Amaral Júnior, Luciana Maria de Oliveira Sá Pires, and Christiane Lucena Carneiro (Cham, Switzerland: Springer Press, 2019).

30   Doug Palmer, "Lighthizer: No One Misses WTO Appellate Body," Politico, December 10, 2020, https://politi.co/3n87HU3.

Constitution for tariff adjustments, had provided the executive branch over several decades to adjust tariffs under certain conditions. Some of these were fit for the Trump administration's purposes. Others would need to be stretched substantially in their legal justifications to fit Trump's intentions, such as the need to find a U.S. legal authority to use had the administration followed through on his reported threat of new auto tariffs on Germany over its policy toward Iran.[31] Because some of these legal authorities were often drawn from older U.S. trade laws and viewed as mostly inconsistent with the newer WTO rules, U.S. administrations had nearly universally avoided their use following the start of the WTO. Instead, the Bill Clinton, Bush, and Obama administrations turned to using other trade tools and options, including stepping up the use of the WTO dispute system to go after unfair foreign trade practices. In contrast, the Trump administration showed little restraint in restoring the use of these older tariff authorities that were still on the books. It did so irrespective of America's WTO commitments.

Some U.S. industries rushed to take advantage of the Trump administration's readiness to impose protective tariffs. Soon after the administration began, manufacturers of solar panels and residential washing machines filed petitions under a rarely used authority, Section 201 of a 1974 trade law, to seek tariff protection. The aim of Section 201 was to enable domestic industries to seek temporary protection from global imports if substantially harmed by them. Petitioners had first to prove the harm, which included a lengthy process for multiple U.S. agencies to investigate the claims. One of these was the U.S. International Trade Commission, which Lighthizer generally disliked and regularly fought against for its denials of anti-dumping and other claims that he advocated for in his law practice. Another drawback to using Section 201 was that the duration of tariff protection, even if granted by the U.S. government, was limited.

A comparison between the handling of these new Section 201 claims by Trump administration and by previous U.S. administrations underscores the Trump administration's detachment from concern with the WTO rules. When approached by steelworkers and producers in the late 1990s, the Clinton administration studied but eventually turned down requests to use Section 201, in part citing concerns that doing so was

---

31   On making tariff threats to achieve foreign policy goals, see, e.g., Patrick Wintour, "Germany Confirms Trump Made Trade Threat to Europe over Iran Policy," *Guardian*, January 16, 2020.

not consistent with America's WTO obligations. The George W. Bush administration surprised many by eventually deciding in 2002 to proceed with the claims. It used the authority to impose tariffs on steel imports, seemingly to help manage congressional pressure to defend America's steel industry from unfair trade in order to create political space to advance other free trade priorities. This action drew strong complaints from steel users in America and from foreign governments, including close allies such as in Europe and Japan. The Bush administration also fully expected to run into WTO problems with the decision. After long deliberation, however, it approved the petitions and raised U.S. tariffs on imported steel. Then, it waited for the outcome of the anticipated challenge and adverse ruling from the WTO. Once the negative ruling came as expected and retaliation was authorized for the EU, the Bush administration quickly ended the tariffs after roughly 20 months of its initially approved 36-month term, all to avoid authorized retaliation by abiding by the WTO judgment.[32]

By contrast, the Trump administration moved quickly after the solar panel and washing machine petitions were filed. Even with a clear 2003 WTO panel ruling finding against America's prior use of Section 201, once the investigations and other legal processes were complete, the administration applied a mix of U.S. import quotas and additional tariffs ranging from 20 to 50 percent on global imports of these products.[33] The Trump administration's rapid and unflinching use of Section 201 became the first tangible signal of America's new detachment from concern with WTO rules and past rulings.

Two other legal authorities granted by Congress to the executive branch provided more promising pathways to impose sweeping new tariffs on America's imports. Both options allowed the administration to self-initiate, self-investigate, and self-determine the outcome of cases— and then self-administer tariffs as it deemed appropriate. One option, covered in greater detail below, was the use of Section 301 under the 1974 Trade Act, which became the administration's primary tool to wage its tariff war with China but also was used to threaten other countries.

---

32   See Charan Devereaux, Robert Z. Lawrence, and Michael D. Watkins, *Case Studies in US Trade Negotiation, Volume 2: Resolving Disputes* (Washington, DC: Institute for International Economics, 2006), chapter 4, esp. 218–29.

33   For more on the precise quota and tariff outcomes for these products, see Brock R. Williams and Keigh E. Hammond, *Escalating U.S. Tariffs: Timeline*, Congressional Research Service, IN10943, January 29, 2020.

The second tool, which also exploited a built-in loophole with the WTO rules, was Section 232 of a 1962 trade law. Passed at the height of the Cold War, Section 232 authorized the president to raise U.S. tariffs or impose other import restrictions if judged to "threaten to impair the national security." Outside petitioners and the executive branch could both initiate claims, after which the Commerce Department would investigate. The president would then decide the scope and duration of any import restrictions. Because it gave the executive branch broad discretion with little external accountability, it was an attractive option for the Trump administration to pursue broad tariff protections for any U.S. industry sector against global imports. Critically, Section 232 provided the administration the broad legal authority it needed under U.S. law to raise U.S. tariffs on global imports without further approval from Congress.

Section 232's national security justification also provided an argument to claim that its actions bypassed WTO accountability. The WTO rules included a broad exception for governments to take any action necessary to meet their "essential security interests." Generally understood to apply to war contingencies or major natural crises, the exception had rarely been used formally by GATT and WTO members. For the Trump administration, the exception was the loophole it needed to justify almost any tariff hike it wished to implement just by claiming national security need.

Given its narrow national security purpose, previous U.S. administrations had weighed the use of Section 232 only 25 times between 1962 and 2017. In these cases, the president often turned down most stakeholder claims and petitions for investigations under the statute as failing to meet the standard of a genuine national security threat. If a threat was established, other measures besides tariffs were instead taken to respond.[34]

Prior to Trump, the last time Section 232 resulted in actual import restrictions was in 1986–87, during the Reagan administration. Then, the administration took over three years to decide on a Section 232 petition from machine tool manufacturers. Instead of imposing a prohibitive quota to cut off 90 percent of imports, as his commerce secretary reportedly recommended, Reagan decided to delay implementation in favor of negotiating a softer voluntary export restraint (VER) with four

---

34   For a full list of filings and cases, see Rachel F. Fefer et al., *Section 232 Investigations: Overview and Issues for Congress*, Congressional Research Service, R45249, May 18, 2021, appendix B.

trading partners to cut their machine tool exports to America.[35] VERS emerged as an often-used, informal tool for Reagan, who regularly touted free trade but also relied on VERs to respond to domestic calls to protect various U.S. industries from imports.[36] Forcing America's trading partners into VERs allowed it to avoid the more direct, harsher use of tariffs or quotas that Trump championed. Eventually, Japan and other trading partners frequently forced into accepting VERs would later succeed in making them explicitly prohibited under the trade rule changes that created the WTO.

By contrast, Trump's commerce secretary, Wilbur Ross, showed no hesitation in dusting off and stretching the Section 232 national security rationale to fit Trump's tariff policy objectives. Ross, whose agency was responsible for administering Section 232 cases, initiated Section 232 investigations on steel and aluminum just several weeks after taking office, setting the process in motion for the new president to approve his first major tariff action. Quick, positive findings from these investigations seemed all but assured as Trump directed Ross to rush to complete the investigations in only 30 to 50 days instead of the 270 days allowed by law.[37]

It did not go as smoothly as planned. As part of the investigation procedures under U.S. law, stakeholder opinions had to be gathered before any final decision was made. Steel consumers who would face paying higher prices due to the tariffs on their purchases, unsurprisingly, stood in opposition to the views of steel producers, which expected to benefit from them. Opposition to imposing sweeping tariffs on imports also came from within the administration, including the Department of Defense, over concerns about the impact of the tariffs on America's security relationships. Many American security treaty allies, from Canada and other North Atlantic Treaty Organization (NATO) allies to Japan and South Korea, would also be hit with substantial tariff hikes on their steel and aluminum exports in the name of protecting America's national security. In light of this contradiction, security agencies insisted that

---

35   See Stuart Auerbach, "Reagan May Ask Japan to Restrict Machine-Tool Shipments to U.S.," *Washington Post*, March 5, 1986. Also see The White House, "Machine Tools and National Security," National Security Decision, Directive Number 226, May 21, 1986, declassified memo, https://www.reaganlibrary.gov/public/archives/reference/scanned-nsdds/nsdd226.pdf.

36   Ronald Reagan, "Statement on the Revitalization of the Machine Tool Industry," December 16, 1986, https://www.reaganlibrary.gov/archives/speech/statement-revitalization -machine-tool-industry.

37   Reagan, "Statement on the Revitalization."

pathways to exempt security treaty allies be provided to avoid rifts that jeopardized essential U.S. national security interests in other ways.[38] The president's own top economic advisor also registered his strong concern with blanket approaches to imposing these tariffs. Facing internal and external dissent, Ross resorted in the summer of 2017 to call on a group of steel industry CEOs to rally for the tariffs to pressure skeptics in the administration.[39]

Instead of the quick tariff hike decision that Trump expected, internal deliberations dragged into late fall. Options weighed to mitigate some of the impacts on America's allies included providing possible special treatment for them and allowing domestic steel and aluminum users to obtain tariff waivers for imports of specialty steel products that domestic producers were unable to provide to meet demand.

The steelworkers' union, which claimed to have pushed the administration into the Section 232 investigation, lost patience and threatened to raise "a lot of hell" if the tariffs were not imposed quickly.[40] At the same time, it also lobbied hard for the administration to exclude just one U.S. ally—Canada. Since the union also represented Canadian steelworkers, it appeared to be no accident that the union, as with multinational corporations, adopted positions sensitive to its foreign interests.[41]

Democrats in Congress also accused the administration of being all talk and no action on tariffs. Some congressional Republicans expressed various concerns, from harming domestic steel–using constituents to alienating allies over a China problem. With just days left on the 270-day statutory clock for the investigation, Trump brought congressional leaders to the White House in early 2018 to confront them over their remaining resistance to the tariffs.[42]

Ross issued final reports just before the legal deadline for a decision, and Trump agreed a few weeks after to impose 10 percent tariffs on imported aluminum, covering approximately $11 billion in imports, and

38   Isabelle Hoagland and Jenny Leonard, "Sources: Section 232 Steel Report Facing Defense Department Objections," World Trade Online, December 8, 2017.

39   Jenny Leonard with Isabelle Hoagland, "Sources: Ross Tells Steel CEOs to Put 'Visible Pressure' on White House, Urge 232 Action," World Trade Online, July 21, 2017.

40   "USW President: Union to Raise 'A Lot of Hell' if 232 Action Isn't Taken Soon," World Trade Online, November 15, 2017.

41   See, e.g., United Steelworkers, "USW: Canada Must Be Exempt from Tariffs," press release, May 31, 2018.

42   Isabelle Hoagland, Jenny Leonard, and Jack Caporal, "Trump, Lawmakers Debate Section 232 Remedies in White House Meeting," World Trade Online, February 15, 2018.

25 percent tariffs on steel and certain steel products, covering just under $16 billion in imports.[43] Tariffs were initially to be applied globally, except to Canada and Mexico, which were in the midst of renegotiating their three-way North American Free Trade Agreement (NAFTA) with America. Before the tariffs were implemented, avenues for negotiations with other trading partners were also opened, including with South Korea, Brazil, and Argentina, which eventually reached their own arrangements in the form of hard U.S. import quotas on their steel exports. Australia was eventually excluded altogether, but efforts to reach deals with Canada, Mexico, and the EU floundered, and they were folded into the worldwide tariff hikes implemented on June 1.[44] With some modifications, these tariffs and quotas on imported steel and aluminum remained in place long into the Biden administration's term.

United Steelworkers cheered the initial move, which seemed to exclude Canada, but then sharply criticized the final decision to also include Canada in the tariff measure.[45] U.S. steel and aluminum trade associations also cheered the move.[46] The American Federation of Labor and Congress of Industrial Organizations (AFL-CIO) union, representing a much broader group of union workers, was also supportive.[47] Just as with the Bush administration's Section 201 tariffs on steel 15 years earlier, downstream users and consumers of U.S. steel and aluminum lodged their strong opposition to having to accept the higher costs resulting from the decision, an expense that threatened their competitiveness.[48] Gary Cohen, Trump's chief economic advisor who fought against the

43   Brock R. Williams and Keigh E. Hammond, *Escalating U.S. Tariffs: Affected Trade*, Congressional Research Service, IN10971, January 29, 2020.

44   Canada and Mexico eventually were removed from the global tariffs but given their own arrangements as a result of the package to finalize the updated NAFTA.

45   United Steelworkers, "Administration Action on Steel and Aluminum Vital to Protecting National Security," press release, March 1, 2018; and United Steelworkers, "USW: Canada Must Be Exempt from Tariffs."

46   American Iron and Steel Institute, "AISI Comments on Section 232 Signing," press release, March 8, 2018.

47   AFL-CIO, "Steel and Aluminum Tariffs Good for Working People," press release, March 1, 2018.

48   See, e.g., U.S. Chamber of Commerce, "Association Letter Urging USTR to Lift 232 Steel and Aluminum Tariffs," letter to U.S. Trade Representative Robert Lighthizer, November 26, 2018, https://www.uschamber.com/international/https-www-uschamber-com-letter-association-letter-urging-ustr-lift-232-steel-and-aluminum-tariffs-0.

approach for various reasons, resigned.[49] This win for domestic steel and aluminum producers was just that—a win for those U.S. industries. Whether it was a win for the rest of America was hotly debated.

U.S. security treaty allies in Europe, Australia, and Japan responded with complete dismay, refusing to accept America's argument that their exports represented a national security threat to the United States. Several of America's most irritated allies, like the United Kingdom (UK) and in the EU, joined America's strategic rivals China and Russia by quickly imposing retaliatory tariffs instead of waiting first to adjudicate and receive WTO-sanctioned authorization. Retaliation in the form of higher tariffs was initially applied against nearly $25 billion in America's annual world exports; these were scaled back to $9 billion in trade in 2019 after Trump eventually lifted the 232 tariffs on Canada and Mexico months after they agreed to an updated North American free trade deal.[50] India, China, Russia, the EU, and the UK also requested WTO dispute panels toward the end of 2018 to seek a WTO ruling, doing so even as it had become clear around that time America might be intentionally aiming to break the dispute system by starving the WTO of new appeals judges.

Stretching Section 232 to fit the administration's purpose also led to movements on Capitol Hill to consider reining in tariff authorities it had previously granted to the president.[51] Some in Congress stressed that America's defense industry accounted for only 3 percent of American steel use, straining the legitimacy of using national security as a justification.[52] Others expressed concern with the impacts of the tariffs, with one key member equating their use to the early days of chemotherapy, which could "often do as much damage as good."[53] The debate continued as the impacts of the tariffs were felt, with competing sides citing competing studies showing the trade restrictions either helped or harmed U.S.

---

49 Dan Mangan, "Gary Cohn Resigns as Trump's Top Economic Advisor," CNBC, March 6, 2018.

50 Williams and Hammond, *Escalating U.S. Tariffs: Affected Trade*. Mexico retaliated against approximately $3 billion in U.S. exports, and Canada against approximately $12.5 billion in U.S. exports. The EU, China, Turkey, India, and Russia maintained their retaliation until the EU eventually suspended it in exchange for a separate deal.

51 Jenny Leonard and Anshu Siripurapu, "Hatch Calls 232 Action 'Misguided'; Flake Offers Legislation to Nullify Tariffs," World Trade Online, March 15, 2018.

52 Hoagland, Leonard, and Caporal, "Trump, Lawmakers Debate Section 232 Remedies."

53 On the various arguments on Capitol Hill, see Hoagland, Leonard, and Caporal, "Trump, Lawmakers Debate Section 232 Remedies in White House Meeting."

jobs and overall economic welfare and that downstream users either faced only marginally or significantly higher steel and aluminum costs.[54]

Many also pointed out that the tariffs failed to have much impact on their primary target, China. Only 2 percent of steel imports into America came directly from China because of America's already high anti-dumping and other temporary tariffs on its steel exports.[55] With the impacts of the Section 232 action instead mostly falling on exports from other countries, including security treaty allies, the administration justified their use to counter the effects of China's state-funded steel overcapacity on depressed global prices. It also cited the need to plug individual country holes through which Chinese steel would find a tariff-free route into the U.S. market.

America's use of Section 232 on steel and aluminum, leading to tens of billions of dollars in tit-for-tat tariff wars with several major countries, was America's first major hit against the WTO system. Others were still to come.

These actions also created an entirely new Pandora's box, further jeopardizing the WTO system's future. In the view of most countries, it was one thing for America to provide tariff protection for America's steel and aluminum producers. It was another for Washington to go on to claim that, because the decision was based on America's national security criteria, these tariffs and other restrictions also automatically met the WTO's "essential security" exception and thus could not be challenged by its trading partners. Other means were available under the WTO rules to impose temporary tariff increases; America's decision to invoke the WTO's national security exception over using other means was viewed as an unfair abuse of that loophole.

For decades, America joined other countries in taking a narrower view of the use of this WTO exception. The GATT and WTO agreements permit each member to implement trade measures "which it considers necessary for the protection of its essential security interests," but also

---

54   Many studies showed conflicting results and narratives depending on their methodology. For two studies of the impact of tariffs imposed from Section 201, 232, and 301 actions in 2018, see Mary Amiti, Stephen J. Redding, and David E. Weinstein, "The Impact of the 2018 Tariffs on Prices and Welfare," *Journal of Economic Perspectives* 33, no. 4 (Fall 2019): 187–210; and Adam S. Hersh and Robert E. Scott, *Why Global Steel Surpluses Warrant U.S. Section 232 Import Measures* (Washington, DC: Economic Policy Institute, March 24, 2021).

55   Michaela D. Platzer, Rachel F. Fefer, and Heidi M. Peters, "U.S. Steel Manufacturing: National Security and Tariffs," Congressional Research Service, In Focus IF11897, August 12, 2021.

adds further language on the context for such measures, which is to permit such actions that relate to "fissionable materials," "traffic in arms, ammunition and implements of war," or those "taken in time of war or other emergency in international relations." America invoked a few such measures after the rules and exception were set, whether to impose trade sanctions on parties engaged in international conflict or to respond to the 1973 Arab oil embargo. These situations responded to an external threat and were thus generally uncontroversial, seen as being in line with GATT and WTO rules, and not challenged formally.

For the WTO system, invoking national security to apply Section 232 tariffs for steel and aluminum—but with no demonstrated wartime need and with only approximately 30 percent of domestic needs for steel coming from imports—opened a slippery slope for other countries to claim their own exceptions for almost any reason they believed necessary to meet their broader and self-defined national economic security aims.[56] The invocation of questionable national security claims meant the WTO would confront legitimacy issues when dispute panels were asked to rule on the validity of a country's national security justification. Thus, the opening of this Pandora's box holds enormous implications for maintaining support for the WTO. Understanding this, WTO members long avoided taking actions that raised such questions and avoided bringing dispute claims to challenge its use by another country.[57] That is, until the Trump administration showed little restraint in opening this box to protect its domestic steel and aluminum production, regardless of the consequences.

After allies and others challenged the validity of this action, Lighthizer, followed by President Biden's trade ambassador, Katherine

---

56   No mention of wartime shortages is mentioned in the overarching investigation findings. See Bureau of Industry and Security Office of Technology Evaluation, U.S. Department of Commerce, *The Effect of Imports of Steel on the National Security: An Investigation Conducted under Section 232 of the Trade Expansion Act of 1962, as Amended*, January 11, 2018, 2–5. Import penetration percentage figures are drawn from p. 7.

57   Even if invoked, use of the national security exception was broadly understood among GATT and, later, WTO members to be ideally resolved outside of the use of the dispute settlement mechanism. Allowing cases to proceed to a panel decision or, under the WTO, an Appellate Body decision, was avoided. The first WTO dispute system filing on the issue was a 2016 case filed by Ukraine against the Russian Federation over discriminatory restrictions on the transit of goods across Russian-controlled or influenced territory. Russia invoked Article XXI to mount its defense. WTO, "DS512: Russia—Measures Concerning Traffic in Transit," panel report, adopted April 26, 2019.

Tai, pointed the blame back at them for retaliating without explicit WTO authorization and for accusing America of undermining WTO rules by unreasonably stretching its definition of national security interests to justify these tariff increases.

Even with broad international blowback and foreign retaliation against its use of Section 232, Secretary Ross continued to expand the effort into other industry sectors. His department launched Section 232 investigations into uranium ore and related products (which might have been a more internationally convincing place to start) and later into titanium sponge, both of which were less globally available and traded but still critical for certain defense industry applications. These products appeared more closely aligned with a potentially legitimate national security issue. Yet, the administration ultimately stopped short of invoking tariffs on these products, choosing instead to take other actions to help shore up domestic production and availability.

Another Section 232 investigation, more than any other, galvanized global perceptions that the Trump administration was completely unhinged on tariffs and the justifications it was ready to use to impose them. Ross's surprise May 2018 launch of a Section 232 investigation into the impacts of imported automobiles and auto parts on America's national security interests stretched to the breaking point the credibility of the administration's stance on the justifiable use of Section 232, and it was met with particularly loud jeers, including from major U.S. business associations, U.S. automakers among them.[58] A few politically important but muted cheers came from America's steel and auto worker unions.[59] Some also viewed the announcement as Ross's desperate bid

---

58   See, e.g., Matt Blunt, "Statement of Governor Matt Blunt, President of the American Automotive Policy Council; Hearing on Section 232 National Security Investigation of Imports of Automobiles and Automobile Parts," American Automotive Policy Council, July 19, 2018.

59   The autoworkers union urged caution over how import restrictions may be applied but supported the investigation's overall aims. International Union, United Automobile, Aerospace & Agricultural Implement Workers of America, "Public Comments on Section 232 National Security Investigation of Imports of Automobiles, Including Cars, SUVs, Vans and Light Trucks, and Automotive Parts," June 28, 2018, https://www.regulations.gov /comment/DOC-2018-0002-1995. United Steelworkers expressed broader support: see United Steelworkers, "USW Supports Section 232 Investigation on Imports of Autos and Auto Parts," press release, May 29, 2018.

to regain influence in the Oval Office after being sidelined by Trump over his widely panned trade agreement with China.[60]

Many focused on the dubious assertion that U.S. automobile production, which remained within a relatively steady band throughout the 1990s and into the 2000s, could possibly pose a national security risk.[61] Although automobile imports steadily rose over the decades as the U.S. market grew, the top sources of those imports were, except for the case of Mexico, all top U.S. defense treaty allies—Canada, key countries in Europe, Japan, and South Korea.

It was well known in the administration that Trump wished to slap tariffs on imported autos through any means, or at least have the leverage at the ready to do so. Beyond the automobile sector's significant political and economic importance at home, auto imports also were a major contributor to America's enormous annual trade deficit.

Abroad, Ross's Section 232 investigation announcement triggered new fears that Trump was ready to use whatever tool available to escalate America's tariff threats, even against a handful of allies that also happened to be major auto-exporting countries. With this investigation, foreign governments could more easily make the case that the administration's trade posture was, in fact, not only about targeting China but also a broad, menacing, and growing global threat aimed at America's friends and foes alike.

The incredulity of threatening new tariffs on autos and auto parts imports as essential for America's national security offered even further proof that America was now playing utterly untethered from the WTO rules. As implausible as the administration's case was, the unhinged unpredictability of it all nonetheless still managed to create new leverage over America's trading partners. As outlined in chapter 5, this leverage was spent during most of 2018 and into 2019 to help accelerate ongoing negotiations with Canada and Mexico to agree on a renegotiated NAFTA and push Japan and the EU into engaging in new, separate trade negotiations with America. While maximizing the leverage the investigation created with America's trading partners, the administration chose not

---

60   This view was widely shared among many in the government. On Ross's slipping credibility, see Woodward, *Fear*, esp. 159–61.

61   Annual U.S. motor vehicle production remained between 10 million and 12.5 million units annually, except for 2008–11, coinciding with the 2007–08 financial crisis, and the period 1990–92 during a U.S. recession. Bureau of Transportation Statistics, "Annual U.S. Motor Vehicle Production and Domestic Sales," U.S. Department of Transportation, http://www.bts.gov/content/annual-us-motor-vehicle-production-and-factory-wholesale-sales-thousands-units.

to publish the final Commerce Department investigative report after a year of work to detail the alleged national security threat from imports of autos and auto parts; the investigation ended instead with a brief summary of the overall findings along with Trump's determination that, while a national security threat existed to America's auto industry, no further action would be taken beyond further reviews and pending a report from Lighthizer on progress made in trade negotiations underway with the EU, Japan, and potentially others.[62]

The Biden administration, quick to stress the need to restore America's alliances and commitments, had several avenues upon taking office to move to overturn key Trump-era decisions and reestablish support for the WTO and the international trading system. Beyond seriously and aggressively engaging with other WTO members to find a way to make the dispute process functional again, it also could have moved to sunset Trump's Section 232 tariffs on steel and aluminum or at least phase them down before any initial WTO dispute panel decisions ruled against them.

Instead, the Biden administration's first trade agenda statement, delivered in early spring 2021, only included a brief, polite nod to the WTO, stating America's readiness to "reengage and be a leader in international organizations, including the World Trade Organization." It went on, however, to also stress that America's focus for the organization would be to "implement necessary reforms to the WTO's substantive rules and procedures to address the challenges facing the global trading system."[63] While not the assault on the WTO waged by the Trump administration, it was far chillier than any of the Trump administration's predecessors toward the organization.

Many expected that the incoming Biden administration would match its rhetoric about repairing America's relations and role in international organizations by working to overturn Trump's trade policies. Instead, the administration mostly embraced the status quo, except for burying a couple of hatchets with some allies, that Lighthizer had left in place at the end of the Trump administration's term that were further eroding the WTO and fraying America's relationships. The Biden administration

62   "Adjusting Imports of Automobiles and Automobile Parts Into the United States," Proclamation No. 9888, 84 Fed. Reg. 23433 (May 17, 2019).

63   USTR, "The President's 2021 Trade Policy Agenda," in *2021 Trade Policy Agenda and 2020 Annual Report of the President of the United States on the Trade Agreements Program* (Washington, DC: USTR, March 1, 2021), 4.

branded its trade approach a "worker-centered policy." What became more apparent over time was that it instead was a union-centered, and at times union-directed, trade policy. The unions strongly favored keeping the Trump-era tariffs in place. As a result, steel and aluminum users never gained traction in their argument that the tariffs had caused them years of shortages and other harm from higher steel and aluminum input prices. Invoking their own "worker-centered" argument, these users called on the administration to consider the risks of further losses among the 6.2 million manufacturing jobs in the industries using steel and aluminum as inputs, compared to the estimated gains from an increase of jobs (4,800) from the tariffs in the steel industry.[64]

Ross's successor as commerce secretary, Gina Raimondo, defended the steel tariffs from the early months of the Biden administration, stressing that they effectively responded to the concerns of the steel industry and workers. Raimondo added that while the new administration would need to grapple with the Trump administration's use of national security justification that had riled up America's allies, it also was the case that "simply to say no tariffs is not the solution."[65] The fact that the steelworkers union had already sternly warned the new Congress to steer clear of revising Section 232 to undercut the ongoing protection for the steel and aluminum industries also seemed to matter.[66]

The Biden administration proceeded to recast America's reasons for keeping the steel and aluminum import tariffs and restrictions in place. Originally justified to protect national security, the new administration claimed the tariffs should instead serve other purposes, such as to achieve environmental goals. It eventually opened negotiations with the EU and, subsequently, with the UK on the 232 tariffs. It reached agreements with them to drop their retaliation against hundreds of millions of dollars of America's exports in exchange for new trade-restrictive quotas. America's usual low WTO tariffs were applied to their imports under these quotas, but imports over the quota would still be charged the high, Trump-imposed tariff rate.

---

64   The petitioners also argued that the increase in steel sector jobs had been generally unrelated to the tariffs. "Hundreds of U.S. Manufacturing Companies Ask President Biden to Terminate Section 232 Steel & Aluminum Tariffs," Businesswire, May 6, 2021.

65   Interview with Gina Raimondo, "Commerce Sec. Raimondo on Chip Shortage, Skills Gap, China Tariffs," Bloomberg Markets, July 28, 2021.

66   Thomas Conway, "RE: USW Opposes Efforts to Undermine Section 232," email to U.S. Senate and U.S. House of Representatives, March 13, 2020, United Steelworkers, http://images.usw.org/download/rapid/232_Letter.pdf.

In exchange, the EU promised to clamp down on its steel imports from China and engage in a new negotiation to establish a new global standard to reduce the carbon intensity of steel production. That negotiation aimed to reach an agreement to better align the EU industry's environmental impact with levels in America, to improve its climate footprint while equalizing the costs of production between them necessary to meet those environmental impact standards. America suggested that a successful outcome could enable it to lift Trump's Section 232 restrictions on steel and aluminum imports from Europe.[67] The suggested implication for other steel-producing countries was that criteria set exclusively between America and EU may only set a new, permanent climate benchmark that would allow America to continue to apply steel tariffs on their exports unless the criteria were met.

Heralded by the administration for its climate objectives, the approach and initial deal with the EU on the quota and new negotiation was also concluded in close coordination with representatives of the steelworkers' union. The union defended the approach to its members by stressing that import volumes from the EU would remain at levels lower than those prior to the imposition of the tariffs in 2018.[68] As of the publication of this book, both sides have been unable, after nearly three years of talks, to strike a deal on decarbonization criteria, agreeing instead in December 2023 to continue the suspension of retaliatory EU tariffs, maintain the U.S. tariff-rate quota on its steel and aluminum exports, and keep working on the criteria into 2025.[69] The EU, seeming to lose patience, announced in early 2024 that it would try to seek America's agreement to bring other countries into their talks on environmental standards for the steel industry.[70]

---

67   For a summary of the EU deal, and the range of views in reaction, including supportive union views, see Rachel F. Fefer, *What's in the New U.S.-EU Steel and Aluminum Deal?*, Congressional Research Service, IN11719, November 12, 2021. The UK deal was reached in March 2022. See United States Department of Commerce, "Steel and Aluminum: U.S.-UK Joint Statement," March 22, 2022, https://www.commerce.gov/sites/default/files/2022-03/UK232-Joint-Statement.pdf.

68   United Steelworkers, "USW Supports Interim Arrangement with EU on Section 232," press release, October 30, 2021.

69   European Commission, "EU Prolongs Tariff Suspension for US Products Related to the Steel and Aluminum Dispute," press release, December 19, 2023.

70   Margaret Spiegelman, "Dombrovskis: EU Suggested Opening Technical Steel Talks to Other Countries," World Trade Online, February 1, 2024.

After the EU cut its initial deal and started negotiations with Washington on setting decarbonization criteria as a possible pathway out of the steel and aluminum tariffs and quotas, Japan immediately registered its strong dissatisfaction with being left behind. Unlike the EU, Japan avoided provoking Trump by deciding to not take retaliatory action against his Section 232 tariffs, working instead to secure as many product waivers as possible from the tariffs. After Trump was out of office, that decision seemed suddenly oddly counterproductive after the Biden administration first prioritized cutting deals with the EU and the UK in return for their agreement to suspend their retaliatory tariffs against American exports. Japan pressed intensively and eventually got its own deal on steel tariffs and volume restrictions, the outcome of which was also closely coordinated with and eventually welcomed by United Steelworkers.[71] Unlike America's deal with the EU, however, the issue of aluminum tariffs and the prospect of a potential deal to align decarbonization standards was left only to further discussions.[72]

Other U.S. allies had a more challenging uphill climb. Facing opposition from America's unions, America's other East Asian ally, South Korea, was not offered a similar chance to update the terms of its trade in steel and aluminum.[73] South Korea cut a deal in 2018 with the Trump administration to avoid tariff hikes on steel in exchange for a restrictive, fixed U.S. import quota. The Biden administration's newest deals with the EU, UK, and Japan also included new quotas, but ones that allowed their exporters the opportunity to export more over the quota if paying the higher Trump-imposed tariff rate. Seoul wanted to discuss securing these more flexible terms for its exporters but was not offered the opportunity. Nor did the administration engage meaningfully with other

71   United Steelworkers, "USW Supports Section 232 Deal with Japan," press release, February 7, 2022.

72   U.S. Department of Commerce, "U.S.-Japan Joint Statement," February 7, 2022, https://www.commerce.gov/sites/default/files/2022-02/US-Japan-Joint-Statement.pdf.

73   In the case of South Korea, its trade minister made clear that with the U.S. agreement with the EU and new negotiations underway with the UK and Japan over the 232 tariffs, "... I think it's time for us to be treated fairly and to be on a level playing field among allies an among key trading partners." In response, U.S. Trade Representative Tai referred to the political limits of proceeding with South Korea, noting in a statement "... ongoing strong concerns of U.S. stakeholders" regarding steel and aluminum and America's focus on negotiating (with the EU) a new carbon intensity arrangement in the sector. Madeline Halpert, "Trade Minister: South Korea Wants More IPEF Details, Section 232 Talks," World Trade Online, January 28, 2022. See also Andrea Shalal, "U.S. Not Looking to Renegotiate Trump-Era Steel Quotas with S.Korea, Says Raimondo," Reuters, March 23, 2022.

countries on updated terms, simply leaving in place most of the Section 232 steel and aluminum tariffs and import limitations left behind by the Trump administration.

This hodgepodge of steel and aluminum arrangements with different trading partners, including even among its allies, moved America still further away from the WTO principle of non-discrimination. It also further validated longstanding skepticism of America's argument that the Section 232 tariffs and import restrictions were necessary to meet its national security interests by keeping them in place over the course of two administrations. Critical to America's shifting justifications had been the substantial weight given to the views and concerns of its steelworker and other unions along the way. As the administration attempted to balance the views of its domestic stakeholders with the demands of its allied trading partners, the mishmash of outcomes and agreements only exacerbated foreign relations problems as more allies were offered different or better access and opportunities over others.

Amidst these developments, the first round of WTO challenges against Trump's Section 232 steel and aluminum tariffs finally yielded initial panel-level decisions in late 2022. Since the Biden administration had kept most of the tariffs and other restrictions in place, claims in the WTO against them remained active and thus kept the Pandora's box open. The WTO panel was forced to consider the legitimacy of America's national security defense, finding that its use of the WTO national security exception was not justified in this case. To avoid complying with the decision, the Biden administration simply filed an appeal with the WTO's non-functioning Appellate Body, thus effectively moving the issue into legal limbo.

Biden's trade ambassador, Katherine Tai, strongly rebuked the lower WTO panel ruling, warning that the WTO was "on very, very thin ice." Repeating the familiar sovereignty refrain from America's far Left and far Right critics of the WTO, she warned of a situation where "unelected, not really accountable decision-makers in Geneva second-guess processes that are run through a government like ours which is democratic."[74] America's WTO ambassador further warned WTO members that it "was a mistake to begin adjudicating national security at the WTO" and that "[f]or over 70 years, the United States has held the clear and unequivocal

74   Ana Monteiro, "WTO on 'Thin Ice' with Metals-Tariff Ruling, US Trade Chief Says," Bloomberg, December 19, 2022.

position that issues of national security cannot be reviewed . . . and the WTO has no authority to second-guess [it]."[75]

Other countries could be forgiven for concluding that America was continuing to both have its cake and eat it. Having made no effort to restore the WTO dispute system, the Biden administration seemed very comfortable for well over a year with settling into the status quo of maintaining nearly all of Trump's tariffs while also doing nothing to restore the dispute system to allow claims against them to be fully adjudicated. Only in mid-2022, and after many requests from other WTO members, did the administration at least begin to engage to discuss ideas for improvements to the dispute process. As it engaged, the administration insisted that it would only support fundamental reform of that system, not steps that would only restore the previous status quo. Talks picked up into 2023, but as of mid-2024, prospects for an agreeable solution on reforms remained unclear, with many WTO members continuing to resist America's assertion that there ever was a problem that needed to be fixed in the first place.

UNILATERALISM RESTORED: TRUMP'S TRADE WAR WITH CHINA (AND BEYOND)

For the WTO system, actions that are protectionist in intent and unilateral in approach represent the most significant threats to its viability. America's use of Section 232 and Section 201 tariffs crossed the first line. Its use of another tool, Section 301, against China and select other countries, then fully crossed the second.

Like Trump, Lighthizer shared a firm conviction that threats to raise tariffs gave real and useful leverage in achieving trade policy goals. His belief came from direct personal experience, both as a Capitol Hill staffer and then as one of Ronald Reagan's deputy U.S. trade representatives, in the context of successive American threats of unilateral trade actions against Japan and others during the early 1980s. He also deeply believed that decades of U.S. government efforts to engage and respond through diplomacy to China's growing threat to the survival of multiple American industries amounted to malpractice, essentially allowing China to steamroll over America's economy. Once he became Trump's lead trade ambassador, prior generations of America's

75   Hannah Monicken, "U.S. Appeals National Security Cases to Defunct WTO Appellate Body," World Trade Online, January 27, 2023.

China hands approached him to offer advice, many recommending continued high-level engagement and dialogues to broker deals with China. Lighthizer countered by stressing that such approaches, with no meaningful leverage having first been established and threatened, had only given rise to China's confidence that it could continue to use these dialogues just to keep on steamrolling.

The Trump administration's first foray with China on trade reinforced Lighthizer's point. President Trump's initial meeting with President Xi Jinping in April 2017 yielded agreement to begin another high-level process, the U.S-China Comprehensive Economic Dialogue (CED), along with agreement to pursue a confidence-building negotiation on the front end to make progress on trade matters. Commerce Secretary Ross was tapped to lead for America a "100-day Action Plan" negotiation to demonstrate early progress, with the promise of more progress to come later. With Lighthizer still not confirmed by the Senate until mid-May of 2017, Ross acquired principal control over implementing the president's trade policy during the first several months of the administration.

Drawing from Trump's rhetoric on reciprocity, China also insisted on securing outcomes from the new dialogue for itself as well. After a fast-paced final few weeks of intensive negotiations, both sides reached an agreement in mid-May on ten areas. China secured America's agreement to take new steps to facilitate imports of cooked poultry from China and, in a political victory for President Xi, to send U.S. representatives to China's next U.S.-opposed Belt and Road infrastructure conference. America got a few items, including a renewed promise first made in 2016 to reopen its market to U.S. beef imports, as well as other promises on e-payment services and other financial services; observers noted that China had appeared ready to grant these to the Obama administration but put them on hold after Trump's election.[76] Ross was quickly and widely ridiculed for characterizing his "100-day agreement" outcomes as "more than has been done in the whole history of U.S.-China relations on trade."[77] One former U.S. trade official graded the outcomes instead as mostly "old wine in new bottles."[78]

---

76 See, e.g., Jack Caporal and Jenny Leonard, "U.S.-China 100-Day Plan Focused on Beef, Poultry, Biotech, Epay Issues," World Trade Online, May 18, 2017.

77 Caporal and Leonard, "U.S.-China 100-Day Plan."

78 Claire Reade, "No Rabbits Pulled Out of Hats at the Comprehensive Dialogue. Now What?," Center for Strategic and International Studies (CSIS), August 1, 2017.

Ross and his team re-engaged with China to have better wine to open in time for the first full meeting of the CED in Washington set for July. Vice Premier Wang and delegation met with the U.S. leads, Ross and Treasury Secretary Mnuchin, but joint announcements about the meeting outcomes never came. According to various accounts, Trump exploded and derailed the whole exercise after Ross previewed its expected outcomes in the Oval Office. Trump demanded tariffs on China instead.[79] Two immediate effects followed. First was a high priority placed by the president on teeing up tariffs against China as quickly as possible. Second was Ross's personal fall from favor in the Oval Office.[80]

The episode also brought instant credibility to Lighthizer's argument about the efficacy of dialogues with China when not backstopped with credible leverage. Not only did Lighthizer have the right argument to bring to this table, but he also had the right tool to serve up the requested tariffs and, thus, the necessary leverage. In mid- to late summer, as Ross's China negotiations went off the tracks, Lighthizer turned to instruct his staff to explore the use of Section 301 of the 1974 Trade Act to initiate investigations against China for its unfair trade barriers. He also instructed his staff around the same time to explore the potential to bring Section 301 investigations against Japan and South Korea as a way to hike U.S. tariffs over their trade barriers to U.S. automobile exports.

As a legal tool, Section 301 authorized the president to hit specific countries with higher U.S. tariffs if those trading partners were found to use unfair trade barriers to exclude U.S. exports. The administration could keep these tariffs in place until it was satisfied that the trading partner had removed these practices and barriers. Before imposing tariffs, Lighthizer's agency first needed to announce and conduct a formal investigation into these practices and then conclude they met the statute's standard of "unreasonable" acts or other policies unfair to U.S. exports and trade.

Section 301, therefore, provided broad authority for the executive branch to identify, pursue, and act against almost any practice by any individual trading partner deemed unfair to U.S. exports. The tool was originally passed by Congress in 1974 to provide leverage for the executive branch to pursue myriad unfair practices that the GATT rules did not cover. Like Section 232, it could be initiated, investigated, and decided

---

79   Woodward, *Fear*, 159–60. See also Steven Mufson, "Is Wilbur Ross Still President Trump's 'Go-To Guy'?," *Washington Post*, December 8, 2017.

80   Woodward, *Fear*.

by the administration with minimal outside checks and balances. Also, like Section 232, if tariffs were imposed, they could be left in place at the president's discretion.

Section 301 investigations were threatened or launched during the 1980s and the first half of the 1990s, particularly against Japan. It became a powerful and notorious tool for America's controversial exercise of unilateralism during that era. Notably, however, different administrations rarely actually hiked tariffs using Section 301. Instead, they often resorted to initially using the threat of an investigation as leverage to negotiate with foreign governments to change their practices before any tariffs were ever raised.

Section 301 fell into disuse from 1995 with the creation of the WTO's new and more robust dispute system and other changes to the WTO rules. With it, there was broad consensus that Section 301–type actions would not survive a formal WTO challenge, leading America to include a clear statement to that effect in the legislative package implementing the WTO agreements. It stated affirmatively that even though Section 301 remained a part of U.S. law, the executive branch would no longer use it unilaterally.[81] By swearing off future use of Section 301, America banked heavily on the promise that the new, more robust WTO dispute system would be sufficient to protect its trade interests.

The wisdom of that decision was quickly tested in a 1996 WTO case that America brought and lost against Japan. America claimed that a series of Japan's policies and practices unfairly limited access in Japan for U.S. companies and U.S. exports of photographic film and paper. Many of Japan's practices cited as unfairly exclusionary, ranging from regulations in Japan's distribution sector to its level of antitrust policy enforcement, were not a clear fit with the coverage of the WTO's rules. With the use of Section 301 closed off, America pursued a WTO case instead. It subsequently lost on all arguments, providing an early and painful lesson in the challenges of pursuing its trading partners' systemic or informal barriers through the new WTO.

Lighthizer, by contrast, felt no obligation to uphold America's unilateral decision in 1995 to retire the use of Section 301. His initial request to probe possible Section 301 automobile cases against China, Japan, and South Korea never proceeded to the launch of a formal investigation.

---

81   Section 301 was still used as the legal means by which the United States raised tariffs but limited only to cases where a WTO or other trade agreement dispute panel had first authorized the United States to retaliate.

Instead, the administration began preparing to launch an investigation against China's theft of intellectual property by building on initial work done during the Obama administration to prepare a case for the WTO.

Less than a month after Ross's dialogue collapse with China, news of a coming Section 301 investigation on China leaked to the press.[82] Shortly after, Trump issued an executive memorandum directing Lighthizer to consider a Section 301 investigation into China's intellectual property practices.[83] While signing the memorandum was legally unnecessary, Trump did it for publicity, calling it a "very big move."[84] It also got China's immediate attention. The following day, China responded by insisting it would "take necessary measures to safeguard our legitimate rights" should America launch the investigation. It also stressed that the action, if launched, would be "against international trade rules."[85] The U.S.-China relationship quickly took a frosty turn, with China putting Ross's dialogue and plans for future engagements on ice.

Lighthizer's unflinching use of Section 301 returned unilateralism to America's trade policy after a 30-plus year absence. In contrast with its use in the past, it appeared this time that the Trump administration would begin by announcing tariffs and then move to explore whether China was interested in a negotiation. The U.S. Congress cheered the Section 301 announcement as though a pent-up itch over America's handling of the China threat was finally being scratched. Unions and some in the halls of big business also applauded. Like Trump, few seemed focused on the implications of America's return to its unilateral past, much less on the implications of the action for undermining the WTO system.[86]

Along with it, leadership of the administration's trade policy also quickly returned to Lighthizer and his position as U.S. Trade Representative at the USTR. Congress established both to lead on trade and gave them relevant legal authorities to carry out that mandate. The Departments of Commerce and especially State, which often try to

---

82 Jenny Leonard, "Sources: USTR to Self-Initiate '301' Probe into China's Forced Tech Transfers," World Trade Online, August 3, 2017.

83 White House, "Presidential Memorandum for the United States Trade Representative," August 14, 2017.

84 Isabelle Hoagland, "Trump Directs USTR to 'Consider All Available Options' on Contested Chinese IP Practices," World Trade Online, August 14, 2017.

85 "China Says It 'Will Not Sit Idle' if U.S. Section 301 Probe Leads to Trade Actions," World Trade Online, August 15, 2017.

86 Hoagland, "Trump Directs USTR to 'Consider All Available Options' on Contested Chinese IP Practices."

assert some role in the process, were effectively cut out of trade policy during the remainder of the Trump administration except in cases where they still held some official role, such as Commerce's oversight over Section 232 and anti-dumping laws. Only the Defense Department, the National Security Council, the White House chief counsel, and closely embedded White House staff (including family) remained among the most significant executive branch checks on Trump's trade actions.[87] Reflecting his new "rising star" status in the administration, Lighthizer was quickly accorded an elevated position at the White House. During Trump's November 2017 stop in Tokyo for an official visit, Lighthizer was moved from courtesy inclusion in the president's motorcades and events into some of the transportation bubbles that moved the president at times more quickly than most of his entourage.[88]

The itch that Section 301 scratched in Washington was met with a sense of caution and unease from America's allies. They shared many of the same concerns over China, and if America could successfully force China to change, they also stood to benefit. At the same time, America's unilateral trajectory raised broad concerns about what it all meant for the WTO system and where its use might next be targeted. These fears proved valid when Lighthizer later turned Section 301 against other U.S. trading partners, formally invoking it in 2019 against France and then, in 2020, against nine other countries and the EU to force them to stop their plans to impose a digital services tax viewed as targeted to discriminate against American digital companies. Two Section 301 investigations were also launched in 2020 against Vietnam over currency practices and its imports of illegally traded timber.[89] By the end of the Trump administration's term, Lighthizer had re-normalized America's use of Section 301, completely tossing aside the 1994 voluntary pledge to stop using it with the creation of the WTO.

Lighthizer's Section 301 investigation on China's intellectual property practices was completed the following March, packaged in a nearly 200-page final report that Lighthizer had bound and printed to distribute

---

87   See, e.g., Woodward, *Fear*.

88   Within a few months afterward, Lighthizer's rising star in the administration became widely known. See, e.g., Ana Swanson, "The Little-Known Trade Adviser Who Wields Enormous Power in Washington," *New York Times*, March 9, 2018.

89   Andres B. Schwarzenberg, *Section 301 of the Trade Act of 1974*, Congressional Research Service, IF11346, January 3, 2023, updated January 29, 2024.

to visitors and on Capitol Hill.[90] There was little doubt about what would happen next. Rather than move to negotiate with China to remove its practices, Trump went straight to announcing forthcoming tariff hikes on $50 billion of China's imports—an approximate estimate of the damage caused by its intellectual property theft and other practices. Within several hours, China announced it would hit back with tariff retaliation on the same level of imports from America. The long-anticipated tariff and trade war with China was underway.

Domestic U.S. reactions shifted quickly to unease over which Americans would be caught in the tariff war crossfire—either from higher prices due to tariffs on Chinese imports or from China's retaliatory tariffs that would impact the producers of U.S. exports by closing them off from Chinese consumers. China's tariff retaliation against American agricultural exports quickly became a particularly politically sensitive issue, leading the administration to put together two large compensation packages for farmers with a combined total of $24.5 billion in payments to help offset their lost export markets in China.[91] After pushback from many American users on the range of Chinese imports slated for tariff hikes, significant changes in the lists of products slated for higher import tariffs were eventually made and remade before finally going into effect in mid-2018. China also responded in kind with its own retaliation against America's exports.

Over the next several months, America and China engaged in high-stakes, tit-for-tat escalations in their new hot trade war. Lighthizer insisted that China was responsible for the war by engaging in unjustified retaliation against America's justified actions. Initial rounds of U.S. tariff hikes of 25 percent on $50 billion in China's imports, once quickly matched by China with tariffs on a similar value of U.S. exports, were increased further with a flat additional 10 percent tariff on $200 billion more in imports from China. China again matched this step, and then the next round of tariff threats and escalations ensued. To the world, it looked by any measure exactly like a two-way, tit-for-tat tariff war of America's making.

---

90   USTR, "Findings of the Investigation into China's Acts, Policies, and Practices Related to Technology Transfer, Intellectual Property, and Innovation under Section 301 of the Trade Act of 1974," March 22, 2018.

91   For details on the programs, see Randy Schnepf, *Farm Policy: Comparison of 2018 and 2019 MFP Programs*, Congressional Research Service, IF11289, August 12, 2019.

In late spring 2018, the Trump administration made one attempt to outline a list of demands for China that, if met, could stave off the administration's plan to initiate tariff hikes. These included guaranteed reductions in the U.S. trade deficit with China by $200 billion over two years through new purchases by China of American exports, an end to China's direct support for companies in sectors targeted for future growth, an end to all technology transfer requirements and cybertheft of trade secrets and other U.S. business information, a reduction in China's tariffs to match lower U.S. tariff levels in the wto, the removal of other non-tariff barriers, opening further access for U.S. services providers, and a wide range of additional steps to ensure U.S. intellectual property was protected.[92] China countered with its own list of demands that underscored a deadlock in objectives, pushing both sides toward their inevitable tariff war, with the first round of tariff hikes implemented by America and then China in early July.

By the time Trump and Xi met next in late 2018, these rapid tariff escalations resulted in roughly 65 percent of the value (trade-weighted average) of U.S. exports to China facing new tariffs that rose to nearly 20 percent on average. Going the other way, nearly 50 percent of the value of China's exports faced new U.S. tariffs that averaged around 12 percent. By contrast, America's average wto tariffs on imports from other countries at the time were in the range of 3 percent, while China had an average tariff rate of around 7 percent—a newly reduced rate for other wto members on some products that chose not to engage in tariff wars with Beijing.[93]

China exerted its leverage in the form of immediate, roughly proportional tariff retaliation, after which Trump and Xi agreed at their meeting to a 90-day truce on further tariff escalations and to begin a more structured negotiation to see if differences could be bridged. America announced that its tariffs on China would be hiked further to 25 percent if the results were unsatisfactory.[94] By March 2019, formal negotiations blew past this initial 90-day deadline; with some progress

92   Jack Caporal, "China Rejects New Slate of U.S. Trade Demands as Tariffs Loom," World Trade Online, May 4, 2018.
93   An excellent overview of the play-by-play, along with excellent data on the scope and impacts of the tariffs on various sectors and overall trade, can be found in Chad P. Bown, "The US-China Trade War and Phase One Agreement" (Working Paper 21-2, Peterson Institute for International Economics, Washington, DC, February 2021).
94   Isabelle Hoagland, "Trump, Xi Agree to Suspend Planned Tariff Boost, Continue Talks," World Trade Online, December 1, 2018.

made, however, Trump announced a hold on further tariff hikes. The White House revealed a similar list of objectives to those it proposed to China several months earlier, which included steps to address the Section 301 technology transfer and intellectual property concerns along with cuts to China's tariff rates and non-tariff barriers, refraining from cybertheft, new rules on subsidies for state-owned firms, ending China's currency manipulation, and reducing America's deficit through new purchases by China of U.S. agricultural and manufactured goods.[95]

Negotiations continued until May, when the American side erupted after China pulled back numerous initial commitments it made across several areas of the talks. Viewed as bad faith, Trump announced another round of tariff hikes on China days later—this time, raising U.S. tariffs from 10 to 25 percent on $200 billion in imports from China.[96] Talks ground to a halt until Trump and Xi agreed in June that negotiations would restart, along with further threats from the White House to raise tariffs depending on how things went.

Lighthizer has elsewhere recounted his account of these high-stakes negotiations with his Chinese counterpart, Vice Premier Liu He.[97] By his and other accounts, the negotiations were as businesslike as could be expected given the circumstances. A degree of rapport was established between the two that created the necessary environment for dealmaking, but only if their respective political systems and leaders allowed them to succeed. It all took place against the backdrop of tariffs on hundreds of billions of dollars in trade and stock market gyrations that hinged daily on every word, smile, and handshake in front of the cameras.

An agreement in principle was eventually reached in late December, with the detailed results announced in mid-January 2020. The "U.S.-China Economic and Trade Agreement" became more commonly known as the U.S.-China "Phase One" agreement from the expectation that further negotiations would be held. It covered some of America's previously announced objectives, including commitments on intellectual property and trade secret protection, new services market access issues, and other changes to China's regulations that limited U.S. agriculture exports to cater to America's farmers. The Phase One agreement also contained purchase commitments from China, including for U.S. ag-

---

95   "White House: 'Progress' in China Talks, 'Much Work' Left, Deadline Stands," World Trade Online, January 31, 2019.

96   Lighthizer recounts this pullback in Lighthizer, *No Trade Is Free*, 175–78.

97   See Lighthizer, *No Trade Is Free*, esp. chapters 9 and 10.

ricultural exports of $32 billion over two years as a part of a broader, two-year $200 billion purchase commitment.[98] Importantly, it neglected to address many of the core issues of China's state-driven model that Lighthizer insisted the wto's rules and norms were not equipped to handle, including China's state-directed support for its large enterprises and industrial targeting initiatives. The agreement also reinforced Lighthizer's insistence that America must keep many tariffs in place to fundamentally reset its trading terms with China so long as Beijing would not jettison its state-supported export targeting policies.

Congressional Republicans greeted the outcomes as a welcome start. Democrats, who had made little headway with China on trade during their control of Congress and the White House, still criticized the outcome as Trump's "failed China strategy" accomplishing "nothing for American workers."[99] These reactions ushered in the official start of the 2020 presidential election primary season, as reviews of the deal fell along strict party lines. After the COVID-19 pandemic shut down much of the world just several weeks later, and with presidential campaigning well underway, the U.S.-China trade and tariff war fell into a frozen state. Then, it drifted into an extended Cold War–style truce. Both sides pulled back some on their tariff hikes immediately after the Phase One agreement came into effect, but tariffs remained quite high between them, averaging around 20 percent for each side on roughly 60 percent of their exports to one another. Only some limited modifications were subsequently made to ease a small percentage of the tariffs, such as on essential goods, to respond to the pandemic. Otherwise, these tariff levels remained the same far into the Biden administration, as of the time of this writing.

What goals did the tariff war achieve? The initial Section 301 goal of raising tariffs on $30 billion in imports from China was to hold it accountable for unfair intellectual property practices. If measured by that narrow objective, the tariff war that ensued was partly successful—on paper. China made some commitments in the Phase One agreement to end some practices.[100] Even so, many of China's questionable intellec-

98   Brett Fortnam, "China Deal Includes Promises Not to Retaliate, IP, and Biotech Commitments," World Trade Online, January 15, 2020.
99   Isabelle Icso, "Schumer, Wyden, Brown Question Enforceability, Substance of U.S.-China Deal," World Trade Online, January 15, 2020.
100   Victoria Huang, "U.S.-China Intellectual Property Issues in a Post-Phase-One Era: Interview with Mark Cohen," National Bureau of Asian Research, January 29, 2022.

tual property practices remained, according to subsequent official U.S. government surveys.[101] The fact that the initial $30 billion assessment of harm from these practices ballooned to higher tariffs covering over ten times the amount of trade, or approximately $370 billion in imports, underscored the barely concealed objective of using Section 301 to accomplish much larger objectives.

One of these goals, explored further in the next chapter, was to satisfy Trump's campaign pledges and other pronouncements to cut the U.S. trade deficit. That goal remains mostly unmet several years later. Temporary progress was made when the goods trade deficit with China fell by over 25 percent between 2018 and 2020 as the tariff hikes were fully implemented, a trend also impacted in 2020 by the seismic interruption to global trade from the COVID-19 pandemic. Meanwhile, imports from some other countries picked up quickly over that period. Imports from Vietnam especially soared, appearing to mostly replace some of the dips in imports from China as some of its goods were just shipped through or production moved to Vietnam instead.[102] As global trade recovered, so did America's goods deficit with China, staging a comeback in 2021 and then roaring back to near-record levels in 2022 even as the tariffs remained in place, before falling back substantially in 2023 from that high.[103]

The Trump administration also bet that purchase pledges from China would kick in to further improve America's deficit. China, however, fell dramatically short of meeting those commitments. Scheduled to take place over 2020–21, U.S. goods exports reached only approximately 60 percent of China's promised purchase levels by the end of 2021. Similar shortfalls were recorded in promised purchases of U.S. services sector exports.[104]

---

101   See, e.g., USTR, "2023 National Trade Estimate Report on Foreign Trade Barriers," March 2023, esp. 75–80.

102   The U.S. goods trade deficit with Vietnam totaled $39.5 billion in 2018, rising sharply to $90.1 billion in 2021 and then $116.2 billion in 2022. United States Census Bureau, "Trade in Goods with Vietnam," accessed June 2024, https://www.census.gov/foreign-trade/balance/c5520.html.

103   The U.S. goods trade deficit with China totaled $352.8 billion in 2021, $382.3 billion in 2022, and then $279.4 billion in 2023. United States Census Bureau, "Trade in Goods with China," accessed March 2024, https://www.census.gov/foreign-trade/balance/c5700.html.

104   Chad P. Bown, "US-China Phase One Tracker: China's Purchases of US Goods," Peterson Institute for International Economics, July 19, 2022.

Another objective was to fundamentally reset America's terms of trade with China for the longer term. Keeping much higher tariffs in place corrected for some of the exporting advantages China wielded with its state-supported and other non-market, industrial targeting measures. It also corrected for what some viewed as the grave error of letting China into the WTO, which had afforded it the same permanent tariff rate that America applied to other WTO members. Before China joined the WTO, Congress provided this preferential treatment to China starting in 1979 to improve ties following the start of official diplomatic relations in the mid-1970s. It also kept the power to revoke that rate as leverage, used most often to lean on China to improve human rights and take other actions as it integrated into the global economy. Congress gave up that power when China was offered permanent membership in the WTO in 2001—until Section 301 tariffs began to be imposed in 2018. America's average tariff rate on Chinese imports went from approximately 3 percent before 2018 to roughly 20 percent as of early 2021—equivalent to the rate applied annually on imports from China before voluntarily offering better terms in 1979.[105]

American importers and exporters still caught in the middle of the tariff war attempted, mostly in vain, to continue to draw attention to their circumstances. One estimate found that almost the entire $48 billion cost was borne by U.S. consumers and importers, belying Trump's promise that the cost would be absorbed only by China.[106] Other modeling suggested the impacts ranged more widely among different importers and users.[107] Years after the tariff war got underway, it remained as difficult as ever to see when and how it might end, with lasting implications for the credibility of the WTO system.

Another goal of the Section 301 tariffs was to raise the risks and costs to businesses of continuing to look to China as a manufacturing and export platform to the American market. Anecdotal evidence suggests the unpredictability of the tariff war impacted some investor decisions, with one survey of U.S. businesses in China during mid-2019 finding 53 percent delaying or reducing investments in China due to trade ten-

---

105 Estimates from Bown, "The US-China Trade War and Phase One Agreement."

106 Tom Lee and Tori Smith, "Section 301 China Tariffs by End Use," American Action Forum, January 11, 2021, https://www.americanactionforum.org/research/section-301-china-tariffs-by-end-use/.

107 United States International Trade Commission, *Economic Impact of Section 232 and 301 Tariffs on U.S. Industries*, publication number 5405 (Washington, DC: USITC, March 2023).

sions.[108] Other aggregate data indicate that overall foreign investment in China continued to grow through the period despite the new uncertainty in U.S.-China trade relations.[109]

As a presidential candidate, Biden attempted to paint the tariff war as failing to live up to Trump's promises and rhetoric, starting with failing to force China to end many of its unfair practices. As president, however, he embraced the new status quo on tariffs, which was popular with unions and other domestic producer groups and thus politically valuable. Biden's nominee for his trade ambassador, Katherine Tai, called the tariffs a "legitimate tool" in her confirmation hearing. Months later, Tai continued the same refrain, referring to Section 301 as a "very, very important tool."[110] The Biden administration trimmed back the 301 tariffs on a very select basis only, chiefly to respond to industry and importer claims of shortages and similar problems. As of mid-2023, less than 10 percent of the products on the list of higher tariffs had been removed.

By spring 2022, the administration was seriously considering a new approach. Seeming to begin to soften the ground for an announcement, Biden's deputy national security advisor remarked that the tariffs were "inherited" and questioned the "strategic purpose" of those on items like bicycles and underwear.[111] The plan reportedly was to launch a new Section 301 investigation with the goal of applying new tariffs more tactically to help reshape critical supply chains, as opposed to simply fulfilling Trump's big, rounded-off dollar announcements for new tariff hike announcements. However, that plan never got the final top sign-off, and the Trump-era tariffs on China were left essentially in place.[112] The fact that they remained politically popular with the unions was one strong political reason to leave them as is. The administration also further backed away from America's initial justification for the tariffs—as

108   American Chamber of Commerce in Shanghai, *2019 China Business Report* (Shanghai: American Chamber of Commerce, 2019).

109   See Paul Hannon and Eun-Young Jeong, "China Overtakes U.S. as World's Leading Destination in Foreign Direct Investment," *Wall Street Journal*, January 24, 2021.

110   David Lawder and Andrea Shalal, "USTR Nominee Tai Says Tariffs Are 'Legitimate Tool' for Trade Policy," Reuters, February 25, 2021; Brett Fortnam, "Tai: China Has No Plans for Meaningful Reforms to Address U.S. Concerns," World Trade Online, October 4, 2021.

111   Brett Fortnam, "NSC Official: China Tariffs Should Be Adjusted to Fit Strategic Priorities," World Trade Online, April 21, 2022.

112   On these anticipated developments, see, e.g., Gavin Bade, "Biden's Trade Team: RIP Globalization," Politico, May 8, 2022; and Fortnam, "NSC Official."

leverage to force China to change its behavior. As one administration official stated, "We're not assuming that will happen."[113]

However, as the 2024 presidential election approached, the administration shook off its earlier reticence and announced in May a new series of Section 301–justified tariff hikes on China across several product categories. With representatives of several labor unions and some domestic manufacturer representatives in attendance in the White House Rose Garden, Biden announced his administration's tariff actions against China, which added to the ongoing Trump-era tariffs. Among other products, additional duties of 25 percent would be introduced on imports from China, ranging from steel and aluminum products to rubber medical gloves, with even higher tariffs on other goods, including a 100 percent tariff on China's electric vehicle exports. The new tariffs were "strategic and targeted," Biden argued, a "smart approach" in contrast to Trump's across-the-board tariff hikes on thousands of goods caught up in his escalating tariff wars.[114] By also having decided to only add to (and not reduce some of) Trump's broad Section 301 tariffs, the smartest approach of all seemed to be a political calculation—to avoid ceding any turf with working-class voters in the leadup to Biden's anticipated November 2024 rematch with the "tariff man."

Over the course of the Trump and Biden administrations, justifications for the tariffs often shifted ever further away from their original, stated purpose, which initially had been to confront China's theft of American intellectual property. The Trump administration used the tariffs to attempt to achieve a multiplicity of goals with mixed results, whether to secure China's commitment to purchase U.S. farm goods or to demand improved access for American financial services companies in China. The Biden administration stretched their original purpose further, including by evaluating requests for exclusions from the tariffs on whether they "would aid efforts to shift sourcing out of China in the near term."[115] With little effort made to engage China on further actions,

---

113   David Lawder, "US Review of China Tariffs Won't Depend on Trade 'Breakthrough,' Official Says," Reuters, March 30, 2023.

114   Joe Biden, "Remarks by President Biden on His Actions to Protect American Workers and Businesses from China's Unfair Trade Practices," The White House, Washington, DC, May 14, 2024.

115   USTR, "Notice of Extension of Certain Exclusions: China's Acts, Policies, and Practices Related to Technology Transfer, Intellectual Property, and Innovation," 89 Fed. Reg. 46948 (May 30, 2024).

the administration molded and further expanded the tariff status quo with China to meet its own domestic political and economic objectives.

Both administrations, but especially the Biden administration, also pivoted to other China "derisking" strategies, including tightening export controls, investment screening, and other measures to further unwind economic interdependence. The administration also pursued a series of discriminatory preference programs, covered in the next chapter, to rekindle targeted sourcing and production value chains in America to the exclusion of China. After initially walking out during the Trump administration, America took these and other steps, moving even further away from adherence to the WTO rules.

In September 2020, China predictably won the first WTO panel-level challenge against the Trump administration's Section 301 tariff actions. The Trump administration disposed of it by simply appealing that decision to the broken WTO Appellate Body, and thus into legal limbo. Rather than going to the WTO to pursue the unfair trade practice claims, Washington comfortably revived and embraced tariff unilateralism as its preferred tool to deal with them instead. America's normalization of tariff unilateralism became the most visible sign to the world of how much America's trade policy priorities had changed. Bypassing the WTO rules to confront the myriad challenges posed by China's practices undeniably propelled many of these decisions; a few other countries have since followed in some similar ways by invoking their own tariffs, with various justifications, on China. The Trump administration took that further, however, by threatening unilateral tariffs against a number of different countries, irrespective of whether friend or foe, and over almost any trade complaint. The Biden administration only unilaterally hiked U.S. tariffs on China, but as explored in other chapters, also used other forms of discrimination in its treatment of imports from most other countries. These actions gave China new data points to use to attempt to make its case to the world that America, not China, was the real threat to the rules-based system.

THE WTO'S AMERICA PROBLEM: INTERNATIONAL AND OTHER IMPLICATIONS

In just over two years, the Trump administration hiked U.S. tariffs on nearly 17 percent of U.S. global imports, with the overwhelming

majority—16 percent—originating from China.[116] Its global application of Section 232 tariffs on steel and aluminum was first justified
to shield America from the harmful global price and capacity effects
of China's non-market-driven overproduction, but then the tool was
used to threaten more tariffs on global imports of autos, titanium, and
auto parts. Similarly, Section 301 tariffs were initially used to confront
China over unfair intellectual property practices, but then over scores
of other unfair practices, and then turned and aimed at other Asian and
European trading partners to threaten them over their unfair practices.
America's allies and others quickly recognized that while China may
have been an administration priority, America also had new and broader
inclinations and motives.

The Trump administration's uses of Section 232 and Section 301
tariffs were challenged at the WTO, and initial WTO dispute panels found
each in violation of America's WTO commitments. It was with that very
expectation that the Clinton, Bush, and Obama administrations had
avoided using those legal authorities to increase tariffs following the
launch of the WTO. The Trump administration embraced their use instead, having also shut the door to any WTO-sanctioned consequences by
breaking its appeals system and thus paralyzing the dispute settlement
system needed to authorize the use of retaliatory tariffs by America's
trading partners. In America's new consequence-free edition of the
postwar rules-based system, many countries resorted to retaliating
anyway to meet their own politically needed expressions of trade and
tariff vigilantism. One breakthrough victory was achieved after an initial
WTO panel turned down in September 2021 China's WTO claim brought
against the Trump administration's use of Section 201 to increase safeguard tariffs on solar products.[117] Having lost that ruling, China simply
returned the favor by appealing its loss in that decision to the defunct
Appellate Body, thus moving it into the same state of legal limbo.

It is easy to imagine how it might have gone differently. Although
none of America's trading partners liked Washington's new China tactics,
Europe, Japan, and others also had come to view China's state-driven
model as an increasing threat to the international system. Targeting
America's tariff actions exclusively at China's practices and engaging

---

116   Congressional Budget Office, "The Budget and Economic Outlook: 2020 to 2030,"
January 2020, https://www.cbo.gov/publication/56073.

117   USTR, "WTO Panel Rejects China's Solar Safeguard Challenge," press release, September
2, 2021.

more meaningfully with like-minded countries to confront that problem would have written a different history and potentially helped engineer a different conclusion—one that did not necessarily require dismantling the rules-based system for everybody else. Efforts were made at times with some allies, including one with the EU and Japan together, to discuss what to do about China. Such efforts never meaningfully advanced amid distrust and resentment over America's broader motives.

Global public opinion, of course, never seemed to factor into the Trump administration's calculations for anything it did. Even so, polls tracking views of America from abroad bear out the particularly damaging impact of the Trump administration's choices for its trade policy and tactics, particularly surrounding its tariff policies, on America's reputation and trust abroad. Among several major issues with global implications, from nuclear weapons to immigration to climate change, America's tariff wars and unilateralism ranked as its least supported policy decisions, with 68 percent of those surveyed outside America disapproving in the spring of 2019.[118] These realities created a difficult, if not impossible, political climate for other governments to collaborate seriously with America to improve or reorder the international trading system in a new way.

Lighthizer himself recognized that a bigger opportunity might have been missed, even if only to first secure more solid domestic support for the administration's broader-than-China tariff agenda. "My preference," he later wrote, ". . . was to move forward first with the Section 301 tariffs" on China to cultivate stronger support at home for further tariff wars to come. By starting with Section 232 tariffs on the world, which led to pain for some American exporters after the EU and some others quickly retaliated in kind, the administration left the ensuing domestic debate focused instead on the harder-to-make case for the "efficacy of tariffs in general." Lighthizer conceded that if the administration had tried harder to work with Europe and broker a quota arrangement to avoid retaliation, such negotiations might have succeeded and thus "blunted criticism that the Trump administration was 'going it alone' when it came to China."[119]

As it was, the administration's focus remained firmly on domestic objectives to guide its trade policy decisions, wherever that might take

118   Richard Wike, "The Trump Era Has Seen a Decline in America's Global Reputation," Pew Research Center, November 19, 2020.

119   Lighthizer, *No Trade Is Free*, 272.

them.[120] The "America First" approach to trade received particular support from America's unions and its domestic, as opposed to multinational, manufacturers—those who expected to benefit from the actions and would generally not be directly harmed by the ensuing crossfire of foreign retaliation. The fact that the Biden administration later avoided making significant changes to these policies underscored the degree to which both administrations were competing for the support of these same targeted domestic audiences.

The plurality of Americans saw it differently. Polls in mid-2019 showed 47 percent of Americans viewed Trump's tariff policies as harmful, with only 25 percent viewing them as helpful, a slide from the 40 percent of Americans who initially supported hiking tariffs as they were first being implemented.[121] Popular support remained high for one objective, however. Although 63 percent of registered American voters believed that the two-way tariff war was hurting America more than China, 67 percent supported continuing to confront China over its policies and practices. A substantial majority, 74 percent, also recognized that American consumers were ultimately shouldering the extra cost of the tariffs on China in order to do so.[122]

While of a different nature than challenges posed by China, America's new trade policies were perceived broadly as at least an equivalent, if not larger, threat to the WTO rules-based system. Walking out and then showing little in the way of interest or proposals to fix what it had broken was a pattern that continued far into the Biden administration, deepening that concern. When America did engage, rather than focus on the larger issues that needed to be addressed, it instead drew attention to the need to fix other longstanding WTO procedural shortcomings and grievances. These included issues like a chronic lack of member compliance with meeting the WTO's reporting and transparency requirements. Only in mid-2022 did America finally begin to engage on the issue of dispute settlement reform, as it also made clear that fundamental reform was the only acceptable way to accomplish it. As of this writing, it remains

---

120   Lighthizer summed up his "what if" scenarios with a similar point, writing, "All this said, I continue to admire the fact that whenever it came down to a choice between American workers and foreign interests, President Trump always chose the former." Lighthizer, *No Trade Is Free*.

121   Niv Ellis, "Nearly Half Think Trump's Tariffs Hurt US Economy: Poll," The Hill, May 28, 2019; John LaLoggia, "As New Tariffs Take Hold, More See Negative than Positive Impact for the U.S.," Pew Research Center, July 19, 2018.

122   Max Greenwood, "Poll: Voters Want US to Confront China over Trade," The Hill, September 3, 2019.

unclear but appears unlikely that a breakthrough premised on America's insistence on fundamental reform can be achieved anytime soon.

Walking out as it did triggered an array of other international responses. For China, whose military actions in the South China Sea and other actions had started to give credence to its growing reputation as a scofflaw of the international rules-based order, Washington's actions made it easy to make a similar claim about America for having ignored and undermined the WTO rules and system. Not known for self-reflection, China began to assert that it, in fact, was the most vigorous defender and champion of the rules-based international trading system.[123] Just days into the new Biden administration, China's president continued to make that case by declaring for the Davos jet set, who knew well of China's own discriminatory and self-enriching practices, that "international governance should be based on the rules and consensus reached among us, not on the order given by one or the few."[124]

Defending its right in the WTO to maintain its economic system, a situation from which it had benefited handsomely, Chinese officials also engaged in new charm offensives to preserve the status quo in the WTO. Joining with countries such as Brazil, India, Russia, and South Africa, China more aggressively called for the world to turn back America's threat to the rules-based trading system and "reject protectionism outright."[125] Few Western governments believed that China had actually taken over the high ground as a new champion of the liberal global economic order, but America's actions started to make it look a bit more convincing.

Without concrete proposals from America to reform the WTO dispute settlement system, China also tried to shape emerging discussions over its future. Dredging up a phrase particularly despised by the Trump administration, China stressed the WTO's important role in "global economic governance" and put forward its own WTO reform agenda in mid-2019. Convening a ministerial meeting of several countries to discuss it, China proposed essentially keeping the status quo with some tweaks while continuing to hit against America's practices directly.[126]

123   Among the first of many such statements, see Ben Blanchard, "China Says Supports WTO after U.S. Trade Threat," Reuters, March 2, 2017.
124   Eleanor Albert, "China's Xi Champions Multilateralism at Davos, Again," *Diplomat*, January 26, 2021.
125   Olivia Kumwenda-Mtambo and Alexander Winning, "BRICS Emerging Economies Reaffirm Support for Multilateral Trade under WTO Rules," Reuters, July 26, 2018.
126   World Trade Organization, "China's Proposal on WTO Reform," WT/GC/W/773, May 13, 2019.

Some greeted China's proposals with skepticism. Even so, the effort to at least engage on a solution, which America was not providing, resonated in some quarters. Most WTO members had few complaints with the dispute system and wanted to see it simply restored. Therefore, America's stranglehold on the WTO left its allies and the non-aligned alike with a certain degree of disdain toward America, even if not expressly stated as such, and, by default, some common cause with China.

As America's new approach was received internationally as both cavalier and inflicting irreparable damage, the Trump administration at times took pride in its self-imposed international isolation, rarely bending to change its approach significantly. Instead, it more often mocked critical reactions from abroad of America's actions as pure hypocrisy—an attempt by other countries to hide behind policies that skirted WTO rules and norms and tilted the terms of trade in their favor.

With America's intent to break the WTO appeals system apparent, other governments eventually stepped in to discuss options as the breakdown of the dispute resolution system loomed. Several met in Canada in late 2018 to formally start the effort, a meeting greeted with skeptical indifference from the Trump administration. At times, however, administration officials had challenged other WTO members to "pick a lane" between America's and China's interests, failing to recognize that America was no longer necessarily viewed as the desired lane.[127] Europeans, Japanese, and others who attempted to work with the administration were eventually left to choose their own lane as the administration made clear that it would not be engaging in meaningful collaboration to fix the appeals system.

This effort grew into a configuration of nations known as the "Ottawa Group," comprising ministers from the EU and 12 countries from Europe, Latin America, Africa, and the Asia-Pacific. As the effort gained momentum, the Trump administration continued to dismiss it and sometimes even mock it. Soon after the WTO appeals system was finally choked off, the EU announced an agreement with over a dozen other WTO members, including most of the Ottawa Group countries and China. The agreement was to create a "contingency" mechanism for binding dispute resolution among interested WTO members until a permanent

---

127 Hannah Monicken, "Shea: WTO Members 'Need to Pick a Lane' on Reform Issues," World Trade Online, October 12, 2018.

fix was realized.[128] This voluntary appeals mechanism was agreed upon and launched in the spring of 2020 among 19 WTO members.[129]

By the summer of 2023, 27 WTO members had joined the new system, which today operates similarly to the WTO appellate system. Although only a fraction of the WTO's 164 members decided to join, the group continued to expand. It included several of the WTO's largest economic players, such as the EU, China, Canada, Australia, and eventually Japan. All came together to choose their own lane, in response to America's unilateral decision to break the system for itself and everyone else.

Once in office, the Biden administration's slow-going approach to deciding whether, and if so, how, to genuinely support the WTO and its mission underscored a sharp inconsistency with the rhetoric it used to trumpet its intention to repair and restore America's international standing. Initially, it did little to change the political legacy of the Trump administration's go-it-alone trade actions. After appearing quite content with this status quo for much of its first year, the Biden administration finally succumbed by mid-2022 to its rhetoric and agreed to begin to engage on the topic of WTO reform. These talks inevitably became more challenging as ideas became more concrete. For America's part, it had racked up successive WTO panel–stage losses in cases brought against Trump-era tariffs and other trade actions. The Biden administration now owned those decisions and acted in the WTO to defend them. The backdrop to its discussions about dispute settlement reform became at least as much about America's eventual accountability to the WTO panel findings against it as they were about system reform. In mid-2023, America eventually tabled a set of general objectives, claiming it hoped to have a new dispute system agreed upon and functioning within 2024.[130] It remains to be seen whether America can agree with others on a solution for the dispute system and, even more questionably, whether America will agree to any solution that may ultimately cause it to be held accountable for its ongoing Section 232 and 301 tariff actions.

In terms of the tariff actions themselves, the Biden administration continued to do little to change the status quo other than easing the

128   Jakob Hanke Vela and Barbara Moens, "EU Moves to Outflank Trump on Trade," Politico, January 20, 2020.

129   Directorate-General for Trade, "Interim Appeal Arrangement for WTO Disputes Becomes Effective," European Commission, April 30, 2020.

130   Emma Farge, "U.S. Wants World Trade Organization Dispute System Fixed by 2024," Reuters, January 26, 2023.

terms of its steel tariffs for a few of its closest allies while adding new and higher tariffs on China—even after WTO panels ruled against all of them. Its negotiations with the EU to set environmental standards in steel production have yet to come to fruition after nearly three years of work. Its plodding steps on WTO reform have been generally welcomed by America's closest trading partners as an improvement over the Trump administration, yet America still operates outside of the WTO rules. Resentment among some allies also lingers over an administration that has routinely failed to treat them equally when negotiating new terms of trade to lessen the impacts of ongoing Section 232 tariffs and other restrictions. The longer the tariffs continue, the more the gap in America's treatment of different countries widens, straining the same external relationships it claimed to aim to repair.

Section 301 gave each U.S. administration significant latitude to continue to adjust and change tariff rates as it saw fit. By 2023, these steps had snowballed into calls inside and outside Congress to make higher tariff rates on China permanent by reimposing the higher U.S. tariff rate schedule used for imports from non-WTO members. As of this writing, the Biden administration has not taken a position on such proposals. If implemented, they would constitute a new unilateral move to permanently unwind and revoke, subject only to a presidential waiver, America's tariff obligations with China under the WTO. The proposal was quickly embraced in mid-2023 by some Republican primary presidential candidates seeking the party's 2024 nomination as they jockeyed to avoid losing ground to Trump in the race.[131] As the 2024 campaign continues, the issue may well emerge as a new political litmus test for trade amid Americans' ever-hardening views of China.

The contrast in America's commitment to the international trading system between the end of 2016 and today can only be described as canyon-like in its depth and breadth. The Biden administration has engaged in very limited ways to attempt to repair what the Trump administration broke through tariffs and various tirades, and in some ways has instead only doubled down. Without America's leadership, and then because of the damage America inflicted on it, the system has been left adrift and remains even more dramatically diminished in importance and credibility. The degree to which it still functions and its rules are generally followed is a testament to the majority of its members that

---

131   Bryce Baschuk, "Why There Are Calls in US to Revoke China's Preferred Trade Status," *Washington Post*, August 22, 2023.

continue to value it and view it as mutually beneficial instead of uniquely problematic.

Having rubbed the lamp and let the genie out of the bottle, does America care to put it back inside? The international community has reason to remain skeptical. Even if that goal were pursued earnestly, it is equally challenging to see how it could be accomplished anytime soon. In 2024, the country's two political parties remain locked in their competition for the support of crucial domestic constituents amidst another presidential election campaign, especially to capture the support of unions and union members as well as large numbers of voters in key swing 2016 and 2020 states who remain skeptical or opposed to returning to America's previous trade policies. The next chapter takes a closer look at these domestic political forces and how they have led America to pull the other rug out from under the international trading system—by ending its commitment to advance freer trade through the WTO.

THREE

Walking Out on Global Free and Open Trade

Ministers and delegates gathered at the WTO in Geneva in early December 2016 with the hope of concluding a new tariff-cutting agreement. President Obama's trade ambassador, Michael Froman, attended with other ministers to make on-the-spot decisions to reach that goal. For the history of the GATT and the WTO, it was a minimalist one. Rather than trying to close another GATT-type negotiation of the kind that every dozen or so years delivered a sweeping new agreement on tariff cuts and new trade rules, this vastly scaled-down effort aimed to salvage just a small win—an agreement to lower tariffs on one to two hundred environmentally friendly "green" goods—out of a collapsed global WTO trade negotiation.

That failed, decade-long global effort started in 2001 as the WTO's Doha Development Agenda. The ambitious mandate of the "Doha Round" aimed for new trade-liberalizing commitments across industrial and agricultural goods and the services sector. Negotiations for new trade rules in areas such as subsidies, competition policy, and investment were also proposed as a part of a package outcome. It was the first GATT-style global negotiation since the WTO was formed, and faith in the future of trade liberalization remained high. Expectations were that the negotiations would end by building further on the GATT-turned-WTO framework and extend the essentially perfect track record of reaching similar agreements in the past.

Even so, the challenges were immense. A first effort in 1999 failed to launch the new round of negotiations. That failure was met by cheers from tens of thousands of anti-trade and anti-globalization demonstrators who gathered in the streets around the downtown Seattle meeting venues to oppose the launch of these negotiations. These demonstrations, later dubbed the "Battle in Seattle," stopped some of the meetings in the city and contributed to the failure to reach agreement to begin new global trade-liberalizing negotiations. Two years later, in the city of Doha, Qatar, a greater focus was placed on making growth through trade for developing countries a central theme of negotiations for this new global agreement. This framing, among other changes, helped gain enough support among all WTO members to start the Doha Round negotiations.

After the negotiations were underway, large perception gaps nonetheless remained among WTO member governments. After years of negotiations, these ultimately proved impossible to bridge. These gaps included vastly different views of the appropriate balance of commitments between developed countries, which had locked in much lower average tariff rates, and developing countries—especially the more advanced developing countries—that had been allowed under the GATT to keep higher average tariff rates and make lesser commitments to trade rules. Developing countries insisted that the burden was on developed countries to continue to do disproportionately more, as they had benefited most from global trade. America and other developed countries insisted in return that the Round's development goals could only be achieved through growth from new trade and that advanced developing countries such as India, Brazil, and China would have to do more on liberalization for the negotiations to succeed.[1] The impasse persisted, and America walked out in 2007, after which the Doha Round talks sputtered. Despite several further efforts, the talks never regained enough momentum to truly restart or conclude.

Several Doha Round negotiation goals were pulled out of the rubble and resuscitated as new, stand-alone WTO negotiations. One of these was to liberalize trade for environmental goods. Leveraging traditional trade policy tools to help solve growing concerns with pollution and climate challenges gained support as an effort worthy of trying to advance, based on the idea that free, and thus cheaper, trade in these goods would help encourage their global adoption and production. As a marriage of

---

1   Susan C. Schwab and Mike Johanns, "Statement from USTR Ambassador Susan C. Schwab and USDA Secretary Johanns on Doha Round," USTR, press release, June 21, 2007.

environmental and growth-through-export goals, the Obama administration enthusiastically helped launch the WTO environmental goods talks and push them forward.

Instead of starting the environmental goods talks among all WTO members, a smaller group of members agreed to begin negotiations and invited others to join on a voluntary basis. A few successful tariff-liberalizing agreements had been concluded this way, including for pharmaceuticals, civil aircraft, and information technology goods. In keeping with the WTO's equality of access principle, or MFN treatment, any agreement to cut tariffs among participating countries would make these tariff cuts accessible to all WTO members. Since participants in the environmental goods negotiations accounted for the overwhelming percentage of the trade in this category of goods, the benefits of locking in freer trade were judged to outweigh the downsides of some limited free riding by others not in the deal. Concluding WTO negotiations in this way, among subsets of WTO members for a defined set of goods, also recognized the new, frustrating reality that achieving a tariff-liberalizing agreement among all 160-plus WTO members was no longer likely and perhaps impossible.

An auspicious 2012 outcome from the 21-member APEC forum injected momentum into hopes that a WTO agreement on environmental goods could succeed. APEC forum members, which included China and America along with 19 other Asia-Pacific economies ranging widely in developmental status, agreed on a list of 54 environmental goods and made voluntary commitments to cut tariffs on these products to 5 percent or less. This momentum was carried into the WTO. Between the launch of the WTO Environmental Goods Agreement (EGA) negotiations in July 2014 and the December 2016 Geneva meeting to try and reach agreement, a total of 46 WTO members accounting for approximately 90 percent of global trade in environmental goods were at the negotiating table to reach a deal.

High hopes for this targeted, narrow agreement instead were quickly plagued by some of the same problems that ran the Doha Round negotiations into a wall. After nearly 20 EGA negotiating rounds, the initial APEC list of 54 goods swelled to a hodgepodge list of more than three hundred proposed goods that had drifted further away from the original environmental objective. Indicative of other challenges was an ongoing standoff between the EU and China over including bicycles on the EGA list. With Chinese-made bicycles routinely dumped in the EU market, against which the EU had imposed 20 years of high EU anti-dumping tariffs to protect its manufacturers, the EU remained adamant in refusing to include them in the EGA's tariff elimination schedule.[2]

Ministers met in December 2016 to rally to close the negotiations. By then, the whiplash of Trump's November 2016 election win presented a new and bigger uncertainty. Trump's post-election threats to raise tariffs and promises to pull America out of its climate and environmental commitments created the sense that the EGA effort would slip away if not completed immediately. The urgent need to reach agreement became impossible when China's delegation, perhaps as a ploy to squeeze a win among negotiators worried about the talks failing, showed up with a brand-new list of products to propose. As negotiators pushed to reach a deal, this new proposal dropped into the mix and caused the talks to implode. With it, yet another WTO-era negotiation burned up, failing to escape the gravitational pull that had brought nearly every other back to Earth.

During the 2016 presidential campaign, Trump claimed that he was "a free trader, 100 percent," but only if it were *his* kind of trade.[3] Once in office, his administration then fulfilled broad expectations of where continuing the EGA negotiations might fall on his scale—not his kind. The Trump administration instead put America's continued participation in the negotiations on hold, let the talks drift at first, and then allowed them to slip into hibernation for the remainder of its four-year term. Others could have kept negotiating without America to reach their own tariff-cutting deal. Doing so, however, would come at a politically intolerable cost—with their tariff-cut commitments made available to all WTO members to meet the MFN rule, America would emerge as the largest free rider, and possibly the largest beneficiary, from their deal.

The arrival of the Biden administration in early 2021 raised new hopes among America's trading partners that it would support rekindling the EGA talks for another try. The goal of the negotiation seemed to fit with Biden's strong emphasis on supporting environmental causes. Concluding it also would give some credibility to Biden's promise to re-establish America's support for international organizations following the Trump era.

---

2   Philip Blenkinsop, "EU Extends Tariffs on Chinese Bicycles, Fearing Import Flood," *Reuters*, August 29, 2019.

3   "Who Said What and What It Meant: The 4th GOP Debate, Annotated," *Washington Post*, November 10, 2015.

Instead, Biden's trade ambassador, Katherine Tai, dropped any hopes for helping restart the EGA talks into a bucket of cold water. Turning the Obama administration's arguments for advancing the EGA upside down in the process, she argued in an environmentally themed speech, "For too long, the traditional trade community has resisted the view that trade policy is a legitimate tool in helping to solve the climate crisis."[4] This remark was paradoxical given that the EGA's very purpose and source of international support, including from the Obama administration, was precisely its use of traditional trade-liberalizing efforts to help accelerate the adoption and use of environmentally friendlier goods. Tai's comment also overlooked broad support for the EGA's environmental goals among America's traditional free trade supporters.

Tai instead called publicly to advance another WTO negotiation to limit government subsidies for fishing among WTO members. Like the EGA, this negotiation was also salvaged from the failed Doha Round effort as another stand-alone negotiation. It, too, was a dual-purposed negotiation, fulfilling a trade purpose of limiting subsidies that distorted competition in fish exports while fulfilling an environmental objective of reducing incentives leading to harmful overfishing. It was not a negotiation to liberalize tariffs but another fit-for-purpose use of the WTO system to create new trade-related rules supporting environmental objectives. Even so, Tai nonetheless went on to make a point in the same speech that ". . . the WTO is considered by many as an institution that not only has no solutions to offer on environmental concerns, but is part of the problem."[5]

America's new approach to global trade liberalization was unmistakable—it was giving up on decades of past efforts and walking out. From 2017, America engaged in only very select WTO negotiations on new trade rules while refusing to engage in any WTO negotiation either underway or proposed that included efforts to achieve new goods or services trade liberalization. Walking out on the EGA negotiations but selectively moving forward with negotiations on fish subsidy rules underscored this radically narrowed and diminished agenda for the WTO.

This chapter focuses on why and how America came to abandon its commitment to advancing ever-more-liberalized global trade through the WTO. It starts by describing the key domestic political shifts behind

4   Katherine Tai, "Remarks from Ambassador Katherine Tai on Trade Policy, the Environment and Climate Change," USTR, April 15, 2021.
5   Tai, "Remarks from Ambassador Katherine Tai."

this new approach. Later in the chapter, individual cases and issues will elaborate on America's turn against global free trade and its impact on further eroding the WTO and the international trading system.

AMERICA'S PROBLEM WITH FREE TRADE

As America's 2016 presidential election campaign got underway, there was little outward sign that its longstanding pursuit of freer trade was about to be put on the political chopping block. Before campaigning began in mid-2015, a comfortable majority (58 percent) of Americans still viewed trade as more of a benefit to the country's economic growth than a threat (33 percent).[6] Overall, public support for trade consistently improved throughout the Obama administration, coinciding with a long period of economic growth following the 2007–08 financial crisis. This general support also paralleled the Obama administration's efforts to negotiate two new mega free trade agreements, one with the EU and another with 11 other Asia-Pacific nations.

Only one prominent and nationally competitive primary candidate, independent-turned-Democrat Bernie Sanders, made his steadfast and blanket opposition to the "disaster" of freer trade a cornerstone of his 2016 campaign message and promises. On the Republican side, among the party's scores of primary election candidates, Trump's 2016 campaign rhetoric on trade stood apart with his similar withering criticism of America's past trade commitments as having harmed job and economic security and the quality of life in American communities. Both Sanders and Trump tapped into the fact that even as Americans held overall positive views of the general benefits from international trade, a large reservoir of concern emerged when polls explicitly asked if foreign trade created new and better jobs in America. In 2014, only 20 percent believed that it did.[7] Unlike Sanders's almost uniform objection to freer trade, however, Trump's campaign messages carved out a distinctly different position that wedged in between these two predominant views among American voters, magnifying, on the one hand, the perception of harm

---

6   As presented in historical polling data trends. See Mohamed Younis, "Sharply Fewer in U.S. View Foreign Trade as Opportunity," Gallup, March 31, 2021, and the associated question responses and trends, "Gallup Poll Social Series: World Affairs," Gallup, February 3–18, 2021, https://news.gallup.com/file/poll/342422/210331Trade.pdf.
7   Bruce Stokes, "Americans, Like Many in Other Advanced Economies, Not Convinced of Trade's Benefits," Pew Research Center, September 26, 2018.

to jobs from America's previous "failed" trade policies while lifting on the other hand the expectation that freer trade could be favorable by overturning America's past commitments and assumptions and doing it Trump's way instead.

Trump consistently aimed his sharpest barbs in campaign rallies and debates at Congress's passage of NAFTA that brought new free trade with Mexico and at its 2000 vote to support China's membership in the WTO, pointing to both as particularly egregious mistakes. In a mid-2016 campaign speech on trade, Trump proclaimed, "At the center of this catastrophe [the loss of U.S. manufacturing jobs] are two trade deals. . . . First, the North American Free Trade Agreement, or the disaster called NAFTA. Second, China's entry into the World Trade Organization."[8] These selections tapped directly into longstanding labor union anger and broader public concerns. Polls validated this broader public sentiment, with America's trade with Mexico and China drawing the most concern compared to other countries.[9]

In 2016, Trump's campaign trade rhetoric particularly appealed to the concerns of Republican (47 percent) and midwestern (53 percent) voters, who held disproportionately negative views on the impacts of trade-liberalizing agreements on their communities. In contrast, only 24 percent of Democrats and just 26–27 percent of voters in other U.S. geographical regions viewed trade negatively, underscoring substantial differences in views both by political party affiliation and by geographic region.[10]

Trump's strategically crafted message proved helpful in mobilizing new support among enough of these often bitter and arguably more motivated American voters.[11] Polling on the views of two specific groups in the three key Midwest U.S. states that narrowly tipped the election outcome in Trump's favor—voters identifying as white working class and

8   "Read Donald Trump's Speech on Trade," *Time*, June 28, 2016.
9   Politico and Harvard T. H. Chan School of Public Health, "Americans' Views on Current Trade and Health Policies," 5. The poll found 46 and 34 percent of voters believed trade with China and Mexico, respectively, "hurt the U.S." compared to 27 and 24 percent who believed that trade from these countries "helped the U.S.".
10   Politico and Harvard T.H. Chan School of Public Health, "Americans' Views," 2.
11   See, e.g., comments by Peter Navarro, an advisor to the Trump campaign on trade, who asserted in September 2016 that other Republican candidates were out of touch with party voters on the issue of trade, and especially with China, and that Trump positioned himself accordingly to win their votes. Benjamin Oreskes, "Politico-Harvard Poll: Amid Trump's Rise, GOP Voters Turn Sharply Away from Free Trade," Politico, September 24, 2016.

as from union households (all races)—showed that trade was a major fault line for these voters in their final ballot choices. A large majority of these groups of voters believed that trade causes harm to jobs over its other benefits to the economy, in contrast to nationwide polls in 2020 that showed Americans overall maintained stronger support for trade than concerns around it.[12] Exit polling from 2016 also backs up the significance of these negative views toward trade in Hillary Clinton's loss in the election. Clinton, whose campaign rhetoric on trade called for a less revolutionary change in approach, still won among union-affiliated voters, but only very narrowly so compared to the larger support they gave her Democratic nominee predecessors. A sizable block defected to vote instead for the Republican challenger.[13]

The broad contours of Trump's message on trade, particularly his opposition to past trade commitments, also appealed on a certain level to America's principally left-leaning, anti-globalization activists and their organizations. Long viewed as fringe by the bipartisan political mainstream on free trade, these activists consistently mobilized to oppose almost every new or proposed trade-liberalizing agreement. The most vehement and sustained opposition to trade liberalization came from labor unions, starting from around 1970 over job losses from imports in the textile and steel industries. By the early 1990s, they were joined by other environmental and health advocacy groups, anti-globalization and anti-corporate causes, and social advocacy groups. Labor and environmental groups joined forces and mobilized together to oppose the passage of NAFTA in 1993. These other groups later joined them to march in Seattle in 1999 in a coordinated, unified demonstration under the slogan "No to WTO." While marred by vandalism and clashes between police and some protestors, the large demonstration of mostly American protestors caught the world's attention in 1999 for having contributed to defeating an attempt to launch a new global WTO trade-liberalizing negotiating round. Seventeen years later, their anti-WTO slogans toted around the streets of Seattle calling for an end to more global trade liberalization had been elevated for the first time into a forceful campaign pledge of the presidential nominee of a major U.S. political party. With Trump also aiming to overturn America's past

---

12   Peter L. Francis, "The White Working Class, Union Households, and Trade: Did the Trump Coalition Endure?" *Society* 57, no. 6 (2020): 669–74.

13   See, e.g., Francis, "White Working Class."

trade commitments and approaches, a sizable degree of common cause emerged in overthrowing past trade policies.

Coming as it did from the Republican presidential nominee, Trump's rejection of America's trade orthodoxy radically transformed America's political landscape. Its suddenness was startling to many, including the overwhelming majority of the Republican Party's congressional members and presidential candidates who, up until the 2016 election, reliably supported and voted for free trade deals.[14] The firm footing that free trade enjoyed in the Republican mainstream quickly eroded as Trump pivoted instead to embrace positions more aligned with a tiny, ultra-conservative Republican party wing in Congress.[15] This loose grouping at times voted against trade deals, citing national sovereignty, the trade deficit, offshoring, and other concerns that America's union and other anti-trade activists on the left had often raised.

More importantly, Trump's positions were also in close alignment with another key group—supporters of the Tea Party movement who came to form the core of the Republican party's New Right orientation. The movement emerged in 2009 as a limited government, anti-establishment cause, opposed to taxpayer-funded corporate bailouts and social handouts passed by the Democratic Congress and the Obama administration to overcome the 2007–08 financial crisis. Comprised principally of socially conservative Republican and Republican-leaning voters, separate polls in 2010 revealed another little-noticed fact about its adherents—nearly two-thirds (61 and 63 percent) also viewed free trade deals as harmful to America. This percentage nearly matched the views of the one group that remained most consistently opposed to America's free trade deals—the 65 percent of trade union–affiliated voters who had organized for decades to fight them.[16]

As the new Tea Party movement's anti-establishment agenda began rolling over the Republican Party, a prescient Georgetown trade lawyer with some notable government experience and a penchant for train

---

14   Based on the June 2015 voting record of members of the 114th Congress (2015–16), approximately 90 percent of Republican members of both chambers voted to approve the Bipartisan Congressional Trade Priorities and Accountability Act of 2015, which enabled streamlined congressional consideration of tariff-liberalizing agreements.

15   See, e.g., Seung Min Kim, "GOP Senators Succumb to Trump's War on Trade," Politico, September 22, 2016.

16   See Russell Heimlich, "Tea Party Drives Anti-Trade Opinion among Republicans," Pew Research Center, November 23, 2010; and John Harwood, "53% in US Say Free Trade Hurts Nation: NBC/WSJ Poll," CNBC, September 28, 2010.

wrecks took note, writing to the *New York Times* in late 2010 to suggest that it all might just turn out this way:

The [Tea Party] movement has already forced Republicans to alter their agenda in several policy areas. Should the same thing happen with free trade, America's stance toward open markets and globalization could shift drastically.[17]

So closely aligned were these traditional Left- and New Right–leaning movements in opposition to more-of-the-same free trade that the limited collaboration among them started in 2015 to derail President Obama's 12-country free trade deal in the Asia-Pacific. These efforts reportedly included the left-leaning Teamsters union using Republican lobbying firms to influence key Republicans to oppose the deal.[18] By the 2016 election, the Left's anti-trade "Blue-Green" coalition of labor and environmental activists—first forged in the early 1990s to oppose NAFTA, energized in the streets of Seattle in 1999 to stop a new WTO negotiation, and remobilized in the 2000s to fight Bush and Obama administration–era free trade agreements—was united in cause with America's "new red" movement of anti-establishment Tea Party adherents also eager for a takeover of Washington on trade.

This alignment of views between traditional Left and New Right voters and activists was the political quicksand finally capable of sinking America's mainstream, bipartisan free trade consensus. It was left to two successive presidential elections in 2016 and 2020 and their winning candidates and positions to pull Washington's mainstream bipartisan consensus all the way into the mire. Then, the quicksand hardened, finishing off the job.

Only in the context of America's longer history of trade politics is this pivot less surprising. America's leading political parties, trade unions, and industry groups have nearly all flip-flopped on open trade at one time or another, in line with their shifting economic, political, and ideological priorities. The aberration had been the mostly stable, mostly solidified post–World War II mainstream bipartisan consensus for freer trade. That consensus began in earnest during the 1950s as the Republican Party's mainstream moved to support tariff liberalization policies initiated in the 1930s by Franklin Roosevelt's progressive administration. It lasted into the 2010s, albeit subject to many adjustments

17   Robert E. Lighthizer, "Throwing Free Trade Overboard," *New York Times*, November 12, 2010.

18   Alec MacGillis, "Why Obama's Big Trade Deal Isn't a Sure Thing," Slate, February 2, 2015.

and compromises from around 1970 as its support among Democratic representatives, in particular, became less reliable. The consensus faced collapse in 2017 when not enough Republicans were prepared to oppose Trump, their new party leader, over the issue to continue to support it publicly. It finally lost its pulse in 2021 when Biden, the new leader of America's other major party, fully abandoned it.

Some hoped that this consensus might stage a comeback after the solid bipartisan approval of the renegotiated NAFTA in 2018—a hope that naively overlooked the reality that the updated agreement was about reining in NAFTA's brand of free trade, not creating more of it. By the 2020 election, with Joe Biden facing a primary challenge from the popular, vociferously anti-trade Bernie Sanders and having to defeat incumbent Republican Donald Trump, Biden's presidential campaign avoided any suggestion that it was planning to return to pursuing trade-liberalizing agreements. Once in office, the administration embraced that position even further, making it more apparent that America was essentially closed for business in doing more tariff liberalization and other free trade deals, whether globally, regionally, or bilaterally.

With critical union and other midwestern votes lost to Trump in 2016 again up for grabs, Biden's 2020 campaign pledge to not pursue more trade deals for a long while, if ever, aimed to reclaim support from voters affiliated with traditionally left-leaning unions and environmental and like-minded groups. Their core positions and slogans opposing trade remained unchanged from the Seattle protests two decades earlier, such as "Globalize Worker Rights" and "Save the Earth, End Capitalism." Biden never called for the end of capitalism, although his sharp criticisms of corporate influence and behavior reflected a similar concern. Once in office, he and his administration continued to paint freer trade as something that, because it disproportionately benefited multinational corporations, was thus no longer in America's interest. As Biden kept Trump from outflanking him in his opposition to freer trade, he simultaneously drew sharp contrasts between his positions and Trump's record of supporting other big business interests, from lowering corporate taxes to cutting regulations aimed at protecting the environment.

The Democratic Party's official convention platforms document this evolution in its mainstream trade positions over three presidential election cycles. The party's upbeat, pro-trade message and platform for Obama's renomination in 2012 was overhauled for the 2016 Trump-Clinton matchup, which took a sharper tone on some of the impacts of free trade while keeping a possible lane open for it. By 2020, the party platform went wholly negative, removing all references to the potential benefits of advancing open trade. In its place, a prominent focus was placed on the assertion that self-interested American corporations and cheating trading partners were at fault for corrupting free trade. Calling for a "fair system of international trade for our workers," it said:

> For too long, the global trading system has failed to keep its promises to American workers. Too many corporations have rushed to outsource jobs, and too many countries have broken their promises to be honest and transparent partners. . . . The Trump Administration has failed time after time to deliver for American workers on this crucial issue, siding with corporate interests over our workers and launching a trade war with China that they have no plan for winning—creating incredible hardship for American farmers, manufacturers, workers, and consumers in the process.[19]

Polls in 2020 showed that about half of voters of all affiliations cited trade as a top election issue for them in deciding their candidate.[20] With the two leading U.S. presidential candidates for the first time both disavowing America's longstanding embrace of freer trade, the competition in 2020 to woo votes focused instead on how each would, if elected, detach and pull America further away from that commitment. Even as Trump already owned that policy turf, which remained popular with some voters, the global tariff fusillade his administration launched with fanfare had turned into a trench war–type stalemate by 2020, drawing growing concern and criticism from other farmers, businesses, and consumers disadvantaged from its higher import costs, higher export barriers, or both.[21]

Biden was also open to attack for his past statements and votes on trade. These included votes to approve NAFTA in 1993 and the legislative package in 2000 to allow for China's membership in the WTO, the two most criticized trade votes for America's unions and anti-trade advocates. As vice president, Biden also supported the Obama administration's 12-nation Asia-Pacific region Trans-Pacific Partnership (TPP) trade deal,

---

19   Democratic Party, "2020 Democratic Party Platform," August 18, 2020, 20.

20   Anne Kim, "New Poll: Trade Was a Top Issue for Many 2020 Voters," *Global Trade*, November 20, 2020.

21   LaLoggia, "As New Tariffs Take Hold," Pew Research Center, July 19, 2018. In May 2019, a year after the largest Trump tariff hikes were implemented, 47 percent of Americans believed that the tariff war was hurting the U.S. economy. See Monmouth University, "American Consumers Expect to Bear Cost of China Tariffs," Monmouth Poll Reports, May 28, 2019.

which, as I discuss in the next chapter, encountered vehement opposition among unions and others who labeled it as "NAFTA on steroids."
In these ways, while mixed, Biden's voting record on trade was similar
to Hillary Clinton's own voting and rhetorical record—the same one
that Trump effectively weaponized in 2016 to argue that only he could
be trusted on this issue. The electoral map dynamics shaping up for the
2020 election necessitated that Biden win back the Midwest states that
Clinton lost in 2016, and neutralizing his own record on trade became
essential to improving his chances.

Biden's counter-narrative to Trump's attacks closely followed the
newest Democratic Party platform: Trump's China trade strategy was a
failure, it went, while America's corporations and trading partners had
undermined America's best trade intentions in ways that necessitated a
complete overhaul in approach and assumptions. Fighting unfair foreign
trade practices and opposing corporate power were familiar campaign
refrains from several decades of national elections. When these themes
reappeared in the 2020 presidential campaign, they were intertwined
and sharpened by both presidential candidates in a consistent new
way—one that placed at least as much blame for America's free trade
ills on its multinational corporations as on the unfair practices of its
trading partners.

Trump's frequent assaults on America's trading partners were
matched by his regular callouts against American companies for offshoring, which he argued had been incentivized by the "disastrous" free
trade agreements they sought and that Washington gave them. Biden
took the anti-corporate case much further, similarly accusing America's
multinationals of undermining free trade for their self-gain but then
attacking Trump for showering them with other favors that harmed
ordinary Americans.

America's corporations emerged as soft political targets, with
anti-corporate public sentiment sharply on the rise. In one national
poll, America's "large corporations" had fallen to the bottom of its
list of institutions the American public felt had a positive effect on the
United States, with only 29 percent viewing their role as positive and 68
percent reporting negative.[22] In another survey, Americans' confidence
in "big business" was quickly falling toward historic lows, with only 14
percent of Americans by 2022 having significant confidence in their

---

22   Ted Van Green, "Republicans Increasingly Critical of Several Major U.S. Institutions,
Including Big Corporations and Banks," Pew Research Center, August 20, 2021.

role. Only the U.S. Congress scored lower.[23] Associating free trade with other corporate giveaways supported by "Big Pharma" and other "big" corporate interests picked up new political currency during the 2020 national political campaign.

Tapping into this anti-corporate zeitgeist served other purposes for Biden. On trade, it provided a foil to avoid answering for his voting record, allowing him to point the finger at America's corporations that, he argued, had taken America's best policy intentions for trade liberalization off course. It also finally aligned the core trade positions of the party's new leader more squarely with those of the growing progressive core of the Democratic Party's elected representatives in Washington. Reliably pro-trade Democrats were already quickly becoming an increasingly scarce commodity. Those who remained, organized under the "New Democrats" banner, had long been in step with their party's internationalist, free-trade-leaning nominees for president. As Biden shifted to effectively close the door to more trade liberalization, the caucus was left fully exposed as out of step with the Democratic Party's new, trade-skeptical mainstream position.[24]

While Trump triggered a particularly sharp shift in the Republican Party's mainstream position on trade, Biden moved the Democratic Party's mainstream position in significant ways as well. Mainstream Democrats of the nineteenth and early twentieth centuries supported lower tariffs to benefit consumers, workers, and farmers, unlike Republicans, who often favored higher tariffs to promote the interests of America's industrialization and industrialists. Higher tariffs tended to support fatter corporate profits and more concentrated corporate market power, making the Democrat's embrace of lower tariffs the anti-corporatist trade policy of the day.

At the end of World War II, the Democrats' populist tariff-cutting policies became the cornerstone of America's new vision for advancing global peace through freer, rules-based international trade. America's postwar global economic dominance from the early 1950s led more American companies to prioritize new export and overseas business opportunities, pulling the Republican Party mainstream along with

---

23   See historical polling data between 1973 and 2023 in "Confidence in Institutions," Gallup, 2023, https://news.gallup.com/poll/1597/Confidence-Institutions.aspx.

24   Here, "mainstream" refers to the official policy positions and orientations of the Democratic Party's officially nominated candidates for president, as reflected in the positions of the party's nominating convention.

them. These dual foreign and commercial policy objectives cemented America's new bipartisan trade consensus. The situation became much less straightforward when American industry in the 1970s began shedding jobs and production to waves of new import competition. Even so, the Democratic Party's core free trade orientation survived through the Clinton and Obama administrations, albeit with new caveats and limitations as time passed.

In 2020, the new Democratic Party mainstream position shut the door to free trade and stepped up attacks on America's multinational corporations for successfully adjusting to and taking advantage of it. With it, the party's long emphasis on taking the fight to foreign trading partners to force markets open and make trade fair for America's exports and businesses also went by the wayside. The entire script was flipped, and the implications were seismic. No longer was it a good look, nor was it consistent in policy terms, for the Democratic Party and its new administration to fight for fair access abroad when it criticized and vilified its largest companies and exporters at home for taking advantage of globalized trade.

The abandonment of America's pursuit of freer trade emerged as a winning formula in two successive U.S. presidential election cycles. New approaches were adopted by both winning candidates to respond to the distress of deindustrialized communities across America's Midwest and framed as a needed break away from the trade policies that failed them. It required each winning candidate to finesse their past positions against the new political present to appeal to voters with a revised vision of the future. Trump's initial claims of support for free trade in principle, peppered with new conditions that made it something else altogether, became more muted as his administration's tariff wars were failing to deliver the promised cost-free and decisive "win" for America. Biden criticized this approach and staked out a different vision from the one he often supported in the past, turning the nations toward other approaches that further deepened America's abandonment of freer, rules-based trade while also leaving many of Trump's policies intact. Their shared objective of competing for the support of critical anti-trade voting blocs in key states to win the presidential election in 2016 and 2020 shattered the mainstream bipartisan trade consensus in Washington. How each administration dismantled this decades-long consensus, and the implications for the WTO system and for America's leadership in promoting open foreign markets and global free trade, are explored below.

AMERICA'S RETREAT FROM FREE AND OPEN GLOBAL TRADE

For the Trump administration, walking out of Obama-era trade-liberalizing negotiations in the WTO was less of a conscious decision than a consequence of its core distrust of and objections to the WTO. The administration's presumed thinking was that since America had fallen into a self-dug hole by opening its market in the WTO to countries often playing by different rules, like China, the simplest solution was to stop digging and walk out. As a result, in January 2017, America ceased all ongoing negotiations at the WTO aimed at liberalizing new trade and declined to pursue new ones.

With America out of the business of pursuing more global free trade, the only way to seek new export access was through stepped-up bilateral or country-to-country engagements. One way to accomplish this was through new bilateral free trade deals. However, the Trump administration made limited progress on this front, as explored in the following two chapters. Instead, it relied on a more aggressive form of unilateralism, including its use of Section 301, examined previously.

For example, when Lighthizer met with foreign counterparts, he insisted that a trade balance scoresheet be inserted near the top of his briefing materials; he often referred to the figures as he underscored the importance of taking action to remove a list of trade barriers he also enumerated. Lighthizer shook his counterparts' hands and developed America's relationships while consistently reminding them of the tools he had at his disposal and his boss, who was focused on eliminating trade deficits.

As much as the Trump administration aggressively moved to remove barriers to American exports, it was not always an ally for American companies concerned about their foreign market access. For example, America's pharmaceutical industry initially secured a certain degree of White House buy-in for arguing that they were forced to charge higher prices in America to recoup research investments due to regulations that unfairly lowered drug prices abroad for patented medicines. In return for his sympathy and willingness to help, Trump also clarified that the industry should relocate more of its drug production back to America.

As time passed and no discernable changes were made to return that production to America, their trade claims were supported less. Trump then later attempted to change U.S. policy toward the industry by tying drug prices paid by the federal government to the lower price levels foreign consumers paid in overseas markets, mimicking the very policies the companies had complained about in other countries.[25]

Another set of concerns revolved around help for large online and big box retailers, which the administration viewed as superhighways for consumer goods imports from China and elsewhere. America's customs *de minimis* level raised a related core concern by allowing most internet and other purchases from abroad valued under $800 to enter America tariff-free. The *de minimis* exemption also helped lower customs clearance costs for the government's customs service, as well as for international express carriers and the post office. For the Trump administration, it was a giant loophole for China and others to circumvent U.S. tariffs to ship goods into America's market. As the administration tried to convince Congress to drastically scale back the $800 exemption, America's express delivery industry was left to pursue for itself its goal of persuading foreign governments to raise their *de minimis* levels to much higher levels.[26]

Equally allergic to pursuing more global trade liberalization, the Biden administration pivoted even more sharply in opposition to it once in office. Like the Trump administration, it refused to re-engage in the WTO to negotiate new market opening agreements, including those for tariff liberalization. It took this further by shutting down the handful of bilateral free trade negotiations started by the Trump administration that were still in progress as it departed office. Then, the Biden administration moved further away from America's longstanding goal of opening foreign markets by substantially pulling back on routine efforts to engage and urge countries to remove their non-tariff barriers to U.S. exports.

The Biden administration's trade team messed even further with the standard U.S. trade policy playbook by reassessing basic definitions and criteria for what even constituted a non-tariff trade barrier. Democratic and Republican administrations alike had evaluated foreign practices and applied similar standards over many decades to call out unfair foreign practices, drawing primarily from fundamental GATT and WTO principles of non-discrimination and necessity that America helped establish. These include the overtly discriminatory barriers governments intentionally create to disadvantage imports and foreign companies

---

25 Peter Sullivan, "Pharma Execs Decline Trump Offer for Meeting on Drug Prices," The Hill, July 27, 2020.

26 Lighthizer expands on these and other related concerns in Lighthizer, *No Trade Is Free*, 304–07.

in their domestic markets and other policies that unintentionally may have a similar impact.

There are different ways to define trade barriers; one of the most frequently used definitions for non-tariff barriers, based on the GATT, is a regulation or other measure that is more restrictive toward imports than is reasonably necessary to meet legitimate goals such as the protection of public health, safety, the environment, or to fulfill some other public welfare purpose such as consumer protection. Deciding whether to call out a foreign practice as a barrier involves assessing its actual impact on U.S. imports compared to its effects on a foreign country's domestic products and services and, if there is a difference in treatment, determining whether there is a valid justification for it. Identifying and calling out barriers that run afoul of this test and unfairly discriminate against imports are the routine work of trade officials, and these barriers are generally challengeable at the WTO. For defensive purposes, it also requires assessing one's own government practice before calling out another government for the same or similar practice.

The Biden administration applied a higher scrutiny to these tests and definitions in its deference to a wave of objections from progressives, unions, and others over America's domestic policies and practices. Their calls for new regulation for large businesses, as well as the need to ensure adequate "policy space" to regulate freely for any policy contingency in the future, at times conflicted with these traditional trade barrier definitions and criteria. America's trading partners often make similar claims of the need to keep their own "policy space" in order to maintain subtly unfair and objectively discriminatory treatment of imports. To ensure consistency and adequate policy space in America's policies for new progressive-oriented objectives, which often include calls to target America's large corporations with special restrictions, Biden administration officials began to review and revise language for new trade rules, as well as annual reports listing foreign trade barriers and other statements and positions, to soften or remove issues and arguments that were potentially inconsistent with those objectives. While the Biden administration did not retreat entirely from raising and asking for the removal of foreign trade barriers, it became vastly choosier in selecting those it decided to raise. Once chosen, it then routinely avoided characterizing its advocacy efforts simply as helping American exports and businesses overcome discriminatory foreign barriers, frequently citing other rationales instead.

The Biden administration's resistance to efforts to make trade more open and freer and, by traditional standards, the low priority it put on making it fair for America's goods and services exports was evident in its first annual Trade Agenda statement. Generic mention of the administration's intention to open markets and reduce barriers to America's goods and services exports was initially missing, later added in time for publication except only glancingly so and only after its complete absence from a near-final draft was noted for its drafters. Its Trade Agenda statement gave some attention to a couple of traditional trade policy priorities, including a commitment to routine enforcement of trade agreements, the objective of working with other countries to reform the WTO and to hold China accountable, and the objective of "[s]tanding up for America's farmers, ranchers, food manufacturers, and fishers."[27] Whether the administration was committed to "standing up" for the largest segments of America's economy and export potential—its manufacturing and services industries—was never directly mentioned. Such a commitment would have signaled a readiness to support the interests of America's largest companies and exporters, a position that the administration's political trade officials made clear they were doing everything to minimally avoid saying out loud as they worked to build out the administration's new union-focused, "worker-centered" trade policy.

Instead, the administration's Trade Agenda statement prioritized "extensive engagement with unions and other worker advocates" and that "workers will have a seat at the table in the development of trade policies."[28] It became apparent over time that worker-centered principally referred to unions and union workers, which, in 2022, represented only 6 percent of private sector employees.[29] Other Americans, from entrepreneurs trading online to indigenous community leaders, also made their voices heard at times to underscore the priority they placed on opening new foreign markets through freer trade to boost growth for their businesses. Such calls, however, were nearly uniformly passed over for being out of step with the administration's more accurately

---

27   USTR, "The President's 2021 Trade Policy Agenda," 5.

28   USTR, "The President's 2021 Trade Policy Agenda," 2.

29   Bureau of Labor Statistics, "Union Members—2022," U.S. Department of Labor, press release, January 19, 2023. The remainder of America's union members, which reached a record low of 10.1 percent of all American workers in 2022, were government employees whose jobs were not impacted by international trade.

labeled "union- and progressive-centered" objectives with substantially different aims and motives.

Richard Trumka, president of the AFL-CIO, emerged as an anchor of this strong alliance. Katherine Tai cultivated a close relationship with Trumka on trade from the outset of the Biden administration, as did Lighthizer later in his tenure. Trumka and the unions, in turn, expected a substantial rewrite of America's trade policy priorities and objectives in exchange. Often, this long list included many domestic policy priorities, many of which also had weak or no real linkages to a traditional trade policy and strategy. It also included steering clear of pursuing any new trade liberalization in the WTO or elsewhere. Unions have sometimes claimed to support open trade in principle, but over many decades, virtually never supported new trade-liberalizing agreements from either Republican or Democratic administrations.[30] Tai fully embraced their insistence on the need for a new model for trade policy and trade agreements instead—a theme further explored below and in the following chapters.

In line with its union-centered trade policy, one way the Biden administration responded to demonstrate its loyalty to these priorities was to swear off pursuing any new trade-liberalizing agreements. The administration's rejection of restarting the WTO's Environmental Goods Agreement negotiations was an early signal that America's turn away from global free trade was more than a passing one-administration fad. Other pitches made for new, tariff-reducing agreements were also turned down. One idea was for a new environmental goods–style tariff-cutting negotiation in the WTO on critical health products to help facilitate trade amid the ongoing COVID-19 pandemic.[31] The Trump and Biden admin-

---

30   The renegotiated NAFTA, known as the United States-Mexico-Canada Trade Agreement, eventually received broad union support after many union priorities were included. At the same time, with free trade already established under the original NAFTA, the updated deal only added more conditions to the terms of the free trade already taking place among Mexico, Canada, and the United States. As such, union support for the deal was because it added new restrictions on existing free trade, as opposed to establishing a new free trade area.

31   Various proposals made during the Trump administration included pledges to avoid export restrictions and to eliminate tariffs on essential medical goods. See, e.g., Government of Canada, "June 2020 Statement of the Ottawa Group: Focusing Action on COVID-19," June 2020. Also, Hannah Monicken, "U.S. Says Ottawa Group's WTO Pandemic Initiative Not Needed," World Trade Online, December 17, 2020. The Biden administration also resisted calls from some members of Congress to engage with other trading partners to reduce tariff and non-tariff barriers to trade in medical goods. Margaret Spiegelman, "Carper, Cornyn:

istrations each opted to pass on the negotiation, with the latter arguing that freer global trade had led to an unwise concentration of production for items like rubber gloves and cotton swabs in foreign countries and that tariff liberalization would only exacerbate the situation further. Another proposal was to negotiate temporarily lower tariffs to help American importers and consumers deal with pandemic-triggered supply and shipping shortages. This proposal, too, was met with America's new anti-liberalization yawn.

Another idea floated in 2022 and rejected by the Biden administration was to seek congressional authorization for the executive branch to volunteer U.S. tariff cuts to help support countries targeted by China's use of economic coercion—the practice or threat of cutting off imports from certain countries over policies or positions that Beijing finds objectionable. America's unions immediately blasted the idea after it was aired, making clear their strong opposition to any limited, targeted tariff liberalization for such purposes. Showing deference to these union views, further consideration of the idea was quickly shut down both in the administration and among Democrats in Congress.[32]

A more acute crisis came with America's sudden domestic shortage of infant formula in the late spring of 2022. With shelves quickly emptying and prices soaring, the Biden administration announced and took emergency steps to approve and airlift imports to replace urgently needed demand. Promising that "every tool" was being used to restore supply,[33] the administration nonetheless avoided publicly calling on action by Congress to at least temporarily suspend America's lofty tariffs of up to 17.5 percent (with higher equivalent rates in some cases) to help ease soaring formula prices amidst the supply crunch.[34] In Congress, some prominent progressives introduced spending package proposals to provide relief, while others expressed alarm at the fact that, behind this dairy industry–supported border wall of high tariffs, only four companies

---

U.S. Must Do More to Reduce Trade Barriers on Medical Goods," World Trade Online, September 28, 2021.

32 See, e.g., Thomas Conway, "RE: United Steelworkers Opposes S. 4514, the Countering Economic Coercion Act of 2022," email, August 9, 2022.

33 Associated Press, "Watch: 'Every Tool' Being Used to End Infant Formula Shortage, White House Says," PBS News Hour, May 12, 2022.

34 The White House, "Fact Sheet: President Biden Announces Additional Steps to Address Infant Formula Shortage," press release, May 12, 2022; The White House, "Fact Sheet: President Biden Announces New Actions to Address Infant Formula Shortage," press release, May 18, 2022.

in the United States were producing 89 percent of the supply.[35] A few trade-responsible Democratic and Republican members in Congress, however, finally took the initiative to advance legislation to temporarily remove America's heavy import duties on infant formula.[36] The Biden administration coordinated but waited until after the legislation arrived in the Oval Office for signature before publicly expressing its support for the pause in tariffs.[37] The delay in administration support underscored how even an obvious trade response to help ease a crisis for parents was caught in strong, anti-liberalization rhetoric.

Steps starting with the Trump administration's rejection of wTo-style global trade liberalization initiatives expanded drastically further under the Biden administration, which turned down all new trade liberalization opportunities and then went further by questioning and often turning its back on a pillar of American trade policy long supported by both its political parties—removing foreign non-tariff barriers. Aimed as they were at appeasing their targeted supporters, America's new trade policy became ever more problematic to identify or define by its modern-era trade policy goals and metrics. The remainder of this chapter examines in more specific terms how America walked out on, and in some ways sought even to reverse, its decades-long adherence to advancing more open and fairer, nondiscriminatory global trade.

WALLING OFF THE HOME MARKET:
AMERICA'S EMBRACE OF DOMESTIC PREFERENCES

As much as the Trump administration flirted with pulling America out of the wTo, it appeared more trigger-happy over the prospect of withdrawing from one of its stand-alone agreements. That pact, the wTo's Government Procurement Agreement (GPA), included approximately 50 wTo member governments as signatories with the goal of opening opportunities for their businesses to compete for one another's public procurement contracts. Had it been attempted, pulling out of this agreement would have produced only an economic ripple in the global

---

35   Helena Bottemillier Evich and Meredith Lee, "Infant Formula Shortage Suddenly Topic A in Washington," Politico, May 15, 2022.

36   Earl Blumenauer, "President Biden Signs Blumenauer's Bipartisan Legislation to Temporarily Suspend Infant Tariffs on Imported Infant Formula, Ease Costs and Address Shortage," press release, July 21, 2022.

37   USTR, "Statement by Ambassador Katherine Tai Following Senate Passage of the Formula Act," July 21, 2022.

economy. As a warning signal to the world of America's readiness to tear up its standing trade agreements and commitments, however, action to withdraw would have flashed bright red.

Ultimately, the Trump administration never followed through with an official threat to withdraw from the GPA. It still took a highly antagonistic view of it, signaling a 180-degree turn from decades of Washington's efforts to build on its commitments and grow its membership. Taking a similar view, the Biden administration found new ways to work around the GPA, including by embracing massive U.S. government spending programs in the form of subsidies to businesses and consumers to make purchases of American-made goods. All these steps served a new, common American objective—walling off its market for itself.

Until 2017, America had promoted reciprocal opening of government procurement markets as one means of advancing the GATT and WTO norms of freer and more open, market-based trade among nations. The idea of opening government procurement contracts up to greater international competition was floated in the discussions that founded the GATT in 1947, but concrete talks on developing commitments in this area only picked up traction during the 1960s. Negotiations were eventually launched, but it took around 15 years to yield an initial agreement on government procurement in 1981. That agreement was then expanded and strengthened into the more comprehensive GPA, a process that took about a decade to negotiate before its more comprehensive set of commitments finally came into force in 1995. Because a sizable number of WTO members chose not to participate in this optional side agreement, those that did join agreed to a special set of conditions. These conditions included providing equivalent access opportunities, or most favored nation (MFN) access, only to the participants of this agreement. A process was also established to include new members that wished to participate in these opportunities by agreeing to open their procurement contracts in return.

Most GPA members joined the agreement to take advantage of the new market opportunities it opened for its exporters. On some level, they also at least implicitly welcomed opening some of their procurement to limited international participation to facilitate lower-cost or higher-quality products that more competition could help generate. America's spearheading of and participation in the 1981 GATT procurement agreement, and then in the updated GPA starting in 1995, meant it also had to reconcile these obligations with older procurement laws and regulations still on the books that dated back to the 1930s, collectively referred to as "Buy American" policies. These laws were enacted to restrict, in various ways, foreign participation in U.S. federal procurement contracts. America opened a lane for businesses in GPA member countries to bid on some of these contracts by providing waivers of these Buy American restrictions in exchange for opening their government contracts to America's exporters. Over time, GPA-style reciprocal procurement obligations were also included in America's free trade agreements with individual countries, thus expanding the scope of these special arrangements beyond GPA members. At times, these individual deals provided broader procurement access than the access America agreed to provide under the GPA.[38]

In line with the priority given to opening new markets and opportunities abroad, this approach was broadly supported in the U.S. Congress and advanced by presidential administrations of both parties for over three decades. However, it was not without controversy. At times, opposition to opening the U.S. procurement market in return arose when cases of foreign governments unfairly blocking procurement access to American exports came to light. One such instance came in the late 1980s when U.S. computer and supercomputer manufacturers repeatedly lost local government contracts in Japan to bids of ¥1 (less than one U.S. cent) by Japanese competitors.[39] Some loopholes that enabled such practices were plugged through bilateral agreements and then more permanently closed in the updated GPA agreement reached among all participant countries. However, a perception lingered that America's procurement market remained more open and transparent compared to some of the GPA's other participants, which looked for new ways to game the rules to continue giving advantages to domestic businesses when competing for government contracts in their home markets.

More fundamental opposition to opening U.S. government contract bids to limited international competition, regardless of the access abroad that America received in return, also remained entrenched among some political figures and causes. Unions representing their workers across the metals, materials, machinery, textile, and other industries continued to push political candidates to support stronger Buy American policies, including, at a minimum, no longer adding reciprocal procure-

---

38   For a fully comprehensive treatment of these issues, see Jean Heilman Grier, *The International Procurement System: Liberalization and Protectionism* (Washington, DC: Dalston Press, 2022).
39   David E. Sanger, "Broad Inquiry Is Started on Fujitsu," *New York Times*, November 2, 1989.

ment obligations to new trade deals. Up until the mid-2010s, however, mainstream support for these obligations in Washington remained unchanged. Accordingly, as late as 2015, Congress continued to direct the executive branch to pursue expanded "country participation in and enhancement of . . . the Government Procurement Agreement" in the WTO as well as to "contribute to the continued economic expansion of the United States" through other negotiations, such as through new free trade agreements, and to remove tariff and non-tariff barriers for "government procurement."[40] This support mirrored the mainstream bipartisan view that America was better off continuing to lock up new reciprocal market access rather than ceding foreign markets to other countries doing the same through their trade deals.[41]

Amid the shifting political winds of the moment, and despite its popularity with unions, calls for strengthening Buy American policies did not feature prominently amid the range of other promises Trump and Clinton each made during their 2016 presidential runs to bring more jobs back to America.[42] Once in office, however, the Trump administration moved quickly to attempt to implement tougher Buy American preferences, a theme Trump highlighted in his inauguration address, which also promised to end the "American carnage."

Trump's first executive order on the topic was produced by Peter Navarro, one of Trump's principal advisors on trade during his campaign. Navarro was initially appointed director of a newly created two-person "National Trade Council." Quickly afterward, he was engaged in well-documented fights with other administration officials who sought to limit his access to Trump in the Oval Office.[43] Later, Navarro regained his standing with an elevated title and eventually moved from a basement-level office in the Old Executive Office Building that adjoins the White House into a large, well-appointed office overlooking the White House North Lawn and its "Pebble Beach" press huts.

---

40 Bipartisan Congressional Trade Priorities and Accountability Act of 2015, 19 USC 4201, Sections 102 (a) (13) and 103 (d).

41 See, e.g., Gary Clyde Hufbauer and Euijin Jung, "'Buy American' Is Bad for Taxpayers and Worse for Exports," Peterson Institute for International Economics, Washington, DC, September 5, 2017.

42 Trump did not refer to Buy American in his major June 2016 campaign speech on trade, for example, although he spoke of other ways to bring jobs back, especially in the U.S. steel industry. See "Read Donald Trump's Speech on Trade." Buy American policies also did not appear in either party's official 2016 presidential campaign platform.

43 See, e.g., Woodward, *Fear*, 140–43.

The order Navarro drafted called on Commerce Secretary Ross to develop a plan to mandate that private company–purchased oil and gas pipelines come from American-made sources wherever possible. Attempting to extend the government's "Buy American" purchase requirements to the private sector was quixotic at best. It also predictably and quickly hit a wall of domestic opposition, starting with America's oil companies, which would face higher sourcing costs and probable shortages if subject to such a mandate. The plan that was called for to implement the order subsequently died somewhere between concept and final draft, never reaching the sunshine of the Pebble Beach press corps parked just outside Navarro's office.

Standing before a "Buy American, Hire American" banner, Trump signed his second executive order in April 2017 to limit waivers for procurements that Congress authorized for GPA members. The order also included a directive to federal agencies to probe the impact of America's GPA commitments on the federal government's procurement practices. Beyond its novel interpretation of executive-congressional legal and constitutional authorities, the order appeared aimed at developing the data on foreign purchases necessary to help make a case to unravel America's GPA commitments. No report, however, was issued, and no tangible steps were taken to implement the order.[44] The AFL-CIO president, among other union leaders, later chastised the administration for its lack of follow-through on its big ideas for tightening Buy American preferences: "The Trump administration used the right words but never put in place policies to affect meaningful change."[45]

Never known for quitting, Navarro's third attempt, among other ideas and drafts along the way that ran into legal and bureaucratic walls, gained only slightly more traction. This executive order, finalized in early 2019, called for state and local governments to use American-made industrial products, including basic ones like steel and cement, in their infrastructure projects. While not mandated, a directive was issued to encourage compliance from state and other non-federal government officials.

Navarro's fourth effort on Buy American preferences stuck better. Issued in mid-2019 as an executive order, it was finally implemented as

44 Grier, *The International Procurement System*, 214–20.
45 Richard Trumka, "Biden's 'Buy American' Executive Order Will Boost Economy," AFL-CIO, press release, January 25, 2021.

a legal regulation on the last day of Trump's term in January 2021.[46] It raised the percentage of made-in-America content necessary for goods to comply with Buy American requirements. It also more than doubled the cost difference that had to exist before American procurement officials could legally justify bypassing Buy American restrictions to allow the use of cheaper imported goods. This executive order provoked taxpayer rights advocates, economists, and others, who derided the step and said it would inevitably result in unnecessary extra costs that America's taxpayers would bear.[47] It nonetheless clearly indicated the new direction in America's approach: to set stricter mandates for domestic preferences for procurements with ever fewer exceptions. Significantly, these actions to tighten requirements also avoided peeling back the special access that America had committed to give the roughly 60 GPA and other free trade agreement partner countries with which it had reciprocal procurement agreements.

By late 2018, key decisions on America's government procurement trade commitments had moved over to Lighthizer, who was overseeing the renegotiation of NAFTA with Mexico and Canada. The original NAFTA included a rudimentary government procurement chapter with reciprocal access obligations. Through the renegotiation, Lighthizer had the opportunity to seek changes in these and other procurement terms with Mexican and Canadian officials, but only as long as Congress, which would need to approve the updated agreement, would also go along. Lighthizer held a strongly negative view of opening America's government procurement markets to foreign competition, in line with similar longstanding opposition from America's labor unions. He sought to leave procurement obligations out of the updated NAFTA deal altogether. But with the Canadian and Mexican governments opposed to that step, along with some in Congress, he pivoted to advocate limiting reciprocal access to government contracts on a dollar-for-dollar basis only. In other words, America would no longer provide equivalent procurement bidding opportunities to its agreement partners on a blanket basis and only offer the same absolute dollar value of access to public contracts that America receives in return from Mexico and Canada.

---

46   "Encouraging Buy American Policies for the United States Postal Service," Exec. Order No. 13975, 86 Fed, Reg. 6547 (January 14, 2021).

47   See, e.g., Tori K. Whiting, "New Buy American Executive Order Bad for Taxpayers," Heritage Foundation, Issue Brief no. 4989, August 7, 2019.

The dollar-for-dollar concept flipped upside down the longstanding, underpinning philosophy of the open international trading system: to provide, on a reciprocal basis, equivalent opportunities on equivalent terms. The Trump administration's view of reciprocity, by contrast, was aimed at engineering equivalent outcomes. It reflected the administration's priority of correcting America's trade deficit, which it viewed in zero-sum terms, and was in keeping with its broader view that America and American jobs were consistently on the losing end of the rules and the system it helped create. Lighthizer preferred to end foreign access to American procurement contracts altogether. If access were kept, his view was that it would only be made fair if reciprocal procurement opportunities were defined in dollar terms.

Canada balked at Lighthizer's novel approach, agreeing instead to leave its procurement obligations with America entirely out of the new NAFTA. Giving up on the issue was no real loss for Canada since its exporters and companies could still rely on their continued access to America's procurement market under their respective GPA obligations. Mexico, which was not a GPA member, had a different calculation. Aided by pushback by congressional members against Lighthizer's approach, which would have also caused U.S. companies to lose access to Mexico's procurement market, reciprocal procurement access between Mexico and America was preserved in the updated NAFTA deal.

Had Canada been aware of the Trump administration's on-again, off-again internal planning to pull out of the GPA (or its threatening to do so unless new terms were met), it likely would have made a different calculation about leaving procurement access out of the updated NAFTA deal. Word of the administration's withdrawal plan was eventually leaked to the press in early 2020, coming a few months after the updated NAFTA deal went into effect. It carried further credibility with reports that Lighthizer personally supported threatening to pull out unless the GPA was renegotiated to America's satisfaction.[48] While the administration never pulled the trigger by making the threat official, it remained a possibility throughout 2020—one that seemed ready for announcement at any point to help bolster Trump's reelection campaign efforts to lock down support from union-affiliated and other voters, especially in the Midwest's election battleground states.

---

48   Bryce Baschuk, "Trump Considers Withdrawing from WTO's $1.7 Billion Purchasing Pact," Bloomberg, February 4, 2020.

With the 2020 election approaching, Navarro took one more stab at curtailing America's procurement obligations. This effort aimed, for the first time, to pare back the access America had given through its GPA and free trade agreement procurement commitments. Pointing to supply chain vulnerabilities exposed during the COVID-19 pandemic, Navarro drafted an executive order to remove essential medicines from coverage under these procurement access agreements. Official notifications were made to America's agreement partners that their access would be cut back, drawing predictable objections and preparations, as allowed under these agreements, to counter by withdrawing America's access to their procurement contracts. After the clock ran out on the Trump administration, the issue was passed to the Biden administration, which initially attempted to justify proceeding with these new restrictions. It ultimately capitulated, however, and withdrew the notifications after several trading partners initiated formal arbitration procedures to prepare to pull back their access in response.

Going into its 2020 election campaign, the Trump administration made some progress in tightening up Buy American policies and restrictions to give greater preference to domestic goods over imports, even when substantially more expensive. It also left office having taken only initial, very narrow steps to begin limiting the procurement access it previously opened to its GPA and free trade agreement partners. Aims to dismantle those existing commitments instead ran into sufficient resistance from Congress and elsewhere over concerns that America's access abroad would inevitably also be withdrawn by its agreement partners.

This state of affairs left an opening for candidate Biden, who more forcefully took up the issue in his messages to union and like-minded voters during his 2020 presidential campaign. Biden made strengthening Buy American requirements and regulations a marquee campaign promise in mid-2020, which included an additional pledge of $400 billion in federal government spending for purchases of "American products" to create "millions of good paying union jobs" as well as a pledge to "tighten the rules to make this a reality."[49] Biden's campaign claimed that the plan would not violate America's WTO commitments, although it acknowledged that renegotiating the GPA would be one of the administration's priorities.[50] It did not elaborate further on how it would

49   Joseph Biden, presidential campaign speech, Dunmore, Pennsylvania, July 9, 2020.
50   "Joe Biden Proposes a $700 Billion-Plus 'Buy American' Campaign," Associated Press, July 9, 2020.

accomplish these goals and avoid violating America's wto obligations. The intent of the pledge was clear enough—setting up promises to steer hundreds of billions in government spending and subsidies to bolster America-only, and potentially even union-only, jobs.

Biden moved quickly after his inauguration by signing his first executive action on Buy American policies, kicking off his administration's more aggressive wave of efforts to curtail the use of imports in government-funded contracts. The "Executive Order on Ensuring the Future is Made in All of America by All of America's Workers" tightened calculation methods and further raised the percentage of U.S. domestic content that many goods had to meet to be eligible for government contracts. The domestic content percentage was to be raised in stages from the 55 percent level (in most cases) set by the Trump administration up to 75 percent by 2029.[51] The order did not attempt to limit the access that GPA and free trade agreement partners continued to have in the market. However, it called for U.S. agencies to begin tracking the amounts they were waiving to meet America's trade obligations with these agreement partners. It also created the "Made in America Office" in the White House, led by an appointed "Made in America Director." The administration named a longtime AFL-CIO union official to that post to, among other duties, oversee the process of granting other waivers to these requirements, such as when no U.S.-made products existed.[52]

Later, the Biden administration and congressional Democrats, along with support from a sizable number of sympathetic Republicans, further widened the application of the Buy American restrictions by automatically subjecting all new federally funded infrastructure projects to its requirements. Construction materials were also added to the list of products subject to domestic sourcing and content requirements, thereby substantially expanding the existing scope of products—namely, iron, steel, and manufactured goods—that were already subject to Buy American restrictions. These steps also created substantially greater costs and challenges for many recipients of these funds, whether municipal airport authorities or high-speed rail consortia, requiring them to research and prove compliance with the restrictions to receive govern-

51   Grier, *The International Procurement System*, 357–60. Also, Ian Kullgren, "Former AFL-CIO Trade Chief Named Top White House Trade Advisor," Bloomberg Law, July 6, 2022.
52   "Executive Order on Ensuring the Future Is Made in All of America by All of America's Workers," The White House, January 25, 2023.

ment funding.[53] These steps brought a sweeping number of additional publicly funded projects and the materials used for them under the purview of Buy American restrictions. Up to that point, most of these local entities, depending on government funding contributions or unless separately restricted in another way, had been free to buy from domestic and foreign vendors alike to meet their cost and product specification targets. Since many municipal and other organizations receiving federal funds were not required to meet America's GPA or other international procurement obligations, trading partners such as Canada and the EU howled at the move and threatened to similarly limit their own access to exclude American exports.[54]

As America continued to pursue a range of pathways to eliminate loopholes and ratchet up Buy American–required domestic preferences, the dam mostly held against attempts to dismantle the trade-related procurement obligations that America still had with its GPA and other free trade agreement partners. The legal and international implications of attempting to partially unwind these commitments would have included triggering many trade disputes and a series of protracted negotiations, as called for under the agreements, to realign levels of reciprocal access with each of its agreement partners. From this perspective, straight and complete withdrawal from the GPA agreement would have been the cleaner, more legally pragmatic approach. While seriously considered by the Trump administration, making a clean break from America's GPA commitments also would have resulted in the loss of procurement access abroad for American exports and firms. That prospect posed a different yet equally complicated challenge—stirring up domestic political resistance from American stakeholders that valued the procurement access they still had abroad.

Rather than attempting to renegotiate or end America's procurement obligations with its trading partners, the Biden administration and Congress shifted to a new approach to implement sweeping preferences for American-made goods. Baked into the architecture of massive new government spending programs, tens of billions of dollars in government subsidies would be given to businesses and consumers in America to make purchases themselves instead of flowing through government contracts. These included new subsidies for companies to

---

53   Grier, *The International Procurement System*, 361–67.
54   Grier, *The International Procurement System*, 368–77. Grier covers these developments up through 2022.

build semiconductor production facilities, along with tax breaks and other grants for consumers and businesses to purchase domestically produced electric vehicles (EVs) and other green goods. While bypassing culpability under America's government procurement obligations, some of these new industrial policy–driven goals raised a whole new crop of questions over their consistency with other WTO rules. Particularly problematic to America's trading partners were its subsidies that set country-of-origin restrictions on the goods that could qualify for these government-provided subsidies or tax breaks.

This new industrial policy aimed to fulfill a range of objectives, from big national goals of protecting America's security and technological leadership and combating climate change to domestic economic goals of stimulating new investment and production at home. Attaching domestic content requirements to some of these subsidies also met other political objectives, including catering directly to America's unions, which had long called for U.S. taxpayer money to be spent exclusively on made-in-America goods and services. Public sentiment also leaned firmly in that direction, with nearly two-thirds of Americans supporting that general view, even in cases where American goods may cost significantly more.[55] The WTO rules, however, leaned hard in the other direction by requiring governments, in principle, to treat imports and domestic goods the same.

Especially problematic under the WTO rules—thus illustrating Washington's general disregard for them—were the massive new subsidies offered for purchases of EVs under the Inflation Reduction Act (IRA). The law earmarked a broad range of subsidies and other incentives for consumer and business purchases of designated clean energy and related products, as well as tax credits for new business investment in clean energy projects. These were made contingent on an extensive array of conditions, including a series of domestic content requirements for consumer and some business purchases.

Among the IRA's subsidies, tens of billions of dollars were earmarked to provide generous support to consumers and businesses for purchases of new EVs. The political intent was evident from an early version of the bill, which required such vehicles to be assembled in the United States to qualify for a base subsidy from the government, but then offered higher

---

55   Timothy Aeppel and Chris Kahn, "Americans Want the Government to Buy More U.S.-made Goods, Even If They Cost More," Reuters, March 30, 2021.

subsidies for purchases of EVs made in unionized U.S. factories.[56] After much lobbying by foreign and domestic stakeholders with members of Congress and the administration, the union-made condition ultimately was struck from the bill. The final law, however, still included the requirement that qualifying EVs undergo final assembly in North America (the United States, Canada, or Mexico), in addition to other complicated criteria for battery components and battery assembly that greatly limited the subsidies available for those inputs and assembled batteries made outside of America.

Similar attempts at incorporating union-made criteria had been made years earlier as Congress debated another massive subsidy package for auto purchases. That one aimed to support the U.S. auto industry in the wake of the 2007–08 financial crisis by offering government subsidies to consumers who traded in older vehicles to buy new and more fuel-efficient cars. For the 2009 Car Allowance Rebate System, colloquially known as the "Cash for Clunkers" program, tying the subsidies to vehicles made by union workers was an idea pushed, but one that ultimately did not survive in that bill either, before coming into law.

America's approach in 2009 and 2022 to providing these vehicle purchase subsidies stands out as a clear example of Washington's new lack of concern with its international trade obligations. Because doing otherwise would bring a challenge and near-certain finding of a WTO violation, the 2009 Cash for Clunkers program was opened to consumer purchases of domestic and imported vehicles alike, so long as they met the environmental criteria, in line with the WTO's core nondiscriminatory principles.[57] By maintaining a nondiscriminatory approach to the program, America was then able to go after Japan to force it to change its criteria under its similar program to boost its own industry, which had been drawn up in a way that prevented most of the limited number of American auto imports from also qualifying.

By contrast, in 2022, concern about abiding by the WTO's nondiscriminatory rules was eclipsed entirely by America's new political and economic objectives. The Biden White House embraced discrimination

56   Tom Krisher for the Associated Press, "Biden Bill Includes Boost for Union-Made Electric Vehicles," PBS News Hour, November 11, 2021; and Congressman Dan Kildee, "Legislation to Expand American, Union-made Electric Vehicles Passes Key House Committee," press release, September 15, 2021.

57   Bill Canis, *Subsidizing Replacement of Motor Vehicles: An Analysis of "Cash for Clunkers" Programs*, Congressional Research Service, R46544, September 25, 2020, 9.

against most imports under America's massive new program, touting that
the IRA would create "good-paying union jobs" in America and support
"American workers with targeted tax incentives aimed at manufacturing
U.S.-sourced products such as batteries...."[58]

A second massive subsidy program raised even further questions
about America's commitment to the WTO rules, especially those around
the potential implications of these massive subsidies on trade, such as
by unfairly advantaging U.S.-made semiconductor exports or displacing
imports. The "CHIPS" Act, which enjoyed some Republican support with
its parallel objective of countering China's subsidies and associated semiconductor advances, included billions of dollars in government subsidies
for companies to build new chip production in America. This program
linked "Buy America," "Made in America," and "Secure America" goals
together in a brand-new way for Washington, harkening back in certain
ways to some of the industrial policies used in Japan, South Korea, and
elsewhere to advantage their own semiconductor producers. At that
time, America responded to such efforts with aggressive, trade war–type
tactics that included the use of investment controls, negotiated market
share agreements backed by the threat of unilateral action, tariff hikes,
and WTO actions.[59] In 2022, America reversed course and went even
bigger than many of its trading partners' previous industrial policies in
the sector, setting in motion a new semiconductor subsidies race among
several major chip-producing countries.

America's trading partners, having been in Washington's crosshairs
for decades for their own industrial subsidy policies, greeted its role
reversal under the IRA with enormous pushback and howls of hypocrisy.
The EU and South Korea led the way in lodging the most vigorous public and official complaints, which, in the case of South Korea, was also
accompanied by a major public uproar.[60] Other car-exporting countries
like Japan expressed their concerns just as clearly, albeit with less public

58   The White House, "Fact Sheet: The Inflation Reduction Act Supports Workers and
Families," press release, August 19, 2022.

59   See, e.g., David E. Sanger, "Japanese Purchase of Chipmaker Cancelled after Objections
in U.S.," *New York Times*, March 17, 1987; Leslie Helm, "U.S., Japan Reach Accord on New
Semiconductor Trade Agreement," *Los Angeles Times*, August 3, 1996; and USTR, "United
States Wins WTO Semiconductor Case," press release, June 27, 2005.

60   See, e.g., Leigh Thomas, "Explainer: Why the U.S. Inflation Reduction Act Has Europe
Up in Arms," Reuters, December 5, 2022; and Troy Stangarone, "Inflation Reduction Act
Roils South Korea-US Relations," *Diplomat*, September 20, 2022.

reaction and attention.[61] China, which continues to massively subsidize its domestic industries and uses other exclusionary practices to exclude imports, eventually initiated formal procedures in the WTO dispute process to press its claim against America for unfair discrimination.[62]

Much in the same way the Trump administration took a cavalier approach to the WTO rules with its unilateral tariff actions, which later were judged by WTO panels to have violated the trade rules, the Biden administration came to embrace these domestic content preferences as a cornerstone of its own new industrial policy goals. America's readiness to disregard its obligations sparked similar responses worldwide and fueled a new competition in global industrial subsidies, as elaborated below. The approach also dramatically further eroded the sense that America's Democratic Party–led government was any less of a threat to undermining the WTO's rules and core non-discrimination principles than its preceding Republican Party–led government.

America's dramatic pivot to create a range of stronger linkages between U.S. government spending and domestic production, compared to its previous emphasis on enforcing the WTO rules and promoting reciprocal and fair competition to open opportunities for its exporters in foreign markets, raised broader questions about the implications of this approach for the future. The strength of America's commitment to its international procurement obligations, including whether it would continue to support the expansion of the GPA to include new members, is one of the fundamental tenets of America's trade policy that newly came into doubt. If America stayed in the GPA, would it continue to allow applicants to accede to the agreement or, because new members would open America's procurement market even further to new competition, would it block new members, thus effectively holding the future growth of the agreement hostage to America's new trade politics?

Negotiations between GPA members and applicants seeking to join the agreement often took years. They involved having to reach agreement with each member on issues that included the level of access applicants would make available in their procurement markets. Even as America made it increasingly clear that it prioritized closing off its market, between 2017 and 2023 it agreed to admit three of the dozen or more

---

61   See, e.g., Government of Japan, "Comments by the Government of Japan," November 4, 2022, https://www.mofa.go.jp/mofaj/files/100417179.pdf.
62   WTO, "China Initiates Dispute Regarding US Tax Credits for Electric Vehicles, Renewable Energy," March 28, 2024.

countries seeking to join the GPA. Australia was one, but it already had procurement access to U.S. government contracts through its separate bilateral free trade agreement with America. The UK was another, which sought to restore the procurement access it had with other GPA members before it decided to leave the EU. Therefore, allowing both into the GPA did not provide any truly new access to America's public procurements. America agreed in 2023 to provide new access for just one applicant—North Macedonia. A country of around two million people with a gross domestic product (GDP) equivalent to the metro area of Scranton, Pennsylvania, its GPA accession brought the most negligible of new competition for American government contracts. For the other GPA candidates, America's aversion to further opening its market left them guessing whether the door was, in fact, closed to their future participation in the agreement.

ABANDONING SERVICES LIBERALIZATION
AND SURRENDERING DIGITAL TRADE LEADERSHIP

As Trump was preparing in late 2016 to begin his term, the future of another WTO-related negotiation—this one on services trade—also newly hung in the balance. Similar to the EGA negotiations, those for the Trade in Services Agreement (TISA) were launched in April 2013 by a subset of WTO members to try to salvage another piece of the failed WTO Doha Round negotiating mandate. With America far and away the world's largest exporter of services of any country, totaling $837 billion in 2017, and with an annual services trade surplus with the world of nearly $290 billion, the Obama administration embraced the negotiations to secure more foreign access for America's service suppliers.[63] America's services sector was already among the most liberalized of WTO countries under the WTO's separate agreement on services, creating the opportunity to gain more than it gave in the negotiations.

Roughly a third of the WTO membership participated in the TISA negotiations, comprising 50 WTO member countries organized as 23 negotiating parties with a single EU negotiating team representing its member nations. In terms of size, these countries comprised the large majority of the world's major services-exporting nations and, thus, of

---

63   2017 data from OECD Data, "Trade in Services (Indicator)," accessed March 12, 2024, https://doi.org/10.1787/3796b5f0-en.

global services trade. The negotiations covered a broad range of services sectors, from liberalizing financial services and telecommunications sectors to setting rules on transparency and curbing limits on domestic preferences that countries used to require some services be provided locally. One of the key issues in the TISA negotiations was to set new rules around the emerging digital economy to make access to digital services markets nondiscriminatory and fair.

The decision to pursue negotiations among a subset of WTO members, which were technically conducted outside of the WTO umbrella, avoided the free-rider problem that made small group negotiations for a subset of goods trade more challenging to organize. This is because the WTO's agreement on services trade allowed some exceptions to the usual MFN principle for services-only liberalization commitments among countries, meaning they did not need to be offered to all other WTO members. Some TISA participants hoped that the outcome could serve as a template for further negotiations in the WTO to conclude an updated services agreement among all members.

The negotiations also drew increased attention from various civil society groups, whose anti-corporate and anti-globalization views were often sharpest on issues such as financial services and digital trade. For one, the environmental advocacy group Greenpeace obtained leaked TISA negotiating documents and issued alarming warnings that the agreement would result in "opening . . . [services markets] to foreign businesses and removing barriers for trade."[64] But this was no discovery as it was essentially the central goal of the WTO system, a goal to which over 160 countries had voluntarily committed themselves by joining the organization. These targeted critiques of TISA tended to reflect the broad anti-liberalization, anti-globalization, and anti-establishment orientation of these groups.

Among their more specific objections, Greenpeace joined other advocacy groups in criticizing the effort to create new trade rules that harmfully restrained government regulation, thus undermining a country's "right to regulate" to respond to issues such as climate change mitigation. They further claimed that the commitments under negotiation undermined national sovereignty, even as each TISA negotiating party had voluntarily chosen to participate in anticipation of the gains

---

64   Zach Boren, "Leaked: How the 'New TTIP' Could Undermine Global Action on Climate Change," Unearthed, September 19, 2016, https://unearthed.greenpeace.org/2016/09/20/tisa-leaked-documents-new-ttip-undermine-climate/.

from doing so.[65] Other opponents pointed to the objective of forging new financial services sector rules to help guarantee a fair playing field between foreign and domestic providers, warning that these efforts dangerously prevented financial regulators and governments from using the tools they needed to stem financial crises and protect customers.[66]

A focus on negotiating trade rules became a new priority in the GATT from the 1970s and grew in importance over the following decades. America especially spearheaded efforts to add trade rules to help ensure countries that made commitments to lower tariffs or opened services markets to foreign competitors did not turn around to later enact new laws or other measures to undermine that access. As I will elaborate in the following chapters, advocacy groups increasingly targeted them for various reasons as the scope and number of new trade rules accumulated into the early 2000s. TISA, therefore, was targeted by opponents over both its core objectives—advancing new services sector liberalization among its negotiating members and creating new trade rules to help ensure competition in services markets is fair and nondiscriminatory for foreign providers.

Participating governments worked for over three years to advance the TISA negotiations, which, as with other trade talks, proved slow and difficult. Much time and discussion were spent crafting language designed to help ensure nondiscriminatory treatment for foreign providers while also striking the necessary balance, through the use of exceptions or other conditions, to provide governments the flexibility they needed to fulfill their responsibilities to safeguard the health and welfare of their citizens.

By the summer of 2016, enough progress had been achieved to make the final push needed to try and complete the TISA by the end of the year. Leaked texts underscored how far away the talks were from that goal. Still, with most of the issues thoroughly discussed and the positions of various parties clear on many points, the parties agreed to accelerate the pace through further negotiations in September, November, and December.[67] Services business associations from 12 countries and the

---

65   Boren, "Leaked."

66   See, e.g., Ben Beachy, "RE: TISA Leak Reveals 10 Key Threats to Commonsense Financial Regulation," Public Citizen, July 2, 2015, https://www.citizen.org/wp-content/uploads/tisa-finance-leak.pdf.

67   Jutta Hennig, "TISA Parties to Resume Push for Year-End Deal; Key Issues Unresolved," World Trade Online, September 1, 2016.

EU, ranging from Peru to Australia, renewed their support for late-year completion. As the negotiations made progress, AFL-CIO president Trumka began stepping up public criticism to attempt to derail them, making clear that America's trade unions had other plans for TISA that included preparing to block approval by Congress of, in his words, yet another of the world's "corporate trade deals."[68]

TISA negotiators arrived at their December 2016 meeting with a deal that was still too unbaked to finish. Among the many remaining issues, the EU was unable to secure a common position and consensus from its own member countries on some of the proposed rules to ensure the principle of free flow of digital trade information.[69] American and other negotiators had grown particularly impatient with the EU's long delays in making these decisions as it slowly formulated its internal consensus to prepare to enact its own digital economy regulations. America had lost patience and already was posturing to attempt to push the EU out of TISA if needed to finally close the agreement with the other parties that were also ready to complete a deal.

The outcome of America's November 2016 presidential election quickly turned the tables. Instead, with Trump's election, America's own commitment to finishing the agreement quickly was put into doubt. Like the EGA talks, the future of the TISA negotiations hung in the balance for weeks after the election. This turned into months, as the other negotiating parties waited for word from America on whether it would re-engage to finish them. Meanwhile, America's unions and other activists also waited for word, ready to mobilize to attempt to block any of these agreements should they ever be concluded.

Shortly after being sworn into his position, Ambassador Lighthizer pledged to a group of lawmakers that the Trump administration would review TISA and other unfinished WTO negotiations to assess their potential benefits and decide how to proceed. Thirty-five bipartisan House members, including the House Ways & Means Trade Subcommittee chair, made clear their support for keeping America at the negotiating table and moving the TISA negotiations forward, citing the particular ur-

---

68   Richard Trumka, "Trumka Outlines a New Direction on Trade," AFL-CIO, speech transcript, June 28, 2016.

69   Brett Fortnam, "Sources: UK Officials Float Possibility of Smaller Services Plurilateral if TISA Fails," World Trade Online, July 26, 2017.

gency of achieving an agreement on new digital trade rules.[70] Abdicating America's participation in such a major WTO negotiation, especially one that would help its service exporters, bordered on inconceivable to many.

The Trump administration instead turned to other trade priorities, never indicating a renewed interest in restarting the TISA work. With the marginalization of America's commitments to the WTO as its principal goal, the administration, in fact, never gave returning to TISA any serious consideration. When asked about it the following March, some nine months later, Lighthizer remained noncommittal, admitting only that it was probably time to decide.[71] No formal decision ever came as America left the negotiations to drift and then ultimately die. The other negotiating parties could have proceeded among themselves, except that with America now out, the scale of the agreement would have taken a sharp hit in both its logic and significance. Moreover, some of the new rules commitments from the talks aimed at improving the services regulatory climate for services firms, when implemented by the remaining TISA members, may have only disproportionately benefited America's large, internationally competitive companies in those markets without any reciprocal new commitments from Washington.

Other countries eventually grew impatient and stepped forward to try and fill some of the void America had left behind. As strong supporters of the TISA effort, Japan, Australia, and Singapore took the initiative to propose a new, voluntary WTO negotiation—but one limited only to forging new digital trade rules among those that agreed to join. Agreement on rules for the sector already had proven elusive in the TISA context. A particular split remained between the EU's approach and a like-minded approach shared among Japan, Australia, Singapore, and America. Given the importance of the issue and the sector to the American economy, Lighthizer signed off on putting America into these new, rules-only talks. Being in the room where other countries gathered to negotiate rules that could profoundly impact America's leading edge in the sector was judged to be preferable to sitting this one out.

Formally proposed in late 2017 and finally launched in early 2019, negotiations for the WTO's Joint Initiative on E-commerce got underway in the wake of TISA's America-induced midair stall and crash. In

70   "Congressional Services Caucus Urges USTR to Restart TISA Negotiations," World Trade Online, July 13, 2017.

71   *President's 2018 Trade Policy Agenda: Hearing before the Committee on Finance*, 115th Cong. 39 (March 22, 2018).

the interim, the EU had started to roll out its own EU-centric digital economy regulations and requirements. Given the global reach of the internet and digital cloud services, companies providing content across the internet needed to comply with these EU regulations, thus effectively turning EU-centric regulations into some de facto global standards. By abandoning TISA and letting negotiations on digital rules drift for a few years, America lost the venue and momentum it had in TISA to push for its alternative vision and goals for these rules—one that it shared with several other countries eager to enact the same.

America's decision to let TISA drift and die off also opened an opportunity for China to slip into the global rule-making club on digital trade. China did not participate in the TISA negotiations, but the proposed WTO e-commerce agreement was a second chance to sit at the table. Initially reportedly reluctant to join, given its radically different state-controlled mechanisms for data flows and digital content, the EU nonetheless urged China to reconsider. Beijing then announced its intention to join just before the official launch of negotiations. Now at the table, China was able to put forward its opening proposals for rules to allow it to continue to protect and maintain its massive state controls over information flows and keep its digital firewalls in place to keep out foreign content. Meanwhile, America returned to the starting line by resubmitting many of its core digital rules positions it had started with for the TISA negotiations, only to later abandon the whole exercise.[72]

Once in office, the Biden administration did not initially attempt to walk away from or postpone ongoing WTO negotiations. The e-commerce negotiations were already painstakingly slow, having made gains in some areas but still deadlocked on several major issues that revealed the stark differences in positions among China, the EU, and the like-minded coalition of the United States, Japan, Australia, and Singapore. Even as these negotiations continued, the Biden administration began expressing a much more antagonistic view toward some of America's core positions on digital trade in other contexts. This included criticism of some digital rules America included in the renegotiated NAFTA deal, which Congress overwhelmingly approved, and of nearly identical rules in a separate digital agreement concluded with Japan in 2019.

As the administration came into office in 2021, countries such as Australia and Japan remained closely aligned with America on the need

---

72   Henry S. Gao, "Across the Great Wall: E-commerce Joint Statement Initiative Negotiation and China," June 19, 2020, https://ssrn.com/abstract=3695382.

for new and stronger digital trade rules, consistent with other WTO efforts to establish an open, nondiscriminatory, and rules-based international approach. Eager to work with the Biden administration to reach new trade agreements, they sought its support in the WTO digital rules negotiations and proposed joining forces through a separate effort to reach a stand-alone digital agreement in the Asia-Pacific region. Pitched as a new regional standard and an alternative to models put forward by the EU and China, the Biden administration instead turned the proposal down and intensified its internal scrutiny of America's positions on digital rules.

The Biden administration then surprised many with another American about-face, withdrawing advocacy to advance and enforce several of its previous core digital trade objectives criticized by America's union leaders and progressives for unjustly benefiting America's "Big Tech" companies over the interests of ordinary Americans. These trade rules, intended to create a nondiscriminatory environment overseas for all digital providers and any business that collected, stored, and collected or shared international customer and business data, were then targeted for dismantlement. As the administration began to flesh out internally which among them it would no longer support, it began making clear in the WTO and elsewhere that it was preparing a strikingly different approach.

The administration then turned to these activist groups to also write America's new digital trade policy playbook. It especially looked to the AFL-CIO, which released "A Worker-Centered Digital Trade Agenda" in 2023. This document, containing numerous recommendations, began from the premise that "U.S. digital trade policy has prioritized securing increased market access and intellectual property rights for its big technology firms . . ." while making "no reference to worker rights and . . . [without requiring] governments to take any meaningful action to protect individuals' personal data."[73] It claimed that the exceptions under the digital trade rules agreed to during the Trump administration were not expansive enough for governments to take action to protect these legitimate public policy objectives. The paper then set out a range of new policy objectives in two main areas.

The first was to insist on much broader regulatory carve-outs than provided under America's existing digital trade rule model, which aimed at striking a balance between creating exceptions for legitimate gov-

---

73   AFL-CIO, "A Worker-Centered Digital Trade Agenda," February 7, 2023.

ernment objectives while preventing arbitrary or other discriminatory actions by governments. The paper's recommendations insisted that much broader exceptions were needed to maintain this balance. These included, for example, allowing governments to intervene to restrict cross-border data flows without the need to demonstrate a legitimate policy need, permitting mandates for localized data storage within a country's borders for certain kinds of information, and giving governments more blanket powers to force private firms to disclose their proprietary software source codes.

The second area of objectives was to advance the union's domestic priorities for regulatory and legal changes by insisting they be folded into America's international agreements on digital trade. These included adding "strong and enforceable labor standards" to all new digital trade agreements, incorporating new requirements for governments to enact regulations on the handling of personal data, allowing governments to mandate data localization of certain categories of information, keeping out provisions that might further facilitate call-center offshoring, allowing for governments to more freely access source codes and algorithms in the name of preventing worker abuse, addressing digital surveillance by employers of employees, addressing "abusive labor practices in the technology sector," clamping down on online intellectual property theft from independent creative professionals, and addressing other artificial intelligence and cybercrime objectives.[74] This extensive list of principally domestic objectives also dovetailed directly with the AFL-CIO's simultaneous new big push to unionize employees across the digital and e-commerce technology sectors to grow its membership.[75]

The Biden administration pulled directly from the union-drafted priorities as it began negotiations in early 2023 with over a dozen Asia-Pacific countries to forge a new kind of trade agreement, covered further in chapter 5. Then, in October 2023, it announced it was officially withdrawing America's own core digital trade negotiating positions in the WTO e-commerce negotiations on data transfers, data localization, and source code rules—the same rules it had advanced and defended since the start of the talks.[76]

---

74   AFL-CIO, "A Worker-Centered Digital Trade Agenda."

75   See, e.g., Olafimihan Oshin, "New AFL-CIO Leader Eyeing Tech Sector for Organizing," The Hill, June 12, 2022.

76   Hannah Monicken, "U.S.: E-commerce Talks Should Focus on What Can Be Done by Year's End," World Trade Online, October 26, 2023.

Claiming that the sudden reversal was necessary to make room for new tools to regulate the evolving digital economy, the administration's surprise move was met with loud objections on both sides of the aisle in Congress.[77] Democratic senator Ron Wyden blasted the move for "leaving a vacuum that China . . . will be more than pleased to fill," insisting that America's existing model for digital trade obligations provided Congress all the flexibility it needed to regulate the sector for legitimate reasons as it saw fit. He added: "USTR's unilateral decision to abandon any leverage against China's digital expansionism, and to oppose policies championed by its allies . . . directly contradicts its mission as delegated by Congress."[78] Senator Mike Crapo, a Republican, blasted the move as well, accusing the administration of having "misled" Congress and adding that the decision "is choosing to side with China over the 8 million Americans who work in the digital economy and generate 10 percent of U.S. GDP."[79] The move was applauded and cheered as long overdue, however, by Democratic progressives in Congress, along with their union and other allies, in terms that welcomed it as much for the administration's policy choice as for being a long overdue strike directly against the size and influence of America's big tech companies.

Amid increasingly rancorous debates in America over everything from efforts to enact online privacy and new protections for gig workers to taking bold steps to regulate artificial intelligence and reining in the market power of America's large technology companies, the Biden administration justified its decision to topple almost twenty years of efforts to craft and advance nondiscriminatory digital sector trade rules as necessary to create its new "policy space." The digital trade rules were developed as the internet grew over the course of three presidential administrations from both political parties, and Congress overwhelmingly approved them in trade agreements passed during that period. They were debated and developed to strike a similar balance as with other trade rules, which was to both permit legitimate, nondiscriminatory actions by governments to regulate in the public interest while prohibiting other arbitrary, discriminatory actions that foreign governments used to disadvantage American exports and companies abroad.

77 "Quote-Unquote: U.S. Demurs (and Wyden Remonstrates) on WTO Digital Trade Talks," World Trade Online, October 26, 2023.

78 "Quote-Unquote: U.S. Demurs," World Trade Online.

79 Dan Dupont, "Finance Republicans Say USTR 'Misled' Congress on E-Commerce; Agency Disputes," World Trade Online, October 27, 2023.

After the administration aligned its positions with those of labor unions and progressives, the market-opening aim for the digital rules was further delegitimized as a corrupt benefit to America's Big Tech companies disguised as a trade-supporting goal. Typical among these reactions was that of Senator Elizabeth Warren to the decision: "We need to make clear that digital rules favoring Big Tech monopolies are a non-starter for the U.S. in any trade agreement...."[80] Other business groups covering a wide range of industries from small app developers to independent and mainstream movie and music industry associations, as well as civil society groups promoting causes from civil liberties to an open and accessible internet for all, disagreed, expressing the opposite view: the change in position was an unnecessary and harmful setback to efforts to promote nondiscriminatory rules with multiple benefits, from discouraging government censorship to preventing unjustified and discriminatory treatment of U.S. businesses abroad.[81]

In subsequent chapters, I explore in greater depth how America came to spend decades developing rules for the digital economy only to abandon them. Beyond another bewildering display of America walking out on its longstanding positions, it provided one more signal to the WTO and the world that America's drift away from adherence to open, nondiscriminatory, principles-based trade would only continue to manifest itself in new and likely unexpected ways.

GLOBAL FREE TRADE'S AMERICA PROBLEM: INTERNATIONAL IMPLICATIONS

By 2023, the view from the WTO's offices on the shore of Lake Geneva of the future of the international rules-based trading system had never looked as bleak. The WTO, already struggling to maintain its relevance

---

80   "US Drops Digital Trade Demands at WTO to Allow Room for Stronger Tech Regulation," Reuters, October 25, 2023.

81   Letter dated November 7, 2023, to Mr. Jacob Sullivan and Dr Lael Brainard from 45 business associations, available via link in the following report: "Business Groups Unite to Decry Shift Away from WTO E-commerce Proposals," World Trade Online, November 7, 2023. See also letter dated February 26, 2024, from the American Civil Liberties Union, Center for Democracy & Technology, Freedom House, Information Technology and Innovation Foundation, Internet Society, PEN America, and Wikimedia Foundation to The Honorable Antony J. Blinken, The Honorable Gina M. Raimondo, and The Honorable Katherine Tai, available via link in the following report: "House Small Business Chair: Digital Reversal Will Hurt Smaller Business More," World Trade Online, February 27, 2024.

and effectiveness, faced yet another series of crippling challenges from its leading protagonist. These started with launching global tariff wars and then hobbling its dispute function. As covered here, America also threw in the towel and walked out on the other goals it set for the international trading system—advancing new global trade liberalization and fostering more open, nondiscriminatory trade through rules-based initiatives. This was a bipartisan shove from Washington, with both the Trump and Biden administrations routinely taking potshots at the wisdom and legitimacy of these goals as they instead prioritized erecting new walls to America's market, abandoning ongoing trade-liberalizing negotiations to leave them to drift and then die, and walking back from previous positions in rulemaking negotiations aimed at furthering the WTO's principles of nondiscrimination.

It took very little, in fact, for America to essentially pull the curtains shut on global trade liberalization. The Doha Round's collapse had already shown the geopolitical improbability of concluding new, GATT-style global tariff liberalization deals. Despite that, and up to 2017, America kept pushing for narrower WTO-related deals among smaller groups of countries with a critical mass. Services and environmental goods negotiations were some of the efforts that still seemed possible to achieve, even as each inevitably became its own tortured exercise that again cast doubt on the potential for new successes. Once America simply walked off the field and remained seated on the sidelines, most of these efforts, too, collapsed.

With America on the sideline, the WTO's core trade liberalization agenda virtually evaporated. Due to the MFN principle, other countries were reluctant to reach their own smaller group agreements in the WTO only to allow America's large exporters to free ride on their concessions. For countries still committed to reciprocal market opening through the WTO, America's abandonment of global trade liberalization highlighted the crippling result of just one major player at the table calling it quits. Washington's decision to sit out global trade liberalization in the WTO effectively ended the game for everyone else.

America's retreat cascaded downhill in other ways. As it flirted with pulling back on its commitments in the WTO and elsewhere on government procurement, it ramped up new restrictions to limit other foreign access to America's federally funded procurements. Once a leader in working to expand the WTO's government procurement agreement's liberalization agenda and scope, America's new trade policy instead left open to question whether and under what conditions it would support any expansion of the GPA to open its procurement market wider in exchange for new procurement access abroad.

The Biden administration and the Democratic Congress further upended America's commitment to nondiscrimination by embracing domestic preferences criteria to direct massive new government spending toward American-made goods. The billions of subsidy dollars they approved to help consumers and businesses purchase domestically made EVs and their batteries avoided running afoul of America's procurement obligations, but they blew new holes in America's commitment to providing equal treatment for imports. The justification used to exclude most imported vehicles and vehicle batteries from these subsidies was a need to respond to China's own subsidies and help wean America off dependence on its exports. However, a different motive seemed to be at work when the U.S. subsidies were made available to American production and imports from only a handful of countries under starkly uneven terms among America's security allies and others. Electric vehicle battery imports from Europe would not qualify, while some South Korean–made EV batteries could; finished EVs made in Mexico and Canada could potentially qualify for consumer subsidies alongside those made in America, but not those made elsewhere. After America's allies complained, bitterly at times, limited adjustments were made to open some new avenues. Even so, the extensive discrimination in treatment among WTO members symbolized Washington's new choices on trade. America's trading partners, from Italy to Japan to South Korea, were motivated to set up their own subsidies with their own criteria, which at times were similarly engineered to make it difficult or impossible for America's exports to qualify. All these developments further accelerated the unraveling of the legitimacy of the WTO and its core goal of promoting nondiscrimination and, with it, more open and freer trade.

Swearing off opening America's market further to imports, as a new policy objective, extended to even the narrowest domestic needs and circumstances. Congress finally took the initiative to pass a temporary tariff break to ease price spikes caused by shortages of critical infant formula needed to nourish America's youngest demographic. However, the Biden administration's public body language made it clear that it aimed to avoid taking ownership of the decision in Congress. Other ideas, such as offering tariff cuts to countries that found themselves bullied on trade by China, were among limited trade liberalization proposals also relegated to America's new political dead zone—a place that its unions and other anti-trade opponents had at long last successfully created to kill them off.

The reality underlying these decisions to reject further liberalization and claw back access and commitments that America had already made was rooted in America's political map and in the electoral strategies over two presidential election cycles deemed necessary to win the White House. At the time of this writing, the same dynamics remain in play as the parties' candidates compete for the presidency in November 2024.

Both Trump and Biden, in striking alignment, pursued and prioritized a long-held top goal of America's labor unions and many of their members—putting a stop to opening America's market any further to the world. Where achievable, both candidates also worked on another union objective—pulling back or simply reneging on America's past market-opening commitments. In other areas, the candidates and their administrations diverged, sharply at times, around other open trade objectives. The Trump administration routinely and aggressively pursued more open markets for U.S. exports by going after most foreign trade barriers, occasionally using threats against the trading partners that refused to remove them. The Biden administration, in contrast, proceeded cautiously, showing some favor toward working to remove barriers to U.S. farm sector exports while taking a much less active posture toward barriers facing U.S. manufacturing and services exports, actions that unions and other progressive advocates had disparaged at times as unfounded favors to America's multinationals.

Differences also appeared in their approaches to new WTO trade rule negotiations. One of these concerned digital trade. After choking off services liberalization negotiations, Lighthizer agreed to put America into new digital-only negotiations to keep others from setting trade rules for America's leading and dominant industry. Among these were China, which used its digital policies to poach foreign technology and surveil its citizens, as well as the EU, which, depending on one's perspective, either had developed a set of farsighted consumer protection regulations or a toolkit to effectively wage discriminatory digital protectionism against American firms in the name of consumer protection. The administration's digital trade rules were developed over the course of three administrations, repeatedly vetted by executive branch agencies along the way, and overwhelmingly approved by Congress in the updated NAFTA—but then unraveled by the Biden administration just three years later during the midst of efforts to conclude WTO digital rule negotiations. Members of the WTO were left guessing which established position America would turn its back on next.

The same question was asked by those Americans who wondered where their government's trade policy, including even its most routine export advocacy efforts, had gone. Whether the U.S. government would continue the deep-rooted bipartisan support for American exports and competitiveness abroad or instead subordinate these goals to other domestic criticisms and reform priorities became a function of which of the two progressive Left/New Right mainstream views on trade occupied the Oval Office. More is explored in the following chapter on their differences over trade rules, disagreements that tended to either freeze the linear progression of U.S. trade policy or cause it to become increasingly erratic.

In just seven years, America's new trade policy trajectory had left the country at fundamental odds with many of the principles and objectives it had long championed. The cumulative effect was to further sink the WTO's importance and relevance, leaving it little to negotiate and achieve short of efforts to preserve its relevance and future. Amid low expectations for making progress on its traditional trade agenda, the WTO's ministerial gathering in the winter of 2024 appropriately put the issue of institutional reform at the top of its agenda instead. Even with that shift in focus and emphasis, the meeting still ended with virtually no new agreements. This followed an epic effort in mid-2022 that attempted to show that the WTO could still reach new negotiated agreements, but that ended with a handful of minor or otherwise incomplete deals and further evidence of the crisis facing the organization. One agreement allowed WTO members to break private company patent rights to produce essential COVID-19 vaccines but was not reached until well after global vaccination rates had peaked and demand for the vaccine was rapidly falling. The WTO also reached a new partial agreement in mid-2022, after 20 years of work and discussions, to limit global fishery subsidies. To achieve a partial outcome, members left on the table much of the difficult work that still could not be bridged after almost two years of additional work to reach a compromise in time for the 2024 meeting.

As the Biden administration heaped praise on the new WTO agreement to limit government subsidies for fishing, it was passing out billions in new U.S. government subsidies, including with powerful preferences given to American-made EVs, their batteries, and other environmental goods. The Biden administration justified all these in terms of their essential environmental sustainability and economic security.[82] WTO Director General Okonjo-Iweala provided a sober reminder of the rules of the road in the GATT and the WTO—any government subsidy that harmfully distorts trade makes that subsidy equivalently problematic. Those used by rich countries to advantage their domestic producers, she continued, tend to beget the use of subsidies by other countries to meet the same goals, inevitably spiraling into a "subsidy race to the bottom" both for the WTO system and for the majority of countries that lack the financial resources to keep up.[83] It was a less-than-subtle calling out of the large subsidies offered by China to its producers, and a calling out of America for responding with its own large payments and credits. The EU, Japan, India, and others followed, funding their own similar subsidy programs. Instead of holding these accountable through the WTO to de-escalate the subsidy race, the programs proliferated, leading all involved to pursue their interests in ways that were increasingly unconstrained by the WTO rules.

America's new trade policies and politics have accelerated and deepened the fragmentation of the rules, norms, and other principles it once championed for the international trading system. It is fair to observe that, despite paralysis and fragmentation, since trillions of dollars of goods and services continue to be traded annually, the WTO system remains mostly intact for now as its members continue to honor, in the main, their core obligations under it. Others see evidence that the WTO is just a few more tugs at the string away from fully unwinding for good. Okonjo-Iweala framed the threat to the WTO's future, one which by seeming implication a few members including America bear principal responsibility for, from the perspective of WTO's developing country members, whose sense is

. . . that rich countries who have benefited immensely from the multilateral trading system to develop their economies now no longer want to compete on

82   See, e.g., USTR, "Remarks by Ambassador Katherine Tai at Signing of the United States' Instrument of Acceptance of the WTO Agreement on Fisheries Subsidies," press release, April 11, 2023; and USTR, "Statement by Ambassador Katherine Tai Following Congressional Passage of the Inflation Reduction Act of 2022," press release, August 12, 2022.
83   Ngozi Okonjo-Iweala, "Interview with World Trade Organization Director General Ngozi Okonjo-Iweala," *Fareed Zakaria GPS*, broadcast transcript, September 24, 2023, https://transcripts.cnn.com/show/fzgps/date/2023-09-24/segment/01.

a level playing field and would prefer instead to shift to a power-based rather than a rules-based system.[84]

This chapter has argued that the starting point for America's detachment from freer trade and lack of consensus on new trade rules began in the mid-2010s amid deepening political and economic conflict and division at home. These often polarizing forces pushed America away from its longstanding pursuit of a core set of trade objectives and norms, resulting in a striking new bipartisan consensus opposed to new global trade liberalization and mired in new and irreconcilable internal debates and dissensions over many trade rules and other objectives. Beyond the WTO, these factors also led it to walk out on and then away from its own marquee free trade deal with 11 other Asia-Pacific nations. That decision, while leaving an enormous American foreign policy crater across that region in its wake, also helped elevate an unconventional presidential candidate to the White House. The next chapter tells this story.

---

84   Bryce Baschuk, "WTO Chief Criticizes Rich Nations for Protectionism," Bloomberg, September 4, 2023. The quote is from WTO Director General Ngozi Okonjo-Iweala.

FOUR

Walking Out on
Free Trade in the Asia-Pacific

A second day of meetings in late September 2014 lasted barely an hour before Japan's top negotiator gathered his papers and declared that he was walking out and flying home.[1] Eager to push the Trans-Pacific Partnership (TPP) negotiations to conclusion by year-end, America's top negotiator, Obama's trade ambassador, Michael Froman, waited many weeks for his Japanese counterpart, Akira Amari, to agree to meet to find a way forward on a core issue for any free trade agreement negotiation—tariff elimination.[2] The other ten countries in the negotiations had also waited for many months, looking for some signal that the two largest economies in the TPP had reached a deal on Japan's agriculture tariff liberalization, so the overall negotiations could enter their end game.

Japan had joined the TPP negotiations over a year earlier, in August 2013, as the twelfth Pacific Rim country to participate. Strong opposition from its farm lobby, successive government changes, and recovery from its devastating March 2011 triple earthquake, tsunami, and nuclear disasters were among the hard political and crisis realities that had led

---

1 For a U.S. account of the meeting, see Mitsuru Obe, "Despite Bold Japan Trade Pledges, U.S. Still Wonders: 'Where's the Beef'," *Wall Street Journal*, September 27, 2014.

2 Obe, "Despite Bold Japan Trade Pledges, U.S. Still Wonders." Also, on Froman's eagerness for a meeting, see "USTR代表、閣僚協議打診TPP交渉巡り" [USTR representative consults with ministers on TPP negotiations], *Nihon Keizai Shimbun*, September 9, 2014.

Japan to stay out of the negotiations after they kicked off in early 2010. Once finally at the table, its participation brought new energy and importance to the TPP undertaking. It also added new layers of challenges and problems. Among these had been Japan's refusal for over a year after joining the negotiations to agree to more meaningfully liberalize its home market for farm goods, triggering calls from America's congressional leaders to conclude the deal without Japan unless it changed course.[3]

Compared to the endless attention that Japan demanded from America as it weighed whether to join the talks, something was clearly off when word came from its top TPP negotiator that he was simply too busy to meet to finish them. Even as Froman waited, Amari had managed to work into his busy schedule a casual cruise down the central canal of the Venetian island of Murano, stopping at a glassware boutique. After repeated requests to meet, Amari finally agreed to fly to Washington in mid-September 2014. Once there, he quickly got to the point of Japan's seeming ambivalence toward reaching a deal—Japan had gone as far as it would in opening its agriculture market, he declared; if America could not accept that and still insisted on reducing the access it offered Japan in response, perhaps there was no longer any deal to reach. One Japanese negotiator even accused the American side of "sabotage" in the press for pulling back on the access it had already offered Japan on auto parts.[4]

What Amari signaled was Tokyo's expectation that its politically important farm sector deserved special treatment, separate and different from the full access it expected from others in return. While Japan offered tariff liberalization for hundreds of farm goods, it refused to go any further than only cracking its door open to new imports for hundreds of others. Trade in these goods instead would be managed perpetually using various tools that included keeping significant tariffs in place, erecting scores of byzantine import quotas covering meticulously differentiated categories of products, and extending state-administered monopoly control over purchases of some imports and over to whom and when they would be sold into the market. It was a managed trade outcome from a country that expected free trade in return. Rather than

---

3   See, e.g., Daniel Enoch, "Nunes Says US Must Push for Tariff Elimination in TPP Talks," *Agri Pulse*, June 11, 2014.

4   "交渉5時間TPP空転、強まる漂流リスク、米国、「車部品の関税維持」、日本、譲歩の「新提案」不発" [5 hours of TPP negotiations go nowhere, increasing risk of drift; U.S. "maintains tariffs on auto parts," Japan's, "new proposal" for concessions misfires], *Nihon Keizai Shimbun*, September 26, 2014.

pushing through a second day of meetings intended to discuss ways for Japan to improve its offers, Amari opted to walk out before the lunchtime sandwiches were even served.[5]

This Washington meeting was their second to end prematurely with a meal left unserved. Nine months earlier, at a Tokyo hotel restaurant, Amari pitched an early "deal-closing" offer on access to Japan's agriculture market. With all TPP leads headed to Singapore to attempt to close most of the remaining issues, Japan convinced a top American negotiator that a stop in Tokyo to meet Amari on the way would be worth Froman's time. After hearing Japan's pitch, however, Froman could only balk at the woefully weak offer, fearing that even mention of it to the other countries in the negotiations could lead them to pull back on their own liberalization offers and unwind the political commitment all had made to achieving a high liberalization target.[6] That tense meeting broke off with the multi-course *kaiseki* dinner left sitting in the kitchen. A misfire in assumptions over what would be an acceptable deal from Japan on agriculture, labeled a "bureaucratic miscalculation" by one Japanese newspaper, only backfired instead, derailing the deal-closing momentum Froman was trying to create.[7] Expectations for significant progress in Singapore quickly flopped after Japan's officials made clear to other delegations they would not make a meaningful offer there on agriculture to help move the TPP closer to its conclusion.[8]

The TPP negotiations drifted slowly forward for months afterward. Several other major issues remained unresolved, as well as many lesser ones. Hopes were raised for a while after Japan and America reported a "milestone" breakthrough on agriculture access in spring 2014. However, they faded after Japan tacked on conditions for that access,

5   Kate Higgins-Bloom, "Food Fight," *Economist*, October 6, 2014. A key Japanese negotiator smugly suggested to the press that lunch had been hidden to be used as a reward for Japan's negotiating posture. The reality was that Japan walked out before lunchtime ever arrived.

6   "日米、関税分野持ち越し TPP経財相「5項目譲れぬ" [Japan, U.S. hold off on tariffs; TPP and Economic and Fiscal Policy Minister says "will not compromise on five points"], *Nihon Keizai Shimbun*, December 2, 2013.

7   "TPP, 日米最終決戦は14年春'妥結か漂流か?" [Japan, US final TPP battle in the spring of '14: Deal or drift?], *Nihon Keizai Shimbun*, December 25, 2013.

8   Before departing for Singapore, Japan's minister made clear to the media that he "will not negotiate one millimeter what is non-negotiable." See "TPP閣僚会合7日開幕、「実質合意」へ議論" [TPP ministerial meeting to begin on the 7th, discussions on "substantial agreement"], *Nihon Keizai Shimbun*, December 7, 2013.

putting a deal further out of reach.[9] This situation led Froman, during the summer of 2014, to ask for a meeting with Amari, essentially to revisit the same basic problem they first discussed at the Tokyo restaurant months earlier.

Walking out of his September 2014 meeting with Froman helped Amari burnish his reputation as a tough negotiator back home. A call soon after by Japan's prime minister for a snap parliamentary election in late 2014 pointed to another motive for the move—playing for more time. Having missed the target of achieving at least a framework deal in Singapore in late 2013, and with the TPP talks struggling to regain traction following it, Froman began a new push in mid-2014 to flesh out "landing zones" with TPP countries on major unresolved issues. The goal was to tee up as much as possible on a handshake basis to finalize the entire deal soon after America's November 2014 congressional midterm elections. Froman had hoped to agree with Amari on these landing zones with the U.S. political calendar in mind.

Japan, meanwhile, had its own political schedule. Amari's ruling party was quietly readying for a surprise snap parliamentary election, revealed just several weeks before voters went to the polls in mid-December 2014. Making further concessions to Froman on farm goods access in the lead-up would risk losing support from key rural constituents and harm the prime minister's party standing. Accordingly, weeks after walking out in Washington, Amari made it crystal clear that he did not share Froman's optimism that a TPP deal could be completed by the end of the year, stating flatly, "There is no prospect for an agreement (between Japan and America) on market access at the moment."[10] Amari's ruling party emerged from the election with its substantial majority in Japan's

---

9   Japanese officials widely made clear that the talks were stuck on agricultural issues like beef and pork access, months after the "milestone" outcome in April. See, e.g., "TPP日米関税協議、溝埋まらず 牛・豚肉など"[TPP Japan-U.S. tariff talks fail to bridge gap on beef, pork, etc.], *Nihon Keizai Shimbun*, September 10, 2014; and "経財相、来週訪米USTR代表と会談へ"[Economic and Fiscal Policy Minister to visit U.S. next week to meet with USTR], *Nihon Keizai Shimbun*, September 18, 2014. On the April progress, see Doug Palmer, "Obama, Abe Find 'Path Forward'," Politico, April 25, 2014.

10   Clint Richards, "Japan Can't Ratify the TPP This Year," *Diplomat*, October 29, 2014. Amari also signaled his expectation that no further progress would be made before the end of the year, calling it a "red traffic light" if a deal was not reached during his meetings in Washington. See Yukihiro Sakaguchi, "TPP,24日に日米閣僚協議　甘利し「今回を最後に"[TPP, Japan-US ministerial meeting to be held on 24th; Amari: "This will be the last time"], *Nihon Keizai Shimbun*, September 24, 2014.

parliament intact, and Prime Minister Abe also remained safe in his job. However, one price of the Japanese strategy was several more lost months of progress in the TPP negotiations.

When Japan was ready to deal again later in 2014, it brought a new set of demands for its top export sector—automobiles.[11] Its focus was on the percentage of a finished auto's content that had to be sourced from among the TPP countries for it to qualify for the agreement's tariff breaks. Opportunities to source auto parts and components among the TPP members were extensive, with six (Vietnam, Malaysia, Mexico, Japan, Canada, and America) of its 12 members having large auto parts industries. With so many options to source parts within the TPP region, their automakers that export to TPP countries should more easily be able to meet higher content percentage rules for their finished vehicles. With tariffs cut to zero, higher content rules also would incentivize more parts trade among them, to the exclusion of suppliers in other countries.

Japan, however, had other ideas. It instead demanded lower percentage content rules for its autos and auto parts to qualify for tariff-free trade within the TPP region. Its goal was to make the content rules weak enough for Japan's automakers, some of which had important suppliers in non-TPP countries such as China and Thailand, to be able to meet them and still export tariff-free with little disruption to their own supply chains. The demand directly conflicted with America's position, made clear several months earlier, wanting higher percentage rules—more in line with those in agreements like NAFTA and the domestic job-creating expectations of its labor unions. Japan's sudden and inflexible official position erupted into a major new point of contention between them, one that Japanese officials insisted for several months afterward to be nonnegotiable and ended in a compromise that profoundly upended support in America for the deal.

These vignettes from among the hundreds of give-and-take moments in this major, multination free trade negotiation underscore how all sides in the TPP were frequently stretched to their political limits. They waited for the right moment to put down their best offer, which was rarely their

---

11   At least one more senior lead and one TPP-wide ministerial meeting were held before the end of the year, but virtually no progress was made. See, e.g., "日米TPP「着実な成果」 関税協議終了、来週に交渉再開" [Japan-US TPP "steady progress" toward conclusion of tariff talks; negotiations to resume next week], *Nihon Keizai Shimbun*, October 16, 2014; and Tsukasa Hadano and Yukihiro Sakaguchi, "TPP打開、なお困難 年内の合意「厳しく」" [TPP breakthrough remains difficult; agreement by the end of the year "tough"], *Nihon Keizai Shimbun*, October 27, 2014.

best offer. They made issues hostages to gain leverage and engaged in strategic tradeoffs to preserve the red lines they most cared about. They adjusted their moves to be sensitive to their own political calendars. They also had to manage their domestic politics simultaneously, which often turned out to be their most challenging negotiations. It was nonstop three-dimensional chess, both among the 12 countries at the table and afterward, as each returned home to face negotiations with their political leaders and stakeholder groups. All the negotiators had to leap off their own political cliffs in one way or another at certain points as the clock kept ticking until something happened to finally call time.

These examples also point to two substantial causes for why the TPP agreement, once finally completed in October 2015, landed with such an ominous thud in Washington. First was the inauspicious timing of its conclusion, delayed past its sell-by date amidst America's already intensifying U.S. congressional and presidential campaigns for the November 2016 election. Several presidential candidates from both parties had already voiced their opposition or skepticism; after the TPP was done, they found more reasons to oppose it openly. A rising tide of congressional leaders and members, many of whom were also up for election, joined in by making clear they would not support it at all, or at least not without considerable changes. Then, less than three weeks before the 2016 presidential election, Trump made killing off the TPP a centerpiece of his final pitch to working-class voters; while stumping in union-heavy Pennsylvania, he doubled down on an earlier campaign pledge to immediately pull America out of the TPP if elected.[12]

The lengthy time it took Japan to finally move to a place on agriculture that America could begrudgingly accept and potentially explain at home, and one that more closely approached the high tariff elimination commitments made by all other TPP members, added to pushing the negotiation timeline out and into this red zone of America's politics. Another significant delay came from the U.S. Congress's inability over much the same period to pass legislation to authorize the negotiations and agree to hold an amendment-free, up-or-down vote on any final deal. Each proved to be among the lengthier, more problematic drags on the overall negotiation timeline.

The second was the political toxicity of the eventual compromise reached with Japan on the TPP's auto content rules, which, among other

---

12   Donald Trump, "Presidential Candidate Donald Trump Remarks in Gettysburg, Pennsylvania," C-Span, October 22, 2016.

criticisms of the agreement, quickly emerged as a particularly prominent and potent lightning rod. America's labor unions made it a top rallying call in their opposition, pointing out that if, as the Obama administration argued, the TPP was a chance for America, instead of China, to write the new rules for trade in the Asia-Pacific, how was it possible that America would benefit from the agreement if it allowed half the content of a car to be made in China? Trump picked up the line days later, wielding it as his top argument to attack Clinton's past support of the TPP and then as his top reason to withdraw from it.

The TPP debate in America marked a watershed moment in its trade policy. This chapter explores in greater detail why America walked out and then away from the TPP, turning its back on its vision for an America-centered, rules-based free trade area in the Asia-Pacific region. The episode exposed the new fragility of America's bipartisan postwar trade consensus, one that America's new mainstreams on the Left and the Right replaced to then reject the Obama administration's claim that its new trade rules would make free trade work better. This chapter also later explores the implications of this withdrawal for America's trade and foreign relations, impacts that continue to reverberate today. For the other 11 TPP members along the Pacific Rim, America's abandonment of the deal, after having arm-twisted each to go as far as they would to accept these rules, was an indelible act of betrayal, one that smashed America's credibility and raised fundamental questions about its commitment to the region and the future of its trade policy. After rejecting both its own trade policy goals and trade agreement partners, would America ever be able to agree with itself, much less with its trading partners, on a new vision for mutually beneficial trade?

AMERICA'S PROBLEM WITH THE TPP

President Obama announced his administration's intention to negotiate the TPP agreement in late 2009, delivered in a single sentence midway through a long speech in Tokyo laying out his "pivot to Asia" foreign policy. In it, he argued America's destiny was tied to Asia and presented a lengthy list of ways that America would engage with the region's countries in fuller recognition of their shared interests. By simply committing to work with a "broad-based membership" to meet "high standards worthy of a 21st century trade agreement," his TPP announcement seemed small amidst the bigger moment.[13] It appears even smaller in retrospect, given the outsized importance it came to play in that foreign policy. Later, the TPP came to be referred to at different times by different officials and commentators as the "centerpiece" of America's strategic engagement in the region.

Making it a centerpiece also raised the stakes. If successful, it would help check China's growing dominance by surrounding it with a free trade area that set new rules, from fair competition with state-owned businesses to transparency obligations to help turn the tide against China's version of the rules it aimed to spread to govern trade in the region—rules that left its state-driven model plenty of policy space to work around. The TPP also would be an open platform, welcoming to new participants ready to meet its updated rules to benefit from a free trade area accounting for 40 percent of global GDP. At home, the Obama administration responded to domestic critics of America's past free trade agreements by aiming to make the TPP "transformational" by incorporating the strongest trade agreement commitments yet in areas like labor rights and environmental protection. It also would continue to cater to centrist, business-friendly growth goals of opening new access for America's businesses and exporters in many fast-growing markets in the region, along with adding new rules to help them compete fairly. Collectively, it aimed to create a mutually beneficial economic compact among a group of countries committed to economic interdependence based on traditional and new, American-influenced standards for trade that left China on the outside.

The vision for this new trading order in the Asia-Pacific was attractive enough for many countries to decide to participate. America and the TPP's original four Pacific ("P4") nations of Singapore, Chile, Brunei, and New Zealand were joined for the launch of negotiations by Australia, Peru, and Vietnam. Later, Malaysia, Mexico, Canada, and then Japan joined as the negotiations were underway, forming the 12 countries later known as the TPP-12. Other countries, from South Korea to Costa Rica, also began openly mulling eventual membership. It quickly gained strong momentum and support around the Pacific for its strategic and economic merits. Globally, the TPP emerged as the most important trade agreement negotiation outside of the WTO.

As a political gamble at home, the TPP's large and expanding membership presented multiple new challenges for the Obama administra-

---

13   Barack Obama, "Text of Obama's Tokyo Address," *Wall Street Journal*, November 13, 2009.

tion. Negotiating with Singapore, Chile, Australia, and Peru raised few new congressional or other U.S. stakeholder concerns, as they were already free trade agreement partners with America. Including New Zealand added a politically potent concern for U.S. dairy farmers, given its state-supported monopolistic model for the production, marketing, and export of dairy products. The inclusion of Brunei as one of the original P4 members provoked civil society groups opposed to its human rights record. Adding Vietnam and Malaysia, the former a single-party, communist country with a bustling private economy, raised human rights as well as new labor rights concerns for many American advocacy groups. Their inclusion also raised strong criticism from America's labor unions and environmental groups over the impacts of opening the U.S. market further to cheaper imports from countries with much lower wages, labor standards, and weaker environmental regulations. Adding Canada and Mexico fulfilled Obama's 2008 election promise to renegotiate NAFTA but raised further concerns and expectations around fixing almost everything about America's most controversial and disliked free trade agreement. Japan brought additional layers of concerns over its long and dubious track record of genuine openness to imports, its historic state-supported export prowess in automobiles and other manufactured goods, and its past track record of currency manipulation to boost its exports.

America's engagement in this negotiation began with the original P4 countries during the George W. Bush administration. It fit neatly into that administration's aggressive efforts to advance free trade, which outdid itself by signing agreements with 17 countries over its eight-year term. Other negotiations were also launched during that administration but never concluded for various reasons; among them were an ambitious 34-country free trade agreement of the Americas and individual negotiations with Thailand and Malaysia. These efforts were buoyed by the reliable support of Republican majorities in Congress across much of the Bush presidency. Many Democrats in Congress were routinely critical, but a sizable number still supported many of the agreements. Even as the number of reliable free trade supporters in the Democratic Party continued to dwindle, as measured by the party's official positions in its convention platforms, this pro-trade group represented the party's mainstream view on trade into 2016. These "New Democrats" were an important voting block for the agreements and critical to maintaining America's postwar bipartisan trade consensus, particularly after the 1992 NAFTA with Canada and Mexico began to fracture the party on trade.

The Bush administration ran out of time to make much progress
with its new Asia-Pacific free trade effort. It took the incoming Obama
administration about ten months to decide to pick it back up, along with
its rebranding of the negotiation as the TPP.[14] As important as its strategic
goal for the TPP of anchoring America within a new Asia-Pacific trading
order came to be, the Obama administration hardly gave this foreign
policy goal any mention in public for a few years. Instead, it stressed
the opportunity to take advantage of growing Asian markets and how
the agreement would enable America to leverage new opportunities for
higher-quality, higher-paying export jobs at home. It also stressed the
need to maintain America's competitiveness in a region where other
large trade deals were increasingly excluding America from access to
the world's fastest-growing markets.[15]

That last point deserves further emphasis and explanation. By 2009,
with the WTO appearing unable to deliver a new global tariff-cutting
agreement, more countries turned to pursue free trade agreements instead. The Bush administration recognized and touted these agreements'
economic and foreign policy benefits. It also viewed them as a means of
putting pressure on countries holding out in the WTO Doha Round tariff
negotiations to either compromise and join more global tariff-cutting
or lose access to the U.S. and other key markets from smaller free trade
agreement deals that excluded them. The Doha Round failed in spite of
it, but the Bush administration's policy of "competitive liberalization"
through new free trade agreements put America squarely in the new
global race to lock up better access to export markets.

With America and other major trading nations seeking new free
trade deals, even more countries abandoned WTO-centered trade policies to pursue their own to avoid losing out. Free trade agreements
are an exception to the WTO's most-favored-nation (MFN) rule, which,
in principle, requires countries that lower their tariffs for one or some
countries to do the same for all other WTO members. As long as the free

---

14   Initial talks in 2007 led to a Bush administration announcement in early 2008 of its
intention to negotiate with the P4 countries of Chile, Singapore, Brunei, and New Zealand.
The P4 concluded a basic free trade agreement in 2005 (the Trans-Pacific Strategic Economic
Partnership Agreement), after which the United States expressed interest in joining further
negotiations. After Barack Obama's election, the effort was put on hold by the Obama administration for further review until the decision was made in late 2009 to proceed.

15   USTR, "Economic Opportunities and the TPP—Increasing U.S. Exports, Creating
American Jobs: Negotiations for a Trans-Pacific Partnership Agreement," fact sheet, December
2009.

trade agreement liberalizes nearly all trade among agreement partners, the exception allowed countries to treat each other more preferentially than they treated other WTO members.[16] Over just a few years, the scramble to negotiate new preferential trade deals emerged into a new competition that resembled a tariff-cutting arms race across the globe.

As of 2000, 82 such agreements concluded over several previous decades were in force worldwide. This increased quickly to two hundred agreements by 2009. By the time the TPP was completed and signed in early 2016, the total number approached three hundred.[17] Many were individual country-to-country deals; others were larger, region-wide efforts. One notable example at the time was the discussion of a new regional free trade area in the Asia-Pacific that would exclude America. Negotiations for that agreement—the Regional Comprehensive Economic Partnership (RCEP)—were launched in 2011 after almost ten years of planning among China, Japan, South Korea, Australia, India, New Zealand, and ten countries in Southeast Asia. As much as the TPP had its own broader strategic and economic value, the goal of pursuing the TPP was also motivated by the same concern—either America negotiates to keep and grow its access to Asian markets, or it will be locked out by other agreements, lose access, and fall behind.

Beyond their export goals, countries routinely select free trade negotiating partners for foreign policy and other strategic reasons. For America, it also required finding willing trading partners prepared to meet its unusually high expectations and standards for these deals. These included a readiness by its free trade agreement partners to fully liberalize their markets to American exports with virtually no exceptions and to agree to an extensive set of trade rule commitments that often required them to change their own laws and regulations to meet them. Washington's ever-expanding set of demands for its free trade agreements significantly narrowed the pool of negotiating partners ready to accept the political difficulties and consequences at home of meeting U.S. expectations.

---

16   The exclusion for free trade agreements from the GATT and WTO's MFN rule was included in the original GATT agreement to accommodate the fact that some of the founding members already had their own preferential agreements. The GATT agreement tightened up the conditions for such agreements going forward to encourage further tariff reduction commitments to take place among all the GATT participants.

17   World Trade Organization, "RTAs [regional trade agreements] in Force," WTO Regional Trade Agreements Database, https://rtais.wto.org/UI/PublicAllRTAList.aspx.

Amid this global frenzy to lock up export markets and bolster strategic relationships through preferential trade agreements, neither the Bush nor the Obama administration viewed choosing to sit on the bench as a legitimate policy choice for America. The Bush administration demonstrated a deeper philosophical belief in free trade and its benefits. Still, it converged with the Obama administration in a shared outlook that America could best serve its interests by leading to shape foreign trade and international affairs instead of waiting and reacting to others that shaped them instead. This objective guided America's pursuit of free trade agreements during this period, and not the goal of aiming to expand globalization per se. To justify the economic case for these agreements, the Bush and Obama administrations consistently stressed the opportunities that opening new markets created for American exports. Implicitly, this also meant the need to avoid falling behind other countries striking their own free trade deals that gave their own exports an advantage.

In most cases, both administrations also could make the case that America was getting more new access abroad from these agreements than it was giving. Having liberalized more aggressively than almost all other countries from decades of leading global GATT tariff agreements, America had already eliminated tariffs for WTO members on over 45 percent of its roughly 11,000 goods categories. Where tariffs remained, most were only in the 2–6 percent range. Those tariffs that remained high (15 percent or greater) accounted for only 2.7 percent of these goods categories. As a result, America's overall average tariff across all goods was quite low by the 2010s, at around 3.4 percent.[18] Since nearly all other countries had higher average WTO tariff rates, insisting on going to zero on all, or virtually all, goods through a free trade agreement most often ended with America giving relatively less in new access than those having to eliminate their higher average tariffs.

Insisting on absolute free trade across all goods, or very near to it, was particularly important to cultivate support for free trade agreements from America's farm goods exporters. With exceptions in a few protected commodity sectors, many U.S. farm producers are export-oriented. Yet the tariffs they faced on their exports abroad were often among the highest. Setting the strong expectation that America's agreements would end

---

18   WTO, ITC, and UNCTAD, *World Tariff Profiles 2013* (Geneva: WTO Publications, 2013), 10–11. Figures taken from summary tables for all products, based on 2012 data for average tariff rates.

with nearly all tariffs lifted was a welcome position rewarded with their enthusiastic efforts to lobby Congress to approve these agreements. Their advocacy was important to many House members, but it was especially influential with senators, whose state-wide elections meant they always paid close attention to rural voters. For U.S. manufacturing companies, views on pursuing full tariff liberalization more extensively cut both ways, depending on their exposure to import competition, ability to access foreign markets, and other corporate capabilities and strategies tied to their sourcing and supply chains and own global operations. In general, the largest multinational companies in manufacturing and services were internationally competitive and positioned to compete in a globalized environment. Therefore, they were often also supportive of these agreements. However, some at times still registered strong opposition to liberalizing U.S. tariffs, such as the U.S. auto industry's opposition to free trade deals with Japan and South Korea over intense competition in the U.S. market from their imports and the complicated barriers to U.S. exports in their markets.

America maintained these high expectations for tariff liberalization in the TPP negotiations, insisting on essentially complete free trade on all goods after several years.[19] Few other countries had the same, highly ambitious expectations for tariff elimination. Those that did, including Singapore, Australia, and New Zealand, also had low average tariffs in the WTO on their imports. Most other countries instead left some room in their "free" trade agreements to keep limited tariff protection for a few particularly vulnerable or politically sensitive domestic sectors in place.

Other countries left quite a bit more room than that. Developing economies often liberalized much less under these agreements, consistent with the WTO's approach that allowed the same. Among advanced economies, Japan, Norway, and Switzerland also routinely liberalized substantially less than their peers in their free trade deals. In virtually all its agreements, Japan held back from liberalizing tariffs on roughly 10 percent or more of its goods categories.[20] In its 2009 deal with Switzerland, Japan even opted to keep its high tariffs on imports of

---

19   In 2013, average tariff rates (MFN applied rate for WTO members) among TPP countries were: Australia 2.7%; Brunei 2.5%*; Canada 4.3%; Chile 6%; Japan 4.6%*; Malaysia 6.5%*; Mexico 7.8%; New Zealand 2%*; Peru 3.7%; Singapore 0.2%; and Vietnam 9.5%* (*denotes countries with which the United States did not yet have a free trade agreement before the TPP and thus represented actual new market opening commitments for U.S. exports). WTO, ITC, and UNCTAD, *World Tariff Profiles 2013*.

20   WTO, ITC, and UNCTAD, *World Tariff Profiles 2013*, 186–88.

Swiss pineapples and bluefin tuna.[21] Lacking a tropical climate and an ocean, it probably did not matter much to Switzerland to leave it that way. It nonetheless underscores the degree of entrenchment that Japan and others often bring to tariff negotiations. Having routinely excluded so many products from its previous agreements, Japan arguably had the furthest to go among TPP members to break with its precedents to meet the agreement's expected high liberalization commitments.

Trump often directed political attention and public anger at the unfairness he saw in America's commitments in the WTO, particularly at the fact that America's average tariff level for global imports was stuck further below, and sometimes well below, those of almost all its trading partners. The solution he called for—prohibited under WTO rules and requiring congressional authorization to implement—was to raise U.S. tariffs on a country-by-country, product-by-product basis to achieve absolute tariff reciprocity with each of America's trading partners.

The Bush and Obama administrations shared a similar concern over this asymmetrical disadvantage. Their approach, however, took the opposite tack to leveling the competitive and trade playing field. Rather than raise U.S. tariffs to match others, as Trump later proposed, they used free trade agreements to eliminate them with individual countries. Setting all tariffs at zero is another means of achieving a reciprocal outcome that erases America's average tariff disadvantage with these trading partners. This approach also reinforced America's commitment to adhering to the WTO, given that free trade agreements are the only practical means allowed under its rules for a country to eliminate broad tariff rate disparities with its trading partners.[22] Creating more reciprocal opportunities through preferential trade would, over time, also tend to increase trade flows between them and shift away from others. This would only hold true if (similar to what Trump claimed to be a fatal flaw of the TPP) these agreements prevented exports from a third party outside of

---

21   Ministry of Foreign Affairs of Japan, "Agreement on Free Trade and Economic Partnership Between Japan and the Swiss Confederation, Annex I," https://www.mofa.go.jp/region/europe/switzerland/epa0902/annex1.pdf.

22   Individual countries could also equalize their tariffs by lowering them at the same point in the context of global WTO tariff negotiations, although those lower levels also would have to be agreed to by other WTO members and offered to all of them. Or the United States could raise its tariffs with one partner, but in the expectation that the partner would later be authorized to retaliate by raising its tariffs further in response. These options, while possible scenarios, were not feasible within the bounds of WTO rules.

the free trade deal from disproportionately benefiting by "coming in" as a significant source of inputs in the agreement partners' supply chains.[23]

While free trade agreements became a widely used tool for establishing preferential tariff-free trade with key trading partners, garnering sufficient political support for free trade agreements also steadily became more difficult in America, as it had in many other countries. As the 2010s began and the TPP effort was relaunched, America's ability to eventually pass free trade deals in Congress seemed to remain intact. The key to securing the needed votes often depended on including ever-more extensive trade rules that responded to the goals and concerns of domestic producers, labor unions, and other stakeholders.

Cause for optimism as the TPP negotiations got underway was rooted in concurrent progress being made to overcome congressional opposition to four free trade agreements negotiated by the Bush administration. Passage of these four deals—with Panama, Peru, Colombia, and South Korea—was initially blocked by Democrats after they retook power in both chambers of Congress in 2007. To find a path, Democratic congressional leaders agreed to work with Republicans on a set of changes to the deals, after which the Bush and Obama administrations began working with each trading partner to renegotiate and update the original terms. These forced renegotiations often created tremendous further political risks and credibility issues for America's free trade agreement partners with their own stakeholders since, after making a range of compromises to secure the initial deal, they were expected to agree to yet another list of U.S. demands.

These changes agreed to between Democratic and Republican leaders in Congress principally called for stronger core obligations in the areas of labor rights and environmental protection. In the case of the Bush administration's deal with South Korea, Democrats also blasted it for failing to ensure fair market access for American cars, citing decades of official and unofficial government policies that kept U.S. cars out. Difficult renegotiations with Seoul ended with a series of additional trade rules and, for Seoul, less favorable concessions on U.S. auto tariffs added to the updated deal presented to Congress. By the end of 2011, all four agreements passed with these revisions included, winning broad support from Democratic members.

---

23   Charlotte Alter, "Transcript: Read the Full Text of the Fourth Republican Debate in Milwaukee," *Time*, November 11, 2015.

Insisting on renegotiations to fix or go back to get more from America's agreement partners emerged as Congress's political playbook for passing free trade deals. It was first successfully deployed with NAFTA in the early 1990s when the Clinton administration went back to negotiate a side letter with Mexico and Canada that added new rudimentary labor and environment commitments. Tacked onto the original agreement reached by the George H.W. Bush administration, it was enough to rally some Democrats to pass the deal over the strong objections of unions and environmental groups. The playbook was then rolled out again almost two decades later, amid similar circumstances of changes in administrations, to pass the George W. Bush administration's four agreements with Panama, Peru, Colombia, and South Korea.

After the TPP was concluded in 2015 and with support flagging in Congress to pass it, expectations rose that Congress's renegotiation playbook would be dusted off once again to get it through. This time, however, forging consensus on the revisions and additions that a U.S. administration would need to force other TPP partners to accept had grown more daunting. Expectations on both sides of the aisle in Congress not only had become vastly more expansive, but many of the "must-have" fixes put forward by one side increasingly collided with demands from the other. These conflicts often tracked major unresolved policy debates in Washington over America's own policies and practices, whether over disproportionately boosting Big Labor or benefiting Big Pharma. With America's 2016 House, Senate, and White House campaigns already in full swing, establishing America's standards for the TPP increasingly devolved into a series of proxy battles over the desirability of those same standards at home. These domestically driven debates pulled at the seams of the bipartisan consensus that needed to be stitched together to get TPP passed.

Amid these deep policy divisions, opponents on the New Right and the progressive Left nonetheless also found themselves in striking alignment against the TPP on other grounds. These externally focused concerns centered around the deal's perceived failures to defend American jobs, whether by inadequately incentivizing more production in America or failing to close off loopholes for TPP members and for third parties, such as China, to take unfair advantage. Exhibit A for these critics of the progressive Left and the New Right was the TPP's unacceptably weak content rules for autos and auto parts. They also aligned in their opposition to other TPP outcomes viewed as far too weak to defend American jobs and production from unfair foreign practices, including commitments made to help prevent TPP members from engaging in currency manipulation to boost their exports and rules attempting to rein in the preferences countries can give their state-owned businesses to provide them advantages. Both camps routinely pointed to these and other examples to attack the administration's claim that TPP was the new, high-standard trade agreement model that would work better for all Americans.

Criticisms of the TPP also erupted in the form of allegations regarding how and by whom these new rules for trade had been written. Anti-TPP advocates, especially those on the progressive Left, consistently referred to the TPP as the "corporate trade deal," a charge belied at times by the range of producer groups that likewise criticized the deal for failing to meet their expectations and objectives. Unions, environmentalists, and other stakeholders similarly pushed for their priorities to be included in the deal. Some welcomed the administration's progress; most, however, derided the outcome of its efforts and opposed the TPP for falling woefully short of fulfilling their specific and lengthy set of expectations and objectives.

Both from efforts to balance the priorities of competing domestic groups and from failures to meet stakeholder demands when other TPP countries refused to agree to them, the debate over the TPP triggered a broader reassessment of what the nation's trade policy should aim to achieve writ large. Building a broader coalition necessary to support a free trade agreement was no longer possible by attempting to accommodate the core interests of various constituencies in the final outcome. Instead, these interests and demands were colliding in the same issue space and proving increasingly irreconcilable amid America's increasingly polarized domestic politics. With Congress unable to arbitrate and broker compromises over many of these same issues in the realm of domestic policy, the TPP became both a new target and a new platform to debate a range of divisive domestic issues. As the next section explores, it was no longer clear that America could agree on the "high standard" rules it expected and wanted for itself, much less confidently and reliably express those it expected from the world.

AMERICA'S PROBLEM WITH WRITING THE RULES FOR TRADE

The post–World War II international trading system began with a bigger idea than global tariff liberalization. It was also to include a slate of new rules for trade to go with it. America set out to create this core set of new codes and norms, along with a new International Trade Organization (ITO) to help participating countries oversee it all. An agreement with these elements was reached among 56 countries in 1948. As a harbinger of difficulties to come with the TPP decades later, however, America ultimately could not follow through on its end to bring the ITO into force when the ambitious agreement stalled out awaiting approval in Congress. The ITO agreement eventually faded into obscurity, becoming the only one of the four major postwar international organizations championed by America to fail to be established. The three that were— the International Monetary Fund (IMF) for international finance, the World Bank for international development, and the United Nations for international peace and security—all faced dramatically fewer acutely competing American domestic interests.

The ITO charter agreement became especially mired in opposition and ambivalence in the U.S. Congress over these newly proposed global rules for trade. Many were novel at the time, particularly in the form of new international obligations. Some were pragmatic. Others were more ambitious. All were shaped by the lessons of "beggar thy neighbor" tariff escalations and economic nationalism that helped stoke a world war, from the competition waged to corner trade in natural resources, the advantages that nations accorded their military-industrial conglomerates to conduct the war, or from targeted postwar reconstruction priorities aimed at preventing a return to war.

With the demise of the ITO, the simpler GATT agreement, a stop-gap deal to get the ball rolling on tariff liberalization before the ITO could be completed and ratified, emerged instead as the foundational agreement on which the new international trading order was built. Beyond its tariff-cutting commitments, the GATT also included a much slimmed-down version of the ITO's core trade rules and principles. Especially important among these were the trading system's two core commitments on nondiscriminatory treatment: the MFN rule requiring GATT members to accord similar treatment to all GATT members, and the national treatment rule requiring that members treat imports from GATT members similar to domestic goods. Some further ITO obligations were also included, albeit often in slimmed-down form, including general commitments to avoid non-tariff barriers as well as more specific rules on the use of tariffs, quotas, and exchange controls. Other rules included in the ITO were mostly or completely left out of the GATT, including limits on international commodity agreements, government assistance for domestic economic development, state trading enterprises, cartels, and other restrictive practices. The GATT also included a more limited range of exceptions than those included in the ITO.

Reactions from business, union, and civil society groups to the ITO charter ranged widely. One top concern for some U.S. producer groups was the ITO text's support for full employment objectives, as demanded by the UK's Labour Party government. These groups viewed recognition of the goal in the charter as inconsistent with the development of an open and freer international trading order, which, as they saw it, necessitated a move away from wartime government planning and toward free markets. A more specific concern was a broad exception sought by the UK in the charter to allow governments to use measures, such as import quotas, as they deemed necessary to maintain full employment. This was viewed suspiciously as a blank check for governments to erect just about any new barrier they saw fit to discriminate against imports.[24] America would again face a similar issue decades later when the Biden administration invoked discriminatory trade measures to fulfill the full employment–style demands of America's labor movement. This time, the perceived inconsistency that America rejected in the 1940s of allowing countries to use trade barriers to pursue employment goals was settled in the opposite direction to meet its own goal.

America also came full circle from the ITO debate decades later in another respect—when the TPP became the only other major foreign trade agreement signed by America after 1945 to fail to pass Congress. Unable to even get a congressional committee vote for the ITO charter, the Truman administration eventually withdrew it from Congress in late 1950, two-and-a-half years after it was signed. The failure to secure enough support in Congress, as one contemporary observer put it, would sound strikingly familiar in the TPP context decades later:

On the one side were arrayed many groups which had a special concern about one or another of the hundred-odd Articles contained in the Organization's charter. Some of these groups had genuine ideological differences with one provision or another . . . while others were simply fearful...(of) the continuation of the policy of reducing tariffs. On the other side . . . were the formal, inhibited presentations of an Administration trying vainly to explain a strange, complex and highly technical agreement.[25]

---

24   See, e.g., Diebold, *The End of the I.T.O.*, 16–17.
25   Raymond Vernon, *America's Foreign Trade Policy and the GATT*, Essays in International Finance, no. 21 (Princeton: Princeton University, October 1954), 6.

After a couple of decades of GATT-centered agreements that mainly focused on further tariff reduction, America once again took up the cause of establishing a more extensive set of global trade rules. Its principal motive was to address the fact that as global tariffs fell, there was a growing need to negotiate to remove the restrictive, non-tariff barriers wielded by America's trading partners to continue protecting their markets. Washington's urgency accelerated with a seemingly sudden unstoppable rise in imports and America's trade deficit after Nixon floated the dollar in 1971. New and growing large imbalances in both foreign access and U.S. trade flows raised important industrial competitiveness and national financial concerns. These also gave rise to potent political pressures, including the sudden emergence of unified opposition to freer trade from America's labor unions.

Most members of both political parties strongly supported the need for new trade rules to make freer global trade fairer for America. Exactly how best to do it and whether it could effectively be done was another question. Franklin Roosevelt put his finger on the true nature of the problem of writing detailed rules to combat these measures when he once reportedly remarked, "Reducing a nontariff barrier is like dynamiting fog."[26] Decades later, after some of organized labor's long-sought labor rights were finally written into the rules of trade agreements, an AFL-CIO representative spotted the same challenge: "On labor in particular, [the TPP] continues to put forth some vague standards, which question whether or not they could be enforced. . . ."[27] Despite the challenges, America proceeded to demand and negotiate new trade rules, both directly with individual trading partners as well as together among all GATT members.

To take on individual countries, Congress gave the executive branch in 1974 the potent tool of Section 301 authority, which, as discussed earlier, allowed the use of tariff and other trade threats to force them to remove such barriers. Japan was a particular focus of concern at that time: between 1970 and 2000, America concluded approximately one hundred separate agreements and other packages of commitments with Japan alone. Some of these covered removing various barriers in individual product sectors, e.g., pollock or supercomputers, while others sought to dismantle systemic policies that excluded imports, or

---

26   Paul Lewis, "The Trade Bill: Its Real Impact," *New York Times*, December 22, 1974.
27   Celeste Drake, quoted in Kristi Ellis, "Labor, Environmental Groups Say TPP Flawed," *Women's Wear Daily*, November 10, 2015.

to tamp down on Japan's export surges. America used the tool with a broad range of other countries from the 1970s into the 1990s to seek similar agreements.

America also pursued new trade rules in the GATT to reduce non-tariff barriers abroad and strengthen its right to invoke trade defense measures with temporary tariff hikes on unfairly cheap or subsidized imports. The 1973 launch of the GATT's Tokyo Round was the first opportunity to get started, ending in a package deal in 1979. Beyond another round of tariff reductions, the outcomes included a new rules agreement to prevent the arbitrary use of national technical and industrial standards in government regulations to exclude imports, new limits on the use of import licenses to discriminate against foreign goods, and beefed-up rights to invoke trade defense measures against unfair imports. It was a slow but successful start.

America pushed for more trade rules during the next GATT round, which got underway in the mid-1980s and finally concluded almost a decade later. These Uruguay Round agreements included new commitments to protect intellectual property and added requirements that members use only science-based reasons to add restrictions to limit imports of plant and animal products. They added further to the rules that allowed countries to respond to unfairly dumped or subsidized imports. In other areas, America failed to make any progress; for example, quick and broad opposition from other GATT members killed off its attempt to begin negotiations on labor rights rules. America proceeded to develop an even more ambitious trade rules agenda for the next WTO round. Once that effort—the Doha Round— eventually collapsed and failed, some of these rules efforts were broken off and pursued as separate stand-alone WTO negotiations covered in the previous chapter.

These efforts in the GATT and the WTO were slow and difficult, always ending in less-than-hoped outcomes for America after compromises were made among scores of countries with different priorities and economic and legal systems. With careful drafting, negotiation, and regular executive-congressional consultations, U.S. negotiators were broadly successful in crafting proposals and negotiating outcomes that avoided Congress's initial concern of having to change U.S. laws and practices to comply. Over time, stakeholders, Congress, and successive administrations increasingly expected that America's laws, regulations, and norms would be projected into, and not threatened by, new trade rules. America's leadership of the international trading system and its insistence on these rules afforded it the opportunity to set and drive these priorities.

Expectations that new rules would make trade fairer for America became inseparable from the task of seeking domestic support for new tariff-liberalizing agreements. Stepped-up monitoring and enforcement of these rules were the other critical pieces to maintaining domestic support for these agreements. These three goals—opening new markets, identifying and removing barriers and unfair practices, and rigorously enforcing trade rules—formed the core objectives of America's external trade policy, as demanded by the legislative branch and pursued by the executive branch. Along with engaging domestic stakeholders to consult on these objectives, they also constituted the four criteria by which America's trade negotiators' annual workplace performance was assessed.

Free trade agreement negotiations gave America the opportunity to push for trade rules on a scale far beyond what was possible with the WTO's 160-plus members. Starting with the fundamental GATT and WTO rules and principles as a base, further obligations in the free trade agreements were layered on in ways that yielded much greater specificity and coverage; new rules were also created whereas none had been possible to add in the WTO. Congress and stakeholders came to expect more "WTO-plus" rules with each new free trade agreement. When the TPP negotiations were launched, the Obama administration branded it the new "gold standard" for trade—a phrase dropped into a speech by Secretary of State Hillary Clinton and then famously turned against her in her campaign for the White House after the TPP was concluded.[28]

Once these WTO-plus rules were added to a free trade agreement, Congress and stakeholders expected that each successive agreement would further add to or improve on many of them. Failure to convince a trading partner to include all rules from prior U.S. agreements became a benchmark against which to criticize the outcome—regardless of whether all were needed or even relevant with each new agreement partner. As newer rules were added to each successive agreement, and then more added on top, they cumulatively came to define a uniquely American brand of rules-based trade.

Expectations soared in Congress and among U.S. stakeholders that America's agreement partners would accept rules that aligned with America's laws and norms and change their own to comply. In exchange

---

28   Ian Culgren, "Yes, Clinton Did Call TPP the 'Gold Standard'," Politico, October 9, 2016.

for the opportunity to secure tariff-free trade with the world's largest market, in Washington's view, it was only reasonable to expect its agreement partners to accept trade rules sufficiently equivalent to the level of access, legal protections, transparency, and nondiscriminatory treatment that their firms and exporters enjoyed in America. A similar expectation emerged, especially from the Left, that these same partners would also commit to similar levels of worker and labor rights and environmental protection standards as additional trade rules, which, among other justifications, were aimed at reducing labor and production cost advantages that otherwise gave their exports to America a competitive edge.

When providing its authority to the executive branch to negotiate agreements with new trade rules, Congress asserted its constitutionally derived oversight over foreign commerce to guide how they should be written. Lacking the capacity to negotiate with foreign governments, which under the constitution falls under the executive branch's power to conduct foreign relations, Congress began in the late 1800s to grant periodic, limited authority to the executive branch to negotiate tariff agreements with select trading partners. As Congress considered in the early 1970s how to expand this authority to allow the executive branch to also negotiate a suite of new trade rules, it recognized that, depending on how they were drafted, these rules could require Congress to amend U.S. law for America to comply with them.[29] Congress addressed this concern in its 1974 Trade Act by including extensive requirements for the executive branch to consult and seek guidance as it conducted these negotiations. Among these were regular consultations with congressional members on negotiating texts and objectives and a new system for engaging with other domestic stakeholders to seek advice on negotiating goals and technical matters. The Act also required the executive branch to seek further advice from the public, the private sector, and other nongovernmental organizations, and from a wider array of federal agencies and state governments before and during negotiations both

---

29 Congress was also motivated after the Johnson administration negotiated outcomes in the GATT Kennedy Round negotiations that would require changes to U.S. customs and anti-dumping laws. To curtail this in the future, beyond new consultation requirements, Congress also required the use of an accompanying implementing law for each new agreement that spelled out exactly what Congress was prepared to change and what it would not be doing to meet the obligations in the agreement. For a short but clear overview of this negotiating authority and its evolution, see Ian F. Fergusson, *Trade Promotion Authority (TPA) and the Role of Congress in Trade Policy*, Congressional Research Service, RL33743, July 2, 2015.

to help inform negotiators of optimal outcomes and to better ensure consistency between the negotiated outcomes and existing U.S. federal and state law, regulations, and practice.

Congress included in the 1974 Act a list of its objectives, expectations, and limitations for trade negotiations, which it further expanded each time the executive branch was given a new temporary delegation of negotiation authority. The 2015 version of Congress's guidance, which it did not pass until over five years after the TPP talks had kicked off, included over 13 pages of legislative text outlining "Trade Negotiating Objectives." Setting these objectives for free trade agreements required Congress first to negotiate and agree with itself, which often proved an extraordinarily arduous process, before passing to the executive branch the challenge of convincing its free trade agreement partners to agree to them as trade obligations.

The 1974 Act also added other requirements for executive branch consultations and reporting, congressional oversight, public engagement, pre- and post-negotiating procedures, deadlines, and procedures for the passage and implementation of agreements. In return, once submitted, Congress's consideration of the final agreement was to be shielded from further amendments and given a straight up-or-down vote. This was intended to provide some certainty to the negotiations so that compromises made between America and its negotiating partners to reach a final deal, at least in theory, would not be reopened to further negotiation after the agreement was submitted to Congress for approval. As it happened, and regardless of the difficulties of reopening finished deals with foreign countries, Congress often later demanded these changes anyway as a precondition to taking a no-amendment vote to approve them.

Had these objectives and requirements spelled out by Congress truly reflected what was necessary and sufficient for it to approve the executive branch's trade agreements, it would have been a more worthwhile exercise. By the 2000s, the reality was that Congress itself disagreed on a number of issues that either were not part of its formal guidance to the executive branch or were drafted with intentionally vague language to paper over legislative compromises. Whether final negotiated outcomes were ultimately in alignment with the expectations of Congress came to depend entirely on which party was holding power in which chamber at the time an agreement was concluded and ready for debate. It also depended on the individual views of the trade committee members and chairs, on lobbying and publicity efforts by various stakeholder groups to shift narratives, and on the prevailing political winds of the day. For the TPP, meeting the priorities and objectives expressed by members in 2010, or even those previously incorporated and approved in past agreements, seemed to make little difference in gaining sufficient congressional support by the time the negotiations were complete in 2015. Stakeholders and congressional members pocketed the outcomes they expected as they were accomplished, only then to expect even more in many cases before supporting passage of the deal.

Given the scores of federal agencies, congressional committee staffers and members, state governments, industry and civil society stakeholders, and others involved in the consultation process, along with the parade of shifting expectations over time among them, no single entity or group could ever genuinely or unilaterally write America's rules for trade as they wished. This was Congress's intention when it established in 1974, and then added to later, this extensive new structure of requirements and input. However, each agreement had to ultimately meet core administration priorities and enough of the competing priorities in Congress to secure the majority needed for final passage.

As trade rules became more important, expectations from stakeholder groups for engagement with executive branch negotiators often exceeded what Congress required, spurring further efforts beyond these requirements for even broader outreach and consultation. During the TPP negotiations, the executive branch added on periodic public negotiation updates and reports, explanations of controversial issues under negotiation, "stakeholder day" outreach efforts at negotiating rounds, and the creation of additional official trade policy advisory bodies, including one exclusively for labor union representatives. As public awareness spread of the extensive scope of trade rules under negotiation in the TPP, expectations for even more expansive consultation and transparency efforts continued to multiply.

Some congressional members and nongovernment stakeholders took these expectations to a new level by demanding that the confidential TPP negotiation texts, whether America's proposals or the positions of all negotiating parties, be made public as the negotiations progressed. If these demands were met in full, the practical effect would have been to make the whole negotiating process unsustainable. No foreign negotiating counterpart would accept their detailed positions being made public by another government, but each certainly would have welcomed America undermining its negotiating leverage by publishing its official proposals in order to watch the ensuing domestic debate force U.S. negotiators to reveal and discuss in public their tactics and their priorities within them. The longer the TPP negotiations dragged out, the louder and more extreme such demands became, fanned further at times by incorrect or misleading allegations from Washington advocacy groups and sometimes members of Congress. They also reflected how branding the TPP as a new model for trade further raised the stakes among those who were alarmed that their causes and priorities were at risk on the negotiating table.

Once a deal was reached among the twelve countries, many specific criticisms in America of the outcomes reflected a new concern opposite to that of the early 1970s. Then, Congress feared that negotiating new rules to discipline foreign non-tariff practices might also necessitate America to change its laws and approaches. By the mid-2010s, with so many America-centered trade rules in its agreements and even more added to the TPP, the concern emerged among some critics that passage of the deal would make it impossible to later make changes to them in America. A similar tension arose in another direction. Where TPP rule outcomes were criticized as insufficient, they became a litmus test for critics to claim that the administration either had failed to force its trading partners to accept them or was insufficiently committed to America's own standards to push for them. Either way, the administration's goal of a bigger and better new "model" for trade raised the stakes for what was included or omitted from the TPP—once added in or left out, it would set the terms both for free trade with America's agreement partners and for America itself for decades to come.

The following brings into focus several specific examples of how these shifting perspectives, political alignments, and concerns ultimately undermined the support for continuing to build out America's own rules-based model through the TPP. In all cases, the objectives and assumptions used to advance Washington's bipartisan mainstream on trade came unwound amid the new politics of trade in America, whether because the agreement's outcomes with its trading partners fell short of meeting the expectations of the Left or the Right in some way or because the rules that were included stirred their own opposition amid rising domestic policy disagreements over America's own policies or practices.

Automobile Content Rules

As raised above, negotiated outcomes with Japan to set the content rules for automobiles eligible to benefit from TPP-region tariff preferences emerged as a top target for TPP critics in America on both the Right and the Left. The criticism was effectively wielded in different ways, from having opened the door for China to benefit from the deal to encouraging and perpetuating globalization at the expense of prioritizing auto and auto parts jobs in American communities. It was quickly seized upon by candidate Trump, who had already bashed the agreement for other reasons, and it later became his administration's most often-used example to insist that the TPP model was such a terrible deal for America that withdrawal was justified.

Negotiations to set the automotive content rules were shaped by the strong views of America's unions and their legislative supporters, the interests of the major automobile and auto parts producers in America, and the positions of other TPP countries and their own stakeholder interests. They also were guided by the axiom that a very high percentage content rule, or one that is too strict in its methodology, would make sourcing too difficult or costly for most finished auto exports to qualify for a free trade agreement's tariff breaks. In contrast, a content rule with a percentage that is too low or too lax would fail to ensure that the gains from new trade under a free trade agreement accrue overwhelmingly to the member countries themselves. These stakeholders all held competing views over what this appropriate balance should be.

America's auto production supply chains were shaped from the mid-1990s by the product content rules in NAFTA, which required a higher degree of integrated production in North America to qualify for tariff-free trade than most free trade agreements require. NAFTA's high North American content requirements also meant that America's automakers were well accustomed and able to source from existing parts suppliers in Canada and Mexico, as well as in America, to meet the rule. With Mexico and Canada also in the TPP, a NAFTA-equivalent content rule would require little or no supply chain changes by North American automakers to export their finished autos tariff-free under the TPP.

By contrast, Japan's automakers and their suppliers from the late 1990s moved more parts production to scattered countries in Asia, including several outside the TPP region such as China and Thailand. This facilitated their cost competitiveness by sourcing cheaper components abroad while keeping much of the high-end parts production and final assembly in Japan. Compared to North America–based automakers, some based in Japan would need to make new supply chain investments and adjustments to comply with higher TPP content requirements by moving more parts sourcing and production to the TPP region.

America's labor unions valued these NAFTA rules yet also insisted they should be further tightened in the TPP to encourage even more production and jobs in America. Among different methodologies, the most widely used NAFTA auto content rule was 62.5 percent, meaning that nearly two-thirds of the value of an automobile had to be sourced in North America before it could be exported tariff-free among the three NAFTA countries. Another methodology, also allowed under NAFTA, used a lower percentage rule based on different assumptions that focused more on an automobile's actual components and manufactured content to the exclusion of other associated costs such as shipping and marketing. These two methodologies were mostly equivalent in their requirements. However, the way the rules were written in the early 1990s meant that the 62.5 percent requirement, in fact, more closely approximated a 55 percent rule since automakers were given a degree of latitude to declare without proof that some content was coming from the NAFTA region.

Tightening some of the flexibilities in NAFTA and pushing for a higher percentage for the TPP was a top union and Democratic Party priority for the negotiations. The three main American auto and auto parts unions—the steelworkers, autoworkers, and machinists—took the position in 2013 that the TPP auto content rule should begin at the NAFTA rate of 62.5 percent (with some loopholes also plugged), increasing to 68.5 percent after four years, and then reaching the final rate of 75 percent four years after that.[30] By contrast, in nearly all cases, Japan's trade agreements included a flexible 40 percent content rule, using the primary methodology in NAFTA, and 30 percent using the other methodology. Japan insisted on the same 40/30 percent levels in the TPP to ensure its automakers could continue to fully benefit from the agreement as they had under most of its other trade agreements.[31]

Among the TPP members, several countries—Japan, America, Canada, Mexico, and Malaysia—had substantial final auto production and assembly plants within their borders, and thus, all had the most direct interest in these rules. They, along with Vietnam, also had significant

30   International Association of Machinists and Aerospace Workers, "IAM, USW and UAW Join to Ensure Fair Trade in TPP," press release, October 31, 2013; and United Steelworkers, United Auto Workers, and International Association of Machinists, "Proposed Trans-Pacific Partnership Rule of Origin Provisions for Assembled Automobiles and Light Trucks and Transitional Mechanism for Certain 'Green' and Fuel-Efficient Automotive Components," October 31, 2013.

31   Steven Chase, "Canada, Mexico Drawn into Deal-Breaking Auto Talks in Trans-Pacific Negotiations," *Globe and Mail*, August 5, 2015.

auto parts production.[32] America signaled to Japan and others for many months that it expected a high percentage content rule. It also shared the target numbers it expected to officially present once the broader negotiations had finally advanced in other areas.

After America made its proposal official, however, Japan claimed to be shocked by the position. Japan engaged America directly to lodge protests as their talks moved to a stove-piped channel between their senior negotiators. With Japan taking a hard-line position, little progress was made for several weeks. Japan further elevated the topic to a "crisis" issue, insisting that it would not agree to more stringent content rules because doing so would make it impossible for some of its key industrial exports—autos—to qualify for tariff-free export treatment and thus benefit meaningfully from the deal.

Rather than bring the discussion into the larger room, where the interests and positions of Canada, Mexico, and potentially Malaysia were in closer alignment with America's position, the American side instead worked through its channel with Japan into the spring of 2015. With Japan remaining inflexible, America developed and proposed novel approaches to try and first bridge the gap directly—a process that ultimately turned into an exercise in America negotiating with itself. The U.S. side watered down its own proposals until they reached a level that Tokyo could live with. Then, as the price for accepting them, Japan leveraged something more from America for its automakers—a faster timeline for eliminating U.S. tariffs on Japanese autos. To gain U.S. support for its bid in 2013 to join the ongoing TPP negotiations, Japan had previously acquiesced to America's insistence on only eliminating its tariffs on Japanese auto imports in accordance with the longest tariff elimination period of any other product agreed under the TPP.[33] When the final TPP deal came together in 2015, the longest agreed period among the tens of thousands of tariff commitments in the TPP was 30 years for a dozen or so types of confectionery food products. Instead of automatically incorporating a corresponding 30-year tariff elimination period for Japanese autos, per their initial agreement, America gave Japan more favorable terms: its 2.5 percent tariff on Japanese cars was

---

32 Australia also had one remaining auto plant, but which in 2013 was slated to close within a few years. "GM Scraps Historic Holden Car Brand in Australia," BBC, February 17, 2020.
33 With this agreement, which also covered other issues, America expressed its support for Japan's candidacy for the TPP. See "U.S.-Japan Bilateral Negotiations on Motor Vehicle Trade and Non-Tariff Measures," USTR, Washington, DC, April 2013.

instead scheduled to begin to fall in the fifteenth year of the agreement and reach zero in year 25.

The auto content percentage rule that Japan accepted in return bumped the final percentages up to 55/45 percent for each methodology, or 15 percent higher than its own initial 40/30 percent proposals. These higher percentages, however, provided a much more flexible means of meeting these higher thresholds.[34] Japan then left it to America to spend its negotiating capital to bring other TPP members on board to agree with the flexible methodology and the 55/45 percentages.[35]

A weak case could be made that these content rules approximated the NAFTA rules after considering the full range of other factors unique to each agreement and approach. Because of their NAFTA-oriented production networks, American automakers would still easily meet these rules to export tariff-free to TPP markets in Asia. For TPP critics in America, they weakened the NAFTA content rule requirements aimed at keeping auto jobs in North America and did nothing to force automakers to boost those content levels over time instead of sourcing parts from China or elsewhere.

Mexico and Canada saw it the same way. It was late in the talks, as TPP negotiators were meeting in mid-2015 to finish the agreement, that the private U.S.-Japan deal on auto content rules was finally revealed to their officials. The pushback was immediate and strong. In addition to the shock and resistance from the last-moment disclosure, Mexican and Canadian negotiators opposed it for falling substantially short of NAFTA's content standards.[36] Of particular concern were the looser content rules agreed for all auto parts, set at 30 percent and well below the NAFTA standard. They also opposed America's idea of a flexible mechanism to enable Japanese and other TPP region automakers to more loosely tack on another 15 points to their content calculations for finished autos. The ensuing blow-up became a principal reason the TPP negotiations failed to close in July 2015.[37]

Mexican and Canadian auto and auto parts industry representatives made their own concern and anger public, asserting that the private

34   "AFL-CIO Warns TPP Could Have Weakest Auto ROO Ever; Blasts Loopholes," World Trade Online, August 27, 2015.
35   Chase, "Canada, Mexico Drawn into Deal-Breaking Auto Talks."
36   Chase, "Canada, Mexico Drawn into Deal-Breaking Auto Talks."
37   See, e.g., "TPP Ministerial Ends Without Deal as Talks Rupture Over Autos," World Trade Online, August 1, 2015.

U.S.-Japan deal, if followed, would cost their workers many jobs and harm their manufacturing from new auto parts production moving to non-TPP countries like China and Thailand. Instead, they called on their governments to insist on NAFTA-level content rules for vehicles and parts.[38]

Key American labor union leaders exploded with greater outrage over the U.S. compromise with Japan. Having first learned about it from the angry public statements made by the Mexican and Canadian negotiators, the president of the AFL-CIO, who was completely blindsided, fired off a letter to the administration to make clear these and other points.

... Canadian and Mexican negotiators are holding out for a ROO [rule of origin, or content rule] no less than 50 percent, while our own government has reportedly struck a deal with the Japanese government for a level of 45 percent for automobiles and 30 percent for auto parts. ... If this report is accurate, I want to convey to you my deep disappointment and anger that the U.S. government has so little regard for American jobs and the health of our manufacturing sector.[39]

The fact that even Mexico's industry expected to lose auto jobs to low-wage countries in Asia under the deal was particularly politically damaging to the administration's case for the TPP. Democratic senators Brown and Stabenow, along with Senator Portman, a Republican who had served as President Bush's trade ambassador, went on the record to remind the administration of their expectations for keeping and growing auto jobs in America. They insisted on auto content rules that at least met NAFTA standards with their loopholes filled, ensuring the tariff-staging-formula commitment with Japan was met in full for both auto and truck tariffs, securing enforceable rules to prevent currency manipulation, and establishing extensive new rules to remove top

---

38   Joanna Zuckerman Bernstein, Luis Rojas Mena, and Dave Graham, "Mexico Carmakers Seek 50 Percent Regional Content in Trade Deal," Reuters, August 17, 2015. Also, see the letter from Flavio Volpe, president of the Automotive Parts Manufactures Association (Canada), and Oscar Albin, executive president of the Industria Nacional de Autopartes (Mexico), to Canadian Minister for International Trade Edward Fast and Mexican Minister of Economy Ildefonso Guajardo Villareal, August 20, 2015, available at "Canadian, Mexican Industries Seek TPP Rule of Origin for Auto Parts of 50 Percent Using Net Cost Method," World Trade Online, August 24, 2015.

39   Letter from AFL-CIO President Richard Trumka to U.S. Trade Representative Michael Froman, August 21, 2015; see "AFL-CIO Pushes Froman for Strong TPP ROO for Autos; Blasts Lack of Transparency, Supporting Data," World Trade Online, August 25, 2015.

non-tariff barriers to American auto exports to Japan.⁴⁰ The final TPP outcomes still fell short of their demands.

After several more weeks of four-way negotiations, a final agreement on the auto content rules for the TPP was reached in time for the handshake deal among TPP trade ministers in early October 2015. The result kept the final 55/45 percentage rules, according to each methodology, but tightened up the content requirements for auto parts and made the flexible terms less so for the finished automobile content thresholds. The 45 percent content rule outcome, in turn, became the basis for the widely used, and perhaps the most devastating, criticism of the TPP: that China had been effectively written into the deal, gifted with the potential to produce more than half of any car that qualified for the TPP's tariff-free treatment. Opponents of the deal on the New Right and the progressive Left matched the labor unions in criticizing the outcome as so egregiously harmful that it alone was sufficient grounds to oppose and block the entire deal from congressional approval.

Currency
In its negotiating objectives for the TPP, Congress, for the first time, directed the executive branch to include rules to discipline currency manipulation

in order to prevent effective balance of payments adjustment or to gain an unfair competitive advantage over other parties to the agreement, such as through cooperative mechanisms, enforceable rules, reporting, monitoring, transparency, or other means, as appropriate.⁴¹

Among TPP countries, Japan, Vietnam, Malaysia, and Singapore had records of intervening in markets to devalue their currencies, a policy used at times to help tilt the competitive trade balance in their favor by making their exports cheaper abroad and foreign imports more expensive at home. When these practices were called into question, financial officials routinely marked their turf by insisting that any discussion of these issues take place strictly among themselves and were

40   Letter from Senators Sherrod Brown, Rob Portman, and Debbie Stabenow, to U.S. Trade Representative Michael Froman, September 10, 2015; see "Brown, Portman, and Stabenow: Trans-Pacific Partnership Must Support, Boost U.S. Auto Manufacturing," Sherrod Brown, U.S. Senator for Ohio, press release, September 10, 2015.

41   Bipartisan Congressional Trade Priorities and Accountability Act of 2015, 19 USC 4201, Section 102.b.(11).

not to become a matter for trade officials and their meetings. Many in Congress viewed that approach as having failed to hold America's trading partners accountable over many decades, giving rise to a new consensus among some Democrats and Republicans that new trade rules for currency practices were long overdue for trade agreements. They also expected that including currency rules in the TPP would serve another purpose—to send a clear message to China and others that America's new rules-based standard for trade would take a stand against unfair currency manipulation.

While not unsympathetic to the problem, the Obama administration remained cautious about seeking a solution. Its top concern was that adding detailed, binding trade rules could also harmfully curtail potential future policy options to ensure America's financial stability. It often pointed to the experience of America's massive bailout spending in the wake of the 2007–08 financial crisis to rescue its financial institutions, the auto industry, and others from financial ruin as an example where concerns about staying within the limits of new trade rules may have limited a U.S. administration's freedom to act without concern of triggering claims from its trade agreement partners. It also recognized the slim prospect of convincing all the TPP countries to agree to add currency obligations to a trade agreement for the first time. Obama's treasury secretary argued, "If a trade agreement is required to come back with a currency discipline that is enforceable through trade mechanisms, I don't think there is another country in the world that would agree to that. . . . It's a poison pill in terms of getting agreement on TPP."[42]

Those advocating for new trade rules on currency pointed to existing IMF rules, to which America and other TPP members had already subscribed, that already made important differentiations among types of currency market intervention by governments. Specifically, these rules defined and discouraged interventions intended to change the terms of trade, as opposed to financial policies aimed at legitimate financial policy needs to secure financial system stability and employment. Proposals using the IMF criteria as a basis for trade rules that specified acceptable and unacceptable currency actions were floated in public by Democrats

---

42   Jack Lew, Secretary of the Treasury, quoted in William Mauldin, "White House Threatens to Veto Trade Bill over Currency Measure," *Wall Street Journal*, May 19, 2015.

in Congress and the Big Three American automakers as a solution, along with proposals for new trade sanctions to enforce adherence to them.[43]

Large, non-partisan U.S. think tanks such as the Peterson Institute of International Economics also supported the objective of adding currency rules to trade agreements, finding that currency manipulation had inflicted enormous harm to jobs and other American interests.[44] One widely used estimate put the annual job losses attributable to currency manipulation by foreign governments at anywhere between one and five million as of around 2010.[45] Other commentators weighed in on the advisability of including currency provisions in the TPP with opposing or more cautious views.[46]

Many Republicans also agreed on the need for new rules, but a significant number remained cautious over whether enforceable sanctions were an appropriate remedy for violations.[47] The issue of how far to go split straight across party lines, with 34 Democrats, 12 Republicans, and two independents lining up in favor of a tougher approach that included trade sanctions, but falling just short of the majority in the Senate needed to include the proposal in the final 2015 bill that set objectives and authorized the negotiations.

For a long time, Congress was mostly kept out of the loop on the options the Obama administration was weighing internally to propose in the TPP. Other TPP countries were well aware that the administration

---

43 See, e.g., Robert E. Scott, *Trans-Pacific Partnership Agreement: Currency Manipulation, Trade, Wages, and Job Loss*, Economic Policy Institute, January 13, 2016; and Vicki Needham, "Currency Manipulation Plan Gets Key Endorsement," The Hill, November 10, 2015.

44 C. Fred Bergsten and Joseph Gagnon, *Currency Manipulation, the US Economy, and the Global Economic Order*, PB 12–25 (Washington, DC: Peterson Institute for International Economics, December 2012). Also, C. Fred Bergsten, *Addressing Currency Manipulation through Trade Agreements*, PB 14–2, (Washington, DC: Peterson Institute for International Economics, January 2014).

45 Bergsten and Gagnon, *Currency Manipulation*.

46 See, e.g., Washington Post Editorial Board, "Adding 'Currency Manipulation' Rules to a Trade Bill Is Too Costly," *Washington Post*, February 18, 2015; and Mireya Solis, "The Answer Is Still NO on Currency Manipulation Clause," Brookings Institution, commentary, January 15, 2014.

47 Senate Majority Leader McConnell asserted that most of the Republicans in the Senate opposed enforceability as a viable option. See Mauldin, "White House Threatens to Veto Trade Bill." On the various views in the Congress, see, e.g., "Hatch: Responsible Currency Amendment Will Strengthen TPA Bill without Threatening Trade Deals," United States Senate Committee on Finance, press release, May 20, 2015; and Manu Raju, "Portman Takes Friendly Fire from GOP," Politico, May 18, 2015.

would almost certainly propose something. In expectation of that day and to draw their own red lines, officials from some TPP countries made remarks in the media insisting they would never accept including currency obligations in the final TPP agreement itself.[48] The administration waited until the closing months of negotiations to finally float its proposed approach with them, which was in the form of a non-legally binding side letter to be concluded separately from the main trade agreement.

Leaving the issue exclusively to the Treasury Department to handle with its financial policy counterparts, the side letter proposal included some basic principles and voluntary commitments, such as a pledge to not engage in competitive currency devaluation. Arguably, the only meaningful provisions were transparency and other reporting commitments by which countries would share internal data that could reveal hidden government interventions in currency markets. Some observers welcomed the commitments as a meaningful improvement.[49] Others derided the side letter as falling far short of the expectations many in Congress held for enforceable obligations. The debate reflected a genuine difference in views, both within Congress and with the administration, of what was possible and best for the country.

Foreign developments did not add credibility to the administration's attempt to sell its softer approach to currency commitments. In mid-2015, as the TPP was nearing completion, China intervened in currency markets, reminding the world that it would continue to play by its own rules. This led to renewed calls in Congress for the administration to take a strong stand in the TPP negotiations as a matter of principle and as an example to currency manipulators of the shifting tide toward adding currency disciplines to trade rules.[50] In August 2015, Vietnam, a TPP member, also devalued its currency by 1 percent just as the negotiations were weeks away from conclusion, a gesture received in Washington as a sign that it, too, appeared ready to continue to do as it wished.[51]

---

48 On these views, see United States Senate Committee on Finance, "Hatch: Responsible Currency Amendment."

49 Fred C. Bergsten and Jeffrey J. Schott, "TPP and Exchange Rates," in *Trans-Pacific Partnership: An Assessment*, ed. Cathleen Cimino-Issacs and Jeffrey J. Schott (Washington, DC: Peterson Institute for International Economics, 2016).

50 "Trumka Calls for Clinton to Take Position on TPP, but Withholds Own Stance," World Trade Online, September 10, 2015. See also the letter from Brown, Portman, and Stabenow to Froman.

51 "Vietnam Devalues Currency by 1 Percent Relative to USD, Drawing Further Ire of TPP Critics," World Trade Online, August 21, 2015.

Once the final October TPP handshake agreements were published in text form in November, Japan's finance minister, Taro Aso, provided more fuel for critics in America by making clear that the letter would not tie Japan's hands, either. "There won't be any change," he asserted, to Japan's yen policies.[52] After Trump withdrew from the TPP, citing as top reasons its weak outcomes on currency and auto content rules, which were both resolved in Japan's favor, Aso subsequently, and with no seeming understanding of the irony of doing so, committed to help the new U.S. president and his administration better "understand" the economic benefits of rejoining it.[53]

In America, the Obama administration's decision not to press for stronger currency rules gave opponents more ammunition to criticize it for failing to deliver the high-standard agreement promised. Had it pushed TPP members to agree to hard obligations on currency, it also may have proven a deal-breaker issue for America with its negotiating partners. As it was, the administration instead chose a substantially softer approach that added some tools but preserved for U.S. financial officials the flexibility they insisted on maintaining to respond to future financial contingencies. That decision proved instead to be a deal-breaker in the eyes of many in America, especially among its labor unions and political figures on the Left and the New Right, which added it to their list of reasons to oppose the TPP as a bad deal for America.

Worker and Labor Rights
Further opposition from some Americans to the TPP centered on the criticism that its agreed rules supporting worker and labor rights were inadequate, both to protect workers in TPP countries and to counter low labor standards in some countries that enabled businesses to exploit the cost advantages of producing there and exporting back to America more cheaply. Labor unions and their allies in Congress had initially mobilized in the early 1990s to press their demands for new labor rights protections in NAFTA. Two decades later, the issue reappeared prominently over the effort to pass the Bush administration's free trade agreements with South Korea, Panama, Colombia, and Peru through a Democratic-controlled Congress. To overcome broad opposition in the

---

52   "TPP Deal Won't Have Binding Power on Japan's Forex Policy—Finance Minister Aso," Reuters, November 5, 2015.
53   "Japan's Aso Says Will Seek U.S. Understanding of TPP's Benefits," Reuters, January 23, 2017.

party, key trade committee Democrats met with Republican colleagues to work out a compromise in 2007. That compromise, which came to be known as the May 10th Agreement, included a set of additional commitments on labor and environment; congressional Democrats, in turn, made assurances that, if these commitments were accepted by each country and added to the agreement, Congress would move to vote to approve the free trade agreements.

Among the labor commitments in the May 10th Agreement were obligations to adopt and maintain laws supporting the freedom of association and the right of collective bargaining, to prohibit and eliminate exploitative labor practices such as child and forced labor, and to meet other core labor standards identified by the International Labour Organization (ILO). These commitments were to be made binding and subject to trade sanctions under the agreement, as with most other trade rules, if they were violated.

The obligations were also carefully drawn, as with other trade rules, to avoid creating obligations that America could not itself meet. To this day, for example, America has not ratified the majority of the ILO's many conventions for a range of reasons, although it asserts that it meets the ILO obligations through other domestic laws and practices. One 2007 assessment found that substantial changes to American federal and state law, in fact, would be necessary to ratify five of the eight core ILO labor conventions, including the right to organize and bargain collectively.[54] Careful wording was therefore developed for America's trade agreements that required countries to "adopt, maintain, and enforce" five of the labor standards,[55] as opposed to needing to ratify and enforce the relevant ILO conventions. The five included in Congress's May 10th Agreement were, in abbreviated form, the freedom of association, the right to collective bargaining, the elimination of forced labor, the abolishment of child labor, and the elimination of discrimination in employment.[56]

---

54   The assessment was conducted by a presidential committee in 2007. See Cathleen D. Cimino-Isaacs, *Worker Rights Provisions and U.S. Trade Policy*, Congressional Research Service, R46842, July 16, 2021, 11–12.

55   Labor standards as stated in International Labour Organization, "ILO 1998 Declaration on Fundamental Principles and Rights at Work and Its Follow-up, 2022," https://www .ilo.org/resource/conference-paper/ilo-1998-declaration-fundamental-principles-and-rights -work-and-its-follow.

56   The "May 10th Agreement," titled "Peru & Panama FTA Changes," is an attachment in a letter to United States Trade Representative Susan C. Schwab from the Chairman of the

The labor obligations in the TPP met the conditions of the May 10th Agreement, which were incorporated into Congress's official trade agreement negotiating objectives for the executive branch to follow for the TPP. Congressional Democrats, however, asserted that the state of labor rights standards in Mexico, Vietnam, Brunei, and Malaysia necessitated numerous additional rules and obligations for the TPP. These included, for example, explicitly extending the protections to include migrant and other foreign workers in TPP countries. Another was to require all TPP members to fully comply with all labor obligations before America brought the TPP into effect. An additional demand was for more robust and direct enforcement mechanisms for labor rules to prevent backsliding.[57]

The administration attempted to accommodate many of these extra demands, including by developing supplementary labor consistency plans with Malaysia, Brunei, and Vietnam. These written and agreed plans helped clarify in greater detail how each country would implement many of the obligations in the TPP labor chapter. The Vietnam plan was more extensive than the others, including steps the government would take to allow independent labor unions to emerge for the first time.[58] While the obligation was deemed a significant concession by Vietnam and a sign of historic progress by some, unions and others still criticized the outcome as outrageously insufficient, particularly due to its allowance for Vietnam of a five-year transition period to comply with the individual obligation to allow independent labor unions to form federations.

Some Republicans, on the other side, criticized the labor plan with Vietnam as exceeding the agreed terms of their May 10th Agreement with Democrats by specifying these additional, detailed commitments that Vietnam would need to take to achieve compliance with its TPP

Committee on Ways and Means and the Chairman of the Subcommittee on Trade, U.S. House of Representatives, May 10, 2007.

57 These concerns and expectations are expressed in greater detail in a May 2015 letter from 14 Democratic senators to the U.S. Trade Representative and the Labor Secretary. See "Sens. Brown, Cardin, Schumer, Stabenow, Casey, Franken, Markey, Baldwin, Peters, Udall, Blumenthal, Schatz, Merkley, and Warren Call for Strong Labor Standards in Trans-Pacific Partnership and Implementation of Standards in TPP Countries," Sherrod Brown, U. S. Senator for Ohio, press release, May 11, 2015.

58 For a broad overview of the TPP labor chapter outcomes in comparison with other U.S. free trade agreements, see, e.g., Cathleen Cimino-Isaacs, "Labor Standards in the TPP," in *Trans-Pacific Partnership: An Assessment*, ed. Cathleen Cimino-Issacs and Jeffrey J. Schott (Washington, DC: Peterson Institute for International Economics, 2016).

labor obligations. The criticism mirrored a familiar disagreement with Democrats in the domestic U.S. context, with Republicans insisting that individual U.S. state governments be left to decide their own approaches and Democrats pushing for more prescriptive and union-friendly nationwide standards. In this case, the Obama administration aligned with the positions of the unions and Democrats by pressing for these additional commitments from Vietnam and others, igniting the ire of some congressional Republicans.

Labor unions also roundly criticized the TPP's mechanism to enforce labor obligations. The mechanism essentially followed the same dispute resolution procedures that American trade officials used to bring against other alleged violations of the agreement. Union critics, however, made clear that they no longer trusted leaving it to the discretion of future administrations to enforce the labor rules. For the TPP, they insisted on an entirely different mechanism for labor chapter obligations, which allowed impacted private parties to self-initiate claims of a violation of the agreement instead of depending on the government to do the same.

Beyond the challenge of getting TPP members to agree to a trade agreement enforcement process that any aggrieved private party could initiate, meeting this demand also would allow for private parties to trigger the same complaints against America's patchwork federal and state labor laws and for lack of enforcement against the practices of companies operating in the United States. By putting America on the hook for such private actions, the approach failed to get political traction, adding another to the list of unmet union and Democratic Party demands. Democrats and unions pressed the issue again later, during the Trump administration, as a condition to secure passage of its renegotiated NAFTA deal. In that case, Mexico agreed to introduce a modified version of this new special labor rights enforcement mechanism to help get the updated deal passed, one that that was written to not allow for its use against practices in America except in a narrow circumstance. [59]

Another often-cited deficiency of the TPP among U.S. labor unions was Mexico's refusal to agree to a separate TPP labor consistency plan with America. Mexico committed to the TPP's labor obligations and to taking actions separately to comply with the agreement's various

---

59   The United States is subject to labor obligations under the agreement, but only when formal complaints are filed by the governments of Mexico or Canada. The ability for private parties to file complaints to use this separate, special enforcement mechanism for alleged workplace violations in the United States, by contrast, is narrowly limited.

obligations. It also began discussions with the Obama administration about its plans for compliance after the TPP was signed. Once the TPP was fully implemented, Mexico would have to go as far as to amend its constitution, in addition to multiple other laws and regulations, to allow for the genuine emergence of collective bargaining by independent trade unions. As a political and legal concern, however, its government refused to sign a special separate plan as Vietnam and some others had done to spell out the manner by which it would achieve these reforms. Instead of waiting to judge Mexico by its actions to follow through to implement its TPP commitments, U.S. labor unions instead cited the Obama administration's inability to secure Mexico's upfront agreement to these specifics as another reason to oppose the deal.

Many of the U.S. labor unions' expectations for additional labor commitments, from allowing self-initiated claims by workers and other groups to extending trade agreement labor rights to illegal foreign workers, reached at least as deeply into national laws and systems as any other trade rule. These expectations also mirrored similar sovereignty and regulatory independence issues that the unions raised as objectionable in the context of other TPP trade rules aimed at disciplining foreign trade barriers. If free trade agreements were "corporate deals," as the unions insisted, the unions aggressively pursued their own "union deal" that reached at least as far into the economic, legal, and social systems of America's trading partners—and arguably even deeper. These demands, at times, also aimed at setting new legal standards for America to meet. Echoing debates being waged in America over appropriate policies toward union rights and union privileges, union-friendly and progressive Democrats slammed the TPP labor obligations as failing to meet the mark they expected. Opposition from the other side of the aisle was that they instead had been taken too far by exceeding their May 10th Agreement with Democrats and potentially also created new obligations for America to meet for itself.

Foreign Investor Protections

Even as they sought their own private right-of-action procedure to enforce the TPP's labor obligations, the unions, progressive Democrats, and others roundly took aim at a similar concept that already existed in a large number of America's investment and free trade agreements aimed at protecting the rights and property of its overseas investors. Governments have provided different forms of protection over many centuries for their citizens and businesses that invest overseas.[60] These protections evolved out of unequal colonial and commercial treaties from the eighteenth into the early twentieth centuries and included, at times, the threat of military action by the large powers in defense of these investments, which says a great deal about the state of world affairs during that time.[61]

Top of the list of host country interferences with a foreign company's investment was its use of expropriation—the takeover of a foreign company's assets without compensation. Other less egregious forms of interference might include arbitrarily and indefinitely closing the only public road leading to a foreign-owned factory, or imposing arbitrary regulations to exact some sort of corrupt favor or pressure the foreign investor to provide some noncommercial benefit.

The modern approach by which governments began providing protections for their investors was based on a model investment agreement that first emerged in Europe around 1960. One early version of that agreement, unsurprisingly drafted by corporate representatives of oil (Royal Dutch Shell) and banking (Deutsche Bank) firms, perpetuated the presumption that capital investments were a benefit to the developing countries of the world that necessitated special legal protections going above local law and customs often viewed as inadequate. These concepts were incorporated into investment treaties that European countries negotiated with a large number of developing countries. American corporations then sought similar protections to their European rivals, and by the early 1980s, America began including investor protection concepts into its new bilateral investment treaties (BITs) across the globe.[62]

As America later began to negotiate new free trade deals, these same investment protection concepts were incorporated into these agreements, forging even deeper trade and investment partnerships. Instead of

60   One scholar has traced the concept of investor-state arbitration back as far as a dispute between the Suez Canal Commission and Egypt under the reign of Napoleon III. See Jason W. Yackee, "The First Investor-State Arbitration: The Suez Canal Company v Egypt (1864)," *Journal of World Investment & Trade* 17, no. 3 (2016): 401–62.

61   One authoritative historical overview is provided by Kenneth J. Vandevalde, "A Brief History of International Investment Agreements," *UC Davis Journal of International Law & Policy* 12, no. 1 (2011): 157–94, https://jilp.law.ucdavis.edu/archives/12/1/brief-history-international-investment-agreements.

62   On these earlier developments, see, e.g., Simon Lester, "Liberalization or Litigation? Time to Rethink the International Investment Regime," Cato Institute, Policy Analysis no. 730, July 8, 2013.

expecting unilateral commitments from the foreign country, as was commonplace in the 1800s, these late twentieth and early twenty-first-century investment obligations applied both ways. Excepting America from these same obligations was viewed as unnecessary because of the manner in which they were drafted and because its modern laws and due process protections were deemed sufficient to avoid foreign investor allegations of arbitrary mistreatment in America.

Setting aside whether the original intentions of these protections are or were defensible, these investment obligations became commonplace in investment and trade agreements around the world. The core elements of these obligations were also routinely included in America's free trade agreements, per Congress's directives setting out trade agreement objectives when providing trade agreement negotiating authority to the executive branch.[63] One notable exception was the 2005 U.S.-Australia free trade agreement, in which Australia refused to take on some of these standard investment obligations. More specifically, it insisted on excluding the private right of action mechanism—or investor-state dispute settlement (ISDS)—in the agreement's core investment obligations.

The ISDS set of rules allowed companies or individuals of one of the countries in the agreement to directly file claims as plaintiffs against another government party to the same agreement over official actions that they alleged unfairly impeded their investments. Several tests had to be met, which, in very general terms, typically required proof of either expropriation, discrimination, or other arbitrary and unfair treatment of the foreign investment compared to other investments. Once filed, an independent panel of experts heard claims, typically through international arbitration organizations such as the International Centre for Settlement of Investment Disputes, affiliated with the World Bank. Judgments rendered by these panels, if they included a finding for the plaintiff, could require compensatory damages paid by the host government to the investor. ISDS was unique in the architecture of international trade agreements as a mechanism provided by governments for private claims against a government outside of its own legal system. Other trade agreement violations, by contrast, are handled through a standard government-to-government dispute procedure.

---

63   For Congress's negotiating objectives under its 2015 grant of authority for the TPP negotiations, see Bipartisan Congressional Trade Priorities and Accountability Act of 2015, 19 USC 4201, Section 102.b.(4).

Negative attention to ISDS was triggered around 2000 by ever more creative and aggressive legal claims brought by private companies against governments, gaining further attention in America after a claim was also brought against the United States shortly thereafter under NAFTA. Opposition to it intensified in America, Europe, and elsewhere after some of these claims sought compensatory damages for regulatory or similar policy decisions intended to protect health, safety, and the environment. These concerns led America to undertake a comprehensive review of its investment agreement obligations during the early 2000s to assess whether changes in the legal wording were necessary to close off exposure to such claims. The template was updated as a result, both for BITs and free trade agreements, to better defend against them. The EU also developed its model to similarly ensure it provided adequate protection against increasingly numerous and frivolous private company claims using the ISDS mechanism worldwide.

American officials asserted that their model legal template used for ISDS across its agreements struck the right balance between protecting the U.S. government from unwarranted claims while providing important protections for American investors abroad. As claims were rising worldwide, they argued, America's existing ISDS model was still working as intended, with none of the dozen or so cases filed against the U.S. government having succeeded.[64] To be safe, however, some limited updates were still made to the model.

Opponents to the TPP on the New Right and the progressive Left meanwhile zeroed in on ISDS, calling it a cancerous threat to America's sovereignty and its legal and regulatory freedom and then using these as alarming arguments to mobilize others against TPP approval. They asserted that ISDS interfered with the ability of regulators and policymakers to make decisions against the interests of foreign corporations to safeguard human and animal safety and environmental protection in America. With the same or nearly identical ISDS obligations already included in scores of other agreements over several decades, they raised the specter that approving them again in the TPP nonetheless amounted to a new existential threat to a wide array of public interest needs and causes, from regulating carcinogens to preventing environmental degradation and countering climate change. Beyond citing a limited

---

64   See, e.g., "ISDS: Important Questions and Answers," USTR blog, March 2015, https://ustr.gov/about-us/policy-offices/press-office/blog/2015/march/isds-important -questions-and-answers-0.

number of examples outside the United States where similar challenges had succeeded, often based on earlier and less precise legal drafting of the obligations, they did not present evidence to support their claim that their concern was more actual than theoretical for America's regulators. For progressive lawmakers and their expanding anti-corporate legislative goals, however, ISDS appeared to be viewed as a threat to pursuing their own domestic policy goals—including those that may necessitate discriminating against specific groups of firms or investment projects to achieve.

One typical criticism came from the Sierra Club, which asserted that ISDS ". . . would empower big polluters to challenge climate and environmental safeguards in private trade courts. . . ."[65] The United Steelworkers claimed it would give ". . . foreign corporations greater substantive and procedural rights than domestic firms to challenge government policies intended to protect the public interest."[66] Others, like the Teamsters, stretched some key facts even further, inaccurately claiming that TPP included ". . . a secret pro-business trade court, with international trade attorneys as judges that could kill any federal, state or local law that might reduce present or future corporate profits."[67] In fact, the TPP procedures for ISDS required published records and hearings to be open to the public. In addition, while rulings by these international investment arbitration panels could demand potentially large compensation amounts to be paid to foreign investors when governments were found to act in discriminatory or unfairly targeted actions against them, any findings against a government could not compel it to change its laws or practices.

Most Republicans long supported ISDS and disagreed with these criticisms of it as uninformed and excessive, insisting that ISDS be kept in America's trade agreements to protect its overseas investors. Many also opposed the Obama administration's decision to explicitly exclude from the TPP agreement the right of the tobacco industry to bring any ISDS claims. The administration added the exception in the hope it would lessen opposition to the TPP, especially among Democrats who

65   Quote from Michael Brune, Executive Director of the Sierra Club, in Sierra Club, "ICYMI: Environmental Groups Warn of Threats of Trans-Pacific Partnership," press release, October 5, 2015.

66   United Steelworkers, "USW Opposes American Job-Killing Trans-Pacific Partnership," press release, November 5, 2015.

67   International Brotherhood of Teamsters, "Dem Platform Firms Up Anti-TPP Language," press release, July 19, 2016.

had grown increasingly uncomfortable with ISDS amid growing outright opposition from their progressive colleagues and other organizations. Had the TPP ever been put to a vote, it was a bet that was unlikely to have paid off, for the exclusion also gave traditional supporters of ISDS on the Republican side a reason to criticize and potentially oppose it. Congressional Republican leaders warned that unless the tobacco exception was removed, the administration should prepare to lose as many as 15 votes for the TPP from southern House members—a margin that might prevent the agreement's approval.[68]

A small group of other congressional Republicans, meanwhile, viewed ISDS differently from their colleagues and joined progressives and unions in their blanket criticism of it to oppose the TPP. This small party faction, which included figures such as Senator Jeff Sessions from Alabama, more broadly viewed America's foreign trade obligations as dangerously surrendering U.S. sovereignty to international tribunals, starting with the WTO's dispute settlement procedure. Some even viewed these commitments as unconstitutional. This wing of the Republican Party was further elevated by the rise of the Tea Party and New Right movements starting around 2010. With Trump's nomination by the party and his election as president in 2016, many of their views coincided with those of its new party leader and emerged as the party's new mainstream on trade.

Opposition to ISDS was also boosted by Trump's trade ambassador, who echoed sovereignty concerns but went further to make clear his antipathy to ISDS, for a different principal reason. In Lighthizer's view, ISDS needlessly helped support American companies to invest and offshore abroad, making it a government-arranged political risk insurance program for them. His opposition to ISDS was an instant hit with unions, progressives, and others, coming as it did from an individual able to exert more influence to change the course of official U.S. policy on the issue than anyone else in the debate. With the withdrawal from the TPP ending the debate in the context of that agreement, Lighthizer continued to campaign against it by attempting to exclude ISDS from the Trump administration's renegotiated NAFTA. That effort ultimately failed to persuade enough Republicans to go along with his approach and still support passing the updated deal. However, further refinements were made to the ISDS model and its legal provisions for that

68 "Reichert Says about 15 Republicans Will Oppose TPP over Tobacco," World Trade Online, December 3, 2015.

agreement, including further limits on its scope of use. As highlighted in the next chapter, the issue of how to handle ISDS was also dealt with in the context of the Trump administration's renegotiation of America's free trade agreement with South Korea.

These standoffs over ISDS were emblematic of other rapidly shifting political views and alliances toward America's trade policy and agreements. Since the TPP never came before Congress for a vote, this particular debate failed to come to a head before Trump signed his directive to withdraw from the agreement. Politically, however, the issue remains no less supercharged. Members of Congress from both parties have joined with unions, public interest groups, and others to continue to oppose ISDS, following decades of support in Congress and its direction to the executive branch to include it in trade agreements. Some in Congress now insist that America's ISDS commitments in other investment and free trade agreements remain such a dangerous threat to policy sovereignty that the Biden administration should immediately seek to renegotiate each of them to unwind America's ISDS obligations with approximately 50 different countries.[69]

The debate over ISDS also reflects a familiar trend described elsewhere, which is the increasing tension and disagreement in America between those who strongly favor more trade rules to challenge arbitrary acts of discrimination by foreign governments against American exports and investment, versus the opposing camp that has come to view some of these same rules aimed at upholding nondiscrimination as now interfering with America's ability to meet legitimate public needs at home. America's negotiators believed they had the right template to do both successfully, while opponents disagreed and continued their campaign to retire ISDS as a relic of America's misguided past. They also revealed another objective of ISDS opponents: to free up the policy space to legislate a more expansive and potentially discriminatory agenda in America, allowing them to target corporate activities as they see fit.

Views and positions toward ISDS dramatically transformed in just a few short years and cut across different wings of both political parties

---

69   In a letter to Katherine Tai and Anthony Blinken, Elizabeth Warren, Lloyd Doggett, and 31 other senators and members of Congress, "We therefore ask that your agencies investigate any and all options at your disposal to eliminate ISDS liability from existing trade and investment agreements." See Elizabeth Warren, "Senator Warren, Representative Doggett Call for Elimination of Investor-State Dispute Settlement System, Action on Behalf of Honduran Government," May 2, 2023, https://www.warren.senate.gov/imo/media/doc/2023.05.02%20Letter%20to%20Tai,%20Blinken%20re%20elimination%20of%20ISDS.pdf.

in remarkably new and consequential ways. New Right Republicans and progressive Democrats found themselves in close alignment over their view that ISDS unduly infringes on America's sovereignty, a claim that progressives pushed further by framing the stakes as a systemic risk to the government's ability to stop corporations from harming the environment or human health. Lighthizer and others on the New Right aligned with progressives, unions, and others over the claim that ISDS harmfully incentivizes corporations to move American jobs abroad by helping them protect their investments in riskier, less developed countries. The traditional pro-business Republican Right, joined by a few moderate Democrats, saw all these concerns as excessive and continued to support the need to maintain ISDS as a longstanding and justified means of protecting both the smallest and the largest U.S. investors abroad. ISDS was never without critics, but after decades of support and explicit direction from Congress to include it in U.S. trade agreements, the shift in this landscape and the impact of opposition to including it in the TPP were as sudden as they were surprising in the debate.

Pharmaceuticals and Access to Medicines

Of all the prominent issues raised by opponents to the TPP, one was of particular significance to a single, specific U.S. industry and its congressional supporters and critics. It was also highly controversial among other TPP members and became one of the last issues to reach a compromise during the negotiation's final moments in early October 2015. The issue, pressed by America, was to secure agreement among TPP members on a defined period of "data protection" for biologic medicines.

Biologic drug developers pay for and use their data to demonstrate the safety and efficacy of drugs to obtain regulatory approval. America's practice was to offer developers 12 years of exclusive use of this data before other makers of similar medicines were allowed to also use that data to market and sell their competitive products. In the TPP negotiations, America was alone in seeking the commitment of the other TPP members to provide the same 12-year period. Their own terms of data protection varied widely, with some providing five or eight years and others having no established period or legal requirement for this type of protection for biologics.

Past efforts to secure high standards of protection for America's innovators through its trade agreements were broadly supported on Capitol Hill over several decades. These efforts began in earnest in the early 1980s. They grew out of a growing alarm over the theft of America's intellectual property by foreign competitors as an industrial competitiveness concern and, as pirated and counterfeit goods proliferated around the globe, a trade concern. America responded by pressing for a GATT agreement for intellectual property, which was eventually achieved in 1994. The agreement, known as TRIPS (Agreement on Trade-Related Aspects of Intellectual Property Rights), added to the international system's set of core rules on non-tariff barriers. It also provided a significant number of caveats and exceptions, particularly for developing countries.

America's free trade agreements provided a better platform to go much further to build out these protections in their trade rules, both to plug the GATT agreement's loopholes and to add many other requirements. The model continued to evolve, but America's negotiating objective consistently was to bring the intellectual property regimes of its trading partners as close as possible to the level of protection that their companies and innovators could enjoy in America. By the time TPP talks began, the intellectual property chapter in America's trade agreements mostly accomplished that goal by including commitments from its trading partners that included enforcing laws to prevent the production and imports of counterfeits and providing more similar periods of copyright protection for creative works such as books and movies.

As imposing as these obligations often were for America's trading partners, including these high-standard protections in trade agreements was supported by American business groups and (with some important exceptions) its labor unions. In its 2013 convention resolution, the AFL-CIO affirmed the importance of intellectual property protection for the nation's economic growth: "The U.S. economy produces many products for which IP [intellectual property] is critical, from movies, television shows, sound recordings . . . software, medicines, fiber optics, specialty steel. . . ." It then reaffirmed the role of trade agreements in protecting these innovations but with a clear caveat in the specific case of pharmaceuticals: "Trade agreements must support the livelihoods of the creators of intellectual property while also promoting legitimate competition—particularly in the area of generic medicines."[70] Unions joined other American critics of intellectual property protections for large pharmaceutical companies by pointing to a range of legal maneuvers

70 AFL-CIO, "Resolution 12: America and the World Need a New Approach to Trade and Globalization," in *AFL-CIO 2013 Convention: Adopted Resolutions and Constitutional Amendments*, 2013 , https://aflcio.org/resolutions/resolution-12-america-and-world-need-new-approach-trade-and-globalization.

and precedents the industry used to, in their view, unfairly extend their patent rights and other protections beyond reasonable periods of time.

For the subset of pharmaceuticals known as biologics, U.S. law was amended in 2009 to provide creators with 12 years of data protection, a right reincorporated the following year in the Affordable Care Act that launched Obamacare. Key Republicans, including Orrin Hatch, who chaired the key Senate committee with oversight over trade policy, made abundantly clear their expectation that, like other areas of intellectual property rules, America needed to press hard to achieve agreement from all TPP members on the same 12-year term, just as it aimed to achieve U.S.-levels of protection for other types of IP.

As the negotiations progressed, several TPP members began publicly speaking out in opposition to America's position, bringing greater attention to the issue among American and other international industry critics. Civil society organizations such as Doctors Without Borders were particularly vocal, more directly attempting to reframe the issue as one of fair access to medicines.[71] These and other criticisms expanded further the range of arguments, attention, and vocal opponents over the issue.

Opponents used the TPP debate as a proxy forum to further ignite a new effort to roll back America's own term of protection. These opponents were especially concerned that if locked into an international agreement like the TPP, the 12-year term would become next to impossible to later reverse under U.S. law. They cheered and pointed to a shift in the Obama administration's position, which called for only seven years of protection in its 2012 budget request to Congress. That step helped reopen a debate in America on the appropriate term length, based as it was on the fiscal implications of the high and increasing cost of biologics for federal healthcare programs.

America's opponents were boosted by the fact that several other TPP members, many with their own public healthcare systems, were also adamantly opposed to providing a 12-year term of protection in their own countries. In the end, and after facing particularly strong opposition from Australia, which had only a five-year term, the furthest America could stretch TPP countries was to reach an agreement on an eight-year term, with a caveat. In a nod to Australia's resistance, a five-year term was allowed if accompanied by other regulatory measures that cumulatively resulted in a total eight-year period.

---

71   Medecins Sans Frontieres/Doctors Without Borders, "Doctors Without Borders Launches Ad Campaign to Highlight Health Dangers of TPP Trade Deal," press release, April 23, 2015.

Soon after this final compromise was reached and the TPP deal was announced in October 2015, Senator Hatch made clear that the outcome on biologics would have to be renegotiated for the TPP to have a chance to gain enough Republican votes to pass through Congress.[72] As the chair of the relevant committee, he could also ensure that consideration of the TPP, if submitted to Congress for approval, would face a rough road without an acceptable modification.

The administration engaged with Hatch and other Republicans over the weeks and months after the TPP deal was reached to discuss options to gain their critical support to pass it in Congress. After the TPP sputtered, the brokered compromise that was reached never became public but appeared to include steps to ensure all TPP countries, including Australia, effectively met at least the full eight-year commitment, however that was accomplished.[73] Australia was more focused on its own politics, however. In the midst of a national election campaign, its government claimed its TPP commitment would not change its existing five years of protection, adding that nothing would be changed that might result in price increases for the medicines.[74] Domestic U.S. critics were also preparing to oppose another part of the rumored deal with Hatch, which was to enshrine America's 12 years of protection in Congress's implementing law for the TPP that would be approved alongside the agreement. Labor and civil society groups fired off their warnings to Congress that it must use the pretext of a trade agreement with foreign governments, and especially one where they had committed only to an eight-year term of protection, by once again locking in America's 12-year term of protection under yet another U.S. law.[75]

All sides were gearing up for the coming battle in Congress when Trump's November 2016 election win and pledge to withdraw from the TPP changed everything. With Trump as party leader, the majority of Republicans who otherwise had remained quietly supportive of trying to find a way to get the agreement passed instead ran out of runway. Despite Trump's threats to withdraw, Senator Hatch nonetheless con-

72   Needham, "Currency Manipulation Plan Gets Key Endorsement."

73   "Debate on Biologics Emerges in Australian Election; Ambassador Warns of U.S. TPP Delay," World Trade Online, May 23, 2016.

74   "TPP Outcomes: Biologics," Department of Foreign Affairs and Trade, Government of Australia, fact sheet, November 25, 2016.

75   See, e.g., the statement of the AFL-CIO, Consumers Union, and Doctors Without Borders in "Quote-Unquote: Biologics (Two Sides), Climate Change, Brexit, China Steel," World Trade Online, November 3, 2016.

tinued to project confidence in finding a way to still get the TPP done. When asked about the wisdom of his efforts to hold up the agreement's approval in Congress for many months over his objection to its outcome on biologics, he simply stated, "I think we're going to get the biologics fixed."[76] Just a few days later, Trump signed the order to withdraw America from the TPP, erasing the partial gains made in the TPP on the issue Hatch had championed on behalf of the U.S. industry. The Trump administration subsequently included a biologics term of protection in its renegotiated NAFTA, reached in 2018, only to drop it in the final, revised agreement with little hesitation after Democrats insisted it be removed to help get it passed.

AMERICA WALKS OUT ON ITS GOLD STANDARD FOR TRADE

With critics mounting new and greater challenges to the TPP from all sides, the first litmus test of its support in Congress came in late spring and early summer 2015. Just a few months before the final compromises were made among the TPP-12 countries to conclude the deal, Congress finally began to move forward with its bill to renew authority for the executive branch to conduct trade agreement negotiations. Instead of passing the bill and spelling out congressional expectations as the negotiations got underway in 2010 and 2011, congressional leaders avoided the political risks of taking a vote until it was clear that the TPP negotiations were in their true endgame.

Even so, executive branch negotiators still met often with Congress to solicit input as the negotiations progressed between 2010 and 2015. These regular oral briefings and consultations were held in closed-door meetings between executive branch negotiators and congressional trade committee members and their staff, as well as with individual congressional members and their staff. Negotiation updates were provided and discussions were held on the detailed, confidential U.S. negotiating proposals before they were presented and then updates were provided on the challenges of achieving agreement on them as the 12-party negotiations progressed. The meetings also were an opportunity to discuss proposals made by other countries in the talks.

By the time the TPP negotiations approached their conclusion in 2015, congressional members had a good sense from these exchanges

---

76   Jenny Leonard, "Finance Members Meet with USTR Pick; Hatch Pledges to Push for TPP," World Trade Online, January 12, 2017.

of what had been agreed, as well as a somewhat clear sense of the major challenges that remained. The level of information sharing was not perfect, as the administration sometimes hedged on being fully open—or not open at all in limited cases—about the status of all the negotiating challenges around some of the most difficult remaining issues. Similarly, participants from the legislative branch side often held back complete candor on which outcomes would be supported or opposed.

Even as information flowed back and forth between the administration and Congress about the negotiations, Congress's failure to pass a bill giving the executive branch a new grant of negotiating authority until the very endgame of the TPP talks led to other impacts along the way. One was to raise questions and doubt among TPP members over the degree to which they could count on congressional approval of the final agreement, particularly in light of Congress's reluctance to pass a bill to grant the Obama administration authority to negotiate it. The fact that it had not been passed was regularly raised by TPP members as a justification for waiting to make their biggest political concessions in the negotiations. Another impact was to provide for those opposing the TPP an opportunity to raise alarm and mobilize to against it by first pressuring Congress to defeat the bill authorizing the administration to negotiate it. These opponents failed, and the bill to grant negotiating authority and provide Congress's official negotiating priorities was approved narrowly in the House 218–208, but with a wider margin in the Senate of 60–38. In the ensuing weeks, as final compromises were made among the TPP countries to complete the agreement, these opponents were already well assembled and mobilized to wage their next battle—opposing the passage of the final agreement.

With the benefit of hindsight, some have suggested that the TPP would have succeeded in Congress had it acted sooner to approve its bill to authorize the negotiations. The December 2013 meeting of TPP ministers in Singapore was scheduled to make a major push toward concluding the agreement, with the hope of also unlocking momentum in Congress to take its first step by passing its negotiations authorization bill early in 2014. That scenario, however, came apart for two reasons. First, Max Baucus, the Democratic chair of the Senate committee overseeing trade and a strong TPP proponent, was nominated in mid-December to become U.S. ambassador to China. Boxed in after his nomination from forcing this controversial vote with his colleagues, decision-making on the vote to authorize the TPP negotiations shifted to Senate Majority Leader Harry Reid, who personally opposed the

TPP and other free trade deals. He insisted on waiting until after the November 2014 congressional elections for the vote to avoid losses and splits in the party.[77] Republicans still won control of both houses in that election and, once in power, finally moved the bill forward. That bill passed with virtually no textual changes from an earlier Baucus-drafted compromise bill that had sat idle since late 2013. Second, the major breakthroughs at the negotiating table needed to create momentum to complete the deal were still not in sight. Japan's reticence to meet the requisite level of tariff elimination, which had sapped momentum from the TPP ministerial meeting in Singapore in late 2013, lingered as one major roadblock. Complicated and still unbaked discussions over many of the trade rules were another, as U.S. negotiators insisted these had to be in the final deal to secure Congress's approval.

As it was, the TPP agreement and its promise of a new trading order for the Asia-Pacific was finally agreed to in October 2015, about five and a half years after negotiations began. The final text, which required further negotiation to transcribe the final handshake deals into legal text, was published in early November 2015. The beginning of the end of America's relentless march toward freer and more open trade also began around this same time, rooted in the political opposition and domestic disagreements surrounding its 30 chapters and estimated 1,121 pages of trade rules, along with its 61 side letters of further obligations and softer promises.[78]

The agreement's other several thousand pages covered the free trade part of the agreement in the form of highly detailed tariff and services liberalization commitment schedules. Opposition to the TPP from the Left and newly from some on the Right was always at least in part, and sometimes in full, about these tariff liberalization commitments from the very beginning. Even so, tariff liberalization figured very little into the ensuing political debate, which instead almost exclusively took place over whether the administration had fulfilled its grand promises for a new kind of free trade deal that transformed the rules of trade.

With few surprises on its tariff outcomes, there was little new to criticize in the TPP that was much different from America's other free trade agreements. The standard formula, replicated for the TPP, im-

---

77 Manu Raju and Burgess Evertt, "The One Fight Harry Reid Surrendered," Politico, May 22, 2015; and "Harry Reid's Trade Veto," *Wall Street Journal*, January 29, 2014.

78 "TPP Parties Release Text, Including Access Schedules, 61 U.S. Side Letters," World Trade Online, November 5, 2015.

mediately brought the majority of America's remaining tariffs to zero, a commitment that it insisted upon from other TPP members. Tariffs on each member country's most sensitive import products would still be phased out, but over several to many years. A handful of goods were accorded other outcomes, such as quantitative restrictions, most of which were also to be phased out over time. Even the better deal America gave Japan on auto tariffs to get a little more on auto content rules raised surprisingly little open criticism from those stakeholders and congressional members that more simply just strongly opposed any reduction in the 2.5 percent U.S. tariff for Japan.

Negative reactions to the tariff outcomes instead came from agriculture exporters, which had grown accustomed to better access from free trade agreements than achieved with Japan. Japan liberalized the least of all the TPP agreement partners, which predictably softened support for the TPP among several American farm groups, including its rice grower and dairy industry associations, which openly questioned the deal's value.[79] Other farm goods producers that initially expected more from Japan still felt some important access was opened for them and opted to lobby Congress to approve the agreement.

The Obama administration touted the elimination of eighteen thousand different product tariffs on U.S. exports to the Asia-Pacific region as its top pitch to the American public to seek support for the deal.[80] While this and other accomplishments received predictable applause from a broad base of America's internationally competitive agricultural, industrial, and services businesses, compared to other free trade agreements, business support for the TPP was overshadowed by hesitation or criticism coming from other, more narrowly defined segments of the business community. Among these, some of America's larger pharmaceutical, tobacco, auto, digital services, and financial services companies, in particular, hesitated or resisted expressing support due to their objections to certain TPP rules outcomes. Some withheld support in order to call for Congress to insist that the administration renegotiate them. These

---

79   USA Rice, "TPP Agreement Signed, Rice Concerns Remain," press release, February 4, 2016; Tom Suber, "Pros and Cons of TPP for U.S. Dairy Industry," U.S. Dairy Export Council, U.S. Dairy Exporter Blog, January 14, 2016.

80   The Obama administration led its overview of the agreement's outcomes with the new eighteen thousand "tax cuts" that the TPP would eliminate on American exports abroad. See, e.g., Office of the Press Secretary, "Fact Sheet: How the Trans-Pacific Partnership (TPP) Boosts Made in America Exports, Supports Higher-Paying American Jobs, and Protects American Workers," The White House, October 5, 2015.

objections sapped life from the business community's usual support for new free trade agreements. As a result, its support for the TPP was never able to find its typical strong and more unified footing. Criticism also came from import-sensitive American producers who registered their opposition to more new free trade agreements and the tariff-free imports that came from them.

Meanwhile, the agreement's more entrenched opponents, from labor unions to issue advocacy groups of all kinds, quickly ramped up their own broad, blistering arguments. Instead of offering acceptable remedies, they issued blanket repudiations of the administration's assertion that, with new gains in labor and environment trade rules, free trade could ever be made to work better. Controversy also enveloped negotiated outcomes in multiple other areas, including in areas beyond those discussed previously (auto content rules, currency, pharmaceuticals, and investment).

The administration's branding of the TPP as the new model for trade in Asia emerged as its greatest target for the counterpunches made against it. The model is one that Congress directed, sought additions to, and approved for other free trade agreements over several decades across different administrations. With rules originally aimed at curtailing non-tariff and unfair practices to make trade fairer for America, the model pushed into new areas over time in response to demands that Washington's trading partners more closely align their level of environmental and labor protections to those in America. It was a model that began incorporating new rules in other areas, such as to discipline unfair practices by state-owned enterprises and to accommodate and support the use of competition policy among agreement partners against anti-competitive acts and the abuse of corporate concentration. It was a model that continued to meticulously and extensively build on prior efforts to maintain and project America's policies, priorities, and approaches into the international trading system without America having to change its laws to meet them. By the time of the TPP, however, rather than advance the model further as a new bulwark against China's attempts to set its terms for trade in the region, the updated U.S. model instead came into conflict with America's new lack of confidence in it. Suddenly, America was too queasy to board its own ship.

With the anti–free trade movement on the verge of a breakout success in its goal of sinking the TPP, others in Washington who ordinarily favored these agreements only further added to its troubles by poking holes in it and then insisting on further repairs to it. A sense of impending déjà vu that America would make more demands of its trading partners and seek to renegotiate the agreement loomed over its future as America's stakeholders busily prepared and put forward their lists of must-have additional changes. The growing likelihood that Washington would again insist that America's trading partners accept its new, one-way demands to pass the agreement in Congress made for difficult political dilemmas for them at home. The practice was giving America a new reputation of being incapable of honoring a deal, harming its international standing.

Aware of Washington's renegotiation playbook, political leaders in the other TPP country capitals grew concerned as the agreement faced trouble in Congress, especially as they worked to build support and tamp down domestic opposition to the politically unpopular decisions they made to agree to it. For example, Japan's top TPP negotiator announced shortly after the deal was finished that Japan would not be reopening the final text.[81] Even if America could agree on a slate of additional changes to secure enough votes to pass it in Congress, these and other comments raised the specter that other TPP countries might still be unwilling to accommodate them.

In fact, the TPP never made it that far in Washington. As opposition, criticism, and demands for changes to the TPP proliferated, the usual pathways for compromise, if achievable, seemed to grow only more irreconcilable with one another. The old renegotiation strategy—doing a little more for labor here and then a little more for business there—might not get it done this time. Instead, alignments between the New Right and progressive Left centered around anti-globalization and sovereignty themes, as well as their growing domestic policy-driven conflicts over other TPP rules, had scrambled the usual pathways to achieve the vote margins needed for these agreements. It also revealed the sharp new tension between what America expected and wanted from others and what it was willing to agree upon and accept for itself.

For example, many Democrats, joined by some Republicans, slammed the agreement's outcome on currency as unacceptable for failing to protect Americans from unfair manipulation by its TPP partners, giving no credence to the concerns of its own financial authorities that adding tougher enforceable obligations would excessively tie their hands. Some of the same Democratic critics then chastised TPP rules in another area for doing just that, zeroing in on the agreement's trade

---

81   Stanley White, "Japan's Amari Says Not Willing to Renegotiate TPP Trade Pact," Reuters, October 9, 2015.

rules to better ensure transparency and nondiscriminatory treatment and reduce other barriers to U.S. financial services providers. These rules had appeared in previous agreements, but in the case of the TPP, they were cast in anti-corporatist tones as a giveaway to Big Finance and an existential threat to the ability of financial officials to regulate domestic financial markets in the public interest.[82]

Similar attacks were stepped up by Democrats, unions, and other progressives against other TPP rules for narrowing and jeopardizing the regulatory and legislative flexibility needed to address everything from food safety to environmental protection concerns. Many of these were the same or newly updated trade rules from prior free trade agreements, developed over several decades through close coordination with U.S. regulators to preserve their ability to regulate for legitimate purposes, and routinely included in the trade agreements approved by Congress. These were the rules that members of both parties had long expected and demanded to preserve sufficient legal and regulatory flexibility and to give U.S. trade officials the tools they needed to target patently unfair practices and discrimination facing American firms and exports. For the TPP, the anti-corporate progressive Left attacked the validity of these rules as a dangerous reinforcement of the status quo in America that they intended to overturn, often framed with the intent of beating back corporate influence.

Other critics and opponents of the TPP came at this issue from the other direction, arguing that its rules were not strong enough to guarantee American firms and exports the same level of transparency and nondiscriminatory treatment abroad that America provided to foreign companies and imported goods in the U.S. market. Accordingly, some Republicans leaned in to expect fixes to the TPP to achieve equivalent rights to those in U.S. law for innovative biologic drugs, and to seek the removal of an exception for financial institutions to the TPP rule that ensured the right of firms to store and share their customer and other data with overseas affiliates across national borders. At the same time, some Republicans also criticized other TPP outcomes for "overreach," including the agreement's labor consistency plan for Vietnam, and for unjustifiably excluding and denying tobacco companies the same invest-

---

82   Typical of these are in a letter from three U.S. senators to Trade Representative Froman. See letter from Senators Elizabeth Warren, Edward Markey, and Tammy Baldwin to U.S. Trade Representative Michael Froman, Elizabeth Warren (website), December 17, 2014, https://www.warren.senate.gov/files/documents/TPP.pdf.

ment protection provisions that other companies could access. Labor and environmental advocates and their Democratic Party supporters, too, had their long lists of criticisms of incomplete TPP outcomes that failed to guarantee the adoption of U.S.-level standards for their priorities.

Many of these criticisms of the TPP boiled down to political debate stage issues that were familiar in the context of America's gridlocked politics: unaffordable drug prices vs. support for American innovation and new medicines; excessive vs. inadequate environmental regulations; the prioritization of offensive vs. defensive trade policy objectives to leverage better-paying jobs in America; setting uniform rules to protect consumer data privacy vs. allowing firms to innovate and operate more efficiently; supporting the mobilization of labor unions vs. leaving it to workers to decide what was best for themselves; and standing up to big business to rein in excesses vs. supporting these and other businesses, where appropriate, to help add new jobs and stay competitive. As an omnibus package that reopened these and other contentious domestic debates, and amid America's gridlocked, issue-driven politics and intensifying 2016 congressional and presidential campaigns, the TPP was dropped into this volatile environment with the pitch that it was America's gold standard model for the world, raising the stakes in every direction for those still engaged in fighting over these issues at home.

In the early days of the 2016 presidential campaign, Trump had been the first prospective Republican candidate to go on the record to oppose the TPP. His position came in a series of statements made in April 2015, several weeks before he formally announced his candidacy and almost six months before the deal was complete and its final outcomes announced. Trump began by invoking currency manipulation, a long-standing, top concern of the American auto industry and autoworker unions: "The [TPP] is an attack on America's business. It does not stop Japan's currency manipulation. This is a bad deal." These messages increasingly resonated with the party's New Right, leading most other Republican candidates—many of whom had routinely supported free trade in the past—to express their skepticism and then, in most cases, to eventually oppose it. As a first mover among the Republicans, Trump quickly owned the policy turf and the argument amid the scores of remaining candidates.

Among the Democratic presidential candidates, Bernie Sanders, who converted from an independent to join the party to run for president, had the most consistent anti–free trade record of anyone in Washington. In a way, his very candidacy was his statement in opposition to the TPP, as it was against other Washington policies viewed as benefiting large corporations to any degree. Candidate Clinton attempted to leave political space for the TPP through much of 2015, insisting that she would wait until the deal was finished to take a position on it. With Trump and Sanders each having already peeled away many Midwest and union voters opposed to trade deals, Clinton announced two days after the TPP was completed that it failed to meet her expectations and standards. Soon after, she sealed key labor union endorsements to help win her party's nomination by promising not to support it even with further updates or improvements, essentially pledging that the TPP would not become her administration's Trojan horse.[83] Whether her promise was true or not, the fact that few seemed to believe it was enough to turn it into an effective political weapon against her candidacy. Having supported it as Obama's secretary of state, and then switching to a neutral stance as a candidate for the Oval Office, only to finally claim to oppose it once it was done, the evolution in position left Clinton vulnerable to charges that she had been too weak on the TPP and therefore a weak proponent of the interests of American workers.[84]

As the prospects for the TPP became ever more turbulent as the 2016 presidential and congressional campaigns unfolded, the Obama administration quietly worked with supportive congressional members, particularly with Republicans whose overwhelming support would be essential for passage, to keep a path open for approval after the campaigns were over. Their targeted timing for approval by Congress shifted to immediately after the November 2016 election, during the short lame-duck period for Congress that lasts from election day until the sessions of both branches of Congress end in late December.

To prepare, the Obama administration worked behind the scenes with select TPP partners to work out an additional set of consistency plans in several TPP issue areas to be announced just after the presidential election. These plans would not require changes to the agreement. Instead, like the labor plans reached with a few countries, each would specify in greater detail their plans to fulfill their agreement obligations in other areas, such as intellectual property. The goal was to reinject momentum back into the case for the TPP to attempt quick congressional

83 See, e.g., Doug Palmer, "Clinton Raved About Trans-Pacific Partnership Before She Rejected It," Politico, October 8, 2016.

84 See, e.g., Annie Carni, "Clinton Friend McAuliffe Says Clinton Will Flip on TPP, Then Walks It Back," Politico, July 26, 2016.

passage during the lame-duck session, accompanied by the support of a few congressional leaders to take on the task of attempting to push it through. The plan, however, became moot after Trump's win on November 8. Trump's renewed pledges that, if elected, he would pull America out of the TPP over its failure to protect U.S. auto employment and defend other jobs from unfair practices like currency manipulation stopped Republican congressional leaders in their tracks. Rather than still attempt to pass it, there was little choice other than to pull back on their plan and avoid a confrontation with the incoming president, now their new party leader.

THE (FAILED) FOREIGN POLICY CASE FOR THE TPP

Abroad, the vision for the TPP continued to attract interest from countries that had sat out the initial negotiations and agreement. Once concluded among the 12 members, discussions picked up elsewhere in anticipation of the next stage, which was to invite and include new countries to expand membership in the agreement. At home, however, America's vision had been at risk of floundering as congressional support to pass it became ever more unclear. Having first attempted to sell the TPP at home for its economic benefits, the Obama administration later began instead to lean hard on making a strategic case for passage to build support for it at home. Its argument centered on the unacceptably high reputational and foreign policy costs to the United States for failing to pass it.

In his January 2016 State of the Union address to Congress, Obama borrowed a refrain used years earlier by Japan's prime minister to justify his decision to bring Japan into the negotiations:[85] "With TPP, China doesn't set the rules in the region, we do." Weaving the TPP into the foreign policy themes of his address, Obama added—to lukewarm applause from Senate and House members—"You want to show our strength in this century? Approve this agreement."[86] By the time of his party's 2016 convention five months later, as delegates gathered to

85 Prime Minister Abe pointed to the TPP's rulemaking as a key reason that Japan had to be in the agreement. Abe Shinzo, "Press Conference by Prime Minister Shinzo Abe," March 15, 2013, https://japan.kantei.go.jp/96_abe/statement/201303/15kaiken_e.html. Obama administration statements on the TPP referred to the agreement as a "21st century" accord that would set high standards; direct references to "setting the rules" for trade in the region only emerged in public statements and press releases from late 2015.
86 "Obama Calls on Congress to Approve TPP, But Doesn't Highlight It Up Front," World Trade Online, January 14, 2016.

nominate Clinton as his successor, chants of "stop TPP" erupted across the convention floor.

With support flagging in so many directions, the Obama administration and the foreign policy establishment stepped up efforts to elevate the foreign policy case for the TPP. Eight former defense secretaries wrote to congressional leaders in April 2016, arguing that the TPP was "a choice between leading the world toward a future that supports U.S. values and interests, or standing back and allowing others—most likely China—to write the rules of the road for Asia in the 21st century."[87] Obama's secretary of defense was already on the record: ". . . passing TPP is as important to me as another aircraft carrier."[88] Other former secretaries of defense and state and former military commanders hit the road later in 2016 to make another push.[89]

The administration's reliance on the foreign policy case got some sympathy but little traction, for the foreign policy case had effectively already been torn apart with just a few potent criticisms of the agreement's outcomes. The most effective of these pointed to the auto content rules as evidence that far from containing China, the TPP instead would only benefit it, as argued by the United Steelworkers:

[The] TPP is sold as a way for the United States to write the rules of trade before China does. In many areas, the agreement fails this objective and the language on rules of origin [on autos] will put a smile on the faces of China's leaders. China didn't get to write the rules in their favor because our American negotiators did it for them.[90]

In the fourth Republican primary debate, Trump proclaimed, "The TPP is a horrible deal. It's a deal that was designed for China to come in, as they always do, through the back door and totally take advantage of everyone."[91] The president of the steelworkers union piled on, calling the TPP "a dagger twisting in the heart of American manufacturing . . .

---

87   Quoted in Jennifer Rubin, "Opinion: TPP Opponents Are Ignoring National Security," *Washington Post*, April 29, 2016.

88   Prashanth Parameswaran, "TPP as Important as Another Aircraft Carrier: US Defense Secretary," *The Diplomat*, April 8, 2015.

89   Jackie Calmes, "Obama Readies One Last Push for Trans-Pacific Partnership," *New York Times*, August 21, 2016.

90   Leo W. Gerard, "USW Pres. Gerard Statement on TPP Coming to Closure," United Steelworkers, press release, October 5, 2015.

91   Alter, "Transcript: Read the Full Text of the Fourth Republican Debate."

[that] does nothing to stop international rule breakers—and countries like China will once again be the winners."[92]

Both also closely mirrored one another in other ways. One was their mutual criticism of the TPP's unenforceable side agreement on currency, citing it as one major failure of the agreement. The United Steelworkers declared: "The TPP would not stop currency manipulation,"[93] and Trump argued that ". . . currency manipulation is the single greatest weapon people have. They don't even discuss it in this agreement. So I say, It's a very bad deal, should not be approved."[94] Others on the Left joined in, such as Congressman Brad Sherman, a House Democrat, and stretched the criticism even further for the message he believed it sent to China: ". . . the President will try to sell this deal as a method of containing and combatting China. But China is a big beneficiary of this deal, because it enshrines the idea the currency manipulation is allowed. . . ."[95]

Representative Sandy Levin from Michigan, who long fought against orthodox trade agreements and the foreign policy arguments used to sell them, summarized well one overall perception:

There are geopolitical aspects to TPP, but trade agreements must be able to stand on their own two economic feet. An agreement that is not in our economic interest cannot be in our national security interest because our national security depends on our economic strength, including in manufacturing.[96]

Levin also stressed that foreign policy objectives cannot be the overriding reason for these agreements, recalling that in 1962, Congress moved the lead on U.S. trade policy from the State Department to a new office within the Executive Office of the President for this specific reason: ". . . because of the notion that trade was something beyond diplomacy."[97]

Whether to forge new agreements or confront unfair trade practices, trade policy decisions are inseparable from and an important extension of America's foreign policy. The issue Levin pointed to, and that faced the case for TPP, was the critical need to begin with its economic case to then define a range of broader trade policy choices and directions that

---

92 United Steelworkers, "USW Opposes American Job-Killing Trans-Pacific Partnership."

93 United Steelworkers, "USW Opposes American Job-Killing Trans-Pacific Partnership."

94 Alter, "Read the Full Text of the Fourth Republican Debate."

95 Rosa DeLauro (website), "DeLauro Joins Members of Congress and a Broad Coalition against TPP Ahead of the State of the Union," press release, January 11, 2016.

96 Jack Caporal, "Rep. Levin Warns Trade Backlash Will Extend Past This Election Cycle," World Trade Online, September 29, 2016.

97 Caporal, "Rep. Levin Warns Trade Backlash Will Extend."

would be supportable and sustainable. With insufficient buy-in from key constituencies for the Obama administration's economic case, any attempt to pivot to sell it as essential to America's foreign policy interests would prove insufficient and probably only backfire instead. As the ultimate arbiter of the nation's trade interests, Levin pointed out that Congress's support for the economic case needed to come first, before the vision thing could come next.

Most of American history proved Levin correct. Only for a short period, from the mid-1930s to the early 1960s, did Congress take a backseat by handing the executive branch great discretion over tariff policy. Initially at the behest of President Roosevelt, the economic case was made for pulling back from the infamously high Smoot-Hawley tariffs, which were passed by Congress and signed by Republican president Herbert Hoover in 1930, through new congressional authority to allow the executive branch to negotiate reciprocal tariff-cutting deals with key trading partners. After World War II, this authority evolved into the executive branch's tool to pursue further tariff-cutting negotiations multilaterally in the GATT and advance the development of an international trading system. With Congress's concurrence that lowering global tariffs helped advance America's economic development, the goal also fulfilled President Roosevelt's foreign policy vision for a postwar order of advancing freer trade globally to contribute to a stable postwar peace. Trade as a foreign policy tool was in its heyday from the 1940s to the early 1960s, coinciding with the acceleration of the Cold War.

After the State Department aggressively cut America's tariffs by around 80 percent in agreements with foreign trading partners,[98] Congress's patience with the department's approach to these "reciprocal" deals ran out after the department's officials consistently gave up more market access than it was getting from these partners in return. In 1962, Congress took the executive branch's tariff negotiating authority away from the State Department and put in the hands of a new trade office attached to President Kennedy's White House. It did so in the pursuit of much better deals, with more oversight and more genuinely reciprocal outcomes—ones that would prioritize America's economic interests at least as high as other goals.[99]

---

98   Alfred E. Eckes, Jr., *Opening America's Market: U.S. Foreign Trade Policy Since 1776* (Chapel Hill: University of North Carolina Press, 1995), 177.

99   Eckes, *Opening America's Market*, chapters 5 and 6.

Pulling America's trade policy back closer to the will and expectations of Congress was reestablished alongside the extensive new advice-and-consent approach between the branches established with the 1974 Trade Act. This arrangement, described earlier, evolved further with each successive grant of new trade negotiating authority as Congress responded to evolving constituent demands and new national trade priorities abroad. A partnership with the executive branch was essential to negotiate and achieve these outcomes with foreign governments, but it was often difficult. This congressional-executive approach to the conduct of trade policy was often difficult and fraught with problems, starting with differing priorities among the political parties. In terms of output, it also proved to be the most lasting and productive arrangement for the conduct of trade policy in American history.

With it, America turned away from the erratic approach that characterized Congress's mostly independent tariff-as-trade policy that prevailed before the mid-1930s. Prior attempts by the executive branch from the mid-1800s to negotiate some tariff deals with foreign governments were uniformly rejected by Congress, including those aimed at simply trying to keep up with preferential trade terms that other countries had secured in America's key export markets. This goal of securing equivalent treatment abroad for its exports from its trading partners, or the principle of MFN access, later emerged as a cornerstone of the American-led postwar trading system. Later, it was blasted by Trump as the handiwork of America's incompetent negotiators for not insisting on absolute, country-by-country and tariff-by-tariff reciprocity.

As with the TPP much later, attempts by presidential administrations over a century ago to play the foreign policy card with Congress to sell it a trade deal also tended to end badly. In one early case, the executive branch sought congressional approval of its mid-nineteenth-century tariff deal with the German Customs Union. The Senate balked at the tradeoff—new access for American exports of tobacco, lard, rice, and cotton in return for tariff cuts from Washington on a large number of manufactured goods. President Tyler's secretary of state then leaned in on the foreign policy case to change minds, arguing that the deal would bring "great changes in the commerce of the civilized world, and lay a solid foundation for an intimate and close commercial and political union between the United States and Germany." Not approving the deal, he added, would further affect the "standing of the government abroad."[100] Congress still refused it, just as it did with similar executive branch agreements in the 1850s and 1860s with Mexico and Hawaii and in the 1870s and 1880s with Mexico, the Dominican Republic, and Canada. Congress then continued to raise and lower tariffs, as it had, in response to constituent demands and changes in the congressional balance of power.

It was from these failures that Congress began a brief experiment in the 1890s to provide the executive branch with its guidance for certain negotiations, along with a more formal grant of authority to negotiate deals on behalf of the U.S. government. This early model of congressional-executive coordination was periodically approved and evolved into the more far-reaching authority used later for the TPP and other trade agreements.[101] However, only a handful of deals were ultimately approved in the early days of this new congressional-executive effort. Those that were approved often later were only scrapped by its trading partners after Congress switched majority parties and hiked tariffs up all over again. Of the approximately 20 limited tariff-cutting agreements negotiated by the executive branch between 1844 and 1909, only three were both enacted and brought into effect for at least a period of time.[102]

America's history shows that a bipartisan consensus for freer and more open trade, based on an alignment in the belief that it can be shaped in its terms and rules to hold greater economic opportunity than harm for America's advancement and growth, is the essential formula for advancing that goal. Foreign policy objectives can sometimes aid in sealing a deal, and moments of national mobilization may give the foreign policy case more weight than is ordinarily the case. As long as Congress has the final word, however, and where that consensus and belief in a deal's economic merits do not exist or cannot be forged, no foreign policy justification alone has been able to save trade deals that need congressional approval.

INTERNATIONAL AND OTHER IMPLICATIONS

Three days after taking office on January 20, 2017, Trump ended America's internal debate over the TPP when he followed through on

---

100   Eckes, *Opening America's Market*, 65.

101   Eckes, *Opening America's Market*, 70–74.

102   Eckes, *Opening America's Market*, 62–67; Douglas A. Irwin, *Clashing over Commerce: A History of US Trade Policy* (Chicago: University of Chicago Press, 2017), 309.

his pledge to sever America from it, signing an order instructing the U.S. Trade Representative to withdraw America as a signatory. The formal withdrawal letters, signed and delivered on January 30 to each TPP member, stated that America no longer intended to become a party to the agreement and had no further obligations relating to it. Trump's order also indicated that trade would remain "of paramount importance" to his new administration, which intended to instead "deal directly" with countries individually when negotiating new trade deals.[103]

In America, while many of the political fights over the TPP quickly dissipated after America's withdrawal, they nonetheless remained embedded in the ensuing debate over what kind of trade policy should come next. For the other TPP countries, many of which had made sacrifices and put their political credibility with their citizens on the line in order to complete it, America's withdrawal decision had the look of superpower self-indulgence, one that turned its back on its commitments in the Asia-Pacific while ceding valuable ground to China's aggressive efforts to dominate and shape the regional economy with different trade priorities designed to meet its own political and economic interests and system.

America's withdrawal also had the immediate impact of killing the TPP agreement for its other members. According to its terms, the TPP could not come into effect for any of the 12 members until at least six of its members, comprising at least 85 percent of the group's combined GDP, first secured all necessary approvals and finished all required procedures at home. Practically speaking, this GDP threshold requirement meant that both America and Japan had to be among those ready to bring it into effect. Once America withdrew, the agreement was dead and could never go into effect.

Another immediate ramification of America's withdrawal was the self-inflicted loss of enormously valuable leverage and the extensive damage to its reputation abroad. Had the Trump administration utilized the leverage it had over the agreement's future instead of just withdrawing from it, it could have, for example, attempted to use that leverage to insist on a comprehensive set of new terms for it. If those would not be met, then withdrawal remained an option. Or, simply by taking no particular action and leaving the TPP's future in limbo, the administration could have exercised greater influence with each

---

103   Donald J. Trump, "Presidential Memorandum regarding Withdrawal of the United States from the Trans-Pacific Partnership Negotiations and Agreement," The White House, January 23, 2017.

TPP member individually to resolve other trade concerns or to insist on progress on a new set of administration priorities. Instead, while fulfilling a critically important and defining campaign promise, withdrawal surrendered leverage and left a foreign and trade relations hole that would require years of new efforts to attempt to fill. These efforts, covered in the next chapter, aimed to regain at least some of what was voluntarily surrendered in January 2017.

Even before withdrawal appeared inevitable, the souring direction of the TPP debate in America had already alarmed the other member governments. Singapore's prime minister provided a typical, somber perspective, stressing in August 2016 that other countries had taken great political risks and made big decisions to participate in the TPP vision. He warned, "[America has] put its reputation on the line," and that not approving the TPP would ". . . set the U.S. back 50 years." He stressed that ". . . if at the end, waiting at the altar the bride doesn't arrive, I think there are people who are going to be very hurt. Not just emotionally, but really damaged for a long time to come." He also underscored the contrast with China, which was ". . . already engaging all of the countries in the region around its own version of trade agreements, and they're sure not worried about labor standards, or environmental standards, or human trafficking or anti-corruption measures."[104]

As the American presidential election approached and the mood turned darker over the TPP's future, retired U.S. Admiral Stavridis remarked that America's exit from the TPP would be equivalent to its "Brexit" from the Pacific region.[105] New Zealand's ambassador concurred, stressing near the eve of the election that ". . . there is no Plan B . . . unless the U.S. anchors itself in the Asia-Pacific region with this agreement, I think there is going to be a much less optimistic future."[106] Universally, America's withdrawal was viewed not only as an enormous rejection of its previous commitment to the Asia-Pacific region but also as handing a win to China, which remained engaged and stepped up its efforts to shape its own terms for trade with the region.

---

104   Brett Fortnam, "Singapore PM: U.S. Failure to Ratify TPP Would Damage Its Diplomatic Relations," World Trade Online, August 2, 2016.

105   "Outside Views: Adm. Stavridis Warns of an 'American Brexit' from the Pacific," World Trade Online, October 7, 2016.

106   "Quote-Unquote: From TPP to Brexit to the Campaign Trail," World Trade Online, October 20, 2016.

The foreign relations harm to America from its withdrawal is difficult to quantify concretely. Still, it became manifest in multiple ways over the ensuing years. It was rooted in a fundamentally profound loss of trust in America and its ability to find a way to keep its word. Regardless of whether Trump administration officials heard it directly or cared to acknowledge it, the harm to trust in America from the withdrawal was deep and remains a point often still raised in engagements with a range of U.S. government officials, business groups, and others. Withdrawal from the TPP continues to resonate and impact national, regional, and global perceptions of America to this day, even as these potential trading partners have, in many ways, moved on to advance their own interests with others.

The remaining 11 TPP members went their own way by reassembling just months after America's withdrawal to discuss salvaging the agreement for themselves. Having already taken political risks to reach an agreement that aligned with America's model for trade, most then faced new political challenges from returning to the table after America suddenly repudiated the deal for being harmful to its economic interests. At the same time, America's clean exit also clarified their options for the future of the agreement. The TPP-11 group officially convened to begin this discussion for the first time in May 2017 on the margins of the APEC trade ministerial meetings in Hanoi—the same meetings where America publicly repudiated the primacy of its commitment to the WTO system.

Having swallowed hard to help bring to fruition scores of the new TPP trade rules that America sought but that Japan had never included in its own agreements, officials in Tokyo remained enthusiastic toward the vision for this new rules-based model for the region. It was the first TPP member to pass the original agreement in its parliament, coming at the end of 2016 and just as Trump made clear that America would withdraw. With the TPP then rendered dead with America's withdrawal, Japan stepped forward to exert its own brand of leadership in America's absence, helping rekindle and lead the discussions to reformulate the TPP. Tokyo, after all, had already done its difficult work at home to pave the way for the TPP, including by budgeting for large domestic support programs to help potentially displaced producers at home.

Through a series of meetings and then negotiations, the remaining 11 members agreed that the TPP deal would be difficult to renegotiate without fully unraveling. They decided instead to remove and set aside over 20 of America's demands that other TPP members had accommodated but not particularly supported. These included several rules in areas such as patent and other intellectual property obligations (including the term of data protection for biologics), express delivery–related commitments, some investment provisions, and transparency-related provisions for government pricing of drugs and medical devices. Other necessary legal and market access changes were also made to reflect America's exit. Overall, however, the originally negotiated TPP agreement survived mostly intact. Less than ten months after America withdrew, the TPP-11 countries agreed to a renamed and only slightly reformulated free trade deal known as the Comprehensive and Progressive Trans-Pacific Partnership (CPTPP) agreement. With it, these 11 countries worked to find a way to refloat the ship that America had abandoned and left listing.

The effort to bring the TPP back to life also attempted, in subtle ways, to maintain political space so that the Trump administration could change its mind and return. This could either come during the process of its renegotiation or, at a later date, once American exporters that found themselves locked out of some key markets were sure to bring new pressure in Washington for America's return. This pressure, in fact, materialized shortly after the CPTPP was agreed upon. It came especially from America's farm exporters, also a key Trump constituency, who anticipated substantial losses of their existing market share in Japan and elsewhere from the new market access Canada, Australia, and other countries secured by completing the CPTPP. Just two months later, in January 2018, this pressure appeared to have some effect when Trump surprised the world by announcing, "If we did a substantially better deal, I'd be open to TPP."[107] Some Republicans in Congress, Japan, a few other TPP members, and several American business and agriculture associations leaped on the comment as a sign of an imminent reversal in position, a brief opening that other administration officials worked quickly to try and shut down. Rather than gravitating toward a genuine reconsideration of the TPP, the pressure to regain some of what was given up was directed instead at pressuring Japan into concluding a new, limited bilateral agreement to give back to U.S. farmers nearly all the agriculture access they had in Japan with the TPP. This is explored in the next chapter.

The CPTPP redux still encountered strong domestic opposition in some TPP-11 member countries. Particular opposition arose in Malaysia and then later in Chile, where enormous anti-establishment protests

---

107   Jacob Pramuk, "Trump: I Would Reconsider a Massive Pacific Trade Deal If It Were 'Substantially Better'," CNBC, January 25, 2018.

erupted in Santiago in 2019 that, to some degree, were also in response to the government's efforts to ratify the CPTPP. Both eventually approved the agreement years later, but only after facing and working to overcome deep domestic dissent. Other governments also faced their own challenges. The CPTPP agreement came into effect for some of the TPP-11 beginning in December 2018 and then, later, among all by mid-2023 as each finally overcame their domestic opposition.

The CPTPP's conclusion also freed up momentum and resources for many of its members to rededicate to negotiations for another regional agreement in Asia, the 16-party negotiation for a Regional Comprehensive Economic Partnership (RCEP). The negotiation, which spanned countries across East and Southeast Asia along with India, Australia, and New Zealand, was long discussed but only started after the TPP negotiations were underway. Once begun, however, the RCEP negotiations moved at a glacial pace and, at times, appeared to essentially stall. After America withdrew from the TPP, the RCEP negotiations picked up again in pace and seriousness, moving from a negotiation that few expected to ever reach a deal to one that gained new energy and purpose. RCEP was eventually concluded and signed in November 2020 by all its original negotiating parties—except India, which, in a similar jarring decision to the one America sent with its TPP withdrawal, dropped out at the last minute before the agreement was concluded, having decided that the agreement would not be in India's best interest. The RCEP agreement was eventually signed (uncoincidentally) just days after America's 2020 presidential election.

America's model and its *in absentia* contribution to the new rules for global trade began to then flourish as the CPTPP continued to attract greater interest from countries worldwide. Fresh from having gone its own way by exiting the EU, Great Britain was one of the earliest to express its desire to attach itself to the CPTPP as a sign of its eagerness to integrate and benefit through free trade with key Asia-Pacific nations. In 2023, the UK eventually became the twelfth member of the agreement. Others stood in line for their turn, with formal expressions of interest coming from China, Taiwan, Ecuador, Costa Rica, Uruguay, and Ukraine. Active discussions in countries such as South Korea, the Philippines, and Thailand were also underway by the end of 2023 to consider the same. America's centerpiece in its pivot to Asia, first announced in 2009, was evolving into the new global trade model that it once championed but then rejected.

The failure of the TPP in America followed a long line of efforts by prior American presidential administrations to negotiate new deals to avoid America losing its place, both commercially and diplomatically, in world trade. Few of these passed in Congress up until the mid-1930s, when in the context of the Great Depression and then World War II, Congress handed great discretion over tariff policy to the executive branch. After Congress reclaimed much of its power in 1974 and struck a new partnership with the executive branch to pursue more complex trade policy objectives beyond tariff liberalization, America's postwar bipartisan political consensus favoring trade liberalization survived with the addition of new rules to ensure its trading partners did not employ other means to undermine America's access to their market or otherwise unfairly advantage their own exports.

This model evolved and greatly expanded with America's pivot to free trade agreements, enabling it to take these rules far beyond what could ever be accomplished with the full GATT and then WTO membership. With America quickly losing faith in the future of trade liberalization in the WTO and then encountering new discord at home over its own rules-based model for its free trade agreements, it found itself again at a new juncture by the mid-2010s. This time, and now sitting on the sidelines as other countries continued to open their markets to one another, America began its search for a new approach. The next chapter looks at this effort to develop a new set of priorities and a new model for U.S. trade agreements, focusing on America's efforts from 2017 to forge new trade deals in the Asia-Pacific.

FIVE

Walking Out and Into a Revolving Door

AMERICA'S SEARCH FOR A NEW TRADE MODEL IN THE ASIA-PACIFIC

D ays after Trump signed the order to withdraw America from the TPP agreement, his skeleton White House trade team paid a visit to America's senior career trade negotiators, many of whom had themselves led different chapter negotiations for the TPP. Joined by the small "landing team" of new administration officials at the Trade Representative's office, Peter Navarro, the director of the White House's new National Trade Council, and Jason Greenblatt, Trump's Representative for International Negotiations, came to share the new administration's direction for America's trade policy, along with instructions and requests for guidance and help.

Billed initially as a staff meeting on plans to renegotiate NAFTA with Mexico and Canada, it moved into an entirely different scope when Navarro began naming a list of 14 countries. The Trump administration, he continued, intended to begin new trade agreement negotiations with each and would immediately begin consultations with Congress to set the plan into motion.

The list included new trade agreements with Mexico and Canada. It was still unclear whether these agreements would be handled together or individually. Additionally, the list included South Korea, with which America also had a free trade agreement, the UK, which had voted to leave the EU months earlier, and Thailand. In addition to Mexico and Canada, it included the remaining nine members of the TPP—Japan, New Zealand, Malaysia, Vietnam, and Brunei, with which America had no free trade agreement, and Chile, Peru, Australia, and Singapore, with which it already did. The fact that the plan included turning a single, five-year effort to finish the TPP agreement into 11 brand-new negotiations with the same countries did not go unnoticed.

With the addition of Thailand, the Trump administration's initial plan and intentions would have expanded the reach of America's trade agreements with Pacific Rim nations beyond even those of the Obama administration. Except for Thailand and the UK, the plan also was about going back to try and fix the past with NAFTA and the TPP.[1] Even the goal of striking a new agreement with a new conservative UK government seemed to be motivated by a desire to help it fix its own past, with many in the administration having welcomed the UK's preparations to pull out of the EU.

Each agreement would be concluded individually with each country, except for perhaps handling Mexico and Canada together. The administration also expected to achieve new goals in all these agreements. These included adding strong currency manipulation provisions and rigid content rules for automobiles and other goods—issues that Trump had highlighted with his criticisms of the TPP. Combined with other new features, the intention was that they would also be negotiated to ensure none of the 14 new deals would ever result in a trade deficit for America.

The focus on individual, as opposed to regional or other multiparty agreements, came straight from Trump's campaign promises. As president, his January 23 order to withdraw America from the TPP repeated the same: ". . . it is the intention of my Administration to deal directly with individual countries on a one-on-one (or bilateral) basis in negotiating future trade deals."[2] The 12-party TPP, he claimed, needlessly diluted America's interests by the compromises made to accommodate all 11 other TPP countries and their interests. Left unanswered was why the Trump administration expected other countries to realistically leap at the opportunity to negotiate with it, with most having just been left at the TPP altar; also unclear was if the administration was ready to make other threats to coax or force these countries to negotiate to complete these agreements.

---

1 America began negotiating a free trade agreement with Thailand starting in 2004, an effort suspended in 2006 and never resumed after the Thai military took over control of the government.

2 "Withdrawal of the United States from the Trans-Pacific Partnership Negotiations and Agreement," 82 Fed. Reg. 8497 (January 23, 2017).

Navarro previewed the ambitious plan on a Sunday television news program soon after, confidently asserting that all was under control since the administration had a plan to quickly recapture the foreign access it had lost by withdrawing from the TPP by negotiating new deals with each individual TPP member. He then called out Japan, Australia, New Zealand, Malaysia, and Thailand as specific targets for new deals.[3]

As internal preparatory work got underway, larger substance and process questions remained to be resolved. Which modifications to America's existing trade agreement model would be made, or would an entirely new one be built? How would the scores of priorities that Congress also expected to be included in that model, some of which, following the TPP's failure, appeared no longer supportable by most of its members, be accommodated alongside the administration's new objectives? Where differences in negotiated outcomes inevitably emerged among these 14 agreements, how would the administration handle the inevitable requests to go back to fix each to meet the additional demands Congress would insist upon to pass them? Would Congress be willing and able to take up to 14 potentially divisive trade votes on the agreements to get them through? Finally, was it in any way possible to realistically complete all 14 agreements in "Trump time" in light of existing manpower and other available resources, multiple legal requirements from Congress with long pre- and post-negotiation waiting periods, regular required consultations and reviewing periods for new negotiating proposals before each round, and a typical negotiating timeline of 24 months for actual negotiations?

These and many other questions quickly came to the fore, both in the minds of career negotiators and in exchanges with congressional trade committee staffers during a first round of consultations that Navarro joined in early February. Some common themes emerged in response to the 14-country plan, beginning with an airing of some of the same fundamental disagreements on Capitol Hill that remained unresolved from the TPP debates. Another was the need to prioritize trading partners and seriously consider substantially paring back the number of planned agreements. Several staffers on both sides of the aisle asked why it would not be easier just to go back to the TPP instead and fix it. Others seemed to welcome the administration's enthusiasm in coming to Congress so

---

3   "Future of NAFTA in Question after Mexico Meeting Canceled: Peter Navarro Provides Insight," Sunday Morning Futures, Fox News, February 4, 2017 (recorded January 31, 2017), https://www.foxnews.com/video/5301885718001.

early and for showing an intent to keep America competitive in global markets. Overriding everything was a shared, palpable unease with how all of this could possibly fall into place and the question of what would happen next.

The next round of consultations with Congress during that late winter and early spring focused on first renegotiating with Mexico and Canada, which the administration came to embrace as its top priority to get started. The administration identified for career negotiators new deals with Japan and the UK as the next two priorities, followed by a renegotiation of the South Korea deal. Further staff work was requested to prepare for these three countries, including to be ready to discuss them with congressional committee members at the administration's next set of consultations.

Of the 14 countries, only three deals with four—Mexico/Canada, South Korea, and Japan—came to fruition. The administration also eventually started full free trade deal negotiations with the UK and Kenya, which were interrupted by the COVID-19 pandemic in March 2020 and then ultimately downgraded into framework talks with no tariff liberalization by the Biden administration. The Trump administration started a negotiation with the EU, as the Obama administration had likewise attempted. It ultimately spun in circles of disagreements over what would be covered in the negotiations before it could start in earnest.[4]

Other agreements included in the administration's initial 14-country plan faded away quickly in priority and attention. Lighthizer, who was not confirmed until mid-May and would be responsible for everything, also had a major agenda to pursue with China and the WTO. The other ten countries initially targeted for new deals were never officially notified of their invitation from the Trump administration to negotiate—an invitation that most, if not all, were probably happier to have never received.

As discussed earlier, walking out entails having a solid tactical plan and enough leverage to successfully change expectations to walk back in on one's terms or, otherwise, be prepared to walk away eventually. The Trump administration's threats to tear up the NAFTA and South Korea agreements unless satisfactorily renegotiated brought that leverage.

4　Among the more fundamental of many other differences, members of the EU parliament insisted that America's tariffs on cars be on the table, whereas EU agricultural tariffs should not be included. See European Parliament, "Trade Negotiations with US Can Start under Certain Conditions," press release, February 19, 2019.

Along with it came a refreshing degree of clarity in the political priorities of many players in Washington. Among producer groups, for example, instead of the posturing and handwringing that some engaged in with the TPP to attempt to get more from that deal, many embraced the much simpler priority of being happy with just keeping the access they already had.

On the other hand, the administration's early and clean withdrawal from the TPP agreement immediately surrendered enormous leverage to accomplish the same with several other TPP members. With the TPP gone, and with no other pre-existing free trade agreement with Japan, Vietnam, Malaysia, Brunei, or New Zealand to make other renegotiate-or-else threats over, the administration discovered it would have to concoct new leverage to arm-twist these into starting a new negotiation. For Japan, and then separately the EU, this meant raising the threat of new tariffs on their automobile and other exports to finally bring them to the negotiating table. Only with the UK and Kenya did the administration rely on the more traditional means of reaching consensus to begin free trade agreement negotiations, which is to foster a shared sense of the mutual benefits for each side from a new deal.

Pursuing its expansive agenda for new free trade agreements also required reaching a consensus on new terms for them that Congress would support. As it consulted with congressional committees and others, the Trump administration began sketching out on Capitol Hill a clearer set of its own priorities—its new model, in effect, for America's trade and its trade agreements. Its starting point was to draw sharp contrasts with some of the negotiated outcomes in America's most recent trade model, the TPP, which it dismissed as a failed, warmed-over version of America's previous model. Gaining support for its model relied on accentuating as priorities the new areas of alignment between the progressive Left and the New Right that had been revealed during the debates over the TPP.

The Biden administration took an even sharper turn to detach itself and America from its past trade model assumptions and goals in its attempt to more fundamentally rewrite them. It retained several of the Trump administration's new priorities but then jettisoned all tariff liberalization objectives, starting with shutting down its ongoing and other planned free trade agreement negotiations in favor of other approaches. Then, it set out to develop and add its own objectives to redefine the core purpose and method for its new-style model agreement through an attempt to negotiate one in the Asia-Pacific. After touting it as a sharp turn away from TPP-style trade agreements by leaving out tariff goals and most other traditional trade rules, the administration's effort nevertheless flopped when union supporters in Congress opposed it for failing to meet their all-or-nothing expectations for new labor rights rules. With it, America first completed a few spins inside a revolving door of its own political making, initially stepping in after walking out on TPP in early 2017 and then finally stepping back out in late 2023 to find itself on the outside and isolated from most other nations over its new approach to trade.

This chapter focuses on America's post-TPP efforts to develop and project a new trade policy model, centering on efforts by both administrations to negotiate new trade agreements in the Asia-Pacific region. Each administration's approach is first explained and examined, followed by three cases to illustrate how they were applied in these efforts: the Trump administration's negotiations and agreements with South Korea and with Japan, and the Biden administration's attempt at a new-style agreement with the region under its Indo-Pacific Economic Framework (IPEF) effort. The major takeaways from these efforts are then examined alongside their impacts on America's trade relations in the region.

AMERICA'S NEW "NEW MODEL FOR TRADE" AND THE MADNESS OF ITS METHOD

After walking out and away from the TPP before the dust could even settle on the incoming president's furniture, attention turned to which might be next to fall prey to Trump's campaign threats to tear up more free trade agreements unless they were renegotiated on better terms for America as well as what, exactly, America would insist be done differently. As it turned out, his administration's new formula for doing these deals "smarter" principally came down to just a few elements. These included setting a revised purpose, adopting a new method, and then either accelerating or throwing into reverse America's previous approaches in just five principal negotiating areas. All these elements were present in its priorities for its initial 14-country plan, its approach to new and renegotiated free trade agreements, and its marketing of those agreements to the American public.

Its approach was most fully fleshed out in the terms of its renegotiated NAFTA with Mexico and Canada, which included the new elements but otherwise essentially borrowed and added to the same trade rules from the just-torn-up TPP model. Other additions to the updated NAFTA deal came only after Democrats took up a range of labor union demands to seek further changes to pass the agreement in Congress. The administration, in turn, worked with Mexico and Canada to accommodate many of these Democratic Party demands, which mainly boiled down to adding further labor rights obligations and an associated new enforcement mechanism.

The Trump administration's revised purpose for America's free trade agreements was rooted in its fundamental belief that they could be negotiated to help fix what, at the time, was a $700–$800 billion annual trade deficit in goods with the world. If strictly using America's trade balance with its free trade agreement partners as a measure of success, America's use of these agreements had *helped* it most often come out ahead, according to one yardstick. In terms of goods trade alone, America had a $71 billion goods trade deficit with all 20 of its free trade agreement partners in 2016, accounting for about 5 percent of its total goods trade with them. This is compared to a deficit of 30 percent of goods trade with its non–free trade agreement partners. If America's services surplus of $80 billion with these same 20 free trade partners was also included, America ran a combined goods and services $9 billion trade surplus in 2016 with all of its free trade partners.

In defining the deficit problem to resolve, however, the Trump administration routinely and selectively discounted the significance of America's services exports. Service exports can include anything from digital services purchased by a foreign client to patent royalties paid from abroad to American innovators to travel dollars spent by foreign tourists in America. These exports all represent dollars coming into America from services-based transactions with foreign consumers. Adding America's services surplus to its goods deficit cut its total deficit with the world by about a third, or to just under $500 billion in 2016 terms. The administration, nonetheless, routinely stuck to citing its goods trade imbalance as its preferred measure of accounting for America's standing in global trade and the success of its trade agreements.

Keeping to this goods-only yardstick, among its 20 free trade partners, America routinely maintained balanced trade or trade surpluses with 16 of them. Goods trade with only four regularly registered large and recurring trade deficits. One is Israel, America's first free trade partner, with which America routinely ran annual goods trade deficits. The administration never targeted this agreement, however, even with a goods deficit totaling $9 billion in 2016 that represented 25 percent of the two-way goods trade. Goods deficits with Mexico, Canada, and South Korea ($63 billion, $11 billion, and $28 billion, respectively, for

2016) instead were targeted; this targeting was accompanied by accusations that the principal reasons for these numbers were the failed models of NAFTA and the South Korea free trade agreement. In relative terms, these deficits accounted for 12 percent, 2 percent, and 25 percent, respectively, of America's two-way trade in goods with each. America's combined $74 billion goods deficit under NAFTA and its $28 billion goods deficit with South Korea quickly became the focus of Trump's renegotiate-or-else threats.

The Trump administration also refused to accept the overwhelming view of economists that a country's total trade deficit with the rest of the world is the direct result of macroeconomic factors related to national savings and investment and other imbalances, and thus ultimately uncorrectable through its trade agreements. Like squeezing a balloon, resetting trade agreement terms with one or a few countries more in its favor would still not solve America's overall trade deficit; according to this view, it would only then *grow* with other countries so long as the macroeconomic factors remained the same. While not a solution for America's overall deficit, Lighthizer and others were correct in asserting that the terms of any individual trade agreement could potentially make a difference in America's deficit or surplus with that particular country. A heavily weighted agreement in America's favor could tilt the balance in trade with that country, at least for a period of time, but often only by imposing terms that were so skewed as to be unlikely to be accepted by others or that would fail to meet WTO-consistent terms for these free trade agreements.

The politics of trade deficits tend to begin with a different set of assumptions. In the political arena, a negative trade balance is easily represented and intuitively understood as a net loss of jobs to imports. Economists have a broad range of views about this simpler presumption.[5] Setting that aside, at least as a political issue, it then follows that any trade agreement advertised to add new jobs but that also contributes to the loss of others (at least in the short term), or that facilitates new export gains but still leads to sizable and acute dislocations from import competition, always has the potential to become a potent political problem.

5   For typical opposing views, see, e.g., Josh Bivens, "Yes, Trade Deficits Do Indeed Matter for Jobs," Working Economics Blog, Economic Policy Institute, May 28, 2015; and Robert Z. Lawrence, "Trade Surplus or Deficit? Neither Matters for Changes in Manufacturing Employment Shares," Working Paper 20-15, Peterson Institute for International Economics, Washington, DC, September 2020.

In countries like Japan, for example, the public's perception of the importance of trade to its economy and jobs has long been shaped by a sense that its routine trade surpluses made trade a net gain for the country and, thus, were something to continue to be pursued. For America, with trade deficits rising and seemingly unstoppable after the U.S. dollar was floated in 1971, maintaining public support for free trade also at times necessitated a political response from Washington in the form of a new model or set of conditions for trade to make it work politically and economically—or at least work better. By elevating the goal of correcting the trade deficit to its top priority, the Trump administration framed it as an economic urgency demanding a head-on political response. Making the reduction and elimination of America's trade deficit its metric for success, however, necessitated a new range of options and priorities for America to pursue to attempt to achieve it.

With this new purpose, the administration's new method was to employ a much more flexible and targeted approach for its negotiations than those used by many of its predecessors and anticipated by Congress. It also often required a readiness to either work around or ignore WTO obligations, as covered earlier, or to walk out on some longstanding domestic and international expectations and norms for these agreements, as covered in chapters 3 and 4. Removing foreign tariffs and non-tariff barriers remained a high priority, for example, but the access to America's market offered in return would be pruned and tailored much more selectively.

The administration's method was most fully fleshed out with Mexico and Canada in the renegotiated NAFTA, which also was given an updated name—the United States-Mexico-Canada Agreement (USMCA). That fully redone agreement left in place NAFTA's tariff-free trade on nearly all goods and even added to it a handful of new two-way opening commitments with Canada for some dairy products. The main updates to NAFTA instead came from the extensive overhauls and additions made to its trade rules. Political support in Congress to pass the USMCA came not because the deal opened many new doors for U.S. exports but rather because these rules were intended to constrain and rein in NAFTA's terms for tariff-free trade. By contrast, negotiations with South Korea and Japan were dramatically more limited in scope and surgical, both in approach and outcomes. The administration also utilized different legal authorities from Congress to achieve those two outcomes, which did not require a congressional vote for approval and allowed for a certain degree of further flexibility in outcomes. Had negotiations with the EU progressed beyond a very early stage, those too may have gone in the same direction as the outcomes with Seoul and Tokyo, in the search for a smaller number of agreeable outcomes instead of a fully comprehensive free trade agreement. All these negotiations also involved the administration's blunt application of leverage to force these trading partners to the bargaining table, ranging from threats to tear up existing agreements (in the case of NAFTA and South Korea) to imposing new tariffs on their auto exports (all). A particular focus on auto trade was another feature of each negotiation, given its overwhelming contribution to America's large goods deficits with these trading partners.

Among the administration's more flexible, more leveraged methods was Lighthizer's effort to set an automatic five-year termination period for the updated NAFTA deal unless all parties explicitly agreed to renew it. Strapping a stick of dynamite and a timer to the agreement served two primary purposes. The first was to maintain leverage into the future, and setting a five-year term meant America's decision would be made during Trump's second presidential term, if achieved. A second purpose of dangling the prospect of America's future withdrawal was to discourage and give pause to American companies when making new investment and sourcing decisions for Mexico and Canada. However, the same uncertainty would also work in reverse for U.S. exporters: a farmer who otherwise would have invested to plant new fields to export tariff-free to Canada or Mexico also would think twice about whether that investment would ultimately pay off. Lighthizer was never able to sufficiently convince Congress, much less Mexico and Canada, to go along with his idea, which was softened to become an automatic progress review after the agreement's fifth year. America still retained the right to withdraw, but there would be no immediate crisis moment to force some decision. Creating the perception that America's trade agreements and their terms may not remain permanent into the future was very much a part of this new method. For manufacturers and farmers relying on these agreements, this uncertainty was also the root of its madness.

Armed with its updated purpose and new method, the administration prioritized five broad areas for major changes to America's trade agreement model. Each area mirrors a key alignment in criticisms of the TPP from both the progressive Left and the New Right, as well as from America's labor unions, whose influence on trade policy choices soared amid the parties' accelerating competition to win crucial votes from their members in presidential election battleground states. Each area also focuses on changing the terms of trade and other incentives for imports into America.

At the top of that list was substantially tightening product content rules for goods to qualify for tariff-free or other preferential treatment. In a clear rejection of the weak outcome from the TPP, a particular priority was put on tighter rules for auto and auto parts production to incentivize more production among agreement parties, along with other conditions to incentivize new production in America. In the case of the USMCA, new auto content rules achieved with Mexico and Canada set that new standard, requiring higher thresholds than the original NAFTA agreement. Its rules also included brand-new innovations, such as specific new requirements for using American-made steel in the cars and new minimum wage requirements in Mexico.

The second area of change, and another contrast with the TPP, was the direct inclusion of enforceable currency obligations in these agreements, along with stronger obligations that pushed well beyond the outcomes achieved with the TPP. Neither Mexico nor Canada were considered currency manipulators. However, the administration still insisted on including a new currency agreement model in the USMCA to meet its own rhetoric and as a model for other agreements. This included bringing currency obligations directly into the agreement text, instead of left to a side letter as with the TPP, and making several advances in the scope and specificity of these rules. Key congressional Republicans continued to resist making actual government interventions into currency and financial markets sanctionable. Still, transparency and reporting requirements added with Mexico and Canada were made subject to trade sanctions along with more explicit expectations and other mechanisms to deal with suspected currency manipulation if it occurred.

A third priority involved rolling back investor protection obligations, specifically the investor-state dispute settlement (ISDS) system for arbitration that sizable numbers of Democrats and Republicans had attacked in the TPP for undermining America's sovereignty, a concern that others on both sides of the aisle had rebuffed as unfounded. The Trump administration also opposed it on the same grounds, but also due to its additional claim that the ISDS system helped incentivize offshoring by American companies by lowering their political risk. The argument was difficult to prove or disprove empirically, but the point that it still potentially *benefited* companies offshoring their American manufacturing was made effectively and became a unifying argument for many. In the case of the renegotiated NAFTA, the ISDS system was dropped with Canada but still included with Mexico at the insistence of congressional Republicans, albeit with a much narrower category of investments eligible for claims.

The fourth major shift in priority reflected the administration's attempt to reverse decades-long, congressionally supported efforts to include government procurement access obligations in these agreements. Here again, Lighthizer and others in the administration turned the case for these obligations on its head by redefining what a reciprocal outcome looks like. He rejected the longstanding goal of reciprocal outcomes that achieve equivalent procurement market opportunities, insisting instead that if access to America's government procurement market was to be provided, it had to be matched dollar for dollar in actual contract value. He fought to keep procurement obligations out of the new NAFTA, succeeding by removing Canada, which still kept its access under the relevant separate WTO agreement, but failing to convince congressional Republicans to allow its removal for Mexico, where no other means of procurement access to its market would have been available.

The Trump administration's fifth priority is best described as preventing China in particular and others from also substantially benefiting from these agreements as third-party free riders. Adding stricter product content rules to agreements was a core means to accomplish this in the case of the USMCA. Another element was the addition of more extensive obligations aimed at disciplining the behavior of state-owned and state-controlled businesses and their access to the U.S. market. The administration also included a notification requirement for the renegotiated NAFTA should Canada or Mexico entertain new tariff-liberalizing negotiations with China. This was to signal America's right to reassess its own commitments if either nation considered opening its market further to China and thus opening new routes for its intermediate goods to find their way more cheaply into the U.S. market. These and other China-focused safeguards were integral to the administration's new approach.

The Trump administration ran into the buzzsaw, however, over some of the other rules it added from the latest U.S. model, the TPP. Facing a Democratic Party–controlled House of Representatives, the administration had to drop some of these outcomes, including removing entirely from the agreement a period of data protection for biologic medicines. Democrats also demanded even more expansive labor rights obligations and a new labor enforcement mechanism as their price for supporting it. These trade-offs appeared to hint at compromises that might have helped the TPP to win support except for other, sharply different circumstances: whereas the TPP newly opened America's market further to imports to gain export opportunities, the updated deal with Mexico and Canada narrowed existing terms of access to the U.S. market and was propelled by Trump's gun-to-the-head withdrawal threat as a catalyst for a forced compromise.

The Biden administration began with its own new purpose and method, and by adding several further negotiating priorities to the Trump administration's own five overarching goals. Its new purpose was to turn more sharply away from America's "corporate trade deals," as criticized by labor unions, in favor of "worker-centered" approaches. One result was that the administration avoided negotiations with any new tariff liberalization for its new-style agreements. When challenged over why America had abandoned negotiating new free trade deals, Biden's national security advisor made clear that his boss was ". . . looking to move beyond the old model of an FTA [free trade agreement] to a model that is actually more geared to today's economic realities and to the lessons of the last 30 years."[6] The administration also aimed to achieve radical reform to other trade rules. To accomplish this, it added a list of additional negotiating priorities, starting with attempts to meet the full slate of organized labor's demands for trade agreements in order to formulate its own definition of what it meant by a "worker-centered" trade policy for America.

Neither administration needed to look far for their playbooks. These elements, from purpose to method to priorities, had roots in the core positions of the anti–free trade movement and particularly in the positions of American labor unions. As their opposition to the existing agreements rose into the 2000s, the labor unions began expressing their priorities with greater coherence as a "people-centered" or as a "new model" for trade. The AFL-CIO especially championed these ideas through a series of convention resolutions and other statements, coalescing into several core pillars that established the outline and many of the details for America's new model. It was thus no coincidence that America's own trade policies, starting in 2017, came to bear an uncanny similarity to its labor movement's "new model."

---

6 The response was to a question over why it might take years to finish the free trade negotiation with the UK started by Trump but put on hold by the Biden administration. Karine Jean-Pierre and Jake Sullivan, "Press Briefing by Press Secretary Karine Jean-Pierre and National Security Advisor Jake Sullivan," press briefing, September 20, 2022.

In 2001, AFL-CIO Convention Resolution 6 blamed America's loss of manufacturing jobs and capacity on its failed "economic and trade policy," which included leaving it exposed due to the effects of "unequal trade agreements that have left our markets open to domination by the predatory policies of our trading partners . . . [that have] kept their markets closed to U.S. exports." Instead of calling, as Republicans and most Democrats had over many decades, for more aggressive rules and other commitments to open these markets to help create U.S. export jobs, its 2001 resolution called for an end to the "race to the bottom" created by trade agreements lacking meaningful labor and environmental protections. The resolution's approach advocated for protective tariffs using Section 201 and Section 301 of U.S. trade law and called for using the trade balance as the "measure of success" in negotiating agreements. It also pushed for more robust Buy American procurement policies and proposed to either renegotiate NAFTA to update its rules on labor, environment, auto trade, and investment, or scrap the agreement entirely.[7]

In 2013, as the TPP negotiations were in full swing, the AFL-CIO updated these goals to expressly call for a "new trade model" and a "new approach to trade and globalization." Resolution 12 of the union's convention that year spelled out the rest of the details of its "people-centered" approach; the Trump administration included many of these in its approach to trade agreements, and the Biden administration included almost all of them.[8] These included prioritizing labor and environmental standards, ensuring the freedom for America to regulate in the public interest, setting strong new rules for state-owned enterprises and on other unfair practices, adding strict product content rules, eliminating ISDS, adding strong currency obligations, rolling back procurement market access and supporting Buy American and other domestic preferences, ensuring "balanced" intellectual property obligations that included ensuring fair access to medicines, and allowing for trade rules that are flexible and responsive to updates and further changes as needed.[9]

In 2017, the AFL-CIO added to its support for more job-creating domestic infrastructure spending by boosting calls for new industrial

---

7 "Convention Resolution 6: An American Economy that Works for All Working Families," AFL-CIO, December 3, 2001.
8 "The Trans-Pacific Partnership: Working Families Need a New Trade Model," AFL-CIO, Executive Council statement, February 27, 2013. Also, "Convention Resolution 12: America and the World Need a New Approach to Trade and Globalization," AFL-CIO, August 26, 2013.
9 AFL-CIO, "Convention Resolution 12."

policy spending and investments to accompany it to "balance trade and share the gains from globalization." These public investments should include creating more room in America's trade obligations allowing the use of Buy American preferences, setting unified standards supporting wages and working conditions for government-funded support for selected industries to invest and create jobs, and demanding equal labor and environmental standards from America's trading partners, or else applying additional fees or tariffs on imports from countries that do not provide similar levels of protection.[10]

Finally, in 2022, the union adopted another resolution to further flesh out a "worker-centered global economic model." This included holding corporations accountable for the worker rights standards all the way down their supply chains, incorporating equity and social justice goals to labor and environmental obligations, utilizing new enforcement mechanisms, and adopting a worker-focused approach to the digital economy.[11]

The uncanny similarity among trade union priorities with those brought into the Trump and Biden administration's models was, of course, no accident. As the battle to win the White House continued, with Trump fighting Clinton and then Biden against Trump, their positions on trade were found squarely within—even at times directly plagiarized from—the core positions of America's leading trade unions. It was the same approach that came to define America's new trade policies toward the WTO, to bring back the use of Section 301 and 201 to fight Chinese and other imports, and to pull away from most traditional efforts to pursue global and regional free trade.

The Asia-Pacific region became a key proving ground for each administration's attempts to redefine America's new trade agreement model.

AMERICA'S RE-RENEGOTIATION:
THE SOUTH KOREA FREE TRADE AGREEMENT

Moon Jae-In was elected president of the Republic of Korea just one day before his swearing-in on May 10, 2017. The election was delayed following the impeachment and then removal of his predecessor, an

---

10   Stan Sorscher, "Did Someone Just Say 'Industrial Policy'?," Huffington Post, blog, February 2, 2017. This originally was also posted on Sorcher's blog on the AFL-CIO site on February 6.
11   "Convention Resolution 9: Building Power for Workers in the Global Economy," AFL-CIO, June 15, 2022.

event that ultimately advantaged Moon's substantial majority win as
the leader of the opposition party. Moon passed on an inauguration
ceremony to immediately get to work to restore a sense of political
stability, repair strife from that episode, and regain confidence abroad.
The most urgent issue facing him internationally was to pursue his campaign promises of peace through dialogue with North Korea, an olive
branch only greeted by North Korea with a series of ever-more brazen
missile launches during his first few weeks in office. Moon's planned
first overseas trip was to meet the new American president to reaffirm
the U.S.-South Korean security alliance and other partnerships, at the
same time sending an important signal to North Korea and China of
South Korea's other core interests.

Instead, what he got from his inaugural visit to Washington was a
rift with America over trade. The official visit began with an informal
meeting and working dinner on June 29, after which Trump touted his
first "very good meeting" where they discussed "North Korea and new
trade deal!"[12] The next morning, Trump told the press gathered for pho-
tos that both countries were "renegotiating a trade deal right now."[13] In
a post-meeting joint press conference, Trump underscored America's
ballooning trade deficit with South Korea since the U.S.-Korea Free
Trade Agreement (KORUS) had come into effect, and the importance
of getting to work to level the playing field for American auto exports
and by ending the dumping of South Korean steel in America. He ended
by stressing that he would "sign a deal" that would be in the interests
of both countries.[14]

President Moon did not address trade in his public remarks at
the White House but, of course, was asked the following day about
Trump's statements. Moon made clear that his meetings had produced
no consensus to renegotiate, calling Trump's comments "outside of the
agreement" from the two-day White House meetings. South Korean
officials pointed to the agreed-upon summit statement, which made no

12   Donald J. Trump (@realDonaldTrump), "Just finished a very good meeting with the
President of South Korea," Twitter, June 30, 2017, 9:44 p.m. EST, June 29, 2017.

13   Donald J. Trump, "Remarks Prior to a Meeting with President Moon Jae-in of South
Korea," June 30, 2017, online by Gerhard Peters and John T. Woolley, American Presidency
Project, https://www.presidency.ucsb.edu/node/329451.

14   Donald J. Trump, "President Trump, South Korean President Deliver Joint Statement,"
PBS NewsHour, June 30, 2017, https://www.youtube.com/watch?v=ghWqp3oL9LU.

mention of reopening the KORUS deal.[15] Moon returned to Seoul with his first major rift with America in full public view.

Trump's unilateral announcement of a renegotiation that was already underway also took American officials by surprise, although the future of the KORUS agreement was well understood to be an open question. Having flown under the radar of Trump's criticisms of other trade deals, KORUS came squarely into the spotlight in an April 2017 interview while the administration was still in its first 100 days. Trump called the Bush administration–era agreement, subsequently renegotiated by the Obama administration and eventually passed in Congress by a large majority, a "Hillary Clinton disaster," adding, "We'll either terminate or negotiate. We may terminate."[16] This followed shortly after Vice President Mike Pence previewed in a speech in Seoul that the agreement potentially had a target on its back. He told the audience, ". . . [W]e have to be honest about where our trade relationship is falling short," starting with the "fact that the U.S. trade deficit with South Korea has more than doubled" since KORUS came into force. He stressed the administration is "reviewing all of our trade agreements across the world" and will "pursue trade which is both free and fair."[17]

These statements put South Korea and others on edge. By the time of Moon's midsummer summit meeting with Trump, however, it appeared that decisions around the future of the agreement would first await the outcome of the comprehensive "performance reviews" of all American trade agreements that Trump ordered in late April and that were given up to six months to conclude.[18] Expectations for the summit were instead for a frank airing of concerns, along with probable "fix these or else" type threats from Trump about the agreement's future. Major decisions, therefore, would come only after several weeks of follow-up work.

South Korean officials did not help their own case; they failed to bring new commitments to address a lengthy list of KORUS-related and other trade concerns, despite concerns shared with them earlier. Seoul

15   Chang Jae-soon, "Moon Says Renegotiation of the US-South Korea FTA Not Part of Summit Agreement with Trump," Yonhap News Agency, July 1, 2017.

16   Philip Rucker, "Trump: 'We May Terminate' U.S.-South Korea Trade Agreement," *Washington Post*, April 28, 2017.

17   Sarah Kim, "Pence Wags a Finger at Korea-U.S. Trade Pact," *Korea JoongAng Daily*, April 18, 2017, https://koreajoongangdaily.joins.com/2017/04/18/politics/Pence-wags-a-finger-at-KoreaUS-trade-pact/3032383.html.

18   "Addressing Trade Agreement Violations and Abuses," Exec. Order No. 13,796, 82 Fed. Reg. 20819 (April 29, 2017).

instead banked on bringing announcements to Washington of a new large energy purchase and more investment by South Korean firms in America as its initial offering to help cut America's trade deficit.

South Korean officials were right to focus on the goods trade deficit as Trump's top priority but wrong to hope they could prevent KORUS from being put at the front of the firing line. Trump's derisory remarks targeting KORUS closely mirrored those from America's labor unions— another failed trade agreement that promised American exports and jobs but instead only ended in a higher "job-killing" trade deficit. America's services surplus with South Korea had risen by nearly 50 percent, or about $4 billion, between 2011 (the year before KORUS came into effect) and 2016, but its goods deficit more than doubled over the same period, rising from $13 billion in 2011 to nearly $28 billion in 2016. Approximately half of that increase, or about $10 billion, came from South Korea's sharply rising autos and auto parts exports to America, and even after the initial Bush administration agreement was renegotiated during the Obama administration to shift its terms in America's favor on automotive trade. Overall, autos and auto parts occupied nearly 90 percent of America's total goods deficit with South Korea by 2016.[19]

As the summit approached, South Korean officials were unaware that quiet plans were already underway to force another renegotiation of KORUS—a plan spearheaded by Navarro but only hinted at in public by Pence and then by Trump during the first few months of the new administration. South Korea's inclusion in the administration's initial plans for a 14-country trade agreement blitz was to be accompanied by a new presidential executive order to set the renegotiation process in motion. That never-released order defined specific objectives for the renegotiation, which would trigger America's withdrawal from the agreement if its terms were not agreed to in full and achieved in a short and defined period. Top among the administration's demands were the addition of enforceable currency obligations, setting new and extremely restrictive product content rules for autos and other industrial goods to qualify for tariff-free treatment, more rules to eliminate non-tariff barriers, and terminating the agreement's ISDS and government procurement commitments. The plan for KORUS, therefore, closely mirrored the five elements the administration set out for all its trade agreement negotiations, which, in the case of the KORUS, was actually a *re*-renegotiation.

19 "U.S. Trade in Goods and Services by Selected Countries and Areas, 1999-Present," Bureau of Economic Analysis, U.S. Census Bureau, March 11, 2024.

Other officials attempted to bring more deliberation and less ammunition to these decisions, questioning the viability of Navarro's take-it-or-leave-it plan for KORUS to meet its primary objective of improving the goods trade deficit with South Korea. With auto trade comprising the overwhelming part of that deficit, the impact of the call in Navarro's draft order for drastically hiking the KORUS product content rules for autos and auto parts under the agreement came into particular focus. Set at 35 percent under the KORUS agreement, a sharp increase in that rate would immediately make it improbable that auto manufacturers—both South Korea– and America-based—could meet it for their finished automobiles if only producing and sourcing parts within and between each country. If unable to qualify, they would no longer be eligible for tariff-free status under KORUS. Auto trade would continue between both countries, but only after importers paid the prevailing WTO tariff rates set by each country.

America's standard WTO tariff of 2.5 percent on ordinary passenger car imports had never been much of a barrier to South Korea's exports or to exporters from other countries. The net cost of the tariff was high, given the high cost of an automobile, but it had been a manageable extra cost of doing business for foreign auto exporters. On the other hand, America's 25 percent tariff rate on pickup trucks and other larger, cargo-ready passenger vehicles is a prohibitively high tariff wall to imports of vehicles in this much narrower category.

Going the other way, with high auto content rules that could not be economically met to qualify for tariff-free treatment, American-made exports would again be subject to South Korea's standard WTO tariff rates of 8 percent for passenger cars and 10 percent for light trucks. Before KORUS, these rates were high enough to disincentivize American-made auto exports to South Korea other than luxury-priced vehicles. After KORUS came into effect and these tariffs and other costly non-tariff barriers were removed, American-made automobile exports to South Korea jumped by 60 percent over the first four years of the KORUS agreement, reaching $1.6 billion by 2016—the year all U.S. auto exports to South Korea became tariff-free.[20] Even so, they remained a fraction of South Korea's auto exports to America, which also jumped in anticipation of

20 International Trade Administration, "New Vehicle Trade Data Visualization: U.S. Exports of New Passenger Vehicles and Light Trucks Total Exports HTS Value HS Basis, Export Value by Country," https://www.trade.gov/data-visualization/new-vehicle-trade-data-visualization.

the scheduled elimination of America's 2.5 percent passenger car tariff in 2016 to reach $16.1 billion that same year.[21]

KORUS did what free trade agreements tend to do—facilitate more exports going in both directions after eliminating tariffs and other barriers. The removal of South Korea's overall higher levels of tariff and non-tariff market protections led to a large jump in some imports from America. In the aggregate, however, those gains had not improved the bottom line that Trump was most focused on—the overall two-way goods trade deficit—as South Korean exports to America also increased. Hiking the auto content rules under KORUS would shift nearly all auto trade back to the ordinary tariff levels, an additional business cost of 2.5 percent for South Korean carmakers. At an 8 percent rate for most American-made auto exports, however, the rate would be high enough to kill off most of the hard-won auto export gains made to that market. The deficit-cutting, job-creating intent of a drastic hike in the autos content rule appeared dubious as a means of improving America's terms of trade.

As for the other demands outlined in the draft executive order, a meaningful agreement on currency practices held greater potential promise for moving the trade deficit needle with South Korea, as might further progress on non-tariff barriers. Its call for removing government procurement obligations would have made little difference since South Korean exporters still had a similar level of access to government contracts under the relevant WTO procurement agreement. Finally, insisting on removing ISDS provisions would have no discernable impact on the overall deficit since South Korea, with its relatively higher wages, was no longer a market that American manufacturers looked at to move their production. Moreover, since South Korean officials would have been just as happy to remove the ISDS mechanism, which had encountered strong opposition at home in the original agreement; insisting on its removal as an up-front condition would only amount to Washington giving up an important bargaining chip it could have used later to secure bigger objectives.

Instead, Trump's one-man renegotiation announcement at the late June summit bypassed all these initial preparations, setting a new series of events into motion. This next stage, from July until December, quickly tested the outer limits of Trump's personal patience. Meanwhile, South

---

21   International Trade Administration, "New Vehicle Trade Data Visualization: U.S. Imports of New Passenger Vehicles and Light Trucks Total Exports HTS Value HS Basis, Import Value by Country."

Korea's initial efforts to delay, or even derail, a formal renegotiation of the agreement in force were quickly replaced by a scramble to confront its own enormous internal legal and political challenges to prepare for it. That period can only be described as highly precarious, with the KORUS agreement capable of unraveling at any moment.

To get the renegotiation ball rolling, per the procedure under KORUS, America requested in mid-July a special meeting of the agreement's minister-led committee. The still-new Moon administration finally appointed its own trade, industry, and energy minister in mid-July, and decided also to bring in a new, specially appointed minister for trade to handle South Korea's new American trade crisis. Appointed trade minister in early August, Kim Hyun-chong was recalled to Seoul from Geneva, where he was into his second of a five-year term as a member of the WTO's Appellate Body.

Kim's urgent return to Seoul was a surprise gift for Lighthizer, creating a new, open seat on the seven-member body that allowed him to more quickly advance his quiet plan, covered earlier, to eventually choke it off by refusing to approve candidates to fill vacant seats. Kim's return to Seoul also put him back in the role he had taken over a decade earlier, one where he had originally pushed Washington hard to consider adding South Korea to America's trade agreement dance card. Later, at the 2007 KORUS signing ceremony, he came to wear a scowl upon just learning that the fruit of his effort had no chance of passing Congress without further concessions from Seoul.

Kim's scowl reappeared ten years later for the first official meeting of trade officials to discuss the future of KORUS held in Seoul on August 22. Lighthizer did not travel to South Korea and only very reluctantly agreed to Seoul's request to open the meeting with Minister Kim via videoconference as a protocol matter under the agreement. The already tense atmosphere became more tense and nearly caused that official launch to fall apart. The KORUS scowl returned, except this time on screen and from both sides.[22] Two working leads from each side were the only officials present in Seoul to hear their short opening remarks. After that volatile moment passed without incident, large delegations from each side joined for a brief photo op and then to conduct the remainder of this first day-long official meeting.

---

22   Jenny Leonard, "S. Korea Says U.S. Did Not Offer Details On Reducing Bilateral Trade Deficit," World Trade Online, August 24, 2017. For part of the story, see Lighthizer, *No Trade Is Free*, 287.

The KORUS agreement enabled this special committee to "consider amendments to this Agreement or make modifications to the commitments therein."[23] For America, the meeting was an opportunity to fully air grievances with the agreement and other unresolved trade concerns and to again officially call for its renegotiation. Seoul was given a couple of weeks afterward to provide all its official responses. It responded by insisting first on a joint study to examine the causes of the bilateral trade deficit and KORUS's potential role in it, a stipulation that its officials characterized to the press as a "precondition" to any renegotiation.[24] South Korea's demand for a "study" progressed no further than America presenting its official trade data at the meeting, rebuffed in turn by Korean officials who presented *their* own official version of their government data. South Korean officials also accused America of cherry-picking facts to make its case, proceeding to only undermine it later by presenting data highlighting substantial gains in American cherry exports as proof the entire KORUS agreement was working well.

As America's negotiators waited for South Korea's official responses, the atmosphere dramatically shifted again in early September when a press leak reported Trump was preparing to sign paperwork to withdraw from KORUS. The decision had actually been made over a week before the leak, just a couple of days after the first committee meeting ended in Seoul. Trump ultimately never signed the withdrawal letter, a draft of which was later published in print.[25] It may have been (as later reported) simply because it was removed from the Resolute Desk and then forgotten.

Other considerations also may have intervened. Internal assessments to game out the trade implications of withdrawal were quickly prepared to provide grist for more consideration among top administration officials. These included the certainty of immediate restoration of pre-KORUS tariff rates and lost gains from the end of its tariff-free imports of American farm goods, along with the related political implications of angering America's farm sector. Other factors included South

---

23   USTR, "U.S.–Korea Free Trade Agreement, chapter 22, article 22.2.3(c)," January 1, 2019, https://ustr.gov/trade-agreements/free-trade-agreements/korus-fta/final-text.

24   Minister Kim also made these points public in a post-August 22 meeting press briefing. See also Jenny Leonard, "Seoul Asks USTR to Postpone KORUS Special Session, 'Objectively' Analyze Effects of Deal," World Trade Online, July 24, 2017; and Jenny Leonard, "South Korea: U.S., in KORUS Special Session, Did Not Offer Details on How to Reduce Trade Deficit," World Trade Online, August 23, 2017.

25   Woodward, *Fear*, xxiii.

Korea's likely restoration of pre-KORUS regulatory and other barriers that disadvantaged American goods and services exports, and potential public boycotts against American exports. Another series of predictable impacts focused on the inevitable damage that a sudden withdrawal would inflict on the bilateral political relationship and security alliance. While the draft withdrawal letter left open the possibility of successfully completing negotiations before the 180-day agreement termination date, many doubted that South Korea could handle the political push-back at home against negotiating after Trump's 180-day withdrawal countdown clock was set in motion. After the leak of Trump's planned KORUS withdrawal hit the headlines, Congress and others aggressively lobbied the White House to convince the administration to pull back from the brink due to the significant harm it posed for these and other American interests.

The leak jump-started South Korean officials into finally coming to terms with the inevitability of the need for haste to agree to a re-negotiation to save the agreement. However, a series of delays from Seoul before it could indicate its readiness to proceed nearly triggered another crisis moment for the agreement's future. Trade Minister Kim eventually agreed to fly to Washington in mid-September to signal Seoul's readiness to negotiate "modifications and amendments" to the agreement, as specified under its terms. The official decision to proceed was communicated at a second special meeting of the KORUS committee, held in early October.

To officially start negotiations, South Korea first had to complete its legally mandated process to prepare for them. That process included providing opportunities for public input, a required public hearing, an economic assessment, and other steps.[26] South Korean officials initially expected that America would also have to follow its own, similar congressionally required process to begin negotiations, but later were informed that the administration already had the authority to negotiate certain changes. Congress provided that authority in the implementing law for the agreement passed in tandem with the KORUS deal, giving the executive branch a range of freedom that included resetting some tariffs

---

26 "Enforcement Decree of the Act on the Conclusion Procedure and Implementation of Commercial Treaties," Republic of Korea Presidential Decree No. 24424, as amended March 23, 2013; "Act on the Conclusion Procedure and Implementation of Commercial Treaties," National Assembly of Korea, Act No. 11717, March 23, 2013.

and changing some rules.[27] Congress still expected to be consulted, but the administration could begin negotiations relatively promptly, followed by a 60-day "consultation and layover" period and a required economic assessment after any agreed, final changes could be brought into force by executive action.

The procedural and time pressures to begin official negotiations thus remained squarely on South Korea to finish its legal procedures, which typically took five to six months. Officials in Seoul moved to meet these requirements as quickly as possible while the Trump administration prepared and waited. Facing substantial pushback from its public, the Moon administration's first attempt to hold a required public hearing was so rancor-filled that it had to be shut down and rescheduled, resulting in an additional delay in completing that step. Every week that passed as it moved through these procedures was another week that risked stoking further impatience from Trump and others in the administration. South Korea's official procedures were finally completed in very late December, taking just under three months and only after expending incredible efforts and political capital to make it possible.

Official negotiations finally got underway on January 5 in Washington, where the American side orally presented an open-ended but extensive list of revisions to the agreement that it expected from the negotiations. This was the first opportunity to formally exchange expectations on both sides before moving to present text-based proposals. A second round took place in Seoul from January 31 to February 1, where the first sets of official, text proposals were presented and discussed for the start of line-by-line negotiations. At this point, seven months had passed since Trump unilaterally announced that negotiations were already underway during his summit meeting with Moon in Washington.

While the final outcomes from the negotiations were referred to later as a "mini-deal," the scope of America's initial proposals was substantially more extensive than what was ultimately agreed. These included the immediate elimination of tariffs on American manufactured goods exports not yet fully phased out by South Korea, lengthy freezes for America's own manufactured goods tariffs not yet fully eliminated (which included its 25 percent tariff on pickup and light trucks), significantly tightened product content rules for autos and some other industrial goods, further revisions to automotive trade rules to improve access

---

27   United States–Korea Free Trade Agreement Implementation Act, Pub. L. 112-41 (October 21, 2011).

for more American auto exports in future years and to facilitate further alignment of environmental standards with America's own standards for autos, a new agreement to end South Korean currency market intervention and enhance transparency, and additional commitments to address a long list of other trade concerns across a range of individual industry and cross-cutting issues from legal services to labor rights.[28]

Seoul, of course, had its list, including signaling its intent to counter the wide range of America's tariff demands, a series of changes to narrow and weaken the agreement's ISDS investment rules, changes to the agreement's provisions on trade defenses relating to anti-dumping and similar measures, and a shorter list of other proposed changes such as to the agreement's product content rules for a handful of textiles.[29]

Preparations were underway for the next round of negotiations, anticipated for late February or early March, to exchange all remaining official text proposals and move into full text-based negotiating mode. Three negotiating rounds in just two months constituted a breakneck pace for an international trade negotiation, all of course intended to meet White House expectations for completing a deal in "Trump time."

Instead, the pressure of the ticking clock led to the renegotiation's third clarifying moment, which came in mid-February. With his patience fully expended, Trump ordered, against the views of his defense secretary, that South Korea be informed that paperwork for withdrawal would be signed unless it promptly agreed to new terms for KORUS. This constituted Trump's third particularly serious threat of imminent withdrawal, prompting a heads-up and invitation to Kim to return to Washington as soon as Lighthizer could meet. Either a deal would be finished, or Seoul should expect to be done with it.

Newly added to this mix was the release on February 16 of the U.S. commerce secretary's recommendation to impose Section 232 tariffs on global steel and aluminum imports.[30] Steel and steel-product imports from South Korea were a major dollar export category and long the focus of American anti-dumping investigations. These investigations also were the focus of several Washington law firm practices, among

---

28 See, e.g., "South Korea Expects Tough Trade Talk, More Pressure from U.S. in January," World Trade Online, January 8, 2018.

29 Dan Dupont, "U.S., Korea Address Autos, ISDS and 'Sensitive' Issues at First KORUS Session," World Trade Online, January 11, 2018.

30 U.S. Department of Commerce, "Secretary Ross Releases Steel and Aluminum 232 Reports in Coordination with White House," press release, February 16, 2018.

which Lighthizer was a leader and knew the industry, history, and circumstances better than anyone. Kim agreed to come as Lighthizer suggested, but also to talk steel and aluminum. Aware that the clock was running out very quickly, Lighthizer offered that mid-March was the absolute longest that discussions might go, if even that long, before their final effort ended in a deal or with a clean American withdrawal from KORUS.

In this renewed high-stakes context, the renegotiated KORUS agreement quickly took shape and soon shed most of America's original ambitions. The South Korean delegation set up camp in Washington at the beginning of March, as soon as Lighthizer was free from his round of negotiations with Mexico and Canada, with Kim and other leads shuttling back and forth to Seoul as needed to consult. Trump also made known on March 2 that he intended to apply 25 percent tariffs on America's imports of steel and 10 percent tariffs on its imports of aluminum in response to the national security threat of these imports, raising the question of whether America's security treaty allies such as South Korea might fare better.[31] South Korean officials expected to talk about it, particularly after learning that Mexico and Canada, which were also renegotiating their trade deal with America, might be offered better terms on steel for doing so.

Lighthizer and Kim reached a deal, officially announced on March 27, after roughly two weeks of work by both teams. The deal covered both changes to KORUS and a separate agreement on steel imports from South Korea that allowed it to avoid Section 232 tariffs but with a new, hard import quota to curtail the volume of its duty-free steel exports. In addition to new terms for steel, South Korean officials could take back to their public a few of the changes for KORUS that it sought. Its proposals for more significant changes to ISDS, which the Trump administration would have accepted if it had its way, encountered pushback from congressional Republicans. They consented to allow some definitions and other terms to be narrowed and tightened to help further prevent frivolous claims, but they balked at more fundamental revisions viewed as undermining Congress's negotiating objectives for the original KORUS agreement. Several of Seoul's requests to revise the agreement's language on anti-dumping and anti-subsidy rule provisions were also included. Congressional leaders and staffers acquiesced to the

---

31   David J. Lynch and Caitlin Dewey, "Trump Finally Gets His Tariffs—and Much of the World Recoils," *Washington Post*, March 2, 2018.

changes that Lighthizer, a champion of maintaining these strong trade defense measures, could comfortably entertain as not meaningfully undermining or weakening those protections.

For America, its dramatically scaled-back package of broader objectives for KORUS focused principally instead on securing better terms for auto trade. Among the few hundred possible tariff acceleration and tariff freeze proposals that were proposed but not yet directly negotiated, the list was quickly narrowed to just one top American tariff demand—freezing the elimination of South Korea's 25 percent tariff on American pickup and light trucks for a total of 30 years under the agreement. The tariff was due for its first cut in 2019 and would fall to zero in 2021. Keeping it in place until 2041, 30 years after the initial agreement came into effect, meant adding 23 more years onto its clock. With America's other tariff proposals shelved, South Korea agreed to this one, unusually long, extension. Additional improvements and additions to the agreement's rules removing non-tariff barriers to auto trade were also made to facilitate the continued growth of American exports to South Korea. The impact of these further commitments had the potential to benefit American exports further, but only over the medium- to long-term. America's intention to tighten auto or other product content rules, although not as drastically as initially proposed by Navarro, to encourage a higher percentage of vehicle production in the United States was also abandoned before detailed negotiations could even begin. With the content rule for autos left at a particularly weak 35 percent requirement to accommodate "Trump time," the steelworkers union expressed disappointment that no progress was made on that issue.[32]

A small handful of individual trade issue priorities on each side from substantially longer lists were also covered, including steps to make customs treatment fair for American exports to qualify for KORUS tariff preferences, ending discriminatory preferences for pharmaceuticals developed in South Korea vis à vis imports, and ensuring no unnecessary delays in processing requests from South Korean textile makers for potential changes to American content rules.

Among these dramatically limited outcomes, the freeze on America's 25 percent light truck tariff held the most potential significance for the bilateral trade deficit. Just how significant that might be depended on a range of possible scenarios, including where South Korean automak-

---

32 United Steelworkers, "USW: USTR's Renegotiation of U.S.-Korea FTA Should Help Save Jobs," press release, March 28, 2018.

ers decided to make light trucks for sale in the American market and, if made in America, whether they did so by adding new production capacity or instead just moving existing model production that would only be exported back to American consumers to accommodate light truck production in the United States.

The U.S. International Trade Commission was tasked with estimating the probable trade impacts of the agreement to freeze the light truck tariff until 2041. It could only speculate in its answer, developing five scenarios that revolved around various assumptions of future production decisions and market share shifts for South Korean firms. It estimated that, in the most probable case, America could avoid 59,000 new vehicle imports annually, although other scenarios ranged from the tariff freeze having no effect on the deficit to having an even more significant impact of avoiding 131,000 in annual vehicle imports.[33] In dollar terms, the agency's most probable outcome equated to avoiding roughly $1.5 billion in annual future vehicle imports.[34] The potential impact of the tariff freeze on jobs was much less clear. One South Korean manufacturer began production and sales of a new pickup truck for the American market beginning in 2021, with the jobs going to its Alabama plant—but moved production of two separate car models back to South Korea in the same year, making the net impact on imports and jobs difficult to ascertain.[35]

The outcome with the greatest potential to positively impact the trade deficit with South Korea was the Treasury Department's parallel pursuit of an agreement to curb Seoul's ability to intervene in foreign exchange markets to advantage its exports. These negotiations had significantly more work still to be done when the Trump time whistle was blown in mid-February. The pace was stepped up, but with the clock suddenly run out, that agreement was not completed by the time the KORUS amendments were announced in late March. The White House fact sheet touting the final KORUS outcomes noted the unfinished state of play: "... the Treasury Department *is finalizing* [emphasis added] an

33   Jeffrey Horowitz et al., *U.S.-Korea FTA: Advice on Modifications to Duty Rates for Certain Motor Vehicles*, Publication Number 4791, Investigation Number FTA 103-031 (Washington, DC: United States International Trade Commission, June 2018).

34   Estimate by the author, using the manufacturer's suggested retail price of the newly introduced Santa Cruz pickup model in the U.S. market in the fall of 2021 ($25,000 per vehicle) multiplied by the 59,000 units estimated to not be imported from South Korea.

35   Sohn Hae-Yong and Song Kyoung-Son, "Hyundai Motor Partially Shifts Production of Sedans to Korea," *Korea JoongAng Daily*, February 7, 2021.

understanding with South Korea" that includes "strong commitments on exchange rate practices, robust transparency and reporting, and a mechanism for accountability."[36]

With the Trump withdrawal threat passed and major leverage lost, the more extensive deal on currency many expected instead started being referred to as an "understanding." The Treasury Department described that understanding later that year as a commitment from South Korea to "begin reporting publicly on foreign exchange interventions in early 2019," a transparency step it "welcomed" in its October 2018 report on foreign exchange practices to Congress. [37] The description failed to mention any actual accountability mechanism, seeming to fall short even of the TPP side letter commitments on currency that Trump often elevated as a core failure of that agreement. By September, the KORUS process moved forward with official notification to Congress of the agreed KORUS elements to prepare for their implementation by year-end. With no evidence of a written agreement or understanding on currency manipulation, some in Congress later wrote to the administration requesting an explanation for what happened to its promised mechanism.[38]

Freezing America's 25 percent truck tariff for more than two additional decades, instead of letting it phase out by 2021, was about preventing an even larger auto trade deficit—and was motivated by one South Korean automaker's plans to begin production in the near term of a new pickup truck for the American market.[39] The more immediate impact on the deficit from this March Madness negotiation scramble, and just before the Trump buzzer sounded, was the separate agreement reached on Section 232 steel. South Korea accepted a hard American import quota that cut its average annual steel exports to America by 30 percent in exchange for America's agreement not to apply its new 25 percent steel tariff on those imports. Welcomed by the steelworkers

36   "President Donald J. Trump Is Fulfilling His Promise on the U.S.-Korea Free Trade Agreement and on National Security," The White House, fact sheet, March 28, 2018.

37   "Report to Congress: Macroeconomic and Foreign Exchange Policies of Major Trading Partners of the United States," Office of International Affairs, U.S Department of the Treasury, October 2018, 1.

38   Debbie Stabenow, "Stabenow, Peters Call on Administration to Support Strong Currency Language in U.S.-South Korea Free Trade Agreement," press release, September 7, 2018.

39   Alisa Priddle, "2019 Hyundai Santa Cruz Pickup Almost Ready," *Motor Trend*, August 18, 2016.

union,[40] the goal of raising Section 232 tariffs or, in South Korea's case, setting an import quota, was incidental to KORUS, aimed at reducing overall steel imports from the world to raise domestic production.

As for the new KORUS deal, in fall 2018 Seoul managed to secure parliamentary approval for the changes, a process complicated again by America's earlier announcement in May of its new Section 232 investigation on autos and auto parts. South Korean officials were particularly concerned that this new investigation carried the potential for even more tariffs on the country's autos, which could make the effort to pass the updated KORUS terms politically impossible. Despite that, South Korea's National Assembly eventually moved forward to ratify the renegotiated deal on December 7.

Because it had stayed within the confines of the renegotiation authority it had from Congress, the Trump administration only needed to proclaim the changes by executive action to put the deal into effect in Washington. That proclamation was issued on December 21, in time for the new KORUS commitments to take effect on January 1, 2019—the original date set for the first of three annual cuts to eliminate America's 25 percent light truck tariff.

RENEGOTIATING ACCESS TO JAPAN

After the shock of Trump's January 2017 withdrawal from the TPP, Tokyo was able to forestall for over a year confronting Trump's expectation for a brand new trade agreement with Japan to slash America's chronic $60 billion-plus annual goods trade deficit. Like Seoul, Tokyo made every effort to avoid it. Unlike with South Korea, however, Trump's early withdrawal from the TPP removed the leverage of threatening to upend that agreement to negotiate different outcomes with Japan. "Trump time" slowly caught up with Japan as well, however, when over a year later, the issue was more clearly and forcefully brought up in a mid-April 2018 meeting with Prime Minister Abe. With less leverage to move that process more quickly in the face of a profoundly recalcitrant Japan, official negotiations still did not finally get underway until one additional year later.

Japan's bob-and-weave to avoid a renegotiation began during the earliest days of the Trump administration. Aware of the administra-

---

40   United Steelworkers, "USW: USTR's Renegotiation of U.S.-Korea FTA Should Help Save Jobs."

tion's intention, with Navarro having already named Japan in his list of trade agreement target countries on Sunday television, Tokyo prepared tactically to steer around it for Prime Minister Abe's first official trip to Washington in mid-February 2017. Trump raised his expectation for a new trade deal, but with other priorities on the agenda, it was not forcefully pushed at the time. The summit meeting joint statement obliquely referred to the demand, pledging "discussions . . . on a bilateral framework." What Japan aimed to focus on instead was found elsewhere in the February joint statement, which was agreement during the meeting on Abe's proposal for a new dialogue. Proposed to help divert and stall pressure for a new trade deal, Japan secured both governments' agreement to instead "engage in an economic dialogue to discuss these and other issues. . . ." Japan did all it could to focus the talks on "other issues" besides trade.[41]

Japan also got more of what it wanted from Abe's first official meeting with Trump, which was a recognition by the administration that Tokyo would "continue to advance regional progress on the basis of existing initiatives."[42] Japan's "existing initiatives" in Asia included continuing to reach a new TPP agreement without America's participation, as well as pushing ahead with negotiations among 16 Asian and Pacific countries to achieve the Regional Comprehensive Economic Partnership trade deal. For Japan, it also meant securing tacit approval from Washington to conclude its free trade agreement with the EU. Japan proceeded to conclude all three agreements for its own reasons and interests, but also did so to add more pressure back on Washington to return and knock again on the TPP door after these deals were completed and American exporters, and especially its agriculture producers, found themselves locked out of its market for many goods. America eventually knocked hard in April 2018, just not on *that* door.

When America walked out on the TPP in January 2017, Japan was walking in on its own modified version of America's vision for a new rules-based trading order in the Asia-Pacific. Japan's slightly different brand included continuing to hold back on providing full access to its agriculture markets and shaping America's trade rules to allow it the space to keep most of its own industrial policy tools and regulatory ap-

41   "Joint Statement from President Donald J. Trump and Prime Minister Shinzo Abe," The White House, February 10, 2017.

42   The White House, "Joint Statement from President Donald J. Trump and Prime Minister Shinzo Abe."

proaches that favored its industries. Abe had taken on and moved past a great deal of domestic opposition to go as far as Japan did. Joining the TPP radically transformed Japan's approach to trade agreements by leading it to eventually liberalize its market at a substantially higher level than ever before (albeit still not fully) and to commit to hundreds of trade rules more advanced than anything it had agreed to before. This, in turn, enabled Japan to begin to propagate these same approaches in its other agreements, stepping into its new role as a key leader setting and shaping the global rules-based trading order as America sat on the sidelines.

Japan could have viewed America's withdrawal as an opportunity to benefit more from the new markets opened by the TPP, but only if it also accepted the loss of preferential access to America's market, something it desired. Beyond these commercial trade-offs, Japan also always wanted America back as part of the TPP for its strategic and geopolitical goals. It worked constantly to engage America in ways that would nudge it in that direction, just as it continues to do today. However, it was a separate question whether Japan would be genuinely prepared to acquiesce and allow other significant changes to the TPP agreement to bring America into it, starting with adding strict automotive content rules and currency-related commitments.

Japan's decision to get the remaining TPP band members back together to save that agreement, but still leave room for America to come back in, meant making some important decisions about a new TPP deal. In the end, the TPP agreement was renamed the Comprehensive and Progressive Trans-Pacific Partnership (CPTPP), which essentially left untouched all TPP commitments except for a handful of new additions to it and by omitting around two dozen obligations that America wanted but others did not. Leaving it virtually the same meant Japan's tariff and other market access commitments remained unaltered. This included leaving unchanged several preferential quotas for farm goods imports that Japan created for America and other TPP members to access together. With America out, the remaining TPP members were able to take and keep Japan's same preferential quota access just for themselves.

With the KORUS renegotiation just finished, NAFTA still under re-negotiation, Section 232 tariffs on steel and aluminum and Section 201 tariffs on washing machines and solar panels implemented, and Section 301 tariffs announced to begin the China trade war, the administration turned again to its plans for a deal with Japan. Lighthizer indicated in congressional hearings in March 2018 that the administration hoped to proceed soon. Tokyo readied its next bob-and-weave in time for Abe's April 18 summit meeting with Trump in Florida.

This time, Prime Minister Abe came with newly elevated hopes of achieving his goal after news leaked of Trump telling U.S. agricultural industry and farm-state political leaders in an April 12 meeting that the TPP was worth reconsidering. Facing the real threat of losing large agriculture markets in Japan after its completion of the CPTPP in November and from its separate free trade deal with the EU the following month, America's agriculture producers were put on edge. In response to these concerns, as one meeting participant described it, "[Trump] just directed Kudlow and Lighthizer to sort of look at what could be done to get us back into that [TPP] agreement" on substantially modified terms. Others described it as an expressed readiness to consider agreements, not strictly bilateral, that might include negotiating a regional alternative to the TPP.[43] Either way, suddenly, it appeared that Japan might instead have the leverage it was counting on to coax America back in, albeit with the undesirable addition of America's new and expansive renegotiation expectations for its trade agreements.

As quick as this opening had come, it seemed shut again just a day later and only five days before Abe's arrival. Trump stated that the TPP would only be possible if made "substantially better," adding that since America already had free trade deals with six of the 11 CPTPP members, he was instead ". . . working to make a deal with the biggest of those nations, Japan, who has hit us hard on trade for years!"[44] With Japan's agriculture market locked up, ministers from Australia to New Zealand threw cold water on the suggestion of entertaining any significant renegotiation of the CPTPP to accommodate America coming back in. One minister from Japan also underscored the difficulty of making virtually any changes to it without the agreement falling apart.[45] It did not ultimately matter, because shortly after he met with Abe in Florida, Trump took to the internet to entirely kill off again the prospect he raised of returning to the TPP: "While Japan . . . would like us to go back into TPP, I don't like

43   Margaret Brennan, Mark Knoller, and Emily Tillett, "Trump Looking to Re-Enter TPP, Says Sens. Pat Roberts, Ben Sasse," CBS News, April 13, 2018; and Anshu Siripurapu and Brett Fortnam, "Senators Cautiously Optimistic about Trump's TPP Directive to Lighthizer, Kudlow," World Trade Online, April 19, 2018.

44   "Quoted: Foreign Trade Ministers on Trump's Latest TPP Comments," World Trade Online, April 13, 2018.

45   World Trade Online, "Quoted: Foreign Trade Ministers on Trump's Latest."

the deal. . . . Bilateral deals are far more efficient, profitable and better for OUR workers."[46]

After Trump's attempt in the summit meeting to force the issue of a bilateral free trade deal, the Japanese side emerged to proclaim the president's agreement to yet another dialogue. The summit's joint statement announced a new round of trade consultations would begin for ". . . free, fair, and reciprocal trade and investment."[47] With no actual agreement on a name for the dialogue and a fundamental lack of clarity on what purpose it would potentially serve, Japan immediately moved to fill that space. Japan unilaterally called it the "Free, Fair, and Reciprocal (FFR) Trade Talks," announcing that the consultations would not be used to discuss a new free trade deal and that their first meeting would not take place until June 2018 at the earliest.[48] Trump, in stark contrast, told the press after the meeting that ". . . we're negotiating. And what I really prefer is negotiating a one-on-one deal with Japan," adding "And we will hopefully, in the not-too-distant future, have a very good deal. . . ."[49] Unnamed Japanese officials even chose to deny to the media that Trump had ever insisted on a free trade deal negotiation with Abe.[50]

The next few weeks did not go much better. As the Abe government was in the midst of seeking to pass the CPTPP agreement in parliament, Japanese officials continued to use various tactics to delay engaging with America. When Washington officials followed up to advance summit discussions for a new trade agreement, Tokyo responded that it was still far too busy with the CPTPP and would have to deal with America and their new dialogue later. At one point, Japan's deputy prime minister, Taro Aso, tried to pin any delays on America, proclaiming to the media that American negotiators were simply too busy with NAFTA renegotiations

46   Donald J. Trump (@realDonaldTrump), "While Japan and South Korea would like us to go back into TPP I don't like the deal for the United States," Twitter, April 18, 2018.
47   "President Donald J. Trump's Summit Meeting with Prime Minister Shinzo Abe," The White House, April 18, 2018.
48   "立場の違い明確に「FTA交渉求める発言なかった」" [Different stances revealed: "No statement demanding an FTA negotiation"], NHK, April 19, 2018; and "日米貿易など協議「FFR」6月以降で調整へ" [Coordination underway for "FFR" U.S.-Japan trade dialogue in June or later], NHK, April 22, 2018.
49   "Remarks by President Trump and Prime Minister Abe of Japan in Joint Press Conference," The White House, April 18, 2018.
50   NHK. "立場の違い明確に「FTA交渉求める発言なかった」."

and had "insufficient manpower" to begin talks.[51] American officials responded to that wildly false, self-serving statement by introducing Japanese officials in Washington to a large team of American trade negotiators who were available and ready to get started, along with a reminder to send back to Tokyo that Washington was, in fact, the one that was waiting.

The process was revived when, on May 23, the Commerce Department announced it was opening a Section 232 investigation into the national security implications of global imports of auto and auto parts imports. Earlier, Toshimitsu Motegi, Japan's minister of state for economic and fiscal policy, had been tapped to lead the new dialogue but was then said to be far too busy with steering passage of the CPTPP through Japan's parliament to get started. After the new Section 232 announcement, he decided shortly thereafter that he had the time for a phone call with Lighthizer. The discussion was friendly but frank. Motegi was left with a few things to think about, including, given the administration's new investigation into autos and auto parts, how Japan ideally preferred to work toward accomplishing Trump's goal of reducing the trade deficit with Japan.

Within a couple of weeks, discussions finally began moving toward setting a day for the first meeting between Lighthizer and Motegi. They eventually met in mid-August after further work on the meeting agenda to frame expectations for exactly what was to be discussed. Lighthizer and Motegi narrowed enough differences during their meeting to finally move the effort into a scoping exercise for the launch of a trade agreement negotiation.

In New York on September 26, five months after their Florida meeting, Trump and Abe officially concurred on a framework for the negotiations. The framework for that deal was worked out between Lighthizer and Motegi in Manhattan. On paper, the agreed-upon English version called for both countries to enter into "negotiations . . . for a United States-Japan Trade Agreement on goods, as well as on other key areas including services, that can produce early achievements," adding that both countries ". . . also intend to have negotiations on other trade and investment items following the completion of the discussions of the agreement mentioned above."[52] However, Japan's translated version

51 "麻生財務相「具体的な協議には時間」日米貿易問題で" [Finance Minister Aso—"Time needed before concrete talks" on U.S.-Japan trade issues], *Nihon Keizai Shimbun*, June 8, 2018.
52 "Joint Statement of the United States and Japan," The White House, September 26, 2018.

for its domestic audience presented a picture of a negotiation that was limited to reaching an agreement only on goods tariffs and other goods market access commitments. The government's translated embellishments to the agreed text even included a different name for the final agreement, which, translated back into English, was the "Japan-U.S. Trade Agreement *on Goods (TAG)* [emphasis added]," an option that was explicitly rejected by Lighthizer. The Japanese version also included a different handling of the statement's mention of adding services to the scope of talks in an effort to downplay it.[53] Official Tokyo then gave it a further spin, insisting that the envisioned agreement would be "strictly limited to trade in goods and is different from a comprehensive free trade agreement."[54]

Awkward tap dancing ensued from inevitable press questions about all these inconsistencies in the agreed text in English with the translated version in Japanese. Beyond that, the differences mattered for two more important reasons. First, this was a clear public indication that Japan had pretty much made up its mind about the scope of outcomes of this unwanted negotiation; they would not go beyond a goods-only liberalization agreement. It became apparent that the government's original intent was to only negotiate a nearly identical agreement on tariffs to the one it reached with America in the TPP. This would give America what it wanted, which was access to Japan's consumers for its farm goods, a market that Australia, Canada, and others were poised to take over with the access they gained from CPTPP. What America would not get —until it came back to the TPP—were other benefits, including tariff-free and other access from the shared TPP quota allocations that CPTPP members had kept for a range of their agricultural exports. In exchange, Japan expected to regain the access it negotiated to America's market in the TPP on autos, auto parts, and other goods—and might be able to do even better in this area by leveraging restored access from the TPP deal to its own farm goods market.

By focusing on tariffs and quotas alone, to the exclusion of the 30 other TPP chapters of rules commitments that aimed to break down other

---

53 The Japanese version subordinated the mention of services into a parenthetical, suggesting that it only might be one of the other "key issues" negotiated in the first stage. For the Japanese version, see "日米共同声明" [Japan-U.S. joint statement], Ministry of Foreign Affairs of Japan, September 26, 2018, https://www.mofa.go.jp/files/000402972.pdf.

54 Prime Minister's Office of Japan, Chief Cabinet Secretary Suga Press Conference, September 27, 2018.

non-tariff barriers , Japan attempted to open the door for America's re-turn to the TPP and avoid new trade rule demands from the Trump admin-istration, such as on currency. Restoring nearly identical bilateral tariff outcomes served another unstated but obvious purpose—it was easier to later slap their tariff-only agreement onto the existing thousand-plus pages of other, already agreed TPP trade rules once America finally later came to its senses to enable it, from Japan's perspective, to return under these conditions as a full member of the agreement.

The second reason Japan's strategy mattered for America was be-cause this goal of reaching a broad, tariff-only agreement was a model that Congress had explicitly rejected and turned away from decades earlier. Covered previously, as America started to run significant trade deficits, Congress began in earnest to insist on the need to bundle tar-iff liberalizing agreements with other commitments from its trading partners to remove their non-tariff and other barriers. The negotiating authority that Lighthizer had from Congress for the NAFTA redo and for other free trade negotiations was heir to this approach, with Congress spelling out a full package of objectives and outcomes on trade rules to accompany any trade agreement that liberalized U.S. tariffs.

Lighthizer well understood that Japan's position of covering only tariff liberalization up front, and thus leaving all other outcomes for some time later, would never fly with Congress. This was the basis for insisting that the phrase "as well as on other key areas including services" appear alongside the mention of goods in the joint statement—to clearly indicate a broader scope beyond tariffs for the first stage of work. Even with it, Lighthizer would still have to convince Congress that a two-stage nego-tiation that also quickly delivered an agreement to regain farm export access to Japan could achieve the same ultimate end if structured well enough to succeed in both stages. It also reflected the administration's new and more flexible thinking and methods, ready to defy preset norms and expectations for a single, comprehensive agreement to achieve its goals. The necessity of Lighthizer's approach to a two-stage negotiation was explained to and reluctantly agreed upon by Japan in the statement language, after which Tokyo then unilaterally set its own expectations for the coming negotiations for its public.

America responded in kind by publicly expressing its expectations. Lighthizer informed Congress on October 16 of the administration's intent to negotiate a "U.S.-Japan Trade Agreement," the name having already been agreed to by Japan. Highlighting concern with "chronic U.S. trade imbalances with Japan," the letter to Congress indicated the administration's aim to "address both tariff and non-tariff barriers" to achieve more balanced trade; it noted that the administration "may seek to pursue negotiations with Japan in stages as appropriate, but we will only do so based on consultations with Congress."[55] America then entered its congressionally mandated 90-day pre-negotiation consultation and preparation period, which included soliciting public input and holding a public hearing, consulting with appointed trade advisory committees, congressional committees, individual members of Congress, and a range of stakeholders from industry to labor to civil society. With this input, the administration released in December its 14 pages of negotiating objectives with Japan, also as mandated, covering scores of goals in roughly two dozen chapter areas that it planned for the upcoming negotiations.[56]

All of this left Tokyo having to figure out how to cover for its own explanations that the agreement would only cover goods.[57] Motegi proceeded to make public his own negotiating objectives in a newspaper interview in late December. Insisting that Japan was "opposed to measures that may lead to managed trade," a position blind to Japan's own insistence on quotas and other state-controlled imports of agricultural goods, he went on to explicitly dismiss some of America's objectives, including adding currency provisions to a new agreement. He clarified Japan's strategy for tariff negotiations: "If America insists on restoring the same tariff reductions on Japan's agricultural goods as in the TPP, Japan will insist on including the same industrial goods outcomes as in the TPP. [We will] fight fire with fire." He went on to also dismiss any focus on services trade, insisting that some services related to the trade of goods, such as customs facilitation, could be added, but that the negotiations would not include traditional services sector issues like finance or insurance.[58]

55 Letter from Robert E. Lighthizer, U.S. Trade Representative, to U.S. Senate President Pro Tempore Orrin Hatch and other majority and minority leaders of the Senate Finance and House Ways and Means Committees, October 16, 2018.

56 USTR, "United States-Japan Trade Agreement (USJTA) Negotiations: Summary of Specific Negotiating Objectives," December 2018, https://ustr.gov/sites/default/files/2018.12.21 _Summary_of_U.S.-Japan_Negotiating_Objectives.pdf.

57 See, e.g., "Opposition Raps Abe for Using 'TAG' to Refer to U.S. Trade Talks," *Asahi Shimbun*, November 6, 2018.

58 "工業製品の関税撤廃、米に求める　茂木経財相に聞く" [Interview with Economic and Fiscal Policy Minister of State Motegi: We will insist on industrial goods tariff elimination from America], *Nihon Keizai Shimbun*, December 30, 2018.

By any measure, expectations for what would finally be negotiated remained fundamentally misaligned when America emerged in mid-January from its 90-day consultation period, ready to finally begin official negotiations. Japan, meanwhile, approached the coming talks with confidence that time and leverage were on its side. With the CPTPP approved and the first round of tariff cuts on farm goods from Canada and Australia already implemented, America's key farm exports to Japan already were at significant tariff disadvantages. Motegi also expressed confidence that Japan would not be hit by America with Section 232 tariffs on autos and auto parts, pointing to language in the September joint statement that no such adverse actions would be taken against Japan while bilateral trade agreement negotiations were underway.[59]

Japan then stalled again, insisting that Motegi could not begin negotiations until after budget deliberations in parliament were concluded in late March. Lighthizer offered to fly to Tokyo in early April, an offer turned down and countered with Motegi's agreement to meet in Washington instead in mid-April. Little progress was made to bridge the lingering misalignment in expectations for the negotiations, which led to another reminder from Lighthizer for Japan to think again about how it preferred to work with the administration to improve the trade deficit.

With Japan still insistent on a goods-only outcome and Capitol Hill generally unwilling to speculate on which subset of elements it needed to be included in an initial agreement to pass it, Lighthizer reconsidered the whole approach. The solution came in utilizing another, much narrower grant of negotiating authority that Congress had also provided the executive branch. This authority was an updated artifact from a century-old provision of American trade law, allowing for very limited tariff adjustments by the executive branch without a congressional vote. The authority also placed many parameters and restrictions on which tariffs could be negotiated and how much could be cut. These included set formulas for how much and how quickly they could be reduced, which ones could be fully eliminated or only reduced, and lists of many products that could not be on the table, which included nearly all agricultural goods. Other legal limits prevented any cuts to tariffs set by dollar amount or commodity weight instead of by a percent of import value. This authority was never intended to be used for

---

59   "茂木内閣府特命担当大臣記者会見要旨 平成31年2月19日" [Summary of Cabinet Office Minister of State Motegi's press conference, February 19, 2019], Japan Cabinet Office, February 19, 2019, https://www.cao.go.jp/minister/1810_t_motegi/kaiken/2019/0219kaiken.html.

a full-scale goods liberalization agreement of the kind Japan wanted, and had it been attempted, pushing its use so far would set Congress on fire. On the upside, taking this route meant that Japan would get a goods agreement it continued to insist upon—except the one it would actually get would be vastly more limited and any outcomes subject to America's quite restricted negotiating parameters.

Going down that route also effectively abandoned the administration's other goals for a first-stage deal with Japan, such as including new provisions on currency manipulation and other negotiations to remove Japan's other non-tariff barriers. The administration could have insisted upon many of these elements, but at the cost of taking much more time and getting into a complicated thicket of issues around whether a final deal with other additions would trigger the need to seek congressional approval.

Lighthizer nonetheless still stuck to his insistence that services should somehow be included in the negotiations. Japan eventually acquiesced to this after the administration pitched the idea of including a deal on digital economy rules to meet that expectation. Given Japan's like-minded approach to America to trade rules in this sector at that time, adding a digital economy agreement along with a separate package of tariff outcomes was a relatively easy-to-achieve and positive means of meeting that end.

Negotiations finally moved into high gear during the summer of 2018 and were completed in late August. The quite limited scope of tariff outcomes in the agreement, tagged as the administration's second "mini-deal," resulted from needing to stay within the narrow tariff authority provided by Congress. It also came from America placing its sole priority on restoring access for its farm exports. The market access packages on each side were balanced out by agreeing to make tariff liberalization commitments on an equivalent $7.1 billion in annual exports for each side. The deal thus liberalized trade in just $14 billion out of the two countries' roughly $200 billion in annual two-way goods trade.

The Trump administration secured most of the access it prioritized with Japan's agreement to reduce or eliminate its tariffs on approximately 600 tariff categories on farm goods. This restored the same level of access for the large majority of these exports that America had given up by walking out on the TPP. It was not the complete list, however, as Japan refused to provide access to some agricultural products, from rice to frozen blueberries, and refused to give America additional quota access for dairy products that it provided to all CPTPP exporters to share among themselves. For Japan, which wanted a much broader goods deal from America than it got, its gains from the deal came from America's tariff reduction and elimination on approximately 250 tariff categories of mostly industrial goods from Japan. However, Lighthizer adamantly refused to include any tariff commitments on Japan's top priorities of autos and auto parts, which, if covered, would have only substantially added to the trade imbalance.

The agreement also set the stage for a next round of negotiations. The agreement text highlighted expectations from Japan that the subsequent round would include talks on its top priorities, autos and auto parts, along with expectations from America that the talks would include negotiations on other agricultural goods, such as rice, not covered in the first round. Japan proceeded to insist to its public that the next stage of negotiations would solely focus on its access to America's auto and auto parts markets. This bout of wishful thinking belied the clear expectations from both sides that were directly added to the agreement text. It also ignored the reality that no U.S. administration would be given congressional authority to negotiate only to liberalize U.S. auto and auto parts tariffs without all other tariffs, along with a full slate of trade rules that included currency rules, also on the table.

The complementary digital rules agreement with Japan, named the U.S.-Japan Digital Trade Agreement, contained nearly the same outcomes as those America included in the renegotiated NAFTA and that were passed by Congress. The administration signed and implemented the digital agreement with Japan as an executive agreement, arguing that it had the authority to do so as the agreement did not adjust tariffs or require other changes to U.S. law. Even as the same package of obligations had passed Congress in the new NAFTA deal, reaching a nearly identical deal with Japan was nonetheless resented by some progressive Democrats in Congress, who later used it as a foil in their opposition to any further digital trade commitments based on that template of new trade rules.

In the September 2019 public announcement of their first-stage tariff and digital agreements, both sides laid out a written timetable to resume negotiations on further tariff liberalization and other outcomes. The agreement called for preparations for the next round of negotiations to begin as soon as four months after the January 1, 2020, implementation date of these first-stage deals.

Internal preparations got underway in Washington in January 2020 to scope out plans for the next stage of negotiations, a goal that

Japan had started to signal that it was less committed to pursuing. As the four-month mark approached, the world shut down in mid-March in response to the worldwide emergence of the COVID-19 pandemic. By the time the gravity and duration of the pandemic were fully recognized and virtual capabilities sufficient to resume talks were made available, America was already deep into its 2020 presidential campaign. Prospects for the anticipated second round of negotiations instead faded, never getting off the ground before the Trump administration left office the following January.

AMERICA'S DECONSTRUCTED TRADE MODEL: THE INDO-PACIFIC ECONOMIC FRAMEWORK

The Biden administration began its term in January 2021 with no apparent interest in pursuing new trade agreements. It, therefore, also lacked the need to think about having an approach, much less a model, for them. Biden campaigned in 2020 on the promise that he would only consider new trade deals after first making "major investments here at home" in areas from education to infrastructure to manufacturing.[60] Once in office, the administration put ongoing free trade negotiations with the UK and Kenya on hold, indicated no interest in moving forward with Japan on a next stage of negotiations, and turned away other proposals from trading partners to negotiate new agreements from regional digital rules to trade-liberalizing negotiations in the WTO. The only deals the administration appeared genuinely interested in were those to settle ongoing tariff battles with a handful of allies and then, later, limited efforts to engage in the WTO for a couple of "mini-deals" that did not liberalize new trade.

The administration instead worked on fleshing out its principles and priorities for a "worker-centered trade policy." As a set of social values and domestic priorities in search of a means to express themselves through America's external trade policies, these left the world to guess for months where it might all lead in more concrete terms.

Some nonetheless remained hopeful the administration would eventually pivot back to new and more traditional trade agreements, whether bilateral, regional, or through the WTO. The success of the

---

60   See, for example, responses from presidential candidate Joe Biden to a union-funded candidate questionnaire. A PDF of Biden's 2020 responses is linked at "Endorsed Candidates: Joe Biden," USW Voices, https://www.uswvoices.org/endorsed-candidates/joe-biden.

renegotiated NAFTA in Congress suggested that some new space for consensus may had been found again. That updated trade agreement model further adjusted the balance between business-friendly export and labor-friendly domestic priorities. Katherine Tai, Biden's new trade ambassador, was at the center of that effort; she had a prior job on Capitol Hill and knew better than anyone where a balance could potentially be found among competing interests.

Instead of pivoting to that new center, however, the administration's trade policy continued to prioritize the fundamentally anti–free trade and broadly anti-corporate views of its trade union and civil society constituents. Avoiding new agreements also avoided reopening politically divisive debates over them, particularly among Democrats who remained skeptical of many of their goals. It also dovetailed with the highly critical views on trade of the Democratic progressives in Congress, who emerged in 2020 as the party's newest mainstream voice on these issues.

The administration attempted to explain its approach in ways that often only raised contradictory distinctions. Tai, for example, frequently invoked the argument used by unions of rejecting the "race to the bottom," which they defined as concluding new trade-liberalizing agreements with countries that had lower wages and labor and environmental standards. On the other hand, Tai also refused to pick up and continue trade-liberalizing negotiations with countries with similar wages and labor and environmental standards as America, such as by simply restarting free trade negotiations with just the UK and Japan. The administration's insistence that it would not join a "race to the bottom" also sent a clear message to developing countries, which in no uncertain terms indicated that America would not be engaging in new trade-liberalizing agreements with them, seemingly no matter what.

The administration's inwardly focused trade policy also came into fundamental conflict with its foreign policy goals. Refusing new trade deals and maintaining nearly all of Trump's tariffs sent one signal to its trading partners, set against the administration's other foreign policy goals of re-engaging with the world in mutually beneficial ways following the Trump administration's "America first" approach. As these contradictions became harder to explain and justify, the Biden administration began developing what amounted to a new theory of global trade disorder and dysfunction in an attempt to more convincingly frame its decisions not to pursue traditional trade agreements. The huge disruptions to trade and production from the COVID-19 pandemic, with shortages of key components causing production delays and supply chains being too concentrated and vulnerable, proved to be a helpful backdrop. These "new challenges" served as both theory and case for the administration's reluctance to move even further in a different direction from what other American administrations had done on trade for generations.

These global disruptions were neither trivial nor insignificant, but they were hardly new, either, over the long history of the GATT-centered postwar trading order. Most of these supply shocks were of the sort that Washington itself could do little to alleviate until production and trade could catch up, beyond stepping in as it could to prevent further supply disruptions, such as by short-circuiting a threatened nationwide rail labor strike or helping speed up customs at local ports to alleviate any backups. Moreover, if set against the vastly more immense challenges of the late 1940s and early 1950s, when America made an intentional policy choice to work with other countries to commit to open, rules-based trade to lead the world out of crisis, the problems of 2020–21 were challenges that policymakers from that time undoubtedly would have preferred over those they were attempting to solve.

Redefining the objective of America's trade policy as a quest to reduce the nation's vulnerability to trade interdependence gave the administration the policy justification to pursue its own brand of an "America first" trade agenda. Like the Trump administration, it put a much greater focus on goals that catered to the demands of America's labor union movement, which centered on reducing imports instead of expanding exports. It also sparked new attention and thinking around what further incentives or other steps could be taken to reduce these perceived risks. These included providing some new incentives for companies to either remain, reshore their operations, or set up new production in America. It also explicitly rejected pursuing new free trade agreements with strategically important and likeminded countries as a tool to redirect its sources of supply chain inputs and other imports.

The fundamental conflicts between the administration's foreign policy goals of engagement and forging new partnerships and its new inwardly focused "worker-centered" trade policy also flared at times between the administration's planners and decision-makers.[61] These conflicts played out in some unproductive ways. For example, with America's new trade policy heading in the opposite direction from past efforts like the TPP, key U.S. foreign policy officials nonetheless contin-

---

61   See, e.g., Alex Thompson, Gavin Bade, Max Tani, and Daniel Lippman, "The Roots of a Tai-Rahm Confrontation," Politico, February 22, 2022.

ued for a time attempting to return to them, even encouraging foreign officials, in some cases, to keep pressing their American colleagues to return to the TPP.

The side that won out was the one that insisted on keeping the administration's emphasis on placating unions and other often fundamentally anti-trade and often anti-corporate constituencies. With it, as covered earlier, America's traditional interests in opening more foreign markets and reducing barriers to American exports were by and large also shelved and pushed to the side.[62] The approach maintained better Democratic Party unity around trade, which had been fractured even further by intra-party disagreements over the TPP. It also kept the electoral map in check by just sticking to candidate Biden's playbook on trade from the 2020 election, which simply had been to avoid opening any opportunity through its trade policy for Trump's New Right to pull away union and other trade-skeptical voters once again.

The administration's trade policy began settling into an ad hoc approach that principally prioritized various efforts to mitigate impacts from America's previous commitments to open trade. This included maintaining and advancing further the Trump administration's goals for curtailing offshoring and globalization and shoring up domestic support for keeping higher U.S. tariffs with its trading partners, or further hiking them, as in the case of China. The Biden trade team also took up a range of new causes to blunt imports, such as through efforts to block imports of foreign-made goods that exploited the use of forced labor, particularly in China.

The administration's foreign policy establishment was not defeated, however. To project a policy of positive engagement with the Indo-Pacific region, it invented and pushed ahead a new American-led initiative to work with interested countries on a broad range of economic and trade-related issues. Under the guise of a new "economic framework" for the region, the concept identified a handful of potential projects for collaboration. As initially announced, these were to define "shared objectives around trade facilitation, standards for the digital economy and

---

62 The issue was fully put to bed in the public domain with the National Security Advisor's speech on international economic policy in April 2023, which made clear the administration would not be pursuing traditional trade agreements with tariff liberalization. See Jake Sullivan, "Remarks by National Security Advisor Jake Sullivan on Renewing American Economic Leadership at the Brookings Institution," The White House, April 27, 2023.

technology, supply chain resiliency, decarbonization and clean energy, infrastructure, worker standards, and other areas of shared interest."[63]

Created to repair the foreign policy hole left by the Trump administration's withdrawal from the TPP and to respond to ongoing calls from foreign countries for its return to that agreement, this new framework concept was greeted at home with both rekindled hopes for, and adamant opposition to, the possibility that it might help lead America back to the TPP. One of these opponents, in rather salty language, dismissed anyone harboring hope that this new effort would be a road back to the TPP as the ". . . last gasp battle for trade team status quo looking longingly at the moldering corpse of the TPP and asking whether it can be reanimated without concern for the policy and political consequences of that outdated, retrograde model."[64]

At the same time, once the announcement was made that America would lead this new effort to set new region-wide trade standards and rules, the administration also suddenly needed to develop a model for the new type of trade agreement model that it aimed to pursue. President Biden opened the door for interested countries to enter America's latest trade policy hall of mirrors in late October 2021 with this announcement, calling for a new "Indo-Pacific Economic Framework" (IPEF). Few could grasp at first what they saw once inside, a matter not helped by the fact that virtually no one in the American government could explain it for some time, either. Announced as an idea still in search of a plan and then, eventually, a model, one observer accurately described it instead as a "hodgepodge of economic initiatives" that was "the best they can do given the political realities in Washington," adding "I don't think anybody's buying it. . . ."[65] Turning it into something that could gain enough international interest to eventually fly as a new model for trade while meeting the goals of the administration's domestically oriented trade agenda would be no easy feat.

To get ahead of its critics and core union constituents, the administration immediately stressed that the one thing the IPEF would not be was another trade-liberalizing agreement like the TPP. As the administration started to develop what it hoped the framework might be, it also

63 "Readout of President Biden's Participation in the East Asia Summit," The White House, October 27, 2021.

64 Madeline Halpert, "Sources: Indo-Pacific Economic Framework Beginning to Take Shape," World Trade Online, January 26, 2022.

65 "US to Develop 'Indo-Pacific Economic Framework'," Voice of America, October 27, 2021.

quickly jettisoned many other traditional trade agreement elements that were typically included to advance America's export interests. Among those that would not make a reappearance for the IPEF were rules to limit the discriminatory use of industrial standards to create non-tariff barriers, commitments to liberalize services, rules for intellectual property protection, and commitments that opened new access to foreign government procurement markets. While helping businesses, exporters, and inventors of all sizes, excluding these elements seemed to be mostly about avoiding criticism that the IPEF was yet another "corporate trade deal" to advantage America's large multinational manufacturing and services companies. Whether it would help serve any export interests at all, including for small businesses, was often left unclear.

The administration eventually asked the public months later to comment on its planned direction for the IPEF, which was to negotiate "worker-centered commitments" on labor, environment and climate, digital economy, agriculture, transparency and good regulatory practices, competition policy, and trade facilitation.[66] Later, when America and 13 participant countries announced in September 2022 their shared priorities for negotiation, inclusivity and technical assistance were added to this rather eclectic and highly selective American list.[67]

The immediate problem with America's new model for the IPEF was that it was no longer about growing or promoting new trade, which remained a core priority of the trade policies of just about every other country in the IPEF and beyond; instead, it principally aimed at fixing a series of America's own domestically defined set of problems with trade. America's insistence that it not include any traditional tariff or other market-access carrots (Tai later called this a "feature," not a "bug," of the new approach)[68] became a particular focus of widespread and deep skepticism over its ultimate viability and chance of success, both in concept and in practice.

---

66   Federal Register, "Fair and Resilient Trade Pillar of an Indo-Pacific Economic Framework," Number 2022-05044, March 9, 2022.

67   "Ministerial Text for Trade Pillar of the Indo-Pacific Economic Framework for Prosperity," linked at USTR, "The Indo-Pacific Economic Framework for Prosperity: Biden-Harris Administration's Negotiating Goals for the Connected Economy (Trade) Pillar," press release, September 23, 2022, https://ustr.gov/about-us/policy-offices/press-office/press-releases/2022/september/indo-pacific-economic-framework-prosperity-biden-harris-administrations-negotiating-goals-connected.

68   "On-the-Record Press Call on the Launch of the Indo-Pacific Economic Framework," The White House, May 23, 2022.

With no real incentive or obvious leverage to attract significant regional interest in the effort, the administration attempted to frame the IPEF as a new collective effort to resolve a series of global problems and elevated issues of universal concern. Some of America's agenda for the IPEF resonated with other countries when framed with that pitch, including the need to deepen cooperation to overcome climate and other environmental sustainability concerns and to undertake new collective efforts to help avoid future supply chain disruptions following those experienced during the COVID-19 pandemic. These topics garnered a degree of interest from America's trading partners in the Asia-Pacific as areas for potential collaboration. Other topics chosen for more targeted domestic reasons seemed oddly stuffed into the same "global challenges" narrative. Adding agricultural issues and competition policy to the agenda for negotiations, for example, were efforts principally aimed at courting America's rural voters and advancing its union-friendly anti-corporatist agenda. America's top IPEF negotiating priority of securing higher standard commitments on labor practices and worker rights was another example, and one that was a less welcome addition to the agenda for many IPEF countries, leaving open the question of what could be reasonably accomplished in that area.

The real challenge facing America's vision for the IPEF ultimately revolved around the modality for these discussions and potential collaboration. Voluntary cooperation was one thing, and the IPEF initiative envisioned just such outcomes in its other areas of work, such as reducing the potential for disruptions to supply chains and promoting the adoption of clean energy. In the trade space, by contrast, bridging differences on issues such as labor practices in the form of hard obligations in trade agreement–style text was a very different type of exercise and commitment, particularly if accompanied by America's expectation of including a means to enforce compliance. In the TPP, the carrot for securing agreement to these was the prospect of new trade and export opportunities from tariff elimination. Whether IPEF members would be willing to accept hard commitments on labor rights in the IPEF without any new trade-liberalizing commitments was widely viewed as the greatest obstacle to its viability as a new trade agreement model.

America's foreign policy establishment got the optics it wanted when the IPEF launched officially in May 2022 with 14 countries, 13 of which agreed to work on the trade-related negotiations. On the other hand, bringing in countries as diverse as Australia, Fiji, Indonesia, and Vietnam into the mix also brought back many of the same problems that had plagued efforts to achieve high standards in the TPP. It was hard to see how reaching a new binding trade agreement in the IPEF would go any better, considering the number of participants and their vastly different levels of development, policy priorities, legal and regulatory approaches, political systems, governmental capacities, and values.

Union leaders also quickly zeroed in on this issue in their recommendations to the administration for the IPEF's objectives, which included their vision for what success should look like at the end. Members of the administration's official labor advisory group on trade negotiations began by asserting that "[f]or far too long, the jobs and economic prospects of American workers have been pawns in the pursuit of foreign policy goals." They identified specific "severe labor and human rights challenges" across several countries likely to join the IPEF, including Thailand, Malaysia, the Philippines, Vietnam, Indonesia, and South Korea. Beyond implicitly questioning the wisdom of including these countries in the IPEF, the group went further to identify anti-unionization efforts by foreign automakers producing in Mississippi and other U.S. states as also highly problematic. By calling out America's own labor laws and protections as similarly inadequate and thus also implicitly disqualifying, their inclusion of these domestically focused demands pointed to the broader agenda they sought to advance at home through this new international trade agreement.[69]

Beyond concern over several of the countries that were participating, the labor advisors' much longer list of expectations for IPEF outcomes included some of the labor outcomes from the TPP, such as enforceable commitments to maintain laws and regulations to abide by the ILO's core worker standards. It included newer outcomes from the NAFTA renegotiation, including a beefed-up version of its special labor enforcement system for private labor rights claims backed by potential trade sanctions. They also sought new outcomes, including a means of holding companies accountable for labor practices along their entire supply chains, and insisted that all labor rules in the IPEF be fully met before any member was allowed to enjoy the benefits of the agreement. With no new tariff liberalization in the IPEF, which they also lauded, it

---

69   Labor Advisory Committee for Trade Negotiations and Trade Policy, "Indo-Pacific Economic Framework (IPEF) Comments of the Labor Advisory Committee for Trade Negotiations and Trade Policy (LAC)," April 11, 2022. Public comments at Regulations.gov, Docket Number USTR-2022-0002-0001.

was unclear what "benefits" there might be for its member countries to enjoy.[70]

The labor advisors further included a lengthy list of expectations for IPEF digital economy rules. These reflected numerous labor union goals for the reform of America's laws and regulations, such as demands for new commitments to prevent companies from digitally surveilling warehouse employees and other workers, obligations to end company "exploitation" of gig economy workers, limits on the collection of personal data by private firms, and steps to address the market power of internet platforms.[71]

The labor union advisors also called for much broader exceptions to digital trade rules included in the renegotiated NAFTA and new Japan digital agreements. In particular, they insisted on allowing broad discretion for governments to regulate the ability of companies to transfer data across borders, to require that certain kinds of data be kept only within the country where originally generated, and more freedom to access proprietary company source code information for their digital products and platforms. The digital rules from those agreements had more narrowly drawn exceptions, permitting regulators to take certain actions while closing off broad loopholes and policies used by foreign countries to either give advantages to their own firms or, in cases like China, to enable online surveillance and aid political repression through preventing access to foreign news and open, global internet chat platforms.[72] For America's unions and progressives, the attempt to strike a balanced approach between preserving room for legitimate regulatory actions and closing off broadly discretionary government actions continued to be slammed as an anti-worker, pro–Big Tech giveaway, and one that had to be turned back through different rules in the IPEF.

The political lines drawn in this debate were as blurred as they had been with other domestic-as-trade-policy disagreements. Progressive Democrats were joined in certain instances by some Republicans, who similarly criticized the technology sector as over-concentrated and legally privileged.[73] On the other side were members from both parties who still

70   Labor Advisory Committee, "Indo-Pacific Economic Framework."
71   Labor Advisory Committee, "Indo-Pacific Economic Framework."
72   Labor Advisory Committee, "Indo-Pacific Economic Framework."
73   This included new and sudden Republican opposition over Section 230 of the 1996 Communications Decency Act that provided internet platform companies broad exceptions from liability for the content of the online posts made by their users. On the broader debate, see, e.g., Lawrence Hurley and David Ingram, "Biden and Republican Senators Join Forces

strongly supported keeping the same digital trade rules model, whether to prevent another competitive American industry from succumbing to unfair foreign practices or to help combat the spread of China-style online political repression.[74] These bipartisan voices insisted that the IPEF incorporate the updated NAFTA and Japan digital agreement rules "as a floor, not a ceiling, in crafting enforceable digital trade rules."[75] Some accused the administration of hiding information that it should have first shared with Congress, but instead covertly unwound these positions unilaterally to change America's model for digital trade rules with its own new rules for the IPEF agreement.[76]

America's debate with itself over digital rules for the IPEF devolved into the familiar microcosm of political division and ulterior motives that had paralyzed support for the TPP. Once the Biden administration had to come up with detailed, text-based negotiating positions to operationalize its more generalized anti–Big Tech platitudes, these divisions erupted once again into another domestic policy proxy war. In the case of tech sector regulations, these divisions had deepened and widened in the eight years after the TPP. With little progress having been made through domestic law and regulation at home to grapple with these issues since then, the positions of both sides had only further hardened and become more irreconcilable.

It also stood as another cautionary tale of how America's volatile trade politics continued to threaten to undermine efforts to use trade to meet its broader foreign relations objectives. As the Biden administration began, and with America's digital trade rule model well-anchored in its updated NAFTA and new Japan agreements, cooperation with its trading partners to develop region-wide approaches and standards for the digital economy initially seemed an obvious way for the administration to re-engage after the turbulent Trump years with its trading partners in the Asia-Pacific. Several governments in the region also

in Attack on Big Tech Before Supreme Court," NBC News, February 18, 2023. On the trade implications, see "House Panel Knocks Inclusion of Internet Liability Language in USMCA, Japan Deal," World Trade Online, October 16, 2019.

74   Jason Asenso, "House, Senate Groups Push for U.S.-led Digital Trade Standards," World Trade Online, March 31, 2023.

75   Thomas R. Carper and Todd Young, "Senators Carper and Young Urge U.S. Trade Representative to Set the Ground Rules for the Digital Economy," press release, October 13, 2023.

76   Dan Dupont, "House Oversight Panel Chair Demands Answers, Documents on IPEF from USTR," World Trade Online, October 12, 2023.

proposed ideas for a regional digital agreement to the administration. These suggestions were echoed by Washington DC think-tank types who, in some cases, only triggered alarm and opposition to the concept by pitching it as America's "path back to TPP."[77] The administration's trade decision-makers instead turned down each of these suggestions and invitations. Intending to put domestically focused union and progressive reform objectives at the center of America's trade policy, any engagement on new digital trade rules would be to fundamentally rewrite the model, not advance the existing one.

This tension was brought into America's goals for the IPEF after its foreign policy decision-makers, eager to respond to these proposals from their regional counterparts, insisted that new digital trade rules be put front and center in the administration's pursuit of the IPEF. To make that more palatable to unions and progressives, other elements were also layered into the trade negotiations framework, including by tacking on new competition policy and labor rights rules as additional core objectives. While a more diluted mix of priorities for the administration to pitch made its plan easier to defend against the inevitable critics on all sides, it made for a less relatable package of goals that was only harder for America's trading partners to digest. A new kind of layer cake lacking the requisite tariff-liberalization icing, America's latest attempt at creating a new-style trade agreement in the Asia-Pacific region took on an appearance more alike a Frankenstein monster than a relatable, coherent model. Whether it ultimately would be accepted across the Asia-Pacific or ostracized would depend on whether America could keep its domestic expectations and debates in check for what is achievable. It also depended on whether America's patient trading partners, many of which supported and adjusted their own policies and regulations to align with America's past trade expectations and models, were also ultimately agreeable to its latest rewrite.

Unsurprisingly, America, not its trading partners, emerged as the weakest link in realizing America's vision for the IPEF. Technically still under negotiation as of this writing, IPEF trade negotiations collapsed spectacularly in mid-November 2023 just as the Biden administration was pulling out all the stops, including marathon negotiating sessions, to try and conclude them. Negotiations were suspended just as the deal

---

77   Matthew P. Goodman, "DEPA and the Path Back to TPP," commentary, Center for Strategic and International Studies, July 15, 2021.

was coming together in time to announce its substantial completion in time for the 21-member APEC Leaders' Summit in San Francisco.

The administration pulled the plug to respond to an urgent political appeal. Sherrod Brown, a long-serving Democratic senator from Ohio and second only to Bernie Sanders in his record of vehement opposition to new trade agreements, had a re-election problem. Joined by a few other Midwestern Democrats also up for re-election the following November, he pressured the White House to not finalize the IPEF trade deal, principally over concerns that it fell short of achieving the strong labor and environment obligations that the administration had promised. That defect, they feared, would become a liability in their efforts to maintain strong support from unions and their voters.[78] With a call to the White House, the administration proceeded to shut down the work of 13 countries. Shortly afterward, Brown proudly took credit for derailing the whole thing to call attention to his own, still pending legislative proposals on trade.[79]

With America's presidential and congressional elections still a year away, and just as with the TPP, yet another American administration was unable to accomplish its new vision for trade in the region—one that, unlike the TPP, did not require congressional approval, avoided liberalizing any new trade, and championed a broad range of objectives aimed at upending or omitting, instead of building further on, most traditional trade policy priorities. The IPEF was to be America's first postwar trade agreement intended to take aim at the free trade models of the past. Instead, it became another example of America's inability to reach a consensus and effectively conclude and implement another trade agreement.

AMERICA'S ATTEMPTS AT FORGING A NEW MODEL FOR TRADE: INTERNATIONAL AND OTHER IMPLICATIONS

Between 1974 and 2016, America defined, constructed, and then continued to build out its trade agreement model with each new iteration.

---

78   See, e.g., Ari Hawkins, "WTO Draft Text Takes Up E-Commerce Moratorium," Politico, February 5, 2024.

79   Sherrod Brown, "Brown Successfully Pushes Biden Administration to Remove the Trade Pillar from the Indo-Pacific Economic Framework," press release, November 15, 2023. See also Gavin Bade, "How Sherrod Brown Rattled Biden's Summit Agenda," Politico, November 14, 2023.

The need for a model was prompted by America's evolving search for ways to make free trade work better. It started with Congress's call for new trade rules to accompany GATT tariff liberalization agreements. Then, it blossomed as America found bilateral and regional free trade agreements to be more leveraged opportunities to push the rules much further than was possible in the WTO.

Starting in 2017, a defining shift in America's trade policy was its rejection of much of that model and its new quest to fix it. The progressive Left's and the Tea Party–turned Trump–New Right's antipathy toward the TPP gave birth to and principally framed this opposition and forced the shift.

The Trump administration took to fixing America's model for trade as if it were an outdated international contract to be renegotiated. Defining America's losses as its trade deficit in goods, it demanded new contractual clauses to overturn 40 years of these losses. These included pursuing ideas such as dollar-for-dollar matching for government procurement, limits on currency arbitrage by finance ministries, and performance requirements for production through new product-content rules. By defining the value of America's trading relationships in actuarial terms, as opposed to one of mutual gains through equivalent opportunities, it needed to adopt completely new methods and tactics that often amounted to its most abrasive policy decisions, whether in the form of actual or threatened termination, or through its use of "mini-deal" amendments that bypassed the company's standard form contracts.

The possibilities and the limits of the Trump administration's pursuit of leveraged negotiations and renegotiations also became clear. With NAFTA and KORUS in effect and generating very large and growing deficits (as well as new export flows from America), the potential cost of a failure to renegotiate that could lead to their termination ultimately proved galvanizing. The renegotiation process for each was touch-and-go at times and entirely distasteful to most, but the stakes no doubt increased the pressure for a successful outcome. This leverage was still limited in important ways, both by the president's own board of directors in Congress, where concepts like dollar-for-dollar procurement were rejected, and by the president's lack of patience, which got in the way in the case of South Korea of getting a bigger deal.

In the case of Japan, the limits of less leverage were more readily apparent. Japan came to hold the agriculture card that America wanted after the president gave it up by exiting the TPP. New leverage had to be created and applied that was sufficient to push for an outcome, but it was one that ultimately fell far short of each side's original expectations. Although the administration started negotiations with the EU, that effort floundered after encountering similar problems to those with Japan. Negotiations with the UK and Kenya seemed better grounded on the promise of mutual benefit but were never completed.

While these negotiations strained in deep ways America's relations with Canada, Mexico, South Korea, and Japan, reaching agreement with each also averted the real danger of damaging political and security rifts with three U.S. security treaty allies and with its southern neighbor. The defense and foreign policy establishments routinely warned about the potential consequences of failure and at times intervened to try to keep these high-stakes trade deal undertakings from inflicting collateral damage on America's security interests. For decades, Japan's government attempted to insist on a separation between its foreign and security policies and its economic and trade policies, even coming up with a term (*seikei bunri*) to brand it. By contrast, the trade warriors in the Trump administration, starting with its leader, viewed it all as part of the same relationship package.

For all the focus on fixing trade deficits as the main criteria, the agreements the Trump administration completed did not achieve much to reduce them. Comparing the goods deficit in the full calendar years before and after each of these agreements came into effect, America's combined deficit with Mexico and Canada increased by $32 billion to reach a record of $157.8 billion in 2021; similarly, its deficit with South Korea increased by $7.2 billion to reach a record of $25.1 billion in 2020. Only the goods deficit with Japan decreased by a total of $8.9 billion, but it still ended at $60.2 billion in 2021.

Overall, America's goods deficit with the world also soared during the four years of the Trump administration, in the wake of the wholly predictable macroeconomic impacts of its large tax cuts and higher fiscal deficits that increased the national debt by nearly $7.8 trillion.[80] America's total goods deficit started at $735 billion in 2016, the year before the administration began, and ended at $901 billion at the conclusion of its final full year in office in 2020.[81]

---

80   Data from Allan Sloan, ProPublica, and Cezary Podkul, "Donald Trump Built a National Debt So Big (Even before the Pandemic) That It'll Weigh Down the Economy for Years," ProPublica, January 14, 2021.

81   United States Census Bureau, "Trade in Goods with World, Seasonally Adjusted," https://www.census.gov/foreign-trade/balance/c0004.html.

In contrast, the Biden administration's approach to fixing America's trade model followed from its inward-focused effort to forge a new social contract.[82] In this analogy, that effort may be best described as a rarely-if-ever-made attempt at turning a stock company into a mutual one. With management's focus less on gains and more on creating and sustaining long-term buy-in, it asked its external partners to make some less confrontational but rather unfamiliar and sometimes unexpected adjustments to accommodate. The direct outgrowth of these adjustments was the IPEF and the oddity that it was evolving into. At other times, as covered elsewhere, these attempts to meet diverse domestic-focused goals manifest themselves in other ways, leading to new discriminatory terms for trade with and among its allies and other trading partners.

Its measure of success for efforts like the IPEF was unmotivated by the actuarial goal of cutting the trade deficit in its pursuit of another one—expanding and maintaining domestic grassroots political support and votes. A more apt yardstick might be the degree to which its approach met the lengthy and diverse list of expectations and concerns of the Citizens Trade Campaign, a group initially forged in 1992 from over four hundred unions and other civil society groups to oppose NAFTA. By that measure, it also had a mixed record of results. By aiming to fulfill in a trade agreement the most ambitious slogans of America's decades-long anti–free trade movement, the administration raised very high expectations for the outcomes that it would achieve.[83] Not for a lack of passion or trying, it broadly failed to achieve the scope of binding labor and human rights commitments from its trading partners

---

82   While this book was in its final phase of edits, Katherine Tai, Biden's trade ambassador, wrote an op-ed to argue the same. See Katherine Tai, "Trade Must Transform Its Role in the Social Contract," *Financial Times*, May 28, 2024. By referring to the 1941 Atlantic Charter's call for a more equitable order through "improved labor standards, economic advancement, and social security," Tai conveniently ignores the Charter's call immediately prior to that U.S.-UK pledge with a call for another joint "endeavor to further then enjoyment by all states . . . of access, on equal terms, to the trade and to the raw materials of the world which are needed for economic prosperity." As the world was sinking into war, these and other principles in the Charter were cornerstones for securing a lasting postwar peace. This book argues that by abandoning the nondiscriminatory principle as a pretext for meeting other goals, the Biden administration is fundamentally undermining this cornerstone of Roosevelt's pledge and vision in the Charter.

83   For a list of these demands, see Citizens Trade Campaign, "Re: Shared Views on the Indo-Pacific Economic Framework (IPEF)," letter to President Joseph R. Biden, March 1, 2023, https://www.citizenstrade.org/ctc/wp-content/uploads/2023/03/IPEF_OrgSignOnLetter_030123.pdf.

that it advertised at the outset, while making only limited gains in its attempts to accomplish new trade-related commitments on climate and the environment. It had more success with meeting demands for deconstructing and withdrawing America's past model trade commitments in other areas, including in areas from digital trade to good regulatory practice, and for fully turning away from and rejecting new reciprocal tariff liberalization.

As doubtful as the viability of the IPEF model had been from its beginning and remains today, the Biden administration, in its enthusiasm to engage economically with more trading partners, decided to negotiate even more IPEF-style agreements to spread its new model approach further. The first was with Taiwan, which fell far short of the free trade deal it had long wanted, but Taipei jumped nonetheless at the opportunity to forge any new partnership with America. As of this writing, free trade negotiations left behind by the Trump administration with the UK and Kenya have also been morphed into soft, IPEF-style trade initiatives. Other plans for an IPEF-type arrangement in the Americas were announced, with the State Department insisting on leading the effort, but these failed to get very far after more than a year under that stewardship. The future of these efforts remains unclear. Other indications suggest that the Biden administration would like to rewrite even more of America's previous free trade agreements, although that has yet to happen thus far.[84]

Where nations share common interests and well-aligned objectives, economic cooperation and engagement of the type the IPEF promised can productively lead to positive outcomes. Pitched as a model for a new kind of binding trade agreement, however, the Biden administration's highly bespoke approach was broadly perceived as lacking coherence and consequence to many both at home and abroad. The administration made no apologies for its "reluctant approach," doubling down on the narrative that it was "writing a new story on trade" shaped by "a very different world."[85] It also turned a deaf ear to criticism from some in Congress and elsewhere that its model and approach were both excessively deconstructed and harmfully neglectful of America's most

84   Brett Fortnam, "USTR Official: Administration Wants to Update FTAs Alongside APEP," World Trade Online, December 16, 2022.

85   Ana Swanson, "Biden's Reluctant Approach to Free Trade Draws Backlash," *New York Times*, April 4, 2023.

basic export and competitiveness interests.[86] For many, it signaled the end of the road for America's pursuit of freer and more open trade, the goal that anti–free trade and anti-corporate movements had fought for decades to achieve.

The credibility of calls on Capitol Hill for the Biden administration to return to traditional, liberalizing trade agreements were undercut by a lack of any tangible signs that Congress was coalescing to mend its own deep rifts over trade. As the administration and Congress pointed at each other to take the first step to show seriousness toward resuming traditional trade agreements, the result was none.[87] Congress could have taken the initiative to express its unified hopes for more traditional trade agreements and, most importantly, passed a new law to provide its negotiating guidance and renew its grant of authority, which expired in July 2021, to the executive branch to negotiate them. The administration could have taken the initiative to propose specific new trading partners and liberalizing agreements to encourage Congress to come to a consensus on its negotiating objectives and provide its negotiating authority. Neither, however, budged.

The failure of the IPEF to prove its concept to date stands in stark contrast to the ongoing work of America's trading partners across the Asia-Pacific, which continue to forge their agreements with each other, whether to liberalize trade or to create their own trade rules without America included to muck it up. Canada's progressive government managed to overcome significant domestic opposition and implement the CPTPP agreement, which remained essentially identical to the TPP model blasted by America's progressives as "put(ting) the profits of multinational corporations before workers."[88] New Zealand's progressive prime

86   See, e.g., Adrian Smith, "Squandering an Opportunity on Trade," The Hill, op-ed, October 5, 2022; Tim Kaine, "Kaine Urges Administration to Strengthen Americas Partnership for Economic Prosperity, Expand Trade in Western Hemisphere," press release, October 5, 2023; and United States Senate Committee on Finance, "Wyden and Crapo Call on Biden Administration to Fight EU Digital Trade Policies that Discriminate against U.S. Workers and Employers," press release, March 9, 2023.

87   See, e.g., Hannah Monicken, "Tai Defends IPEF Approach as Senators Push on Lack of Market Access," World Trade Online, March 31, 2022; and Maydeen Merino, "Crapo: Trade Legislation on Hold Until Administration Pursues New Trade Deals," World Trade Online, September 8, 2022.

88   Typical are the priorities included in public comments submitted prior to the IPEF negotiations by Senators Warren and Casey Jr. See Elizabeth Warren and Robert P. Casey, Jr., Letter to United States Trade Representative Katherine Tai, April 11, 2022, available at Regulations.gov, Docket Number USTR-2022-0002-0001.

minister took the opportunity during a visit to Washington to cautiously welcome the IPEF but went on to praise the CPTPP, which Jacinda Arden said ". . . remains in our view the gold standard" and the best place for America to re-engage with the region.[89] Chile's progressive president, who was highly critical of the CPTPP, nonetheless signed onto it after it was finally passed by centrists and right-leaning members in Chile's senate.[90] The UK's Conservative government also joined as the CPTPP's newest member, as it began making commercial cooperation agreements with individual U.S. states while waiting for America to agree to resume free trade negotiations.[91] Several other countries also await the opportunity to sign on. Separately, several digital trade agreement initiatives have been launched, and some concluded, as America continues to fail to agree at home on what those rules should be. Other trading partners, such as the EU block of nations, also continue to pursue their free trade agreements and models, which further add their own unique elements, in addition to tariff preferences for its exporters, that continue to foreclose American export opportunities to third-country markets in a number of ways.

Seven years after America walked out and then away from the TPP, it seemed no closer to finding a stable and reliable consensus for a new model for trade agreements that could predictably garner support for them both home and abroad. The renegotiated NAFTA seemed, for a time, to be a potential new center, but even that model soon after was picked apart over its digital rules and other issues, and then it was shelved when America gave up on advancing trade liberalization. Limited wins with South Korea and Japan served as another model that was much more flexible and innovative in approach, albeit limited in result. Those limited outcomes were mostly supported in political circles but left some congressional members uncomfortable over the approaches the Trump administration used to achieve them, in addition to its less-than-expected level of consultation with Congress along the way. Whether Congress would again offer tariff negotiating authority to future administrations, or what further conditions it may add to any new authority, remains to be seen.

89   "Live: PM Jacinda Ardern's Visit to US—Meeting President Joe Biden at White House Still to Be Announced," *New Zealand Herald*, May 25, 2022.

90   Patricia Garip, "Boric Is Trapped on Trade," *Foreign Policy*, November 16, 2022.

91   Dan Dupont, "U.S., UK Plans for New Trade Talks Raise Questions About Approach, Timing," World Trade Online, October 6, 2023.

With no interest in negotiating tariff outcomes and asserting that it also harbored no intent to negotiate outcomes that might require changes to U.S. law, the Biden administration initially planned to negotiate the IPEF and others like it as executive agreements to bypass the need to secure congressional approval. Key members of Congress's trade-related committees had different expectations, reminding the Biden administration that Congress must review and vote on any binding trade-related agreement.[92] It made that demand more explicit in the case of the administration's IPEF-style negotiations with Taiwan, passing a law to require the administration to put any final agreement with Taiwan up for a vote in Congress before it could enter into effect.

This put back into focus the question of whether Congress could even muster the votes to approve the administration's new-style trade agreement, which many made clear they did not want in the first place. By intentionally eschewing most traditional trade agreement goals, many on Capitol Hill have remained critical of the administration's IPEF-style model for simply having gone too far in that direction. One senior Democratic senator summed up this frustration as follows: "It is extremely disappointing that this administration is once again proposing proceeding with a 'trade agreement' that will neither benefit the American public, nor respect the role of Congress in international trade."[93] Precedent since 2006 also suggests Congress will insist, regardless of the outcome, on its own, additional changes to approve any trade agreement that comes before it. Familiar domestic-policy-as-trade-policy debates are also certain to erupt once again over IPEF outcomes for digital rules or over labor rights, and disrupt the congressional process even further.

Congress's approval of the renegotiated NAFTA in early 2020 ended a nearly decade-long dry spell since it had approved any free trade deal. The consensus that made it possible was not durable, however, propelled as it was by the unique circumstance of Trump's withdrawal threat. Beyond an emerging consensus around setting new terms for America's trade with China, an external and more unifying objective amid its realigned trade politics, domestic policy–driven disagreements continue to make nearly every other trade decision in Congress nearly impossible. One

92   Yuka Hayashi, "Biden's 'Go It Alone' Trade Deals Draw Warnings from Congress," *Wall Street Journal*, March 19, 2023.

93   Statement by Senator Ron Wyden, Chair of the Senate Finance Committee, in Dupont, "U.S., UK Plans for New Trade Talks Raise Questions ."

area where this is apparent is Congress's inability to renew a system of tariff preferences for developing countries, which it allowed to expire in 2020. The prospects for renewal remain unclear years later. Established in 1974 to help support their development goals by offering tariff-free access to America in product areas that by and large are not produced domestically, instead of finding a path forward, Congress walked out by letting the system expire and then consistently failing to sort out its differences to find a pragmatic compromise to renew the preferences. The next chapter takes up this and related shifts in America's approach to tariff preference programs for developing countries.

SIX

Walking Out on Developing Countries

In September 2023 the U.S. House of Representatives Subcommittee on Trade gathered in a cavernous Capitol Hill hearing room to consider renewing another of America's core commitments to the international trading system—its offer of limited tariff-free access for some developing country exports to the U.S. market. Since 1974, Congress periodically renewed this commitment to over one hundred developing countries to help support their economic development. As long as they met a range of conditions, their exports of over 3,500 types of products, from gold necklaces to rubber gloves and from Christmas tree lights to air conditioner parts, were given preferential tariff-free treatment at the U.S. border. For the least developed among them, exports of 1,500 additional product types also could qualify for similar, conditional tariff-free treatment.

Care was taken to ensure these tariff breaks were limited to goods that U.S. companies, by and large, no longer made in America. If still made domestically, they were generally of a different or higher quality. Any American producer that believed tariff-free imports of one of these goods were harming their business could petition to have the product removed from the list of coverage. Numerous other safeguards were also built in, including a cap on the dollar imports of each product type from individual countries that could receive tariff-free treatment each year, as further measures to prevent disruptive import surges.

With these and other limits in place, the concessionary tariff breaks were approved for only 10 percent, or $23.8 billion out of a total of $238.4 billion, of goods imports from the approximately 120 eligible developing countries in 2018. Set against America's $2.6 trillion in imports from all countries that year, the program provided tariff-free treatment for just under 1 percent of America's total imports.[1]

Although a tiny drop in America's overall import bucket (which, depending on whether made of plastic or metal, also could qualify for tariff-free treatment), the Generalized System of Preferences (GSP) program was nonetheless economically significant for many of these countries. It was especially so for several South and Southeast Asian countries, with exports from India, Indonesia, Thailand, Cambodia, and the Philippines routinely ranking among the top 10 beneficiaries under the GSP program during the mid-2010s. For other countries in the Pacific, such as Tonga and the Solomon Islands, trade under the GSP program accounted for a large percentage of their annual exports to America.

The tariff breaks were also valuable to the American firms and retailers importing the goods, which would ordinarily have to foot a bill from U.S. customs. Avoiding the tariffs allowed them to boost their competitiveness, whether from the cheaper cost of the components they used in their manufacturing processes or from importing goods more cheaply to sell to American consumers. U.S. tariffs on most of these goods were already generally low, averaging just under 5 percent. Even so, the GSP provided an extra incentive that tilted some commercial decisions toward taking advantage of opportunities in individual developing countries that otherwise may have been left untapped. The program also provided incentives to meet other objectives, such as for importers to diversify their sources of supply away from China as a key overseas supplier.

By late 2020, however, this longstanding American commitment to mutually beneficial trade was yet another at risk of crumbling. The GSP program, authorized by Congress but administered by the executive branch, was used by the Trump administration as leverage for its aggressive "America first" trade agenda. The administration insisted that certain GSP countries with which the US had a trade deficit remove trade barriers identified by Washington to maintain their GSP eligibility. It

---

also used GSP to exact retribution for pushback from abroad to Trump's new trade barriers. America's labor unions and others, too, stepped up calls for reining in the GSP's coverage, whether to add substantially more onerous eligibility conditions or to delist eligible GSP countries over a range of practices.

More aggressively attempting to leverage the GSP program in such ways might have had better long-term odds of success in some cases had Congress also proven capable of reauthorizing it. Instead, trade and other dysfunction on Capitol Hill, compounded with ever-expanding expectations for how the GSP should be used as leverage to achieve various congressional and constituent priorities, only paralyzed Congress's ability to extend it. Lacking congressional reauthorization, the GSP program expired at the end of 2020 for all the roughly 120 eligible developing countries. As it lapsed, so too did its ability to be useful to anyone in Washington with an agenda for it. Meanwhile, the EU, Japan, Australia, and others managed to sustain their own GSP programs without interruptions and drama.

By the time of the trade subcommittee's hearing in the fall of 2023, three years of congressional efforts and proposals to renew the GSP had just one consistent outcome—each sputtered and flamed out. As the hearing got underway to try once again to identify a way forward, the subcommittee's Republican chair and Democratic ranking member each lamented the fact the GSP program had been allowed to remain expired for over three years—the longest since it was established. They also pledged, in a bipartisan way, to try and renew it.

Afterward, each proceeded to call on their handpicked witnesses and make statements indicating that to renew it, GSP criteria would need to be even more fundamentally restricted and reformed. This meant adding a slew of additional conditions to make it politically palatable across America's new political alignments and expectations on trade. Given the range of expectations, the degree to which agreement on these was still possible emerged as the larger question. As the hearing progressed, it also became evident that the goal of recommitting America to helping improve livelihoods in developing countries, while also making Christmas lights and other imported goods a little cheaper for some Americans, had been relegated to secondary if not tertiary importance in the process.

These new conditions and expectations for GSP reform included instituting sweeping eligibility assessments of worker and human rights in each country, including on issues as specific as "property and inheritance rights" and "marriage, divorce, and child custody" laws. Progress by GSP beneficiary countries on achieving "equal pay for equal work" was also to be evaluated—a metric that America itself has failed to attain.[2] The steelworkers union, meanwhile, called for hiking the GSP program's minimum domestic product content rule from 35 to at least 60 percent for any goods to qualify for the tariff benefit. It was the approximate autos content rule in NAFTA, popping up again to the warm embrace of some of the subcommittee's members. Others called for layering on completely new criteria, from meeting goals for environmental protection to maintaining open digital economy regimes to securing better access for U.S. agricultural exports.

As the subcommittee members proceeded to air and hang their shiny new GSP eligibility ornaments on this legislative Christmas tree, its branches no longer seemed able to accommodate the imported tree lights to complete it. It was left to the imagination how a poorer country, as defined by World Bank criteria, would manage to meet all of these expectations. Failing to do so could be due to a lack of resources to enforce laws as America expected, or a lack of a sufficiently diversified manufacturing base to meet a 60 percent domestic content threshold for anything other than simply processed natural minerals and materials.

U.S. companies that invested money to reap the GSP program's benefits were left holding another bag. After investing to build a new supply chain with Cambodia to shift sourcing away from China, in line with Washington's rhetoric, one American entrepreneur summed up more succinctly the impact on his business of Washington's inability to simply manage to agree to renew GSP and extend those benefits: ". . . [Y]ou screwed us."[3]

This chapter focuses on the GSP program, both to highlight America's sharp turn in its use and implementation, and the fruitless effort and debate to try and renew it (as of this book's publication). For the Trump administration, which inherited a functioning GSP program from Congress, the story begins with its efforts to weaponize the GSP as untapped leverage with several advanced developing countries. The Biden

---

2 Earl Blumenauer, "Chairman Blumenauer Files Legislation to Update Key Trade Program," press release, December 8, 2020; for the text of the bill referenced, see To Amend the Trade Act of 1974 to Modify and Extend the Generalized System of Preferences, and for Other Purposes, H.R. 8884, 116th. Cong. (2020).

3 Jason Douglas, "Manufacturers Move Back to China as Renewal of U.S. Trade Deal Is Delayed," *Wall Street Journal*, March 17, 2023.

administration, which came to office just after the GSP had expired, had no program to administer but joined with progressive Democrats and unions to clarify their priority list of new conditions for America's trade with the rest of the world. Intended to stop the "race to the bottom," these and other conditions, along with others sought by some producers and Republicans, left Congress unable to reach a consensus to renew the GSP program—leaving developing countries at the bottom of Washington's priorities.

AMERICA'S PROBLEM WITH TRADE PREFERENCES

The GSP emerged from UN recommendations in the early 1970s to fulfill a straightforward idea—a new trade program to help lift the economic conditions in developing countries. It was embraced in America and by many of the world's developed countries. To make it work under the GATT rules, its members, in turn, agreed to make the program a special exception to the core rule on most-favored-nation (MFN) treatment. However, a key condition was added: the terms of each country's GSP program must be "generalized" to apply in a nondiscriminatory way to all developing countries meeting specific national income criteria. This condition was necessary to prevent developed countries from cherry-picking—offering individual developing countries preferential access to the exclusion of others. Otherwise, a free-for-all would ensue with developed countries offering better access to curry favor with a subset of developing countries, leaving other developing countries out and unable to secure the same opportunities. Beyond not supporting the core goal of lifting the economic prosperity of all the world's developing countries, allowing benefits to be offered to some but not all of them would erode and unravel the GATT's core MFN principle of nondiscrimination.

Developed countries had no obligation to offer these GSP trade preferences. If they did, they could set their own terms and conditions so long as these were not tailored to discriminate between some developing countries over others. In a 2002 dispute brought by India against the EU's GSP program criteria, the WTO Appellate Body set the expectation that GSP terms and conditions should support a specific development or trade need of *all* developing countries. In this way, criteria applied by developed countries might still lead to different eligibility treatment among them, but only in the service of an objective that aims to meet the needs of all.[4] This ruling made clear that GSP criteria should not be in service to the domestic objectives of the country offering the benefits.

In keeping with the program's intent, GSP terms were not to be negotiated with developing countries as reciprocal arrangements. That is, developing countries would not be expected to provide their own tariff cuts or similar new market access in exchange for the access the developing countries offered. Developed countries still had multiple other ways to achieve those goals. One way could be to negotiate a reciprocal, two-way free trade agreement with a developing country, so long as it met the GATT and WTO exception that it liberalizes "substantially" all the trade between them. Another, more common way would be to take a dispute to the WTO or engage in other trade diplomacy to resolve a concern satisfactorily.

The actual evolution of trade preference programs and trade arrangements between developed and developing countries proved to be significantly messier than the tidy expectations presented above. The EU, for example, implemented its own GSP program but then proceeded to separately pursue other two-way preferential tariff agreements with some developing countries, which often fell well short of the WTO requirements for comprehensive two-way free trade deals. Some of these have been renegotiated in recent years to improve their overall tariff liberalization commitments by varying degrees. Even so, the EU's patchwork of these agreements continues to perpetuate significant differences in treatment among developing countries.[5]

In contrast to the EU, America's two-way free trade agreements with developing countries are far fewer. Those concluded clearly met from the outset the WTO's requirements of substantially liberalizing all two-way trade. Even so, America still offered better access to a subset of developing countries that it has not provided to all GSP-eligible countries through its patchwork of other trade preference programs. One program, established in 2000, opened America's market wider to over 30 African nations under the Africa Growth and Opportunity Act (AGOA). Another was its Caribbean Basin Initiative, which evolved

---

4   The WTO case is DS246. See World Trade Organization, *European Communities—Conditions for the Granting of Tariff Preferences to Developing Countries*, Appellate Body Report WT/DS246/AB/R (Geneva: WTO, adopted April 7, 2004).

5   A good overview of these EU agreements and their evolution is provided in San Bilal, "EU-Africa Trade Relations and the EPA Process: Ratification and Sustainable Development Perspectives for Cameroon, Côte d'Ivorie and Ghana" (Discussion Paper no. 304, European Centre for Development Policy Management, The Netherlands, September 2021).

since its launch in the mid-1980s with Central American countries to encompass 17 Caribbean island nations. To square these programs with its WTO obligations for nondiscriminatory treatment, America has routinely secured special waivers from the WTO membership to operate them. Each, however, also came with its own patchwork of terms and conditions that continued to evolve as they were renewed or updated, resulting in further differences in treatment and access among recipient developing countries.

Congress's constitutionally derived authority over foreign commerce and tariffs provides it the power to give and take away these tariff preference programs for developing countries. In the case of the GSP, however, Congress instead fell into a routine pattern of just letting it lapse before eventually reconsidering and then mustering the political momentum to renew it for a while longer. One reason was the increasingly complicated politics of trade in Washington as the 1990s unfolded. It also often required packaging the program's extension with other large revenue or trade bills to make it through Congress eventually.

Most of these lapses in the GSP lasted only a few months when they occurred; when the GSP was eventually reauthorized, importers were permitted to file for refunds of the tariffs they paid during the lapse. This allowed American importers and recipient countries to have recurring confidence that, even with a lapse, their decisions to develop new supply chains with GSP-eligible countries would eventually be rewarded in the form of a refund of the tariff costs they paid before the program's renewal.

However, as the GSP program entered its fourth decade, these lapses tended to grow longer. Before the Trump and Biden administrations, the most prolonged lapse had been two years, coming between July 2013 and July 2015 as the Democratic Congress delayed passing the authorization bill for the TPP negotiations, which also included GSP reauthorization. Even as the GSP renewal process became messier and less routine from the mid-1990s, few still questioned the inevitability of reauthorization. With overall bipartisan support still intact, the uncertainty was only when, not if, it would eventually happen. GSP countries and American importers could still invest and sign purchase contracts while counting on its eventual renewal.

A livelier and less predictable issue was what, if any, new conditions might be negotiated and attached to its reauthorization. Conditions for the GSP included various safeguards mentioned earlier aimed to prevent these tariff breaks from directly undercutting American producers, along with others such as setting the product content rule at the GATT-standard rate of 35 percent. Other country eligibility criteria introduced when the program was first approved by Congress in 1974, and that were carried over into each new renewal, included disallowing GSP tariff preferences for exports from certain communist and Organization of the Petroleum Exporting Countries (OPEC)–member countries, countries that had expropriated American-owned investments within their borders without compensation, and countries that were unsupportive of U.S. efforts to combat terrorism.

The original 1974 GSP authorization, coming shortly after the Arab oil embargo of late 1973, also included the following criteria: "[T]he President shall take into account . . . the extent to which such [a developing country] has assured the United States it will provide equitable and reasonable access to the markets and basic commodity resources of such country. . . ."[6] This condition remained essentially latent until the Trump administration, which, over 40 years later, began applying it formally to threaten and kick out GSP beneficiary countries. More on this development is explained below since this shift in approach substantially changed the program's trajectory.

Other criteria and qualifying conditions were added to subsequent GSP reauthorizations over the ensuing few decades, such as excluding countries that fail to protect intellectual property adequately or that provide safe havens for international terrorists. Criteria for upholding and making progress to protect internationally recognized worker rights were added in 1984. These and other conditions provided a degree of leverage to engage and encourage or warn developing countries to improve these conditions; if this leverage was not sufficient, the next step would be to formally consider revoking their GSP eligibility for lack of compliance. In extraordinary cases, such as the case of a GSP country initiating a war or similar dramatic changes in circumstances, other grounds were available for finding a way to delist it more quickly.

With the day-to-day administration of the GSP program left to the executive branch, decisions on when and how to invoke these and other criteria at times also came to reflect the foreign relations and domestic economic priorities of different American presidential administrations. Most of the criteria set by Congress provided broad discretion over when or how to act in response to changing policies and conditions in GSP recipient countries. Input for when to trigger these eligibility reviews routinely came from congressional members and American

---

6   Trade Act of 1974, Section 502(c)(4), 19 U.S.C. Section 2462.

labor, business, human rights, and other organizations. It also came from tracking local developments through America's embassies abroad and other reporting. American citizens and other stakeholder organizations could also file formal petitions to trigger these reviews, which happened routinely and sometimes resulted in changes in eligibility for individual recipient countries.

All of these influences on the process, the potential gaps in it, and the broad scope for discretion that the criteria often provided led to uneven application of the program's conditions among the hundred-plus eligible developing countries. A petition calling to revoke GSP eligibility over the denial of worker rights in one country might trigger that official action, while equally or more egregious violations in another could remain unchallenged. Reviews of eligibility were held routinely, but this sense of unevenness led to an internal, executive branch effort to undertake ad hoc reviews as new evidence came to light instead of waiting for routine reviews to begin.[7] These "self-initiated" reviews, intended to help facilitate a more even application of the GSP criteria among countries, also ended up giving the Trump administration a lever to initiate country-specific reviews to conveniently accomplish its own goals.

Set against this backdrop, the development goals that spurred the GSP program seemed almost a quaint relic of American idealism as these expectations collided with the Trump administration's more caustic, less magnanimous American trade policy. For starters, the simple act of giving tariff-free access to the American market with no similar access gained in return was the antithesis of Trump's "reciprocal trade" philosophy and policy plank. In addition, some of the GSP recipients included the same "shithole" countries that America's new president reportedly made clear that he cared less about when it came to offering support or assistance.[8]

The Trump administration inherited the job of administering the program, nonetheless, and at least initially implemented it more or less as it had been in the past. Early actions included removing some products from coverage while adding others, such as travel goods, to the list of

---

7 The "self-initiated" review process began with an out of cycle review of Bolivia's compliance with GSP requirements for child labor concerns. See USTR, "USTR Announces New Trade Preference Program Enforcement Effort," press release, June 29, 2017.

8 See, e.g., Ali Vitali, Kasie Hunt, and Frank Thorp V, "Trump Referred to Haiti and African Nations as 'Shithole' Countries," NBC News, January 12, 2018.

eligible imports "where there is currently minimal U.S. production."[9] The administration's priorities for the GSP quickly shifted, however, in favor of leveraging it to extract concessions and, at other times, as retribution. The following section focuses on this fundamental change and its short- and long-term implications for America's foreign relations and the future of the GSP and America's other preference programs.

A comparable assessment cannot be made of the Biden administration since Congress allowed the GSP program to lapse just before that administration came into office. When asked, administration officials indicated general support for the reauthorization of the GSP by Congress.[10] Trade Ambassador Tai more proactively and publicly called for a successful renewal of the Africa-focused AGOA preference program, but only with a substantial overhaul of it, in advance of its scheduled lapse in 2025.[11] Noting in each case that the ball was in Congress's court to act, she indicated the administration's preferences for the renewal of trade preferences to meet, in the case of AGOA, new "resilience and inclusion" goals. The administration routinely used such phrases to indicate incentives to diversify trade away from China and promote more production in America, along with a slew of progressive-friendly criteria in areas such as labor and human rights and environmental protection.[12]

FROM RELIEF TO RECIPROCITY AND RETRIBUTION

The critical turning point in America's approach to the GSP came in spring 2018, more than a year into the Trump administration's term. As the administration's Section 232 investigation into the impact of global steel and aluminum imports on America stretched on for nearly an entire year, its trading partners had ample time, as covered in chapter 2, to prepare for the inevitability that came in February 2018—its final decision to slap Section 232 tariffs on America's steel and aluminum imports. With a door opened to the possibility that other arrangements might be set with some countries, America's trading partners waited until March to announce their final responses when it became clear that many of these

9   USTR, "USTR Announces New Trade Preference Program Enforcement Effort."

10   See the statement from a USTR spokesperson in Jason Asenso and Oliver Ward, "Trade Panel Chair: Ways & Means Committee 'Anxious' to Reauthorize GSP," World Trade Online, September 21, 2023.

11   David Lawder, "U.S. Ready to Explore Next Phases of Trade Relationship with Africa, USTR Tai Says," Reuters, December 12, 2022.

12   Lawder, "U.S. Ready to Explore Next Phases."

alternate arrangements would never materialize. Most of the major steel
and aluminum exporters, from the EU to China to Russia, responded
by threatening to levy or immediately moving to implement their own
retaliatory tariffs against American exports. Some decided to also take
America to WTO dispute settlement over its decision, which was still a
functioning and viable option at the time.

India and Turkey joined others in claiming the 232 action was a
WTO violation and prepared their own retaliatory measures to respond.
India notified the WTO in May of its plan to raise tariffs, beginning in
late June, on hundreds of millions of dollars of American exports,
including products such as apples, walnuts and cashews, and motorcycles.[13] Turkey, like the EU and China, chose to begin near-immediate
retaliation by raising tariffs on approximately $1.8 billion in American
exports of rice, nuts, tobacco, beauty products, paper, automobiles, and
other products.[14] America responded to Turkey soon after by doubling
its tariff on Turkey's steel exports, claiming the initial 25 percent tariff
had been ineffective; but, as widely reported, this move also appeared to
be in response to the arrest of an American citizen. Turkey then upped
its retaliation in a further round of tit-for-tat tariff war escalation.[15]

India and Turkey were America's only GSP-eligible countries that
responded to Trump's Section 232 tariffs with threats to retaliate and
raise their own tariffs.[16] Adding important U.S. farm good exports to
their retaliation lists had the intended impact in Washington of riling up
Trump's rural supporters, who feared losing these export markets and
bearing the cost of the administration's first trade war. Some members
of Congress pressed the administration to do more to stem the harm
to farm exporters by making ". . . it a priority to negotiate a solution

13 WTO, *India: Immediate Notification under Article 12.5 of the Agreement on Safeguards to the Council for Trade in Goods of Proposed Suspension of Concessions and Other Obligations Referred to in Paragraph 2 of Article 8 of the Agreement on Safeguards*, WTO Doc. G/SG/N/12/IND/1 (May 18, 2018).

14 WTO, *Turkey: Immediate Notification under Article 12.5 of the Agreement on Safeguards to the Council for Trade in Goods of Proposed Suspension of Concessions and Other Obligations Referred to in Paragraph 2 of Article 8 of the Agreement on Safeguards*, WTO Doc. G/SG/N/12/TUR/6 (May 18, 2018).

15 See, e.g., Shayerah I. Akhtar, *U.S.-Turkey Trade Relations*, Congressional Research Service, RIF10961, August 28, 2018.

16 According to a list compiled by the Congressional Research Service. See Rachel F. Fefer et al., *Section 232 Investigations: Overview and Issues for Congress*, Congressional Research Service, R45249, September 11, 2018, 15.

that shields our specialty crop growers from retaliatory actions. . . ."[17] While a necessary exercise of congressional constituent management, these appeals proved mere wishful thinking amid the dark clouds that had already gathered in America's new tariff wars.

The political problem of agitated farmers caused Trade Ambassador Lighthizer to leap at a suggestion that threatening to pull GSP benefits from India and Turkey was fair play in return. Lighthizer relished responding to countries complaining about the administration's trade decisions by engaging them in his game of "Who is the real protectionist?" Few could win at Lighthizer's game once triggered, as only a small handful of countries could claim to have a similar overall level of openness to international trade and investment as America. Those who criticized the Section 232 tariffs as unfair, except from behind their own wall of tariffs and other forms of protection, became easy targets for Lighthizer. This happened even though most of the world—and some in America—shared the same incredulous view of the Trump administration's action.

In the case of India, which proudly presented itself within the WTO and to the global South as the developing world's champion in opposition to much of the West's vision for a liberal and free trading order, this was a no-contest game. Among a myriad of other measures, India applied an average tariff rate in 2018 of nearly 14 percent on its global imports, but maintained the flexibility under the WTO to hike its rate on all imports up to an average of nearly 50 percent if it chose.[18] Turkey was less protectionist than that, having gradually reformed over many years, which, for a time, was spurred by the hope of eventually joining the EU. Even so, Turkey still maintained an average tariff rate of nearly 11 percent for global imports, or three to four times America's average rate, which it also was allowed under WTO rules to raise as high as almost 30 percent if it wished.[19]

Lighthizer chose to self-initiate GSP eligibility investigations of India and Turkey as his tool to threaten retribution and to make his point with both countries. Initiating these reviews allowed him to up the chance that each might back off their own retaliatory tariff threats while also

---

17 "Washington State Lawmakers Urge Lighthizer to Negotiate 232 'Solution' to Shield Ag Products," World Trade Online, June 13, 2018.

18 WTO, ITC, and UNCTAD, *World Tariff Profiles 2018* (Geneva: World Trade Organization, 2018), 10–11.

19 WTO, ITC, and UNCTAD, *World Tariff Profiles 2018*, 12–13.

creating leverage to seek other concessions from them to lighten their tariff and non-tariff barriers to American agricultural and other exports. To make it all legally sound under Congress's framework for the GSP, Lighthizer for the first time invoked its criteria allowing the executive branch to scrutinize "the extent to which a developing country is providing the United States equitable and reasonable access to its markets and basic commodity resources" as his sweeping, most-anything-goes eligibility criteria for these reviews.

Lighthizer routinely took a much more permissive approach toward America's trade with the world's least developed countries, rarely picking on or targeting them for their barriers and policies. It probably mattered that none had a steel industry or steel exports, either. He had little hesitation, however, targeting the more industrialized countries of the developing world, which, if exporting in large dollar terms to America, he viewed as sufficient grounds to cut them off from receiving any special treatment from America or in the WTO. He especially targeted the more protected markets of countries that ran significant trade surpluses with America. Countries that, in his view, hypocritically pointed the finger at the administration's trade policies as violating WTO rules also received the same treatment.

So it was for India. Once India announced its plan to retaliate against Section 232 tariffs, Lighthizer launched a formal GSP country eligibility inquiry to assess whether it was offering "equitable and reasonable access" for America's exports. With this criterion invoked and released from its box, the contagion spread among U.S. stakeholders that saw it as an opportunity to press their own claims against India for the review. America's medical device industry, for example, sought progress on its complaint against India's price controls for medical devices such as heart stents and knee implants, which India had claimed to be a cost-saving measure (and one that also happened to target U.S. company products).[20] Key American agricultural interests also pressed their concerns, from dairy to poultry to pork, citing an array of barriers limiting their access to Indian consumers. Other American firms raised India's digital and e-commerce policies, which were a sore point they hoped could be resolved through leverage.[21]

---

20   Aditya Kalra and Neha Dasgupta, "Exclusive: India Rejects U.S. Request on Price Caps on Medical Devices—Sources," Reuters, May 2, 2018.

21   See, e.g., Shayerah Ilias Akhtar and Vivian C. Jones, *Trump Administration's Proposed Removal of Generalized System of Preferences (GSP) Benefits for India and Turkey*, Congressional

After the GSP review was announced, India decided to hold off on its planned retaliation and instead play ball with Washington to see if a deal could be reached to escape the Section 232 tariffs and preserve its GSP status.

For these talks, America brought a long list of stipulations to meet the market-opening demands of U.S. stakeholders. The talks went on for a few months and almost worked. However, the results fell short of Trump's expectations, and no final deal was announced. America instead announced in March 2019 that it would pull India's GSP eligibility in 60 days over America's lack of equivalent access, thus denying GSP tariff-free benefits for approximately $5.7 billion of its exports to America.[22] India, in turn, proceeded to retaliate against Section 232 actions as it had planned a year earlier, levying tariffs on nearly $1.4 billion in American exports of nuts, apples, chickpeas, motorcycles, and steel, among other goods.[23] With no deal reached, it also left in place the trade barriers that some American stakeholders had hoped to see resolved. Another effort was made during the latter half of 2019 to try again for a deal, but it was also to no avail. Lighthizer pinned the blame on India, later writing that he had come to conclude, and with no sense of irony, that its government was "just protectionist."[24]

The fate of GSP eligibility for Turkey, which already was retaliating against the Section 232 decision with tariffs on approximately $1.8 billion in U.S. coal, nuts, paper, and other goods exports, seemed more likely to be a foregone conclusion.[25] The first step in the formal review process for Turkey got underway in mid-August 2018, three months after the same for India, amid other complications and strains in U.S.-Turkey relations at the time. The GSP eligibility reviews for Turkey and India were launched based on the same grounds—to examine whether they failed to offer equivalent market access. American producers stepped forward with complaints, as they did with the investigation for India. The review for Turkey ended, however, with a different conclusion. In March 2019 the administration announced that instead of having its GSP status revoked pending changes in its policies toward U.S. exports,

Research Service, RIN11075, March 15, 2019.

22   USTR, "United States Will Terminate GSP Designation of India and Turkey," press release, March 4, 2019; and Amy Held, "India Becomes Trump's Latest Trade Target," NPR, March 5, 2019.

23   Williams and Hammond, *Escalating U.S. Tariffs: Affected Trade.*

24   On the GSP-related issues and negotiations, see Lighthizer, *No Trade Is Free*, 282–84.

25   Akhtar and Jones, *Trump Administration's Proposed Removal.*

Turkey had become "sufficiently economically developed" and thus was no longer eligible to benefit from the GSP program.[26]

The Trump administration's use of GSP eligibility reviews as threat or retribution for unrelated issues, not to mention its use as leverage to identify and pursue a hodgepodge of market access barriers, was probably unprecedented for U.S. administrations and likely against the GATT and the WTO rules. It also whetted the appetite of other U.S. stakeholders who saw it for the first time as a tool to achieve their own goals. From labor unions to business groups, once set loose, America's more aggressive and expansive use of GSP opened a new avenue to press the administration and Congress to use it to take up their lists of grievances.

Most GSP country eligibility reviews since at least the mid-1990s focused on the other, more concrete and targeted criteria set by Congress. These included reviews triggered by the expropriation of American company investments and inadequate protection of intellectual property; ones in support of internationally recognized worker rights; and to eliminate the worst forms of child labor. These reviews at times took on certain market-access fairness and other political overtones. For example, the Obama administration launched one new eligibility review and restarted another for several developing countries in November 2015 over worker rights complaints and petitions, which happened to coincide with its effort to reduce opposition from America's labor unions to the just-completed TPP agreement.[27] The Trump administration consistently demonstrated less self-restraint in its politicization of the GSP, such as when it reportedly delayed restoring partial GSP eligibility for Ukraine, following improvements it made to its intellectual property protection regime to address U.S. concerns, after the national security advisor warned that Trump would disapprove of any action favorable to Ukrainian president Volodymyr Zelenskyy.[28]

Compared to the more expansive "equitable access" criterion that could cover almost anything, denying GSP eligibility over deficient protection of worker and investor rights, and, to a certain degree, for failure to protect intellectual property, were arguably more defensible

---

26   USTR, "United States Will Terminate GSP Designation of India and Turkey."

27   A new worker rights review of Thailand was launched, along with the resumption of worker rights reviews of Uzbekistan, Niger, Fiji, Georgia, and Iraq. See USTR, "USTR Uses Trade Preference Programs to Advance Worker Rights," press release, November 25, 2015.

28   See, e.g., David J. Lynch and Josh Dawsey, "White House Delayed Ukraine Trade Decision in August, a Signal That U.S. Suspension of Cooperation Extended Beyond Security Funds," *Washington Post*, October 24, 2019.

under the GATT and WTO standard of being in the service of promoting a country's development. Gaining more access or insisting on the removal of barriers in exchange for keeping GSP tariff benefits was not a trade-off envisioned as meeting that standard.[29] The Trump administration's use of the "equitable and reasonable access" criteria that Congress had provided was thus a significant turning point for America's administration of its GSP program.

The Trump administration targeted other countries on the same "equitable access" grounds, particularly in Asia. Top examples included Indonesia and, shortly after, Thailand, which was already technically under eligibility review, one that the Obama administration officially opened in late 2015 over worker rights concerns.

In two waves, the administration denied Thailand's tariff preferences for a sizable percentage of its GSP-eligible exports. The first was announced in late 2019, when the Trump administration, acting in support of a long-pending worker rights denial petition filed in 2015 by the AFL-CIO, revoked benefits for approximately a third, or approximately $1.3 billion, of Thailand's GSP-eligible exports. Rather than pull Thailand's country-wide eligibility, the administration maintained tariff-free access for American importers to a subset of Thailand's exports that were not as readily available from other countries.[30] The second wave came weeks later; the administration announced it would open a new review of Thailand's eligibility based on the much broader "equitable and reasonable access" criterion, this time triggered by a petition from America's pork producers over several of Thailand's onerous restrictions on imports of American pork.[31] That review and the lack of progress with Thailand on the complaints led to the removal of tariff-free benefits

---

29   Trump administration officials attempted to make some arguments that agricultural access was in the service of the developmental goal of requiring that it bring its agricultural regulations into conformity with science-based, WTO standards. See, e.g. Brett Fortnam, "Doud: Administration Using GSP to Boost SPS Standards of Beneficiaries," World Trade Online, May 23, 2018.

30   USTR, "USTR Announces GSP Enforcement Actions and Successes for Seven Countries," press release, October 25, 2019.

31   The National Pork Producers Council filed in April 2018 for Thailand, days before the administration launched its first general market access denial review for India. See "USTR Accepts Pork Industry Plea to Review Thailand's GSP Eligibility," World Trade Online, May 17, 2018.

from an additional one-sixth of Thailand's GSP-eligible exports, totaling approximately $817 million.[32]

For Indonesia, the administration launched in April 2018 reviews to assess its "equitable and reasonable access" criterion eligibility, as well as to evaluate its "trade distorting investment practices" and its steps to "reduce or eliminate barriers to trade in services." Indonesia had not formally threatened or pursued retaliation for the Section 232 announcement and, like Japan and some others, was later able to secure product exceptions to the tariffs for some of its specialty steel exports. Even so, America's steel industry remained upset at Indonesia for another reason—its export restrictions on unprocessed nickel, a critical natural resource the global steel industry depended upon as an input in the production of stainless steel. Indonesia's limits had caused a spike in global prices for the mineral over several years.[33] Beyond nickel, numerous American stakeholders had many other complaints with Indonesia over its digital policies, dairy import restrictions, and insurance regulations. The announcement also affirmed that a separate, prior review related to Indonesia's intellectual property protections remained active and ongoing.[34]

With the review docket opened, another free-for-all of market access complaints from American stakeholders ensued in these and other areas. Like India, Indonesia agreed to negotiate with Lighthizer and his agency to try to reach an agreement to keep its GSP eligibility, which in 2017 applied to about $2 billion of its roughly $20 billion in total exports to America.[35] These talks succeeded, with a deal reached in 2020 on improvements to be made to respond to many of these access concerns in order to maintain GSP eligibility. The administration announced on October 30 that the market access reviews of Indonesia would be closed in exchange for its pledge to "continue to work with the

32   USTR, "USTR Announces GSP Enforcement Action, Successes, and New Eligibility Reviews," press release, October 30, 2020.

33   On the export restrictions, see, e.g., American Iron and Steel Institute, "RE: Request for Comments on Indonesia Market Access under the Country Practice Review of the Generalized System of Preferences," public comment USTR-2018-0007-0053, docket USTR-2018-007, January 17, 2020.

34   USTR, "Initiation of Country Practice Reviews of India, Indonesia, and Kazakhstan," 83 Fed. Reg. 18618 (April 27, 2018).

35   Vivian C. Jones, *Generalized System of Preferences (GSP): Overview and Issues for Congress,* Congressional Research Service, RL33663, May 9, 2018, 14.

United States to ensure the successful implementation of these policies for the benefit of both countries."[36]

The administration's Indonesia success story proved short-lived as the entire GSP program approached its congressionally mandated expiration in just two months. A few in Congress attempted to push for renewal in time, but with America's congressional and presidential elections approaching that fall, it became apparent that walking out by letting the program lapse again for a period of time was the preferred option, rather than engaging in another legislative battle to pass it. As of this book's writing, more than three and a half years later, Congress has still failed to reauthorize the GSP program.

Once Congress let the program expire, (and so long as it is not renewed retroactively), countries like Indonesia that went out on a limb to agree to a large number of concessions were left with no incentive to follow through in full on those commitments. Countries like Thailand and India, which never conceded to Washington's demands for changes to their practices to save their GSP eligibility (which, for Thailand, was partial), were left no worse off than others since no country was receiving tariff-free GSP access either. Turkey, which had been kicked out permanently, had not lost out either so long as the GSP remained expired. American importers, who were accustomed to waiting for a few months for refunds in the tariffs they paid once the program was eventually reauthorized, were still making extra tariff payments for three and a half years and counting.

The Trump administration was the first to unleash expectations that GSP could be used as a lever to demand just about anything from America's developing country trading partners, in the process knocking the program off its original, foundational pedestal. Many in Congress came to embrace the same view, for their own reasons and to advance their own agendas, adding even more complexity to Congress's ability to reach consensus on a bill to reauthorize it. Well over three years later, that consensus remains elusive. The following section focuses on these debates and why America failed to find a way forward to recommit to a program that for nearly 50 years has used trade to help lift living standards globally and help American firms compete.

---

36   USTR, "USTR Announces GSP Enforcement Action, Country Successes, and New Eligibility Reviews."

THE GSP IN CONGRESS:
THE ROAD FROM BIPARTISANSHIP TO PARALYSIS

With GSP authorization due to lapse at the end of 2020, the first cloud on the horizon came in a bill dropped by the House Ways and Means Trade Subcommittee chairman in early December.[37] Congressman Earl Blumenauer, representing the trade- and progressive-friendly Portland, Oregon, and the surrounding region, endeavored to meet these local priorities by proposing a bill to renew, but also reform, the GSP. The bill called for extending the program for only five months, until May 1 of the following year, which would have kept it running until more was known about the incoming Biden administration's views on trade.

Blumenauer, who genuinely supported GSP renewal, loaded his bill with an expansive new set of criteria, expectations, reporting, and conditions for that renewal. He proposed adding five new country eligibility criteria to the 15 already established, including new expectations on environmental protection, human and economic rights, rule of law, economic reform, and anti-corruption. Except for the environmental criteria, all had also previously been included in the more concessionary tariff treatment offered to eligible African countries under America's AGOA preference program.

Beyond these criteria, Blumenauer's bill tacked on new and extraordinarily expansive reporting requirements for the executive branch to report on each GSP-eligible country's policies and practices. One called for a joint report from the Trade Representative Office and the Department of Labor every May on the state of gender and labor laws and the legal protections of the nearly 120 eligible countries across nine broad areas, to include access to education, levels of "mobility" and "entrepreneurship," and family law issues. The other was a one-time report, also due in May 2021, to assess the use of GSP benefits and other issues, such as meeting product content requirements to qualify, and steps that could be taken to prevent goods from non-GSP beneficiaries from being transshipped tariff-free to the U.S. market from GSP-eligible countries. It was difficult to imagine how all this could be accomplished in such a short timeline, and it was uncertain how far recipient countries

---

37 Blumenauer, "Chairman Blumenauer Files Legislation"; and To Amend the Trade Act of 1974 to Modify and Extend the Generalized System of Preferences, and for Other Purposes, H.R. 8884, 116th. Cong. (2020).

would go to meet the program's extensive new conditions in exchange for a five-month extension of their eligibility. The bill went nowhere.

Portions of Blumenauer's bill reappeared several months later in the United States Innovation and Competition Act of 2021, a massive two-thousand-plus-page Senate bill that passed that chamber by a bipartisan vote of 68–32 in June. From provisions covering space exploration to discovering the origins of the COVID-19 pandemic, the bill also included a few trade-related articles. Among these was a section to reauthorize the GSP until 2027. The Senate version included a less restrictive approach to new GSP criteria and requirements than Blumenauer's House version, but still incorporated a couple of its extra eligibility criteria and added a new one—whether a recipient country maintained an open digital trade policy framework by refraining from using barriers such as data localization requirements and data transfer restrictions.[38]

The Senate effort to follow through on the GSP and other trade business ultimately flamed out. It began with a process foul: House members chided their Senate colleagues for including a revenue (tariffs) provision in its bill, which, under the Constitution, had to originate in the House of Representatives. Blumenauer and other Democratic members then attempted to still play ball with the Senate by proposing their own, House-originated GSP renewal bill that included their long list of new GSP criteria.[39] It also tightened the existing eligibility criteria for labor rights, requiring GSP countries to effectively provide core rights to workers instead of the prior standard of continuing to progress toward doing so. This adopted the approach labor unions insisted upon for the successfully renegotiated NAFTA that passed Congress in early 2020. The bill added a similar standard on environmental protection, requiring the effective fulfillment of, and not just progress toward, its domestic and international environmental laws and obligations. With these and other "essential improvements" added to the GSP eligibility criteria, the AFL-CIO supported the bill.[40] These dozen or so pages of union- and progressive-friendly criteria for GSP reauthorization were folded into the House's three-thousand-page version of the Senate's 2021 Competes

---

38   United States Innovation and Competition Act of 2021, S. 1260, 117th Congress (2021).

39   Generalized System of Preferences and Miscellaneous Tariff Bill Modernization Act of 2021, H.R. 3975, 117th Congress (2021).

40   William Samuel, "Letter to Senators in Support of Generalized System of Preferences and Miscellaneous Tariff Bill Modernization Act of 2021," AFL-CIO, December 6, 2021.

Act. Leaders in the House and Senate then met in conference well into 2022 to hash out a single version capable of passing both chambers.

As a single conference version of a bill moved toward agreement, the wheels fell off for GSP renewal after multiple differences and divisions erupted over the different trade provisions in the House and Senate bills. The fights covered familiar proxy battles and other territory from prior chapters. Among these, House progressives, for example, adamantly opposed the Senate bill's call for stepped-up digital trade enforcement and new digital trade agreements. Some Senate Republicans opposed the House bill's provisions for renewed and much higher funding for retraining and other programs for workers displaced by international trade without including the other legislative course typically served alongside it—a renewed grant of trade agreement negotiating authority for the executive branch. Other New Right Republicans joined with progressive Democrats to insist on substantially lowering America's customs *de minimis* rate, the tariff-free customs treatment of individual online import purchases of $800 or less that Lighthizer had railed against, but that business-friendly Republicans were against changing.[41]

Instead of allowing these and other disagreements to potentially tank a final consensus on their priority issues, conferees moved to strip *all* the trade provisions out of the conference bill to save its core goal—approving billions in new funding and incentives for China-countering industrial programs from research to the domestic production of semiconductors and other key technologies. With trade tossed out, a pathway was made possible for the rare event that followed—a well-supported, bipartisan (and non-trade) legislative success known as the CHIPS and Science Act.

Bush administration trade ambassador-turned-Ohio-senator Rob Portman, along with Senator Chris Coons, a moderate Democrat from Delaware, made another attempt in late 2022, shortly after the glare of congressional elections had passed but before the 117th Congress was due to adjourn. Expressing confidence that a "grand bargain" on trade was still possible, Portman proposed a bill and then joined with Coons to make the case for it.[42] Noting Congress's failure to reach an agreement

41   See, e.g., Gavin Bade, "With Trump Gone, Republicans Look to Weaken His China Tariffs," Politico, April 22, 2022; and David Dayen, "The Trade Fight That Could Doom Biden's Industrial Policy," *American Prospect*, April 20, 2022
42   Maydeen Merino, "Cardin: Lame-Duck Trade Bill Could Pass This Year—If It's Attached to Something Else," World Trade Online, December 7, 2022.

on trade in the final version of the CHIPS Act, they expressed concern about the ongoing cost of inaction as America continued to be left on the outside of trade deals that others, including China, were concluding. They wrote, "The consequences of failing to open new markets for U.S. exporters, help workers hurt by trade, fight unfair trade practices, and reauthorize expiring trade benefits all add up to two things: fewer good jobs for American workers and weakened U.S. influence around the world."[43]

Portman's "grand bargain" bill attempted to bundle several priorities together for members of both parties, as trade bills had often been handled in the past. Among these were renewed funding for displaced worker support and retraining, renewal of the GSP and other routine tariff programs, and stricter trade defense protections against unfair imports. It also added a narrower grant of negotiating authority for the executive branch to pursue new free trade agreements, limited only to negotiations with the UK and Kenya (already started during the Trump administration) and with Taiwan and Ecuador.[44] The session ended with no action and Portman's retirement from the Senate.

As hope again faded, the new Congress got underway in January 2023 with a slim Republican majority in the House and a razor-thin Democratic majority in the Senate. Hopes for rekindling the longstanding bipartisanship on trade appeared to still have a heartbeat, at least, as incoming House Ways and Means Trade Subcommittee chair Adrian Smith called Republican leadership in the House a "great opportunity" to renew various trade programs like the GSP.[45] As covered in the opening of this chapter, the House Trade Subcommittee called its hearing for later that year, the outcome of which was only to expand the list of demands for GSP reform, with Smith remarking that some of these proposals remained "problematic [and] hard to enforce."[46]

Sensing an opening to tap into Congress's antipathy, particularly among many Republicans, toward allowing Chinese content to find its way into America's market, the steelworkers union advocated for stricter product content rules for tariff-free imports from GSP coun-

43   Rob Portman and Chris Coons, "A Bipartisan Trade Proposal to Support Our Economy," op-ed, The Hill, December 2, 2022.

44   Portman and Coons, "A Bipartisan Trade Proposal to Support Our Economy."

45   Maydeen Merino, "Rep. Adrian Smith: GOP-Led House Offers 'Great Opportunity' to Renew Trade Programs," World Trade Online, January 12, 2023.

46   Jason Asenso, "Reps. Moore, DelBene Push to Raise CNL Threshold for GSP Recipients," World Trade Online, December 7, 2023.

tries. It demanded increasing the percentage rule from 35 to at least 60 percent, calling this and its other conditions non-negotiable.[47] Unless all its demands for GSP reform were met, its witness testified, "the union will be forced to oppose renewal of the [GSP] program to defend American workers against unfair trade practices."[48] As others piled on more demands, with no resolution in sight, one American trade association publicized its estimate that American importers had paid at least $3.2 billion in extra tariffs while waiting for Congress's action to renew the GSP.[49]

Other congressional members took a different tack on the China point. They pressed their view that to use GSP to help open new and divert more existing supply chain channels away from China, it was important to substantially increase the annual monetary caps placed on imports from each of these countries from $210 million to $600 million, with built-in percentage increases after that, so that American companies could shift more significant business in their direction. A bill to make this point and drive a new discussion about what kind of GSP reforms would really help move production and imports away from China was proposed by Republican representative Blake Moore and Democratic representative Suzan DelBene in late 2023.[50]

A bipartisan House delegation from Florida also called for action on the GSP in late 2023, claiming the failure to renew was ". . . crippling U.S. companies that have borne these costs" and had ". . . halted business expansion, hindered job creation, and prevented crucial investments in operations and infrastructure." Led by Democratic Representative Debbie Wasserman Schultz and Mario Diaz-Balart, along with 18 other bipartisan members of the Florida delegation, they bemoaned the $300 million in tariffs paid by Florida businesses as Congress failed to renew it. Beyond the cost to these businesses and other costs for consumers, they stressed the harm to the employment prospects in countries of Latin

---

47 "USW Urges Lawmakers to Improve GSP When Renewing It," World Trade Online, August 31, 2023.

48 Roy Houseman, Jr. (for United Steelworkers) to U.S. House of Representatives, "Re: United Steelworkers Urges Reforming the General Systems Preferences Program and Restarting the Worker Training Program—Trade Adjustment Assistance," letter, August 31, 2023.

49 Coalition for GSP, "Nearly 100 GSP Advocates Press Lawmakers to Renew GSP in 2023," press release, October 20, 2023.

50 Asenso, "Reps. Moore, DelBene Push to Raise CNL Threshold for GSP Recipients."

America, a harm they characterized as a "key driver for migration."[51] They also focused on China, claiming that if Florida businesses were to source their GSP imports from China instead, 99 percent of those imports would be subject to the still-in-place Trump China Section 301 tariffs.[52]

As 2024 began and presidential primary elections got underway, prospects for a bipartisan approach to reauthorize the GSP fell completely apart, just as they did for other trade legislation. The Republican House Ways and Means Committee chair finalized and advanced in April his party's version of a GSP renewal bill; he also added an amendment to include some environmental and labor criteria changes that had limited bipartisan backing in the Senate to try and bring House Democrats on board. Instead, House committee Democrats chided the rushed process, lack of consultation, and refusals to tack onto the bill more of their other trade priorities, such as refunding worker assistance programs. The Republican bill passed the committee, with the Republican majority in support and Democrats opposed.[53] As the election season heated up, the relevant Senate committee in June also made another attempt to secure a compromise with enough bipartisan support to finally renew the GSP program. The future of these House and Senate committee efforts remain unclear, however, as the same disagreements that prevented GSP renewal continue to swirl around these proposals in each chamber.

INTERNATIONAL AND OTHER IMPLICATIONS

The fate of the GSP perfectly paints the picture of the dead end that America's new trade policy has found itself in. After the bipartisan mainstream that advanced open and freer trade for over 70 years was swept away by America's New Right and progressive Left, their shared interest in adding new and ever more conditions to America's imports was insufficient to overcome their sharp disagreements over which conditions to add. Legislators who had forged these compromises on trade over several decades and who believed in the benefits of the GSP program

---

51   Debbie Wasserman Schultz and Mario Diaz-Balart to Jason Smith, Richard Neal, and members of the Ways and Means Committee, letter, November 9, 2023, quoted in "Wasserman Schultz, Díaz-Balart Lead Florida Delegation in Push for GSP Renewal to Boost Local Economy, Lower Consumer Prices," on Debbie Wasserman Schultz's official website, press release, November 10, 2023.

52   Ibid.

53   Oliver Ward, "Ways & Means Panel Advances GSP, de minimis Reform Bills; Democrats Blast Process," World Trade Online, April 17, 2024.

for America and for the developing world made sincere attempts to find a path to overcome those differences. Instead, they found themselves unable to do so for the first time amid demands that were increasingly irreconcilable and expectations that were newly unbridgeable. Congress was paralyzed—a problem that Maryland Democratic senator Ben Cardin identified when, in late 2022 and after various efforts had been tried and failed to pass trade legislation, he lamented: "I don't think there's any way you can have an independent bill on trade."[54] Other attempts to stuff trade legislation into larger omnibus bills were also tried but failed.

Unable to constrain the expansive demands of each side to reach compromises, other trade-related legislation also fell into limbo. GSP reauthorization was routinely packaged with the renewal of other trade programs and authorities. These frequently included funding to help support and retrain workers who had lost their jobs to international trade and other limited tariff breaks for U.S. businesses to lower their cost of intermediate goods inputs used to maintain the cost competitiveness of their own U.S.-based production. At times, these were also packaged with a new grant of negotiating authority for the executive branch to pursue new trade agreements. Congress appeared unlikely to agree on any of these programs, whether proposed independently or as part of a package, for the same reasons that made agreement on GSP elusive.

These impasses were especially acute over any bill that aimed to lower U.S. tariffs, irrespective of the potential benefit, impact, or intent. As such, programs like the GSP remained effectively dead. As long as U.S. tariff cuts are viewed, as many on the progressive Left view them, as tax breaks for greedy large American corporations, or viewed, as many on the New Right see them, as unrequited favors to foreign countries that only suckers would fall for, the entire logic of America's postwar international trading system remains derailed. This is the glasses-crashing train wreck of American impulse that its leaders had attempted to avoid for almost a hundred years, ever since Congress passed America's peak Smoot-Hawley tariffs in 1930. The new Left and Right mainstreams have a ways to go to unwind trade commitments before returning America to 1930-levels of tariff and import protection. However, recent actions covered in other chapters, including hikes of U.S. tariffs up to 100 percent for some car imports and other presidential campaign proposals for 10 percent across-the-board tariffs on all imports and 60 percent

54 Merino, "Cardin: Lame-Duck Trade Bill Could Pass This Year."

tariffs on imports from China, are very strong moves in that direction. In this environment, it is easy to see that securing a consensus support for *lowering* tariffs temporarily on some imports from GSP countries faces an unprecedented, uphill climb.

The impacts on America's foreign relationships have been manifold. The Trump administration's aggressive implementation of the GSP transformed a program aimed at improving America's support for and linkages with the developing world into a weaponized tool of leverage to advance its own trade goals and, in limited cases, even to exact retribution. For the developing world, these actions were received as a direct expression of America's new foreign policy goals and tactics, one that stood markedly apart from America's past approaches and those of other advanced, developed nations. It also worked at sharp cross-purposes with the Trump administration's efforts to improve America's relationships with an arc of nations around China's eastern, southeastern, and southwestern flanks to help thwart Beijing's regional influence and ambition. Using the GSP to target Indonesia, Thailand, India, and others for the reasons it did, instead of relying on other tools and avenues to address administration concerns, worked directly against its own new "Indo-Pacific" strategy.[55]

Once the GSP was repurposed in this way, it opened the floodgates to a hodgepodge of other demands to further use it as a tool of leverage. These demands, in turn, became so extensively politicized that once the GSP expired, it was dead and of no use to the service of any goals, reasonable or not. Beyond reneging on expectations for its routine renewal that had led U.S. companies to invest and count on the opportunities the GSP provided, Congress's failure to reauthorize it only further reinforced for GSP recipient countries the message of America's waning commitment to them—and this time, from its legislative branch as well.

The future of the GSP is left uncertain. The TPP was a vastly different proposition for eventually obligating America to the permanent elimination of virtually all its tariffs with those agreement partners. Renewal of the GSP included vastly more conditional and temporary tariff pref-

---

55   The Trump administration's Indo-Pacific strategic framework emphasizes the importance of boosting ties with Southeast Asia and India for the success of that strategy. The administration's National Security Council strategy, declassified days before the administration's end, can be found at "Statement from National Security Advisor Robert C. O'Brien," The White House, National Security & Defense Statement, January 12, 2021, https://trumpwhitehouse.archives. gov/briefings-statements/statement-national-security-advisor-robert-c-obrien-011221/.

erences for developing countries. Like the TPP, however, it also became stuck in America's new trade policy dead end, unable to move forward.

SEVEN

From America's Opportunity to America's Harm

For decades, America's political leaders maintained an optimistic commitment to building and shaping the global trading system as they advanced more open and freer trade. Their political patience and America's economic capacity were often tested along the way, whether from predatory practices or import surges. To maintain their commitment, they demanded constant adjustments to the system and America's trading relationships. The Trump and Biden administrations were not the first to practice unilateralism, threaten tariffs, demand results-based trade outcomes, employ subsidies, block foreign acquisitions, insist on new trade rules, or demand reciprocity in treatment. Stretching the limits of the rules-based system and adding to those rules when necessary has always been a part of making it fair for America, enabling its leaders to ultimately remain committed to the system.

Pushing back on its trading partners when necessary to keep a lane open to press forward with trade liberalization and new trade rules was a bold and outward sign of America's confidence in its workers, businesses, and its economic strengths and resilience. America's position as the system's leading rule-maker reflected its size, influence, and persistent leadership. It was a privileged position that enabled it to continue molding the system so long as it was still setting the agenda and leading the way. As a leader, America's priorities, legal and regulatory approaches, definitions, practices, and customs were instilled into the global trading system on a scale that other countries often resisted and muted but simply could not match.

Since America's approach was shaped by its norms, values, and experience, these efforts could, at best, be only partly successful globally. Because the trade rules it sought were also necessarily made flexible to accommodate legitimate regulatory and policy needs, they often left ample room for its trading partners to pursue their national goals of tilting trade in their favor. As its trading partners custom-fit them to their own policies and interpretations, America's attempts to propagate these rules and norms often proved to not be as effective as anticipated.

This dynamic led to two great defining clashes in modern American trade policy, both with rapidly growing Asia-Pacific countries. The first was with Japan, especially during the 1980s and into the early 1990s. A security ally but economic rival, Japan's export surges and tools for playing technological catch-up from the 1960s into the early 1990s tested the resilience of America's commitment in unprecedented ways. Richard Gephardt, a Democratic congressman from Missouri, led his party through the worst of those days as its majority leader in Congress. Aiming through it all to still align with America's trade union and middle-class interests, Gephardt and many of his colleagues still managed to maintain space for America's ongoing commitment to freer trade. The optimism these Americans had over the future of the trading system still held for years afterward. Stressing the need to build in more labor and environmental goals alongside dealing with business concerns, he reflected on it in early 2001: "I believe in trade [and] I think the WTO is a good thing. I've always supported international rules in trade. We suffer when we don't have international rules that we can get countries and people to adhere to."[1]

The second great clash came roughly two decades later, with China. Wielding many of the same tools Japan had used but with a vastly larger market, lower-cost labor, and a more extensive and tightly interwoven state-owned and state-controlled economic system, China also molded its priorities and policies on top of the international rules to make its economic advances. With the import surges and job dislocations that followed, America's commitment to the system again came under tremendous stress. This time, at the insistence of Japan and others, America had previously abandoned key tools of unilateralism to create the WTO, including its use of Section 301 and negotiated voluntary export limits.

---

1   Richard Gephardt, interview from *Commanding Heights*.

In exchange, it got the judicial-style WTO dispute mechanism it wanted and needed, which it only later spurned as counterproductive to making trade fair. Walking out on the WTO by unilaterally hiking tariffs and breaking the dispute system met its purpose of successfully reclaiming America's ability to throw its elbow once again, and at just about anyone.

As underscored by the examples presented in this book, China's threat and the political and economic impact of that threat often stressed, to its breaking point, America's commitment to the open international trading system. However, the fact that it broke came as a domestic political response to a broader set of factors. These more fundamental changes were already manifest by the mid-2010s, brought to a head in the debate over the TPP, and cemented by a presidential campaign and election in 2016 that responded to a new zeitgeist that pushed America's trade policy in its new direction. China's challenge further reinforced the urgency of, but did not alone direct, that turn.

<hr />

Two quotes encapsulate the domestic political origins and the significance of America's turnabout. First is the proposition that "no trade is free," the title chosen by Robert Lighthizer, Trump's trade ambassador, for his retrospective on the administration's trade policy. The second comes from Richard Trumka, the late former AFL-CIO president and, for a time, Biden's shadow trade ambassador. Speaking in 2019 about how the Trump-era renegotiated NAFTA still failed workers and needed more work, he stressed: "Unfortunately, the deal we have before us tries to serve two masters . . . the corporate interests . . . and the workers. . . . But here's the thing: You can't serve both."[2]

The politics of zero-sum thinking is generated from "the belief that gains for one individual or group tend to come at the cost of others."[3] The rise of America's sharp domestic political polarization, which became "exceptional" by global standards in the 2010s, has given new focus to the sources and implications of zero-sum assumptions in America's political process.[4] It was spurred further by the rise of the New Right

2   Richard Trumka, "Trumka: New NAFTA Not Good Enough," AFL-CIO, April 2, 2019.

3   Sahil Chinoy, Nathan Nunn, Sandra Sequeira, and Stefanie Stantcheva, "Zero Sum Thinking and the Roots of U.S. Political Divides" (Working Paper 31688, National Bureau of Economic Research, Cambridge, MA, September 2023).

4   Dimock and Wike, "America Is Exceptional in the Nature of Its Political Divide."

movement during the Trump era, but it is not limited to one political party or movement.

Expressed domestically, zero-sum thinking is the fuel giving rise to populist ideology, which "considers society to be ultimately separated into two homogeneous and antagonistic groups: 'the pure people' versus the 'corrupt elite.'"[5] Neither the exclusive domain of the Left or the Right, it is a soft ideology that requires a division between legitimate and illegitimate interests. It is, therefore, both exclusionary and zero-sum. Expressed globally, national leaders of any persuasion can also use zero-sum logic to promote at least a soft form of nationalism. Insofar as zero-sum means only either winning or losing, it can motivate national decision-makers to walk out as a means to assert or reassert control over a nation's external commitments in the name of national sovereignty.[6]

Zero-sum thinking is not based on a particular, fixed political ideology. It most often feeds into other ideologies to justify them. Zero-sum assumptions are used as a tool by the progressive Left and the New Right alike to justify their own experiences and worldviews. By defining the discourse in American politics and the decisions that emerge around their respective poles, such thinking has led, for example, to America's trademark political gridlock at home.

International trade adds a foreign, or external, dimension to zero-sum thinking that has facilitated a surprising degree of alignment between the New Right and progressive Left. Lighthizer's proposition that "no trade is free" defines the zero-sum ideology well along this foreign dimension, where trade is an "us or them" proposition. "Us" is defined as American workers. "Them" are both America's trading partners and, as agents of globalization, its multinational corporations. With these distinctions, both extremes align in their definition of an external problem—the zero-sum belief that America is made worse off by freer trade, which benefits "them." It follows from that presumption that America is also worse off for continuing to play by the rules of its system that led to the problem. With agreement on the problem, the new mainstream of both America's political parties turned to compete

---

5   Cas Muddle, "The Populist Zeitgeist," *Government and Opposition* 39, no. 4 (2004), 541–63.
6   Traditional definitions of nationalism include a great care placed on national identity along with the pursuit of sovereignty. See, e.g., Nenad Miscevic, "Nationalism," in *The Stanford Encyclopedia of Philosophy*, fall 2023 ed., ed. Edward N. Zalta and Uri Nodelman, https://plato .stanford.edu/archives/fall2023/entries/nationalism.

over ways to stem the harm by pulling away from—or walking out on—America's previous trade commitments.

This alignment on the external problem manifests itself politically in both sides' messaging on trade by emphasizing harm over opportunity. With freer trade labeled a "disaster" by Trump's New Right and Bernie Sanders' progressive Left, both Lighthizer and Tai were left with the job of, in Tai's words, "writing a new story on trade."[7] They were pushed and aided by the rise of a new crop of controversy entrepreneurs[8] who aimed to recast and revise prevailing arguments and conventional wisdom over questions such as whether jobs are gained or lost from freer trade, whether free trade deals are good or bad, and whether trade deficits matter or not. There is often little room for nuance in the always contradictory findings put forward on either side of these debates because, in this new zero-sum world, there can only be one correct answer.

Also, this alignment has given rise to policy entrepreneurship for new ways to isolate America from this harm. In terms of both rhetoric and policy, neither side can allow itself to be outflanked by the other in their race to a zero-sum end.

In concrete policy terms, along the foreign dimension of America's new trade policy, it proved easiest for both administrations and Congress to walk out on commitments either not yet implemented or still under negotiation. Walking out on the TPP, which was signed but not implemented, and pulling out of other trade-liberalizing negotiations such as TiSA, were starting points for stemming the harm. Neither negotiation included China, underscoring the importance of America's domestically driven shifts in attitudes as principal drivers of its new trade policy choices. Other global tariff liberalization negotiations in progress, such as on environmental goods, and those newly proposed, such as on medical supplies in the wake of the COVID-19 pandemic, were left to drift and die or otherwise be spurned. Congress's inability to renew tariff-free GSP benefits for poor and other developing countries after the program expired, a failure rooted in the lack of agreement on new conditions for those benefits, also reflected a similar inertia.

In contrast, threats to terminate agreements already in force, from NAFTA to KORUS, and to withdraw from the WTO or just from its stand-

---

7   Swanson, "Biden's Reluctant Approach to Trade Draws Backlash."

8   Adapted from Amanda Ripley's usage of the term "conflict entrepreneur." Amanda Ripley, "We Keep Moving from One Wrong Fight to Another. Here's How to Stop," *Washington Post*, op-ed, December 8, 2022.

alone government procurement pact, risked greater political blowback from various stakeholders whose interests would be more directly impacted. Threatening to "terminate, or else. . ." put the onus on America's trading partners to deliver, making them easy scapegoats for any political fallout at home should these high-stakes threats end in America's withdrawal. NAFTA and KORUS were not terminated but renegotiated; they were updated to deliver on promises, such as providing more breathing room to automakers and autoworkers in America. In the WTO, the choice was made to drastically undermine and weaken those commitments but not to go so far as a formal withdrawal.

The Trump administration's decisions to hike import tariffs represented a bolder political move given the considerable domestic impacts. This included the Section 232 actions against global imports of steel and aluminum, and its Section 301 tariff escalations against China. Trump's tariffs led China, the EU, and others to retaliate against American exports, stoking resentment among exporters caught in the trade war crossfire. In terms of protecting America's market from China's export deluges, public opinion was mostly on the side of acting despite the potential economic costs. Even so, after their implementation, the tariffs were still viewed negatively by the plurality of Americans who recognized they often ended up paying the price. Subsequent studies of the tariffs support these two impacts: the tariffs failed to boost employment in America, but China's retaliation cost jobs for some Americans. Nonetheless, the tariffs helped Trump politically in certain ways.[9] Efforts were made to stem some of the political fallout at home, such as by excluding many medical goods from higher import tariffs after the start of the COVID-19 pandemic and leaving cell phones and other high-demand consumer electronics off the lists of tariff hikes. Many other consumer goods were assessed a lower tariff than those for intermediate goods, steps aimed at avoiding immediate sticker shocks for consumers.[10] Later, and not to be outflanked while still in the midst of his re-election campaign, Biden joined in hiking tariffs even higher on Chinese imports in several industrial goods sectors.

---

9   David Autor, Anne Beck, David Dorn, and Gordon H. Hanson, "Help for the Heartland? The Employment and Electoral Effects of the Trump Tariffs in the United States" (Working Paper 32082, NBER Working Paper Series, National Bureau of Economic Research, Cambridge, MA, January 2023), https://www.nber.org/system/files/working_papers/w32082/w32082.pdf.
10   See, e.g., Tom Lee and Tori Smith, "Section 301 China Tariffs by End Use," Research, American Action Forum, Washington, DC, January 11, 2023.

The heaviest of these tariff costs were most often initially borne by businesses and then passed along to consumers. To stem the harm from lost exports to China's in-kind retaliation against Trump's Section 301 tariffs, American farmers were showered with two massive taxpayer-funded compensation packages totaling $24.5 billion to help rural communities, aiding them "while President Trump works to address long-standing market access barriers."[11] That work remains unfinished, and most of these tariffs on both sides remain in place. In addition, the Trump administration held back from imposing Section 232 tariffs on worldwide imports of autos and auto parts, which, while strongly supported by unions, also would have significant negative implications in other areas, including on most American auto dealerships, auto repair and parts businesses, and consumers who relied on foreign parts—or just preferred foreign cars. Whereas domestic politics was the primary accelerant for imposing some of these tariffs, it also served as a guardrail for other decisions, keeping America's policymakers from taking even more dramatic steps.

This New Right–Left alignment on trade also stopped, quite literally, at the water's edge. If walking out was the remedy for America's external trade harm problems, stark divisions between these groups in the domestic policy arena interfered with their ability to forge alignment on a new model to replace the old approach to advance America's redefined trade interests. Domestic disputes that ended in zero-sum gridlock in Washington also brought these attempts at reform to a standstill.

These disagreements, which boiled down to a deep distaste among both the progressive Left and the New Right of having to live in an America dominated by the other's values and rules, took as their first casualty the efforts to pass the TPP. America's domestic impasses were manifest in nearly every trade policy debate thereafter: Was it justifiable to expect trading partners to enact U.S.-equivalent levels of protection for new pharmaceutical innovations just as for other copyright and patent protection terms? Must the freedom to organize independent unions be added as a legal condition to every new trade agreement and program, regardless of its intent and scope? Efforts to find the right balance for digital trade and financial services trade rules, among many others, provoked similar fierce and divisive debates.

---

11   United States Department of Agriculture, "USDA Announces Details of Support Package for Farmers," press release no. 0114.19, July 25, 2019.

As a result, no durable Right-Left alignment or consensus emerged around a new model for trade agreements. The renegotiation of NAFTA seemed, for a moment, to have perhaps forged a new consensus on many issues. Ultimately, however, these trade-offs failed to hold together as a new American model of compromise for subsequent agreements and initiatives. As a package brokered and approved to stave off Trump's threat to terminate NAFTA, underlying disagreements over its outcomes re-emerged when attempts were made to apply it in other contexts. The failed IPEF and its example of the advent of the trade-lite agreement, America's sudden reversal on digital rules in the WTO negotiations, and disagreements over conditions to tack onto GSP country eligibility are just three demonstrations of how these domestic policy disagreements continue to prevent the emergence of a lasting consensus.

Along its domestic dimension, therefore, America's zero-sum assumptions fueled ideological Right-Left splits that proved insurmountable in identifying which priorities, practices, and norms should underpin new trade agreements and efforts. Trumka's view that trade agreements could not possibly serve the objectives of both companies and workers at the same time perfectly sums up the progressive Left's domestic, zero-sum objective and view, which was, put simply, to promote the goals and membership of Big Labor and stick it to Big Business for its perceived exploitation of workers and as a generator of economic inequality. This view was elevated into U.S. trade policy with the Biden administration's adoption of its "worker-centric" approach, which firmly sided with U.S. labor union goals to upset America's economic status quo. With it, issues such as labor and human rights were elevated in importance far above basic trade policy objectives, such as removing barriers to U.S. exports.[12]

In its domestic dimension, the New Right's zero-sum ideology focused on preserving the societal status quo, including traditional conservative attitudes about how economic gains should be distributed among classes and social groups.[13] This view made room for the Trump administration to intervene aggressively at times with trading partners to support America's longstanding trade policy goals of growing America's exports and removing foreign trade barriers to better equalize

---

12 Shai Davidai and Martino Ongis, "The Politics of Zero-Sum Thinking: The Relationship Between Political Ideology and the Belief That Life Is a Zero-Sum Game," *Science Advances* 5, no. 12 (December 18, 2019).
13 Davidai and Ongis, "The Politics of Zero-Sum Thinking."

conditions of competition abroad for its exports (especially for goods) by firms of all sizes.

With respect to America's trade agreements, the only areas of alignment between the Right and the Left in these zero-sum dimensions were those principally external in their impacts and focus. For example, both groups strongly supported raising domestic product content requirements and adding currency obligations to these agreements, additions that were aimed at stemming cheaper imports from abroad to potentially add jobs at home and that aroused little domestic controversy. Similarly, domestic controversy swirled around the objectives and fiscal impacts of massive new government spending programs such as for electric vehicles, but not around giving domestic products preferences over most imports.

At least reputationally, America's large multinational corporations fared poorly amid the emergence of the foreign dimension of this New Right and progressive Left alignment on trade. When acting as agents of globalization, by diversifying their supply chains or by offshoring production to remain successful at home and competitive abroad, multinationals were viewed and treated as "them" by both the New Right and progressive Left along the two sides' common "us or them" continuum. When generating new jobs in America or export-oriented in their objectives, they were elevated in attention and support by both the New and the traditional Right. To progressives, however, America's multinationals were still not to be trusted for other reasons, whether because they manufactured in less union-friendly, right-to-work states or because of their pursuit of regulatory favoritism in Washington. At the end of the day, they were still the "Bigs," with interests viewed as inherently in opposition to workers.

The progressive Left's view of freer trade in the 2020s also turned their own movement's historical assumptions about tariffs upside down. These views began to shift as early as the 1970s. By the 2020s, reductions to U.S. tariffs came to be viewed as mere tax breaks for big corporations, and higher tariffs as a cost they could easily absorb and pay with little consequence. These views reversed the progressive assumptions that led President Franklin Roosevelt in the mid-1930s to begin to steer America toward decades of successive tariff liberalization agreements with the world. Tariff reduction goals promoted by Roosevelt and prior Democratic administrations were guided instead in their domestic policy dimension as a means of accelerating a wealth transfer from American industrialists, who sought high tariffs to protect their profits, to workers and consumers, who benefited by lower prices and greater industrial competition.

As anti-multinational political rhetoric rose especially on the Left but also on the New Right, a complementary precipitous decline was apparent in public support and trust toward these same institutions.

America's foreign relations have been deeply impacted by this shift. As the global trading system's newest rule-breaker, America pushed far into and found the international limits of tolerance with its new domestically centered consensus and discord. That discord led to policy delays and flip-flops across an array of trade issues, leaving no clear sense that a future U.S. administration would not again just reset and start over by rejecting the policies of the prior administration.

Although this was a new direction for the country, America was hardly alone among WTO members trying to undermine that organization's trade-liberalizing and rule-setting efforts. China, too, was working to ignore or skirt around the agreed rules, but it had a very different model and approach. China also continued to liberalize trade with its trading partners through other agreements, confident of the ability of its economic central command mechanisms to manage liberalization as needed, irrespective of its commitments. America, lacking such informal and discretionary mechanisms, had to resort to applying tariffs and enacting other domestic preferences in plain sight to reset the terms of America's open economy.

In some ways, America's new-look trade policy was more comparable to that of a country like India. Despite starkly different economic conditions and levels of formal trade protection, both are large economies and influential in their external reach. India similarly views full participation in the international trading system and tariff liberalization as inflicting economic harm, in similar zero-sum, domestically driven terms. Like America with the TPP, India also pulled itself out of a mega trade-liberalizing deal just as the negotiations were concluding in 2019, to the great shock and surprise of its 15 negotiating partners across East and Southeast Asia and in the Pacific. Like America, India cited concern that opening its market would harm its domestic industries and result in an unacceptably high trade deficit with the region and the world. It also proceeded to demand the renegotiation of other existing trade agreements, such as with Southeast Asia, out of concern that its trade deficits with them were increasing. It similarly was notorious for blocking consensus in the WTO on new liberalizing agreements, citing its domestic priorities.

Even so, America's turnabout was so sharp and sudden as to be uniquely alienating and especially impactful. Starting with the Trump administration's justification in 2017 that others had made the system unfair and harmful, four years later, America's next administration claimed, in line with its unions, that the system that America shaped was itself the problem and required a major do-over. Seen from abroad, it all looked to be hypocrisy at its worst. America's trademark stresses on the system were one thing, as long as it also continued to support and advance its commitment to mutually beneficial trade; complete abdication and breaking the system to force its domestic agenda was another.

At the same time, many countries remained keenly aware of and exercised their own sources of leverage with America when possible. Countries like Japan stuck firmly to the 2015 version of American rules from the TPP by reconvening the remaining members to complete the agreement in line with nearly all of those same rules. When forced into a new negotiation by the Trump administration over America's lost access to Japan's agriculture market, it used that leverage to avoid agreeing to a new, full-blown free trade agreement with America, and so having to face its new, post-2017 rules and expectations. Countries like South Korea, Mexico, and Canada had less leverage as they aimed to save their in-force agreements, but they still managed to largely stem the most problematic among the many demands made of them.

In the WTO, America walked out on all trade-liberalizing negotiations, broke the dispute system, and bypassed its core most-favored-nation and nondiscriminatory treatment rules to hike tariffs and pursue its new industrial policy. America's size and importance proved to matter enormously to what happened next. WTO trade-liberalizing negotiations did not resume. America finally engaged in discussions to reform the WTO dispute system, but it remained broken so long as America remained dissatisfied with ideas to fix it. The WTO struggled to cope with America's attempt to match China in a new global subsidies race fueled by America's preferences and restrictions on billions of dollars of tax breaks for electric vehicles and other goods, an affront to its nondiscrimination and other core rules. The head of the WTO called it a subsidy "race to the bottom" that only the wealthiest countries could afford.[14] As America turned to suddenly and sharply reject many of its own rules, there was an overwhelming sense that the system would continue to drift so long as America continued to deny it positive support, piling on by adding to its irrelevancy.

In the Asia-Pacific, America's absent leadership, self-imposed alienation, and rejection of prior assumptions that others still supported came amid China's accelerating export expansion and economic influence. In this environment, trust in America's commitment to the region and to forging mutually beneficial ties there suffered a disastrous setback with its withdrawal from the TPP. The Trump administration then adopted a new negotiating style and used unilateralism for its trade engagements in the Asia-Pacific, steps that became as (or more) off-putting to countries across the region as Beijing's leveraged demands on them.

The Biden administration launched the IPEF, a trade-curious-at-best alternative to the TPP, to attempt to restore some trust. America's proposal for this new regional trade framework initially received lukewarm interest because it lacked traditional trade-expanding market opening goals that its trading partners in the region all prioritized, aiming instead at outcomes that supported the administration's political priorities at home in areas like labor, environment, and competition policy. More than a dozen countries invested their resources in a year of planning and another year of negotiations, only for Washington to stop the negotiations it championed in their final hours. The IPEF was intended to replace the TPP model as America's new approach to trade, but instead got hung up on the same all-or-nothing demands for enforceable labor rights commitments that were a rallying call for opposition to the TPP agreement eight years earlier. America's new-style trade agreement thus far has failed to demonstrate its proof of concept—both at home and among its trading partners.

In the meantime, most in the Asia-Pacific moved on with their efforts to further integrate trade through new free trade deals, whether by reforming the CPTPP, finalizing the Regional Comprehensive Economic Partnership agreement covering East and Southeast Asia and Oceania, negotiating individual new free trade agreements, or negotiating their own stand-alone regional trade rules agreements. America's vision of open and rules-based trade mostly endured, but America chose to sit

---

14   Okonjo-Iweala, "Interview with World Trade Organization Director General Ngozi Okonjo-Iweala."

on the sideline instead. America ceded its role as rule-maker for that of rule-taker—one of responding and reacting to a new status quo for regional and global trade that others are now creating in its place.

Instead of opening markets and setting new rules that could prove durable and achievable, America's new trade negotiations agenda with its self-defined "allies and partners" revolved around working out exceptions to its escalating tariffs and new domestic preference measures. Once America moved off and kept moving away from honoring its commitment to the WTO's core nondiscrimination rules of most-favored-nation treatment and national treatment, an entirely new crop of decisions arose around which countries might be given better treatment than others, and on what terms it should set for each. These led to troubled and, at times, perverse choices as America decided, for example, which countries would secure better terms for its steel exports or receive a waiver for its exports to qualify for America's state-funded electric vehicle and battery subsidies. Once discrimination became a feature and not a bug of America's new trade policies, each decision along the way imposed new and different consequences for its trading partners that further complicated America's relations with allies and simply alienated many others.

The Trump administration showed the least concern for the foreign policy implications of its trade decisions, for in many ways, its new trade policy was a cornerstone of its new foreign policy. In some cases, brakes were ultimately applied to pull some decisions back from the cliff's edge out of concern for irreparable damage to follow. As it was with the renegotiation of KORUS and with letting Canada stay in its renegotiated NAFTA deal with Mexico, pulling back often was contingent on reaching an agreement in the final hours. In other cases, like with the TPP, there was no opportunity offered to discuss changing the terms before Trump withdrew from it, only adding to the foreign relations damage. The Trump administration engaged in trade policy roulette with various countries that hoped to beat the house odds to secure better terms for its tariff hikes. The administration eventually granted steel tariffs exclusions for Canada and Mexico after the successful renegotiation of NAFTA, for example, but left South Korea with its hard import quota after its renegotiation of KORUS. The administration also relied on threats of new tariffs on automobile exports to boost the odds of starting new trade deal negotiations with its allies Japan and the EU.

The Biden administration, which proclaimed its intention to repair America's relationships, claimed to take a friendlier approach. It then only created new terms and conditions that *further* discriminated among its key allies and other trading partners. Treaty allies like the EU countries were given the first seat at its table to negotiate new terms for lifting their retaliatory tariffs on steel. In contrast, other treaty allies that chose not to retaliate, such as Japan, had to step up and insist on similar treatment. South Korea, another treaty ally, was never given a chance to update the terms of its Trump-era deal. The EU was given a preferred place at the administration's table to negotiate a new agreement on environmental standards for steel production, with the suggestion that a successful outcome could lead to EU steel becoming fully exempt from the steel tariffs, but no comparable opportunity was provided to others.

The Biden administration also negotiated faux free trade agreements with its preferred trading partners, limited only to terms on critical minerals trade simply to achieve a similar legal status as its real free trade partners, to allow the electric vehicle battery exports of those preferred partners to qualify under its new subsidy programs. Meanwhile, electric vehicles assembled in Canada and Mexico qualified alongside those assembled in America, while those in all other countries could not.

Lack of clarity and deep inconsistency over which countries were provided less negative treatment became a frequent sore point among all.[15] For decades, preferences among its trading partners were created as a result of free trade agreement negotiations, where America offered better terms for trade in exchange for agreement to America's lengthy expectations for trade rules. These amounted to WTO-allowed discriminatory differences in treatment, but in the direction of making trade more open and rules-based. America's use from 2017 of unilateral and global tariffs, along with domestic preferences, relied on a negative form of discrimination that moved in the opposite direction. With it, countries tried to seek exceptions or improved outcomes simply to return to their pre-2017 terms of trade with America.

As long as America continues to discriminate to restrict trade, as opposed to offering reciprocal preferences to expand trade, resetting

---

15   The case of Indonesia is a good example. It has sought a similar faux free trade agreement on critical minerals to the one concluded with Japan in a bid to benefit from subsidy tax incentives for its production of nickel and other materials used in electric vehicle batteries. For the opposition expressed to it on Capitol Hill, see Hannah Monicken, "Harris, in Indonesia, Calls For 'Resilient' Critical Minerals Supply Chains," World Trade Online, September 6, 2023; and Kevin Cramer (with cosigners), "Senators Express Concerns Regarding Critical Minerals Trade Agreement with Indonesia," Office of Senator Kevin Cramer, press release, October 25, 2023.

normalized trade with the rest of the world will continue to provoke new foreign relations problems with its allies and adversaries alike. These decisions also led to similar choices at home, as Washington discriminated among America's industries, businesses, farmers, consumers, exporters, and importers when selecting the products to include or exclude from its import tariffs. All these choices opened new opportunities for interest groups to try and capture favorable decisions from America's policymakers, opening the door for further discrimination among them as well.

A world where zero-sum ideology begets zero-sum tariff and trade policies is precisely the world that America's invention of the international trading system aimed to bring to an end. In recognition of its "position of world economic leadership," President Harry Truman in 1949 described America's commitment "to do its share in re-establishing world economic relations on a sound competitive basis for the mutual well-being of all peoples."[16]

A contemporary observer described the creation of this system as guided by America's foreign policy objective of "a peaceful world order [that] requires economic co-operation among nations and the removal of economic causes of friction" by "nondiscriminatory access to supplies and markets," along with its commercial policy objective of restoring

in a disorganized, chaotic and impoverished world the foundations for a world-wide multilateral and nondiscriminatory trading system, which will permit America private enterprise to compete on equitable terms and will contribute to the general welfare by increasing both the volume and quality of international trade.[17]

Its creators also recognized that countries would need space within the system's rules to make adjustments to accommodate their own economic needs and priorities. They incorporated some flexibilities in the system to allow for it. At the same time, they insisted on tighter adherence with fewer exceptions to the core principles of nondiscrimination, precisely because without sustained, collective adherence to

16   Harry S. Truman, "Truman's Statement on Trade," *New York Times*, September 27, 1949, 3.
17   William Adams Brown, Jr., *The United States and the Restoration of World Trade* (Washington, DC: The Brookings Institution, 1950), 1.

that core commitment, the new system would quickly unwind, and countries would return to tit-for-tat escalations. Later, as its members used the system's flexibilities to pursue their own subsidies, industrial policies, and other means to advantage their exports and improve their industrial and economic development, America confronted many of these problems and insisted on additional rules to help rein in their use. China's heavy mixing of the state in its economy emerged as one of the most intractable challenges for a system that relied on the presumption that its members would engage in less interventionist, more market-based competition.

Once committed to its rules, members of the international trading system were left to make their own adjustments as needed within their borders. Starting with how and to whom the economic gains from trade would be distributed, governments also would need to consider whether to help the workforce adjust over time and what kind of commercial and competitive environment would prevail. It is unlikely to have ever crossed the minds of America's architects of the system that America itself, having just won a world war and emerged as its strongest and most prosperous nation, would later come to struggle to be able to make these fundamental decisions for itself. As America lost its capacity to resolve its problems at home, its two political camps, once unable to agree at home, were able to agree on looking outside its borders for blame. They found alignment around their shared goal of untethering America from its commitments under the system.

Because of its size and historic influence over the international trading system, America's leadership came with a special responsibility that accompanied the particular privileges of its position. It held more influence over the system than others ever could and expected much more of it than others ever did. America's political system and its domestic stakeholders, in turn, grew to demand ever more from America's leverage over the system, which both made it possible to expect everything else from others while avoiding expecting more of itself. As America turned inward on itself and these expectations came into fundamental conflict, America could no longer sustain the system, still less continue to lead it.

Governments in Europe and Japan also face difficult trade politics but retain, for now, a core commitment to advancing the open, rules-based system. There are some new cracks, however. America's subsidy programs have triggered a subsidies race in both the EU and Japan and elsewhere. The EU has also elected to apply tariffs on carbon-intensive imports, which developing countries view as a new, modern American form of protectionism that they do not have the economic resources to overcome. How long the system can maintain its integrity and relevance in the absence of America's commitment to supporting it and abiding by its rules may be its greatest challenge.

⌐⌐ ·· ─────── ◇ ─────── ·· ⌐⌐

Will America find its way back? Perhaps more accurately, *can* it find its way back, since its current and prospective leaders continue to make their case that it should not?

One positive sign is that, despite nearly a decade of the hyper-politicization of trade in Washington, there has been no corresponding collapse in American public opinion toward trade. Support among Americans stands in sharp contrast to the turn its political system has taken against it. Americans instead share a healthy and quite balanced, as opposed to zero-sum, view of both the opportunities and challenges that international trade holds for their country. These views, in fact, only improved as the 2010s progressed. By 2018, a record-high 74 percent of Americans viewed international trade as "good" for the nation. Only 36 percent, however, believed it created jobs and even fewer, 31 percent, believed it helped increase wages. These views were in a similar range to the responses to the same questions in advanced nations in Europe and in Japan.[18] Support has since faded some, but as of 2022, over 60 percent of Americans still viewed trade positively as an opportunity for economic growth.[19]

Even so, this book provides ample evidence of a much more sober political reality ahead, particularly for those still pinning their hope on America somehow waking up and recommitting to the norms and principles it now spurns. Every year, beginning in 2017, America continues dreaming up new reasons and justifications to discriminate against imports and its trading partners. The competition between its political parties continues to drive these proposals forward, just as during its 2016 and 2020 presidential campaign seasons. The Republican candidate for 2024 is pulling from the same playbook, advocating an across-the-board 10 percent additional hike in U.S. tariffs on all imports while renewing

---

18   Stokes, "Americans, Like Many in Other Advanced Economies, Not Convinced of Trade's Benefits."

19   Jeffrey M. Jones, "U.S. Views of Foreign Trade Nearly Back to Pre-Trump Levels," Gallup, March 10, 2022.

his play for auto union member votes by insisting a transition to cleaner vehicles is an existential threat to the entire American automobile industry and their jobs.[20]

The views of President Biden, the Democratic candidate until he later withdrew from the race, were framed just two days after he announced his candidacy. He called for the need to "forge a new consensus" that involves turning away from open, rules-based trade to fix everything wrong with America and the world. If, as the argument continues, the "project of the 2020s and the 2030s is different from the project of the 1990s," it is hard to make the case that it exceeds the challenges of the 1940s and 1950s, when America's progressive political leaders created the open, rules-based trading system to lift the poor and prevent the world's return to the discriminatory and other beggar-thy-neighbor policies of the 1930s.[21]

Meanwhile, reaching a consensus on the domestic issues that underpin America's external positions in international trade remains as gridlocked as ever. From digital rules to worker rights, each side continues to insist it will only be content with achieving 100 percent of what it expects and demands. These debates thus continue to derail the possibility of forging a stable, new consensus for a new model for trade beyond one that continues to further wall off America. Recent history demonstrates that until and unless America can first reach more accommodations over its own economic goals and priorities, it will continue to struggle to find the necessary ground to project a positive and reliable vision for the global trading system.

As America continues to walk out on the international trading system, it does so at the ever-increasing risk that it will also leave the system irreparably broken and irrelevant. It is also likely to continue to do so as long as America continues to engage in its search for itself.

---

20   Jeff Stein, "Trump Vows Massive New Tariffs if Elected, Risking Global Economic War," *Washington Post*, August 22, 2023; and Jonathan Weisman, "Trump Seeks U.A.W.'s Support as the Union Waivers on Backing Biden," *New York Times*, July 20, 2023.
21   Sullivan, "Remarks by National Security Advisor Jake Sullivan."

Index

tariffs (*cont'd*)
  absolute tariff reciprocity as goal
    of Trump administration, 27–28,
    144, 273
  authority granted by Congress
    about, 39–40
  automobiles, 221
  Biden administration and, 6,
    51–56, 72–73, 76–77
  China and, 68, 99
  developing countries and, 14
  new tariff war with the world,
    39–56
  normalization of unilateralism in,
    66–70
  Smoot-Hawley tariffs, 193
  tariff reciprocity by setting at zero,
    144
  TPP and, 183–84
  trade war with China and, 56–70,
    73, 294–95, 298, 299
  Trump administration and, 6–7,
    71–73
  zeroing, 33–35
  See also Generalized System of
    Preferences (GSP)
Tea Party movement, 87–88, 175
Teamsters, 174
Thailand, 280–81, 282
TISA (Trade in Services Agreement),
  114–19
titanium sponge, 49
tobacco industry excluded from ISDS
  claims, 174–75
Tokyo Round, 151
TPP. *See* Trans-Pacific Partnership
  (TPP)
TPP-11, 198–99
TPP-12, 138
Trade Act (1974), 153–54, 194. *See also*
  Section 301 claims
Trade Agenda statements, Biden
  administration, 97

trade agreements
  agriculture and, 142–43
  with Australia, 172
  automobiles and, 143
  Biden administration not pursu-
    ing, 244–47, 260, 262–63
  Bush (George W.) administration
    and, 140, 144, 145–46, 166–67
  with Columbia, 145–46, 166–67
  Congressional authority for,
    145–46, 153–54, 181–83
  Doha Round and, 140
  as exception to most-fa-
    vored-nation treatment, 140–41
  intellectual property and, 178
  investor protections in, 171–72
  IPEF as not, 249–250
  ISDS using, 173
  manufacturing and, 143
  Obama administration and, 144,
    145
  with Panama, 145–46, 166–67
  paralysis about, 288–89
  with Peru, 145–46, 166–67
  separate from WTO and, 140–42
  with South Korea, 145–46, 166–67
  trade deficit not correctable with,
    210
  See also specific agreements
trade barriers, non-tariff trade barriers redefined, 95–97
trade deficit
  assumptions about reasons for, 13
  China-U.S. relations and, 10–11,
    66
  goods versus services, 209–10
  Japan-U.S. relations and, 11–12
  push for trade rules due to, 150, 211
  South Korea-U.S. relations and,
    209–10, 220
  Trump wanting to meet pledge to
    cut, 66, 106, 209–11, 256–58
  USMCA and, 256–57

The authorized representative in the EU for product safety and compliance is:
Mare Nostrum Group
B.V Doelen 72
4831 GR Breda
The Netherlands

www.ingramcontent.com/pod-product-compliance
Lightning Source LLC
Chambersburg PA
CBHW020334270326
41926CB00007B/183